Left Catholicism

Catholics and Society
in Western Europe
at the Point
of Liberation

1943 | 1955

Edited by
Gerd-Rainer Horn
Emmanuel Gerard

KADOC-Studies 25
Leuven University Press 2001

The series KADOC-Jaarboeken
was followed by the series
KADOC-STUDIES.

A publication of
KADOC
(Katholiek Documentatie- en Onderzoekscentrum)
Vlamingenstraat 39
B-3000 Leuven
tel.: 016/32.35.00
fax: 016/32.35.01
E-mail: postmaster@kadoc.kuleuven.ac.be
Internet: http://www.kuleuven.ac.be/kadoc

Cover:
Portrait of the Belgian worker priest Charles Boland.
(Flémalle, M. Cadet)

© 2001 by
Leuven University Press
Blijde-Inkomststraat 5, B-3000 LEUVEN (Belgium)

No part of this book may be reproduced in any form, by print, photoprint, microfilm or any other means without written permission from the publisher.

ISBN 90 5867 093 7
D / 2001 / 1869 / 1

CONTENTS

Introduction
Emmanuel Gerard and Gerd-Rainer Horn — 7

Left Catholicism in Western Europe in the 1940s — 13
Gerd-Rainer Horn

The French Catholic Left and the Political Parties — 45
Jean-Claude Delbreil

Left Wing Catholicism in France. From Catholic Action
to the Political Left: the *Mouvement Populaire des Familles* — 64
Bruno Duriez

Left Catholicism and Christian Progressivism in France (1945-1955) — 91
Yvon Tranvouez

The Milieu of Left Wing Catholics in Belgium (1940s-1950s) — 102
Jean-Louis Jadoulle

The *Témoignage* of the Worker Priests. Contextual Layers
of the Pioneer Epoch (1941-1955) — 118
Oscar Cole-Arnal

Christian Movements and Parties of the Left in Italy (1938-1958) — 142
Antonio Parisella

"Left Catholicism" and the Experiences "on the Frontier"
of the Church and Italian Society (1939-1958) — 174
Giorgio Vecchio

Socialism out of Christian Responsibility. The German Experiment
of Left Catholicism (1945-1949) — 196
Andreas Lienkamp

Multi-faceted Relations between Christian Trade Unions and Left
Catholicism in Europe — 228
Patrick Pasture

From Permission to Prohibition. The Impact of the Changing
International Context on Left Catholicism in Europe   247
Peter Van Kemseke

Left Catholicism in Europe in the 1940s.
Elements of an Interpretation   269
Martin Conway

ABBREVIATIONS   282

BIBLIOGRAPHY   285

INDEX   309

CONTRIBUTORS   313

INTRODUCTION

Emmanuel Gerard and Gerd-Rainer Horn

The Dossetti wing of the *Democrazia Cristiana* in Italy, the *Mouvement Républicain Populaire* in France, the worker priests and the *Mouvement Populaire des Familles* in France and Belgium, Walter Dirks and the *Frankfurter Hefte*; these are some of the phenomena that were part of the Catholic experience in the years after the Second World War which will be discussed in this book. Perhaps it will surprise some readers to find these examples categorized under the label of "Left Catholicism".

The expression "Left Catholicism" in and of itself already raises a number of questions. Some observers consider it to be a *contradictio in terminis*. Usually Catholicism and its diverse political and social offshoot are associated with the Right. "Left" refers to individual and collective attitudes and concepts which hardly seem to be reconcilable with Catholic traditions.

"Left" and "right" are difficult to define. Due to different shifts of meaning over time, they do not have a precise definition. However, broadly speaking, one can differentiate two meanings. Until the First World War the dichotomy refers largely to the demarcation line resulting from the bourgeois revolution(s): "Left" incorporates the Enlightenment and the revolutionary tradition; "right" incorporates the resistance against it. After the First World War the dichotomy between "left" and "right" is increasingly referring to the opposition generated by the social question, notably the struggle for social and economic equality and the resistance against it.

If there exists a strong relationship between political Catholicism and the Right in the first of the above meanings, then its positioning in the Left-Right axis in the second of the above contexts is less unequivocal. On the contrary, here the problem of social Catholicism and Christian Democracy emerges in full view. Closely linked to the Right in the initial period, subsequently these movements belong to the Left as well. The secular Left, considering itself the continuation of the original Left dating back to the era of bourgeois revolutions, always felt it difficult to recognise Left Catholicism. Liberals, socialists and communists acknowledged the existence of a progressive wing within the spectrum of Catholic social and political movements, but situated it on the right side of the Left-Right divide. However, this configuration once again changes after the Second World War and particularly in France under the influence of the phenomena studied in this book.

But other problems also arise in relation to this terminology. In the first place "left" and "right" are political labels, not very appropriate to differentiate between modern and traditional pastoral methods or theological opinions: e.g. worker priests versus classical priesthood, specialised Catholic Action (e.g. the JOC apostolate) versus parochial apostolate. Nevertheless, it has to be said that, ever since the Second Vatican Council, these labels have been used as indicators of both progressive and conservative tendencies within the Catholic Church.

Thus the reader may be warned. The editors and the authors of the contributions are very well aware of the problems resulting from the chosen terminology. They are conscious of the fact that a simple dichotomy is not sufficient to situate persons and groups within a complex configuration of tendencies and movements which partly overlap and thwart each other. Besides, one has to take into account the various national sensibilities. "Left" does not mean the same thing in every country, just like "progressivist" does not mean the same in all the various contexts.

Still, even with this reservation in mind, one cannot deny the occurrence, among Catholics, of a series of phenomena in the years after the Second World War which imply a contestation of traditional concepts and attitudes in the realm of politics, society and pastoral concerns. Catholics seem to be part of the general atmosphere of renewal and - some contemporaries do not hesitate to use the word – revolution. In the context of the Liberation – a term immediately assuming a double meaning – strong Catholic pleas for social and economic reforms changing the balance between capital and labour can be heard; new forms of the social apostolate, in which the situation of the worker's world and the "choice for the poor" becomes determining, emerge; and even - although some engage in it only reluctantly - a rapprochement to the marxist intellectual world can be detected.

Are these phenomena, highlighting the role of labour in modern, industrial society, expressions of the same movement? In the central contribution of this book, G.-R. Horn furnishes an affirmative answer to this question, although not every author shares this view. This issue gave rise to an animated exchange of opinion in the course of the workshop where his paper served as a basis for discussion and out of which emerged most contributions to this volume.

This introduction is not the place to answer this complex question. Nevertheless, it may be useful to make a distinction between conjunctural and even purely incidental political phenomena on the one hand and pastoral and theological developments on the other. The role of the "Left" Catholics in the *Democrazia Cristiana* (Italy), the *Mouvement Républicain Populaire* (France) and the *Christlich Demokratische Union* (Germany), and the origin of the *Union Démocratique Belge* (Belgium) must perhaps be seen as an answer to the temporarily very powerful impact of communism and the Left. Of a different kind, although occuring at the same time, may be the discovery of the secularisation of society, exemplified in the recognition of *France pays de mission*, and the new forms of apostolate which are the result of this evolution: the rejection of the Catholic ghetto and the choice for testimony. The worker priests are concrete manifestations of the new apostolate in which the priesthood obtains inspiration from the world of labour. And here we begin to approach very closely developments in the doctrinal field in which the discovery and the appreciation of Marx start to play a role. The discovery of the early writings of the young "humanistic" Marx in the 1930s certainly contributes to this rapprochement, as the German example in this book demonstrates.

The fact that all these phenomena occur simultaneously must be highlighted in this context. They all seem in one way or the other strongly linked to the war, occupation and Liberation. The war itself forms the background in which new initiatives can come to fruition: the discreditation of fascism is an important element, but also the cooperation between Catholics and non-Catholics, especially socialists and communists, in the Resistance. The noticeable growth of Catholic Action during the occupation undoubtedly affects developments after Liberation. And the phenomenon of the worker priests is likewise linked with the occupation, including their presence within the deportation camps and the communities of forced labourers in Germany.

Because of the sudden disappearance of traditional frames of reference, society after Liberation is in a state of flux. It delivers opportunities and possibilities: it is "a moment of crisis and opportunity". The constellation is most revolutionary in Germany, Italy and France, where the traditional political framework almost entirely disappears. In the same way, the impact of the role of the Soviet Union on an international level, but likewise the aura of Great Britain and the victory of Labour in 1945, cannot be denied. It is striking to see in which way the *travaillist* idea affects postwar discussions in France, Italy, Germany and Belgium. The idea partly emerges in the period of occupation, notably in the midst of Belgian, French and other exile communities in London.

Are the above-mentioned phenomena only indebted to the war, occupation and Liberation? Certainly not. They have their roots in an earlier history, in a whole range of social Catholic initiatives and in intellectual movements which precede the events of 1940. But it is striking that the filiations with prewar initiatives and movements are less straightforward than one might expect. For instance, the main impetus for the Left Catholic enterprise is not provided by the Christian workers movement. On the contrary, the Catholic trade unions are rather opposed to Left Catholic adventures, a reluctance motivated by the old battle of competition with the socialists and by their vested interest in preserving acquired positions. But one should mention here nonetheless that there has always been an anticapitalist component within Catholic social movements, an element which now emerges more prominently within the context of the Left Catholic initiatives.

Catholic Action plays a more important role. Between the two World Wars, it had developed new forms of apostolic methods, characterised on the one hand by action directed at specific social milieus and, on the other, by the distiction between the spiritual and the political planes. This created the possibility to go beyond its classic orientation towards the middle classes and its traditional ghetto mentality. However, one needs to emphasise here the fact that the history of Catholic Action is a highly complex matter, a history with pronounced national peculiarities and sometimes paradoxical turns.

The JOC, straddling the Catholic labour movement and Catholic Action, takes on a special role in the genesis of Left Catholic initiatives. The particular form of Catholic and social engagement developed by this youth movement during the interwar period reaches its apogee in the *Mouvement Populaire des Familles* in France and Belgium.

By contrast, the phenomenon of the worker priests, closely linked with the theology of incarnation, is an entirely novel one. But, in this case too, one has to consider the activist heritage of priests within Christian Democracy and social Catholicism since *Rerum Novarum* and the related discussions about the appropriate nature of this engagement, the dignity of the priesthood, etc. And new forms of apostolate, where social milieus become more important than the parish and where the ministry is more concerned with social inequality than spiritual equality, can be detected already prior to 1940 as well.

The fact that Catholic Action rather than the Catholic workers' movement stimulates Left Catholic initiatives raises the question of the role of "intransigentism" in this particular historical context. The intellectual origins of many Left Catholic departures are located in the fundamental rejection of liberalism rather than a sympathy for democracy, the latter understood as an outgrowth of bourgeois sensibilities. In this respect, the anticapitalist phrases and the solemn declarations about the end of liberalism are illustrative and deceptive at the same time. The contributions to this volume underscore the complex nature of this particular dimension of Left Catholicism.

It is not only the forcefulness with which these phenomena suddenly emerge at the same time and in different countries which is striking. Just as remarkable is the short duration of and the resistance against them. Which factors are responsible for the disappearance of Left Catholicism? This book offers different answers to this question. First, one has to consider the fact that these movements emerge out of a position of extreme marginality, notably an isolation with respect to established Catholic social movements, in particular the trade unions. Second, the international context has to be taken into account. The initially relatively open relationship with the Soviet Union on the international level creates windows of opportunity in the field of domestic politics which, from 1947-1948 onwards, are slowly but firmly shut. Third, this Left Catholicism - a typically urban and male phenomenon - has only minor links with the traditional Catholic strongholds which are largely situated in the countryside. The negative attitude of the Catholic Church and its condemnation of the *Mouvement Populaire des Familles*, the worker priests, communism and pacifism, can definitely be regarded as a reflection of this unfavourable constellation of forces.

However, the impact of these phenomena may not be judged solely by their temporary character. One cannot deny that the programmes and objectives of Christian Democratic parties - founded after the Second World War and dominating the European Right for many years – includes elements of the Left Catholic heritage from the immediate post-Liberation period. (Incidentally, in the post-Liberation years there exists a more general problem of incongruency between a Christian Democratic programme and policy which is geared towards the "Left" and an electorate located firmly within the Right, due to the disappearance of a number of traditional right wing parties.) Also, notions of political pluralism, the renewal of theology and the dialogue with marxism are there to stay and, indeed, forcefully emerge into the foreground of Catholic debates in subsequent decades. Opinions differ whether these Left Catholic phenomena of the years 1943-1955 are antecedents of future developments, but such a view constitutes, at the very least, a challenging thesis.

It is certainly risky to lump together phenomena originally deriving their meaning from one specific national context, but the study of these phenomena as presented in this book opens up new perspectives towards a better understanding and, above all, for future research. The phenomena under observation did not exist in all the countries targeted in this volume, certainly not with the same degree of intensity. Italy pioneered the close cooperation between communists and Catholics. France played a special role because its history of political Catholicism is rather unique. Belgium never experienced a viable Catholic Left in the world of party politics. Germany was at best only marginally affected by any of the pastoral innovations. Up to now, various aspects of Left Catholicism have been investigated within their national context only, but no attempt was made to study these phenomena in a comparative and transnational framework. This is precisely the aim of this book.

***

The idea for this book arose in the context of a Research Fellowship from the Research Council of the Katholieke Universiteit Leuven (K.U.Leuven) that we applied for and obtained from 1 October 1998 to 31 July 1999, in association with the Department of Political Science and the Catholic Documentation and Research Centre (KADOC). In the course of these ten months, one of us, the visitor, was able to devote his time entirely to the study of the phenomenon of what we initially termed "progressive Catholicism" in several western European countries in the 1940s. In-depth study of the available secondary sources, facilitated by the plentiful resources of the various libraries belonging to the K.U.Leuven, was soon followed up by archival research in, above all, Belgium and France.

As part of this joint project, we conceived an international and comparative workshop which was held on 28-29 May 1999 at the KADOC. Participants hailed from Belgium, England, France and Italy. It is out of this workshop that the majority of contributions to this volume arose. As mentioned above, the introductory chapter on "Left Catholicism in Western Europe" originated as a discussion paper that was drawn up and distributed to all participants in advance of the conference. It is reproduced here without many substantive changes, though the author has since carried out systematic additional archival research and plans to publish a single-author monograph on this topic in the near future.

The success of this gathering of scholars convinced us to forge ahead with plans to publish the revised proceedings and to contact a small number of additional scholars for further contributions. We believe that, to the best of our knowledge, this volume constitutes the first-ever attempt to analyse the phenomenon of Western European Left Catholicism, circa 1943-1955, in a comparative and transnational context. It is up to the reader to judge the result.

In preparing this volume, the editors incurred many debts from many individuals and institutions. We want to thank the K.U.Leuven Research Council, the Department of Political Science and especially the KADOC. We would like to express our gratitude to the KADOC's chairman, Emiel Lamberts, and its director, Jan De Maeyer, who also contributed to the success of the international workshop and generously offered to take up this volume in the KADOC-series of Leuven University Press. Special mention should be made of Lieve Dhaene, publications coordinator at KADOC, who provided the indispensable and much appreciated technical support in the final editing of this volume.

LEFT CATHOLICISM IN WESTERN EUROPE IN THE 1940S

Gerd-Rainer Horn

1. Introduction

The years 1943 to 1948 were a historical moment of opportunity and crisis on a continental scale. The closing months of the Second World War and the tumultuous years between the end of the hot and the beginning of the Cold War constituted one of those rare moments in history when age-old ideas and practices were suddenly questioned and often abandoned, when individuals and, seemingly, entire societies were searching for new answers to the multiple crises determining their daily lives. In those brief months and years spanning both sides of V-Day traditional belief systems and longstanding political alliances were shaken up, challenged from within and without and, on occasion, discarded in favour of entirely new ones.[1]

Lest I be misunderstood, let me immediately follow up these opening lines with an important qualification. The opening paragraph is not to be misunderstood as an endorsement of the traditional view of the moment of Liberation/capitulation as a fundamental and radical break in the political, social and cultural history of European societies, propagated by the historiography of the 1950s and 1960s. The myth of the "hour zero", perhaps strongest in the German context, was successfully challenged by the revisionist trend gaining ground in the 1970s, and for some twenty-five years now the dominant paradigm tends to be the view that, certainly below the surface, the lines of continuity between pre-1945 and post-1945 European societies (most definitely in the Western European context) are stronger than ruptures and breaklines. Yet, on the other hand, as Rudi Van Doorslaer has pointed out in a thought-provoking text, particularly when focusing on the mentalities of Europeans living in those trying times, it is not at all so certain that this particular historical moment was experienced by the proverbial "average person" as a time of little fundamental change. "Indeed, in the memory of many people the Second World War has retained its stature as an extraordinary event. Herein lies hidden a contrast with the political history approach tending towards the conclusion that, in actuality, there were few processes of an extraordinary nature to be noticed at that time".[2] Van Doorslaer then proceeds to draw attention to the necessity of highlighting the history of everyday life and the way everyday life was per-

---

1. For some more detailed comments on the concept of "historical moments of opportunity and crisis", see the introductory and concluding comments to my *European Socialists Respond to Fascism*.
2. Van Doorslaer, "De oorlog tussen continuiteit en verandering", 23-24. In this article Van Doorslaer solely addresses the Belgian context. Yet I believe it is easy and indeed imperative to draw similar conclusions for other European societies at that time.

ceived by the individuals directly experiencing the moment of Liberation and its aftermath.

Despite the highly pertinent nature of Van Doorslaer's insights, I believe that such a juxtaposition of a "new" cultural or *mentalitätsgeschichtlichen* approach versus the revisionist political history approach constitutes an overly mechanical diagnosis of a more complex relationship. The original historiographic emphasis on political ruptures and breaks in the mid-1940s clearly must be seen as more than a mere exercise in the ideological justification for the post 1944/45 political elites. There undeniably existed important new departures, making these years into the highly unusual months and years of flux and rapid changes which, I contend, crucially aided in the perception of this period as an extraordinary moment in the minds of most contemporaries. The rise of Left Catholicism is certainly one particular manifestation of the political and ideological ferment of the initial postwar months and years. Of course, the undeniable fact that, certainly in Western Europe, these new political projects rarely won out and were frequently stillborn was just as much a part of this moment of opportunity and crisis as the closure of this moment following the economic revival and the outbreak of the Cold War. Yet to conclude from this that the point of Liberation was either a radical break or merely one dot along a line of continuities would be an overly simplistic analysis of a situation demanding a far more nuanced assessment.

In what follows, I would like to trace the contribution of Catholicism in shaping this particular crisis point in 20th century European history. In particular, I would like to focus on that portion of Catholicism which was most centrally involved in aiming to give new directions to contemporaneous European societies. As was the case with other innovative trends in social thought and practice and/or the world of ideologies and philosophies, this brief flowering of "Left Catholicism" never became a dominant trend and faded in the late 1940s and early 1950s. Yet for several all-important years in the 1940s and early 1950s, Left Catholicism became a powerful challenge on a variety of terrains. A brief explanation of the range of currents that I subsume under the vague label "Left Catholicism" - in the realm of party politics, theology/philosophy, and apostolic/social missions - may exemplify its impact on European societies in the 1940s.

Perhaps most visible to the broader public, political Catholicism experienced a range of new departures and party-political projects pushing the boundaries of Catholic politics further to the Left than in any previous historical conjuncture. Depending on concrete historical circumstances and specific national cultures, such openings to the Left could be timid or pronounced. From the vantage point of Italian or French politics, perhaps, the phenomenon of the *Union Démocratique Belge* (UDB) would appear to be a rather tame manifestation of the leftward evolution of portions of the Catholic public sphere, as, by contrast to French or Italian political Left Catholicism, the UDB consistently upheld the sanctity of private property. Within Belgium, however, the UDB briefly but profoundly questioned the self-certainties and staid traditions of, above all, the Catholic political world. In France, a number of new political departures, ranging from the *Union Démocratique et Socialiste de la Résistance* (UDSR) to the *Mouvement Républicain Populaire* (MRP), initially advocated some form of revolutionary break with established political practice. And, needless to say, in Italy, organisations such as the *Movimento dei Cattolici Comunisti* (MCC), by virtue of their self-definition symbolised in the choice of name, constituted an unprecedented new departure even in the Italian context, less foreign to political extremes than comparatively moderate Belgium.

Within the realm of theology and philosophy, the 1940s witnessed an equally astounding range of innovations. On a scale unheard of in the past, Catholic theology and philosophy paid central attention to dimensions and desires of the human experience which had previously never obtained such central place. The traditional Thomist understanding of the duality of the natural and supernatural here constituted the window of opportunity onto previously largely uncharted terrain. New theologies of human *praxis* saw the light of day. Indeed, concurrent with a sudden interest in the world of labour on the part of secular social scientists, theologies of labour were suddenly propounded on both sides of the Rhine and Rhône. Traditional Catholic social teachings tending to identify the poor as worthy objects ceded places to new visions of the poor as subjects and shapers of their own destiny.

In the world of Left Catholic theology/philosophy, the range of options chosen was similarly varied as in the openly party-political sphere. Most thinkers remained on some level of analysis equally critical of liberalism and marxism, the twin evils of modernism, and thus placed themselves squarely in the Catholic tradition of Leo XIII. But in the 1940s most proponents of such a view did not hide their sympathies for an outward extension of the boundaries of Catholic ideology.[3] Also, with the unforeseen revalidation of the socialist ideal characterising this particular moment of opportunity and crisis in the closing months and the aftermath of World War II, the anti-communism of this Left Catholic milieu left behind its "exclusionary anti-communism" and adopted a "competitive anticommunism".[4] Indeed, for some theologians their engagement with marxist political thought and practice eventually resulted in a far-reaching adoption of many marxist central tenets. Perhaps the most telling indicator of the winds of change in Catholic theology/philosophy was the reaction from Rome. Whereas in the late 1920s, Pope Pius XI focused his critique on a leading representative of the political Right, Charles Maurras, if only for his agnosticism, by the late 1940s his successor concentrated his attention on the perceived threat emanating from the political Left.

Profoundly influenced by these experiments in party politics and the radiance of new theological departures, the 1940s also played host to some innovations within the world of Catholicism which cannot be satisfactorily placed either in the field of politics proper or theology. What may be termed Left Catholic apostolic/social missions emerged out of this creative interac-

---

3. The hierarchical and quasi-monolithic view of most Catholic social teaching after *Rerum novarum* is highlighted in Verstraeten, "De sociale leer van de Katholieke Kerk en de 'Derde Weg'", 51-61.
4. These are the terms coined by Letamendia in his *Le Mouvement Républicain Populaire*, particularly pp. 75-86, citation on p. 80. As is the case with my interpretation of Van Doorslaer's thesis I referred to above, Letamendia developed his analysis for one particular country only (France) and in an exclusively party-political context, but I believe his insights have a far wider purchase within and outside of France.

tion of ideology and political action (of Left Catholic theory and practice), capturing the attention of larger segments of society and indeed the attention of the Holy See. The experience of the French and Belgian *Mouvement Populaire des Familles* (MPF) and the phenomenon of the worker priests best exemplify this third identifiable manifestation of Left Catholicism in the 1940s.

Concretely, I propose to cast light on these three Left Catholic phenomena - party politics, theology/philosophy, and apostolic/social missions - in the order in which I introduced them above. Despite the unquestionable existence of many profound differences within and between these tendencies within and beyond national frontiers, I aim to emphasise their commonalities by tracing what I regard as key similarities or parallels within those variegated strands of thought. For what is most astounding upon reflection on these trends is the degree to which they emerged in a variety of national contexts, but at roughly the same time, with similar emphases - and that they suffered a similar fate.

A note of caution on the question of the historical originality of Left Catholicism in the 1940s. As is the case with all historical phenomena, the various manifestations of Left Catholicism did not emerge from nowhere without the direct or indirect aid of theological and political antecedents paving its way. All these strands of Left Catholicism built on previously elaborated and existing traditions. Indeed, it is impossible to explain the specific form and content of Left Catholicism in the 1940s without, to cite but two examples, studying the cultural immersion tactics of the *Jeunesse Ouvrière Chrétienne* (JOC) developed by Joseph Cardijn in the 1920s or the intellectual impact of Jacques Maritain's *Humanisme intégral*, written in the mid-1930s. My argument is not that Left Catholicism of the 1940s was completely unprecedented or wholly innovative. My aim is rather to point out that the moment of opportunity and crisis of 1943-1948 managed to procure unprecedented societal relevance and exposures to a variety of new approaches in the Catholic world.

2. Catholic Party Politics

2.1. *Politics in Belgium*

The UDB can be traced back to conversations between political activists in a variety of milieus - socialists and Catholics above all - taking place in exile and the underground from 1941 onwards. The political projects that eventually became the UDB were originally part of a wave of interest in creating progressive organisations modelled after the British Labour Party, a development affecting more than just Belgium.⁵ By the time the UDB went public⁶, almost all remaining activists hailed from the progressive Catholic milieu.

Parallel to the birth of the UDB, the traditional Belgian Catholic party underwent a process of reconstitution and renewal of its own. When the *Katholieke Vlaamse Volkspartij / Parti Catholique Social* reemerged after Liberation as the *Christelijke Volkspartij / Parti Social Chrétien* (CVP/PSC), it had not only changed its name, but it had also left behind the legacy of dependency on large occupational categories, the *standen*, as their main building blocks of party organisation. The PSC/CVP had dropped the Catholic label, though unwilling to go all the way towards deconfessionalisation.⁷ With the adoption of its Christmas Program, published in early 1946, the CVP/PSC had firmly established itself as a progressive reform-oriented organisation, including advocacy of elements of co-participation in the running of enterprises and, indeed, the national economy.⁸

Considering that the UDB's programmatic statements in many ways did not differ significantly from the CVP/PSC's *Kerstprogramma*, the question may be raised regarding the rationale for the existence of two separate political parties originating in the Catholic milieu. Indeed, the UDB's blueprint for the Belgian national economy read similar to its larger rival's. Social partnership was writ large in both cases, coupled with a decided emphasis favouring private enterpreneurship. Where the *Kerstprogramma* read: "Private property is a holy right", the UDB stoutly proclaimed: "Authority within the enterprise must stay with the owner".⁹ The key difference lay in the UDB's consistent push for total deconfessionalisation and its equally programmatic insistence on seeing itself as "the party of the Resistance". Indeed, this near-exclusive orientation towards the values emanating from

5. The sole comprehensive survey of the UDB's trajectory remains Beerten, *Le rêve travailliste en Belgique*. For French expressions of "le rêve travailliste", see, for instance, Letamendia, *Le Mouvement Républicain Populaire*, 57-58; Delbreil, *Centrisme et démocratie-chrétienne en France*, 425 and 436; and Wieviorka, *Une certaine idée de la résistance*, 256 and 387. For German interest in the British Labour Party model, see Uertz, *Christentum und Sozialismus in der frühen CDU*, 34-36, but above all Schmidt, *Zentrum oder CDU*, 159-175. This phenomenon of widespread and transnational interest in a progressive, democratic and non-confessional political organisation remains to be satisfactorily addressed, but see Peter Van Kemseke's contribution to this volume for a first overview of this complex issue.
6. Its official founding congress did not take place until June 1945, but for all practical purposes the 1 October 1944 publication of a manifesto firmly placed the UDB in the public eye. See Beerten, *Le rêve travailliste*, 31-32, for some quotations from this manifesto.
7. For a short and precise survey of this evolution, see Gerard, "Van Katholieke Partij naar CVP", 13-27.
8. On the *Kerstprogramma*, see Van den Wijngaert, *Ontstaan en stichting van de CVP-PSC* and the same author's shorter piece, "De lange weg naar het Kerstprogramma". For a view that regards the *Kerstprogramma* as less unequivocally progressive, see Jadoulle, "L'évolution du programme du Parti Social Chrétien / Christelijke Volkspartij".
9. For the *Kerstprogramma* citation, see Van den Wijngaert, *Ontstaan en stichting van de CVP-PSC*, 114. The UDB defense of private entrepreneurship is taken from a preliminary "Programme", drafted sometime before the June 1945 Congress, but widely printed and distributed. I consulted a copy in Centre d'Études et de Documentation Guerre et Sociétés Contemporaines / Studie- en Documentatiecentrum Oorlog en Hedendaagse Maatschappij (CEGE/S/OMA), Fonds UDB, 174 C 19/3, 1.

the Resistance may have ultimately constituted one of the nails in the coffin of the UDB.

While coming closest to building up a fully-fledged party structure in Brussels[10], its major structural and ideological support originated amongst the Catholic trade union movement in Wallonia.[11] But when it came to constituting lists for the first national elections, no efforts were spared to nominate resistance leaders, but very few well-known Walloon labour leaders became candidates.[12] In the end, for a variety of reasons, the first parliamentary elections of February 1946 put an end to the brief experience of the UDB. Though holding two national cabinet posts between August 1945 and January 1946, the electorate shunned the UDB, giving it a mere 2.16% of the vote. By the summer of 1946, the UDB leadership met mainly to discuss its precarious financial straits. By 1947, apart from isolated local survivals, the UDB was effectively dead.

Nevertheless, for two years a competitor had arisen to the left of the newly-reformed CVP/PSC. Never large in membership - in mid-1945 it counted a mere 500 members; on 30 March 1946 it had still no more than 2637 members; later on a former UDB leader claimed that active members and sympathisers may have at one point reached as high as 8-9000[13] -, its radiance far surpassed these paltry figures. Its daily paper, *La Cité Nouvelle*, for some time sold 100.000 copies a piece[14], and its theoretical organ, *Forces Nouvelles*, had a print-run of 8000 copies in late 1945.[15] Its influence could be felt all the way inside the CVP/PSC. Indeed, Van den Wijngaert stresses the pressures exerted by the UDB within and outside the CVP/PSC as an important factor pushing the mainstream Catholic party away from its traditional conservatism and giving the *Kerstprogramma* its decidedly progressive inflection, in particular in regards to its social policy proposals.[16] And former UDB president Antoine Delfosse in 1973 remarked somewhat embittered that the PSC/CVP on Christmas 1945 "indeed copied, but precisely so, our programme"[17], once again suggesting that the UDB's success in gaining a voice for its opinions ultimately helped to undercut its support.

---

10. Beerten, *Le rêve travailliste*, 73.
11. See, by dint of example, the somewhat exaggerated reminiscences of a leading *liègeois* UDB member, Joseph Fafchamps, thirty years after the events: "It is certain that, in Wallonia, the overwhelming majority of Christian labour leaders were active in the UDB". Comment recorded in the transcript of a radio programme, "Dossiers de l'après-guerre - Dossier Van Acker", CEGE/S/OMA, UDB, C 19/27, 59. When reading Fafchamp's comment, it should be kept in mind that the Christian labour movement in Wallonia remained rather small.
12. Beerten, *Le rêve travailliste*, 144.
13. Ibid., 132.
14. This figure is reported independently by Beerten, *Le rêve travailliste*, 29, and Willame, "L'Union Démocratique Belge", 12.
15. Willame, "L'Union Démocratique Belge", 13.
16. Van den Wijngaert, *Ontstaan en stichting van de PSC/CVP*, 29. For another example of the UDB's radicalising influence on the early PSC/CVP, see ibid., 47. For a differing view, citing no evidence for the supposed push in the direction of progressivism exerted by the UDB on the PSC/CVP, see Gerard, "De Christelijke Volkspartij en het Sociaal Pact na de Bevrijding", in particular pp. 329-334.
17. "Dossiers de l'après-guerre - Interview de M. Delfosse", CEGE/S/OMA, UDB, C 19/1, 2.

2.2. French Catholic Political Pluralism

The main postwar French Catholic party, the *Mouvement Républicain Populaire* (MRP), initially portrayed itself as far more radical than the CVP/PSC or even the UDB to the north. Whereas the UDB openly denounced calls for a revolution[18], the MRP boldly proclaimed in its first programmatic manifesto: "We want a revolution...", a slogan subheading every single paragraph in this document.[19] And they went on to underscore: "This revolution requires on the social level a collective and complete organisation of the material security of each and every one, a new reorganisation of private property in order to avoid any further enslavement of human beings to capital"[20], a formula repeated in the Catholic regional press throughout the first postwar months.

In October 1945, the MRP obtained 24.9% of the vote in elections to the first postwar constituent assembly, and it followed up this astounding success with an even higher vote of 28% in the elections to the second constituent assembly in June 1946.[21] While the tone of its party publications had by then certainly moderated somewhat compared to the first post-Liberation months, the MRP was then still regarded as a party of the Left. Of course, the precise nature of MRP "revolutionism" had always been kept purposefully vague. The last of four equally nebulous "definitions" of the kind of "revolution" the MRP advocated in its November 1944 manifesto, for instance, read: "We want a revolution which will give France the means by which completely to realise its destiny". Nevertheless, popular approval of the MRP at the polls created a situation, in which an organisation with a decidedly Left Catholic inflection became by far the strongest representative of French political Catholicism.

By contrast, interwar France had been host to two Catholic parties, the *Parti Démocrate Populaire* (PDP) and *Jeune République* (JR). To some extent, the MRP was the direct descendant of the PDP, as most PDP locals folded into the MRP in the fall of 1944. The PDP's name had become too compromised, as no more than three of its MPs had voted against giving Pétain emergency powers[22], though many PDP members had charted a different course from the very beginning and, by the time of its founding in November 1944, the MRP leadership was firmly in the hands of individuals with solid Resistance credentials.

Jeune République, however, had no need for a name change, and though many of its leaders opted to join with the MRP in 1944, the majority of its membership at its national congress in January 1945 opted for an

---

18. "The UDB wants the reform of the economic system. It does not want a massive upheaval. Violent revolution signifies twenty years of rationing". Thus were the words, printed in bold, of the UDB's "Instructions à nos conférenciers et propagandistes", CEGE/S/OMA, UDB, C 19/15, 6.
19. Ellipses in the original, boldfaced subtitle towards the beginning of "Le Manifeste du MRP", 25-26 November 1944, facsimile reprinted in Letamendia, *Le Mouvement Républicain Populaire*, 65.
20. Ibid.
21. A useful analysis of these two electoral campaigns from the point of view of MRP results can be consulted in Bichet, *La démocratie chrétienne en France*, 67-80 and 99-102.
22. Guerrier, "La Jeune République de 1912 à 1945", 739.

independent course.[23] Instead of fusing with its more moderate rival, *Jeune République* entered electoral alliances with the French Socialist Party (SFIO) and signed a unity agreement with the *Union Démocratique et Socialiste de la Résistance* (UDSR). The UDSR-*Jeune République* ticket returned twenty-five MPs to the first constituent assembly, one of them, Lucien Rose, the former president of the Savoie *comité départemental de libération*, was subsequently chosen to become Secretary of the Assembly.[24]

The MRP, then, though - up to 1947 - considerably more radical than the PSC/CVP to the north, in this early stage of its history had to contend with a serious Catholic rival even further to the Left. And even within the somewhat tarnished PDP, by no means all party locals easily made the transition into the MRP. The Toulouse section joined up with the French socialists instead. A similar defection occurred in Lyon, and Marseille PDP members dreamed *le rêve travailliste*.[25] Left Catholicism, then, was a mainstay of French politics in the immediate postwar months and years.

Simultaneous and interwoven with the above developments in French political Catholicism, a separate though in many ways intimately related strand of Left Catholicism emerged increasingly visible in the Fourth Republic, a current forcefully attracted by the seemingly uncompromising opposition of the *Parti Communiste Français* (PCF) to the reconstitution of the pre-Vichy *status quo ante*. Here the *Union des Chrétiens Progressistes* (founded in 1947) and the journal *La Quinzaine* (founded in November 1950) played the most significant role.[26] Indeed this sudden wave of "fellow-travelling" can by no means be explained by an entire cohort of Catholic political activists' refusal to comprehend the nature of stalinism on both sides of the emerging Iron Curtain. Instead, it can perhaps more fruitfully be understood as a desperate measure by a generation of committed social activists in a world political situation when marxism exerted a strong pull but where non-hierarchical interpretations of it were nearly invisible and officially disdained in both East and West.[27]

---

23. Guerrier, "La Jeune République de 1912 à 1945", 744.
24. Ibid., 752-755. The UDSR, in part originating from a Catholic resistance group, vacillated between an ill-defined socialism and an equally ill-defined Gaullism and included such notable individuals as André Malraux, Henri Frenay and François Mitterand. For some informed comments on this phenomenon, see Letamendia, *Le Mouvement Républicain Populaire*, 70, more importantly Wieviorka, *Une certaine idée de la résistance*, 379-396, but most notably the *thèse d'histoire* by Duhamel, *L'union démocratique et socialiste de la résistance*. But most conveniently see also the relevant pages in the contribution by Jean-Claude Delbreil elsewhere in this volume.
25. Delbreil, *Centrisme et démocratie chrétienne*, 436.
26. On this aspect of French Catholicism the work of Yvon Tranvouez is key, above all his *Catholiques et communistes*. But see also his earlier *Catholiques d'abord*, especially pp. 132-171, his "Guerre froide et progressisme chrétien", 83-93, his "Mission et communisme", 49-69, and, of course, his contribution to this volume.
27. Verlhac, "La jeune génération catholique en 1944 et le Parti communiste", 501-505, is a brief approximation of this problematic. For a rich source on the interplay of political, intellectual and cultural determinants creating the space for "fellow travelling" in the Catholic milieu in post-Liberation France, see also the collection of autobiographical comments by young French intellectuals: "Ceux qui en étaient, ceux qui n'en étaient pas: enquête sur le communisme et les jeunes", *Esprit*, 118 (January 1946) 191-260, and "Le communisme devant nous: enquête", *Esprit*, 121 (April 1946) 572-610.

2.3. The Italian Crucible

But it was in fascist Italy where a similar pro-communist Catholic grouping first emerged, operating in the underground and frequently changing names, some of these labels clearly identifying their ideological proclivities: *Partito Comunista Cristiano* (PCC) and *Movimento dei Cattolici Comunisti* (MCC). Tracing back their roots to the second half of the 1930s, by the spring of 1942 their cooperation with the *Partito Comunista Italiano* (PCI) had sufficiently evolved so that a leading PCC activist, Franco Rodano, was coopted into the Roman PCI leadership structure.[28] By 1943, the ties between PCI and PCC were firmly in place, though the PCC retained its organisational and ideological autonomy.[29] One of the PCC's earliest "media events" was an Easter 1943 mass demonstration on Saint Peter's Square in Rome, which led to the arrest of four hundred PCC members and forced the Pope to cancel his traditional public Easter address, but at the same time catapulted the PCC into the limelight.[30]

Though closely allied with the PCI, the PCC by no means renounced its work with and orientation towards the Christian Democratic fold. In 1943 the PCC became the *Sinistra Giovanile Cattolica*, a more than cosmetic name change. Its intellectual leaders and its working class base continued to operate in the periphery of the PCI. Its student base oriented towards work within *Democrazia Cristiana* (DC), and some did both. Franco Rodano became an editor of the newly reconstituted united trade union federation's daily newspaper; Adriano Ossicini[31] participated in the creation of the *Associazioni Cristiane dei Lavoratori Italiani* (ACLI), founded in August 1944, the Catholic Action group for the working class milieu. The definitive break with the DC, however, occurred already in the fall of 1943 (the group now became the MCC), and it is largely due to DC insistence that the PCC/MCC never obtained a seat on the Roman Committee for National Liberation, despite its eminent presence and implantation in the capital city.[32]

Rome indeed was the PCC/MCC stronghold, and only in Rome did significant numbers of blue collar workers join the organisation. Elsewhere, students and intellectuals provided its membership base. This sociological profile did not significantly change after the merger with the *Partito Cristiano Sociale*, another small Catholic grouping, in the summer of 1944, resulting in the creation of the *Partito della Sinistra Cristiana* (PSC). By now, the PSC, apart from Rome, was present in Lazio, Piedmont, Lombardy,

---

28. Casula, *Cattolici-Comunisti e sinistra cristiana*, 90. On Italian communist Christians and related Christian socialist movements and milieus, see also the contributions by Antonio Parisella and Giorgio Vecchio elsewhere in this volume.
29. Casula, *Cattolici-Comunisti e sinistra cristiana*, 81-94.
30. Ibid., 93-94.
31. Adriano Ossicini, together with Franco Rodano, had been one of the co-founders of the *Movimento di Sinistra Cristiana* (MSC), which, in turn, had developed out of the activities of South Rome youth members of Catholic Action. The MSC was the direct predecessor of the PCC. Ossicini remained a prominent figure in the colourful and influential spectrum of Italian Left Catholics in postwar decades, to become vice-president of the Italian Senate in the 1980s.
32. Casula, *Cattolici-Comunisti e sinistra cristiana*, 100-109, 130-131.

Tuscany and Umbria. Total membership figures are difficult to determine, but in Rome alone in 1944 they counted one thousand members (second only to the PCI with 3000 adherents).[33]

The PSC finally dissolved itself with most members joining the PCI after its final congress in December 1945. With that decision, one of the earliest examples of independent Christian-communist coalescence came to an end, just at a time when some French Catholics began to execute a similar turn. But the importance of the PCC/MCC/PSC goes beyond this trendsetting experience. Carlo Felice Casula notes that, particularly in Piedmont and Lombardy, the leadership team of the PSC and its periphery attracted an extraordinarily high number of intellectuals who subsequently played an outstanding role in Italian postwar public life.[34] Another historian of this phenomenon, Francesco Malgieri, notes that those members entering the PCI, particularly those individuals assuming responsible positions in the party press, introduced a new, more open style of communication into the PCI which remains to be satisfactorily assessed and analysed in all its possible consequences.[35]

After this rupture with Italian political Catholicism, prepared during Mussolini's reign and consummated little more than half a year after final Liberation, it was small wonder that a new Left Catholic current within DC would take some time to emerge. When it did so, it was initially rather moderate, and it never assumed the intransigeance of the earlier "fellow travellers". The group around Giuseppe Dossetti emerged out of a circle of young Catholic intellectuals, some of whom, like Dossetti, had participated in the civilian (or even the military) Resistance; others were more established academics, such as Amintore Fanfani, who had undergone an evolution from moderate supporter of Italian fascism to determined opponent, or Giorgio La Pira, professor of Roman Law in Florence and an expert in Thomist philosophy. Most had had various contacts with the Milanese *Università Cattolica del Sacro Cuore*.[36]

In the course of 1946 the *gruppo dossettiano* began to take shape around the then-Vice President of DC, Giuseppe Dossetti, and evolved to become "decisive opinion shapers with some weight in national political debates"[37], though in 1946 its language did not yet distinguish this group

---

33. Ibid., 142-143 (on the sociology of the MCC); pp. 173-177 (on the merger with the *Partito Cristiano Sociale*); pp. 177 and 191-206 (on the geography of the PSC); p. 131 (on membership in Rome). See also, more specifically on the *Movimento Cristiano Sociale*, Parisella, ed., *Gerardo Bruni e i cristiano-sociali* and Parisella, *Il Partito Cristiano-Sociale 1939-1948*.
34. Casula, *Cattolici-Comunisti e sinistra cristiana*, 197-199 (on the self-dissolution); pp. 192 and 206 (on its radiance within the Northern Italian intellectual milieu).
35. Malgeri, *La Sinistra Cristiana*, 431-432.
36. Useful biographical information on the leadership team can be found in the opening chapter of Pombeni, *Il gruppo dossettiano*, particularly pp. 28-96. The *Università Cattolica del Sacro Cuore* was the sole Catholic university in the Italian state at that time, and indeed even today it remains the sole Italian Catholic university officially recognised by the Association of Italian Bishops and the Holy See. Although in 1943-1945 many faculty members supported the anti-Nazi underground, in the 1930s and early 1940s the university had many ties and entered into many compromises with the fascist regime.
37. Pombeni, *Il gruppo dossettiano*, 202-203.

from the "restorationist centrism of De Gasperi, leaving the latter room for maneuvre".[38] The first open break with party discipline occurred in December of that year, at the occasion of a debate on the usefulness of continuing the tripartite coalition with the communists and socialists, which the embryonic new left oppositionists within DC continued to defend.[39] Paolo Pombeni locates the moment of "a fundamental turn" in the strategy of the Dossetti group in the subsequent year.[40] Realising that it would be more difficult to reform the DC's political orientation than to carry out effective change in the Italian Catholics' cultural domain, the Dossetti group, without abandoning their overtly political designs, founded a journal, *Cronache Sociali*, which influenced Italian public life for four difficult years.

From 1947 to 1951, the *gruppo dossettiano* frontally challenged centrist and conservative tendencies within DC, sometimes opting to step down from party posts, sometimes accepting leadership responsibilities within DC, at other times declining such offers, including cabinet posts. They became DC's most ardent defenders of social justice, consistently attacked *laissez-faire* ideology, without fail defending state intervention in the economy, finally reaching an inner-party highpoint at the June 1949 Venice Congress of DC, where their chief motion garnered 35% of the vote.[41] At the same time, the leading *dossettiani*, among them Fanfani and La Pira, helped determine the contours of the Italian constitution[42] and some eventually became mayors of important urban agglomerations, as did Giorgio La Pira in Florence.[43] In a dialectic all too common for inner-party opposition groups, the *dossettiani* wavered between principled cooperation and overt confrontation with DC's more conservative majority, perhaps thereby ultimately undercutting their ideological influence over significant portions of DC's membership.

The *dossettiani* never purposefully attempted to organise a distinct inner-party faction or tendency. In September 1946, they had founded an intellectual think tank, *Civitas Humana*, and one year later a largely stillborn attempt was made to form a support group for their journal, *Amici di Cronache Sociali*.[44] But the entire leadership team of the *dossettiani* remained singularly disinterested in helping to create an organised political current and thus remained a powerful though curiously amorphous group.[45] And the experience ended in a similarly enigmatic fashion when, in June and September 1951, Giuseppe Dossetti gathered his closest supporters for two gatherings to announce his total withdrawal from politics. It spelled the effective end of the *corrente dossettiano*.[46]

---

38. Galli and Facchi, *La sinistra democristiana*, 44.
39. Ibid., 48, and Pombeni, *Il gruppo dossettiano*, 350-351.
40. Pombeni, *Il gruppo dossettiano*, 388.
41. Galli and Facchi, *La sinistra democristiana*, 90-93.
42. Pombeni, *Il gruppo dossettiano*, 217-306.
43. Galli and Facchi, *La sinistra democristiana*, 115.
44. On *Civitas Humana*, see Pombeni, *Il gruppo dossettiano*, 313-333; on the *Amici di Cronache Sociali*, see Pombeni, *Le 'Cronache Sociali' di Dossetti*, 92-104.
45. See the repeated comments to this effect in Pombeni, *Le 'Cronache Sociali'*, 96, 121, 152 and 211.
46. Galli and Facchi, *La sinistra democristiana*, 117-119.

For as long as it lasted, however, this current engendered much national debate within and outside of *Democrazia cristiana*. An average monthly circulation of three thousand copies sold ensured that *Cronache Sociali* reached a respectable audience. Pombeni's calculations suggest that roughly 9000 individuals at one point or another closely followed the monthly magazine for at least six months in a row.[47] Its genuinely national distribution, reaching an audience down to the level of provincial towns, ensured a resonance for its beliefs.[48] *Cronache Sociali* sold best in regions affected by at least some industrialisation, where marxist parties were forcefully present and acted as serious competitors to DC, where Catholics had been involved in the Resistance, and where they had thus experienced firsthand the solid roots of the marxist-oriented working class Left.[49] In sociological terms, the audience of *Cronache Sociali* included far more than a narrow political elite, but above all reached a young, male, intellectual readership of relatively broad proportions.[50]

Symptomatically, these socio-geographic conclusions overlap to an astounding degree with the findings of Jean-Pierre Gault concerning the readership of the French Left Catholic journal, *Témoignage Chrétien*, at roughly the same time.[51] Given this transnational parallel affecting the French and Italian Left Catholic milieus, it only stands to reason that the Catholic Left was in part a product of ongoing intellectual debates reflecting the atmosphere of industrial Europe, then experiencing the often conflictual but sometimes creative confluence and interaction between Catholicism and marxism in a politico-economic context dominated by liberal capitalism then just beginning to consider its social welfare option. It is to these debates within the Catholic milieu to which I turn now.

3. Theology / Philosophy

3.1. The Duality of the Temporal and the Spiritual

In one sense, the intellectual origins of mid-20th century Left Catholicism can be traced back all the way to the 13th century. For the intellectual revolution effected by Thomas Aquinas consisted not only in rehabilitating the thought of non-Christians for scholarly attention, but, in part resulting from his interest in Greek philosophy, Thomas Aquinas theorised the essential duality of the spiritual and the temporal, the natural and the supernatural. This postulation of two dialectically related, though analytically separate spheres, opened a window of opportunity for subsequent philosophers and theologians. The temporal sphere was always conceptualised as subordinate to the spiritual plane, yet it had now obtained at least

---

47. Pombeni, *Le 'Cronache Sociali'*, 192.
48. Ibid., 60 (national distribution) and p. 73 (for its respectable distribution in provincial Italy).
49. Ibid., 170 and 196.
50. Ibid., 150.
51. Gault, *Histoire d'une fidélité: Témoignage Chrétien*, 76-81. Paolo Pombeni draws attention to this similarity in his *Le 'Cronache Sociali'*, 150.

theoretically an existence independent from the supernatural. And it was up to later generations to lay the stress on one or the other pole in this dynamically interrelated conceptual pair.[52]

The distinction between the temporal and spiritual planes played an important role in 20th-century reconfigurations of Catholic thought, irrespective of political provenance. Thus, ideologically rather moderate Catholic Action groups already in the early 1920s utilised this duality to proclaim a distinction between Catholic and political action. 20th-century Left Catholic thought was equally indebted to Thomism, and indeed its representatives consciously viewed themselves in a direct line of continuity. The modern-day Thomist authority with the largest purchase on his contemporaries was Jacques Maritain, and his *Humanisme intégral* became the standard reference work for neo-Thomist theologians in the mid-20th century.[53] This pathbreaking work offered a 20th-century interpretation of Thomist principles, deeply affected by the contemporaneous relevance of marxist social thought and marxist social movements.

First gaining international fame as theologian and philosopher in the 1920s[54], Maritain soon abandoned his sympathies for conservatism and by the 1930s emerged as the leading Catholic intellectual with distinctly progressive leanings. In early 1934, for example, he authored two public manifestoes, one drawing attention to the injustices meted out to Austrian socialists in the wake of their unsuccessful military attempt to stem the tide of the radical Right on 12 February 1934, the other focusing on the dangers to French democracy in the wake of a semi-spontaneous and violent physical attack on the French parliament by right wing activists six days earlier.[55] Later on in the decade, he repeatedly protested against Francoist violence in the course of the Spanish Civil War. During World War II exiled in the United States, Maritain continued his openly political engagement by broadcasting frequent messages into occupied France.[56]

---

52. The literature on Thomas Aquinas is vast. Given the context of this essay, a useful and precise paraphrasing of his theorisation of the duality of the spiritual and the temporal can be gleaned in the opening paragraph of Maritain, "The Planes of Action", in the appendix to his *True Humanism*, 288-294.
53. Note, for instance, Marie-Dominique Chenu's authoritative comment on this volume: "One knows to what extent its pages, which one could consider prophetic, ...have animated the Christian generation of 1936, of 1940, of 1945". See Chenu, *Pour une théologie du travail*, 35.
54. The author of the first comprehensive biography of Maritain, Jean-Luc Barré, interestingly devotes two thirds of his voluminous study, *Jacques et Raïssa Maritain: les mendiants du ciel*, to Maritain's career up to 1932. But see also Fouilloux, *Une église en quête de liberté*, 57-65, for a brief aperçu of Maritain's radiance in the 1920s.
55. For these two statements, co-signed by other Catholic intellectuals, see "A propos de la répression des troubles de Vienne" and "Pour le bien commun", in J. and R. Maritain, *Oeuvres Complètes*, V, 1020-1021 and 1022-1040. For the international context and the crucial place of these two events within the history of interwar Europe, see Horn, *European Socialists*, 20-23, 122-127 and 140-142.
56. On these experiences, see, amongst others, Bressolette, "Jacques Maritain et la guerre civile en Espagne", 33-42, and Fourcade, "Jacques Maritain inspirateur de la Résistance", 14-57. The radio broadcasts on the Voice of America and other stations can be consulted under the title "Messages" in J. and R. Maritain, *Oeuvres Complètes*, VIII, 381-508.

Humanisme intégral was an organic product of Maritain's engagement for social justice. Published in 1936 - the preface was written literally on the eve of the victory of the French Popular Front -, the volume consisted for the most part of six slightly revised lectures he had originally presented in August 1934 to the summer school of the University of Santander in northern Spain.57 The date and location of these lectures are highly significant, given the - at least in portions - militantly progressive character of the published pages. Of all European countries threatened by political instability and the growth of the radical Right in the 1930s, Spain experienced the highest levels of unrest, and within Spain its northern provinces. Indeed, less than two months after Maritain taught in Santander, a massive working class rebellion gripped northern Spain, a violent revolt spearheaded by a radicalised, voluntarist social democracy. It is therefore highly significant that the very text, which guided an entire generation of progressive Catholic intellectuals, emerged out of the highly politicised context of northern Spain in 1934.58

In *Humanisme intégral*, Maritain further developed the Thomist conception of the duality of temporal and spiritual planes by concentrating on the natural world and in effect stretching the boundaries of worldly affairs to maximal proportions. Paying strict homage to the ultimate primacy of the spiritual, when focussing on the temporal sphere Maritain proved to be an ardent supporter of pluralism and autonomy. In contradistinction to prevailing unity in the spiritual sphere, "on the second plane, on the temporal one, the rule is not union, but diversity. When the objective is the earthly life of men, when it concerns earthly interests and our temporal welfare, or such and such an ideal of the common temporal good and the ways and means of realising it, it is normal that a unanimity, whose center is of a supra-temporal order should be broken, and that Christians who communicate at the same altar should find themselves divided in the commonwealth. It would be contrary to the nature of things, and hence highly dangerous, to seek on this plane a union among Catholics which could there be only artificial...."59

But there was more. Addressing the interrelationship between Catholic action and political action, Maritain postulated: "It seems normal and inevitable that the appropriate organs of action should correspond to new social and political conceptions. The awakening of the Christian conscience to those strictly temporal social and political problems implied by the inauguration of a new *Christendom* will entail, I hold, the birth of new temporally and politically specified political formations, whose inspiration will be intrinsically Christian".60 Considering Maritain's concomitant comments on the role of the modern-day proletariat (about which below), *Humanisme intégral* must be considered a concerted and passionate defense of Catholic political pluralism, at the same time giving center stage to problems and issues pertaining to working class self-emancipation.

---

57. See Maritain's "Foreword", penned on 25 April 1936, in *True Humanism*, VII-IX.
58. On the comparative place of Spanish (and in particular Asturian) politics in 1934, see Horn, *European Socialists*, 53-62.
59. Maritain, *True Humanism*, 297-298.
60. Ibid., 265-266.

Not surprisingly, Maritain's contemporaries read Maritain's volume with utmost interest and attention. In an important review of *Humanisme intégral* - important because of where it appeared and what it said - Marie-Dominique Chenu, in the pages of the *Bulletin thomiste*, pointed to one of Maritain's key accomplishments. Chenu saw *Humanisme intégral* as a programmatic statement aiming to adapt Catholic thought to the challenges of modern society. Chenu drew particular attention to Maritain's efforts to create a space for pluralism, to supersede "the unitary metaphysics of the Middle Ages", understandable and logical in its time, by advocating movement towards "an order characterised by a pluralism more highly developed than in the Middle Ages, a pluralism in the economic, social, political, even religious sphere, inasmuch as, by a normal process of differentiation, the autonomy of the temporal plane comes into its own...."[61]

Ten years after the first printing of *Humanisme intégral*, in the crisis moment of post-Liberation Europe, Maritain's bold pronouncements were echoed throughout the growing sphere of influence of Left Catholicism. In Italy, for instance, the *dossettiani*, frequently paying homage to the intellectual influence of Jacques Maritain[62], defended their course of action as a distinct current within DC in an increasingly militant fashion, as did Giuseppe Lazzatti in a DC leadership gathering: "And this is one of the most important problems: the problem of the relations between the Church and the world. In short, and given that we want to render the Church maximal service, underlying the solution to this problem is our will to work as Christians but in the real world, according to the constraints of the world, which is the field of politics. To reach real liberty in the world means to construct the world according to the rules and regulations of the world...which are reached by following the demands of the world: self-determination from below. By constructing a distinction between political action and Catholic action, we do not mean to question the divine unity of Catholics, as that unity exists on the supernatural level. Instead we are impelled by the recognition that such a distinction operates on a very profound level in this world of human beings we live in...."[63]

3.2. From the Centrality of Humanity to Self-Emancipation of the Working Class

For this circle of neo-Thomist intellectuals, the crucial link or the living embodiment of the duality of the temporal and the spiritual consisted in the existence of humanity. In the words of Emmanuel Mounier, in the 1930s a close collaborator of Maritain, the human individual or the person is "the highest form of existence", and "the evolution of prehuman nature culminates in the creative moment when this achievement of the universe

---

61. The review was published in the *Bulletin thomiste*, 15 (April - June 1938) 360-364, citation on p. 362.
62. On this link, see, most conveniently, Ardigò, "Jacques Maritain e 'Cronache Sociali'", 195-202, and Dall'Asta, "Maritain e il movimento dossettiano", 275-289.
63. Cited in Galli and Facchi, *La sinistra democristiana*, 85-86, first ellipses copied from Galli and Facchi's rendering of the text.

emerges".[64] Created out of the universe in accordance with God's design, each person incorporates and exemplifies the consubstantiality of the temporal and the spiritual, of matter and spirit. However, in contradistinction to individualistic liberalism, neo-Thomists viewed the human being as an organic part of a social community.

Again, as was the case with the theorisation of the duality of matter and spirit, the mere elevation of humanity to central place in neo-Thomist philosophy did by no means automatically entail a conscious choice for social radicalism of a progressive kind. And, indeed, personalist philosophy could and did provide a matrix for any number of political engagements within the entire spectrum of political beliefs. But it created the possibility for various concrete philosophical and practical departures by mid-20th century Thomist philosophers in the direction of progressive social choice. Given the political turbulence of the 1930s and the 1940s, the frequency of such a choice is wholly unsurprising.

For Mounier, for instance, history since ancient Greece has seen a steady, though frequently interrupted, progression of human emancipation, liberating humanity from multiple yokes that have kept it from fulfilling its divine mission to become the truly autonomous master of nature. While much has been accomplished on this road to personal liberty, more remains to be done. In particular, social inequalities continue to hamper the quest for freedom. "Several centuries were necessary to pass from the spiritual rehabilitation of the slave to his effective liberation; the recognition of the equality of souls has still not been translated into an equality of social chances"[65]; for Mounier, then, social liberation is an elementary part of the agenda of human liberation and remains to be acted upon.

Marie-Dominique Chenu also places humanity at center stage, but in a very concrete way he goes beyond Mounier by ascribing a central place within human evolution to human labouring activity. "Just as, within the evolution of the cosmos, human beings are anatomically perfected, so does humanity perfect itself within the evolution of the world; *here labour plays a central role*".[66] "Humanity and the universe: labour lies at the juncture of the two. And also at the juncture of spirit and matter".[67] While Chenu elaborated his theology of labour, a German Left Catholic, Theo Pirker, entitled his own equally innovative programmatic statement: "Towards a Theology of Labour", underscoring the similarity of intellectual and political ferment on both sides of the Rhine.[68]

---

64. Mounier, *Le personnalisme*, 7.
65. Ibid., 10.
66. Chenu, *Théologie du travail*, 24, emphasis added.
67. Ibid., 28.
68. Pirker, "Kleine Arbeitstheologie", 149-166. It shall come as no surprise, then, that, when the Dominican monastery of Walberberg near Cologne reopened its adult continuing education program in liaison with the reconstituted Christian Democratic Union, the second major theme was likewise, "On the sense and value of human labour". (Incidentally, the first topic had been: "The human being and his relationship to community".) See Uertz, *Christentum und Sozialismus in der frühen CDU*, 67.
    The Walberberg monastery was a centre of German Left Catholicism independent of the circle of Bavarian Left Catholics to which Theo Pirker belonged. Pirker's "Kleine Arbeitstheologie" was published in 1949 in the journal *Frankfurter Hefte* belonging to yet another independent grouping of Left Catholics around Walter Dirks and Eugen

Given Left Catholics' focus on human beings and on labour, the next logical step was attention to labouring human beings, or the working class. Analyses of various aspects of working class life constituted indeed a red thread in the work of many leading Left Catholic intellectuals. In this context, it may suffice to refer to a central figure in the milieu of Belgian Left Catholicism, Philippe De Soignie, who, in the mid-1940s, not only devoted much energy to the construction of the Belgian MPF (see below), but likewise penned a number of highly innovative and challenging books. In his *Culture et milieux populaires*, he drew attention to various dimensions of blue collar working class culture.[69] His *Mystique chrétienne et ascension ouvrière* built on his earlier work and accomplished a twofold task. The first portion of the book provided a sociological survey of the economic, social, cultural, moral and religious condition of the Belgian working class; the second half attempted to provide a blueprint for its self-emancipation.[70]

And here we have reached one of the central, if not the central preoccupation of many Left Catholic intellectuals: the liberation of the working class as ultimate fulfillment of humanity's divine mission. This was a topic first broached by social Catholics at the beginning of the 20th century, but now, in mid-century, it took on an entirely different meaning, given the strong presence of marxism on a continental scale, and given the greater willingness of some Catholics to engage in dialogue with, and not just to remain in ardent opposition to, such secular forces. Here again, De Soignie may serve as a useful point of departure. The very opening sentences of his *Mystique chrétienne* constitute a veritable political programme: "This brochure takes the form of a blackboard with two volets. The first is composed of dark colours and depicts the desperate situation of the working class households; by contrast, the second is lit up by a brightly-shining light: the one towards which today's working class is advancing: its social, familial, cultural and religious emancipation".[71] Theo Pirker, in his "Kleine Arbeitstheologie", put it this way: "A Christian revolution must be the permanent revolution against the system of exploitation and oppression, against the deification (*Vergötzung*) of the human spirit".[72] For Marie-Dominique Chenu, the antagonistic relationship between capital and labour "is not a minor dispute (*querelle*) between the rich and the poor but a constitutive foundation of the contemporary economic and social order" that needs to be resolved.[73]

Even Jacques Maritain, usually committed to less openly partisan writings, occasionally let his audience know where his sympathies lay. Characteristically, a section of his *Humanisme intégral* is entitled, "The growing consciousness of the dignity and solidarity of labour", followed by a section on "The historic role of the proletariat", including the following passage unequivocally taking sides in favour of working class self-emancipation: "If the proletariat claims to be treated as an adult person, by this very

---

Kogon. On German Left Catholicism in the immediate postwar era, see also the contribution by Andreas Lienkamp elsewhere in this volume.
69. De Soignie, *Culture et milieux populaires*.
70. De Soignie, *Mystique chrétienne et ascension ouvrière*.
71. Ibid., 9.
72. Pirker, "Kleine Arbeitstheologie", 165.
73. Chenu, *Théologie du travail*, 9-19, citation on p. 10.

fact it is not in a position to be succoured, ameliorated or saved by another social class. On the contrary, the principal part in the next phase of historic evolution belongs to it and its own upward movement".[74] And, in case one may doubt whether this unabashedly radical stance survived the political conjuncture of 1934-1936, in a private communication of April 1943 Maritain once again stated "that the bourgeoisie as a social class has failed and reconstruction must be based on the workers' organisations".[75]

3.3. Voluntarism, Morality, and the Marxist Challenge

It is Jacques Maritain again who at one point approvingly refers to Karl Marx's famous dictum, "Man makes history, but under conditions that are determined". Significantly, Maritain immediately followed up on this quotation with a fitting remark of his own: "Scientific German marxism forgot the first half of this formula".[76] The Left Catholic preoccupation with work and working class emancipation naturally resulted in a serious engagement with marxist thought. For some, amongst them Emmanuel Mounier, it remained a far more central concern of their intellectual output than it did for Jacques Maritain.[77]

What Left Catholic intellectuals loved most in Marx were his writings on alienation. Marie-Dominique Chenu's observations may stand for many others: "It was the contemporary tragedy of humanity suffering enslavement by its own labour that prodded Marx's discovery of the *homo oeconomicus*. His metaphysics of production grew out of the observation of the atrocious conditions by which human beings destroy themselves by that very act by which they should find their ultimate joy: humanity alienates itself through its own labour. We are aware of this grand theme, mystical and prophetic as much as doctrinal, of the communist philosopher. Work exists therefore in a state of dehumanising subversion: the emancipation of labour constitutes the return to humanity. This is the humanism of Karl Marx".[78]

What Left Catholic intellectuals loved least in Marx was not only his solid adherence to a materialist philosophy, but his frequent stresses on the seemingly overwhelming socio-economic constraints against which humanity could rarely advance. Jacques Maritain's acerbic comment on German social democracy's partial appropriation of Marx's statement, "Man makes history, but under conditions that are determined", may appear to exculpate Marx himself. Others within the Left Catholic milieu were less generous.

---

74. Maritain, *True Humanism*, 228-229.
75. Letter by Jacques Maritain to John U. Nef, 4 April 1943 - Archives Jacques Maritain (AJM). Maritain here describes the views of a joint acquaintance (Louis Marlio), whom Maritain characterises as "a good personal friend, an open mind and reflective man, *profondément démocrate et progressiste*", and it is made abundantly clear that Maritain identifies with that view.
76. Maritain, *True Humanism*, 206.
77. Some of the most crucial articles on this topic appear in the posthumously edited anthology by Emmanuel Mounier, *Communisme, anarchie et personnalisme*, which has the advantage of simultaneously drawing attention to the anarchist strand equally noticeable in some Left Catholic thought.
78. Chenu, *Théologie du travail*, 59.

Amintore Fanfani, soon-to-be the economic expert of the *dossettiani*, in 1944 ascribed similar views to marxism *tout court* and pointed his finger at its curious combination of mechanical materialism and messianism. If change is only possible when conditions are ripe, at the same time that change is inevitable when conditions are ripe, then what is the role of human agency in determining its own fate?[79]

Apart from this decidedly voluntarist strain in Left Catholic thought, another point of conflict with marxism was the latter's seemingly blind belief in the liberatory potential of production and planning. This technocratic and productivist orientation could have devastating consequences unless individuals are protected from anonymous bureaucracies by measures ensuring the primacy of human beings over machines by means of decentralised and democratic control over seemingly neutral mechanisms.[80] And precisely here the Left Catholic critique of liberal capitalism and productivist marxism meet up in what Philippe De Soignie, for instance, regards as "the same fundamental error: the one and the other consider work as an independent variable without worrying about what gets produced or the person who does the work".[81] Or, to close with an observation by the German Left Catholic Goetz Briefs, made in a letter to Jacques Maritain: "Indeed, there exists an invisible connection between all-out liberalism and communism; the mechanisms of market constraints and the mechanisms of state domination coexist in a - I would say - dialectical relationship. In both systems human beings constitute merely the building blocks of a process proceeding anonymously".[82]

Again, as is the case with other aspects of Left Catholic social thought, the simultaneous critique of liberalism and marxism is by no means an exclusively Left Catholic attribute and can be found in more conservative social Catholics' pronouncements several decades earlier. But the novelty is a vastly different social and political context and a far greater penchant of individuals, such as Maritain or Chenu, to engage with, rather than primarily to confront, marxist social thought and practice. Equally distancing themselves from both liberal capitalism and mechanical marxism, though frequently evincing rather obvious sympathies for Karl Marx rather than Adam Smith, in the 1940s Western European Left Catholics staked their intellectual honesty and sometimes their lives in the service of humanity. They provided the intellectual backdrop and justification for the new experiments in political Catholicism referred to above. They likewise helped

---

79. This is one of the messages I extract from the citations and paraphrases of Fanfani's 1944 *Storia delle dottrine economiche - il naturalismo* in Galli and Facchi, *La sinistra democristiana*, 304.
80. This passage has benefited from the discussion of the economic beliefs of Maritain and Mounier in De Jonghe, "Het integraal humanisme van Maritain", and Bouckaert, "Mounier en de beweging rond Esprit", with the most interesting passages on pp. 110-111 and 136-137.
81. De Soignie, *Leçons familières d'économie politique*, 34.
82. Letter by Goetz Briefs to Jacques Maritain, 26 September 1936 - Archives Jacques Maritain. Goetz Briefs (1889-1974) began his career teaching economics at a number of German universities during the Weimar Republic, already then closely cooperating with the Christian trade unions. He belonged to the *Königswinterer Kreis*, whose members helped shape the papal encyclica *Quadragesimo Anno* (1931). On Briefs' biography, see, most conveniently, Schröder, *Katholizismus und Einheitsgewerkschaft*, 338-348.

spawn the creation of novel Left Catholic apostolic/social missionary movements, to which I turn now. Perhaps Jean-Paul Sartre was right when, in 1948, he referred to Thomism, marxism and existentialism as the only living philosophies then.[83]

4. Apostolic and Social Missions

4.1. The Worker Priests

Not all Thomists were Left Catholics and not all Left Catholics were Thomists. Similarly, the degree of interest and involvement in matters concerning the world of work, workers and working class self-emancipation differed widely within the spectrum of reform-minded Left Catholic intellectuals and/or social activists. Thus, for instance, I have yet to find a single concrete reference within the voluminous writings of Jacques Maritain to the problematic of the worker priest phenomenon in post-Liberation francophone Europe. Nevertheless, as will hopefully have become clear above, Maritain's opus played a - if not the - central role in stimulating the engagement of post-World War II Catholics with key problems posed by modernism and industrial development. Indeed, the creative ferment of the *nouvelle théologie*[84] can, in my estimation, be measured most clearly and concretely in two specific applications of theology to practice: the worker priest phenomenon and the *Mouvement Populaire des Familles* (MPF).[85]

---

83. This remark, made by Sartre at a conference in Canada, was reported by Étienne Gilson to Yves Simon, who relayed it to their mutual friend and colleague, Jacques Maritain. Sartre had apparently referred to the situation in France. See letter by Yves Simon to Jacques Maritain, 10 April 1948 - Archives Jacques Maritain.
84. A masterful survey and standard reference work for years to come of this "new theology" can now be consulted in Fouilloux, *Une église en quête de liberté*. The term *nouvelle théologie* refers to the diverse and somewhat amorphous assortment of mostly francophone theologians, such as Maritain, Mounier, Chenu, Henri de Lubac and Yves Congar, who were united by their desire to combat creeping secularisation tendencies by means of a "return to the sources of the faith" which, in their view, would have the beneficial twin effects of renewing the Church and furnishing arguments for the ongoing discussion with their contemporaries. In their quest these thinkers engaged in dialogue with Catholics, non-Catholic Christians, members of other religious faiths, and even agnostics or atheists. Most of their writings were published between 1940-1960. Conformity with established theological traditions never stood very high on their agenda, and consequently their pronouncements frequently called forth hostile reactions from the Church hierarchy. Their proximity to the milieu of Left Catholicism covered in this volume varied considerably, though virtually all of them influenced Left Catholics in a direct or indirect manner.
85. In what follows I concentrate exclusively on Belgian and French developments, though the MPF had branches in the Suisse Romande and Québec as well. In the 1940s and early 1950s Italy never witnessed phenomena quite like the MPF or the worker priests, though new strategic approaches towards the working class milieu were developed and applied in practice in Italy as well. Similar to efforts of the *Mission de France*, they stopped short of the experiences of full-time industrial employment. On efforts by the Catholic Church to renew its links with the world of working class labour in Italy, see Durand, *L'église catholique dans la crise de l'Italie*, 471-497.

Interest on the part of priests or priest-seminarians in taking up full-time industrial work emerged in various locations of industrial Europe separate and independent from each other though clearly linked on a transhistorical, intellectual or spiritual plane. As was the case with the *nouvelle théologie*, the time was ripe for such an experiment, benefiting from the atmosphere of post-Liberation openness and optimistic belief in the possibility of significant socio-political changes. The idea of such a full-time industrial apostolic mission was in the air, so-to-speak. What was lacking was "merely" the concretisation of such a perspective which had taken shape in countless reflections and meditations by a variety of creative and committed individuals from Liège to Marseille.

In 1941, the Dominican Jacques Loew became the very first worker priest anywhere - on the docks of Marseille.[86] Yet his proletarian mission initially grew out of the engagement of a fellow Dominican, Louis-Joseph Lebret, whose spiritual itinerary bears some attention, though Lebret never became a worker priest himself. In the late 1920s, Father Lebret was posted to his native Brittany near Saint-Malo where he studied and shared the lives of the local fishermen, then buffeted not only by habitual climatic tempests but by the effects of the Great Depression as well. For some ten years, Louis-Joseph Lebret immersed himself in the community and resolved to do what he could to improve their lives. He involved himself in trade union work. By 1938 he began to study the economic writings of Karl Marx. His marginalia of *Das Kapital* reflect his initial reticence of the materialist philosophy evinced in this work, but Lebret's comments soon began to become less openly hostile. He recognised in these pages the same indignation vis-à-vis the working class condition that he had felt in past years: "I discover on each page the same conclusions I have drawn on the basis of nine years of experience with the social conditions of maritime workers, and I am singularly astounded by the parallels".[87] The more Lebret read in *Das Kapital*, the more critical he became of traditional Catholic social teaching: "This man [i.e. Marx] is definitely a genius", he noted at one point. "Let us measure the backwardness of social Catholicism". "Catholics should have loudly proclaimed those things one hundred years ago".[88]

In 1940, Lebret moved to Marseille, where he continued to work amongst French fishermen but aided in the decision of his assistant, Jacques Loew, to take on full-time work amongst Marseille dockworkers. Loew's mission consisted in the same type of empirical, quasi-anthropological participant-observer enterprise amongst longshoremen that Lebret had specialised in amongst maritime workers for the past dozen years.[89] While Lebret and Loew moved towards missionary work amongst blue collar workers in the southern reaches of francophone Europe, a similar preoccu-

---

86. See, most notably, Loew, *Journal d'une mission ouvrière*.
87. Cited in Pelletier, *Économie et humanisme*, 114.
88. The first of these citations can be found on p. 114, the other two on p. 115 of Pelletier's rich and detailed volume. Another recent biographer of Louis-Joseph Lebret cites a close associate as describing Lebret's daily reading schedule including "fifteen minutes of church fathers and forty-five minutes of Marx". See Houée, *Louis-Joseph Lebret*, 33.
89. On the origins of the *Mission de Marseille*, see also Poulat, *Naissance des prêtres-ouvriers*, 415-443.

pation began to dominate the reflections of a committed priest on the northern edge of francophone Europe.

Two brief internships as a factory worker during his seminary education in 1921 and 1922 had stimulated the interest in full-time industrial work by the Belgian priest Charles Boland. For twenty long years his wishes were rejected by his superiors, who regarded Boland's desire as eccentric and incompatible with the mission of a priest, but in 1942 he finally received permission to engage in factory labour at least one day per week, followed by Liège Bishop Kerkhofs's approval of full-time work in 1943.[90]

Jacques Loew and Charles Boland were only the initial leavening of what became in subsequent years a far less uncommon practice of full-time industrial work for priests. And there existed other strands within 1940s Catholicism independent of Boland and Loew/Lebret, conceptually developing and practically engaging in near-identical paths. Thus, hidden away in the deserts of North Africa, an unlikely spot for the genesis of an apostolic mission amongst the working class poor, the order of the *Petits Frères de Jésus* developed a related concept of full-time industrial work, which, upon moving back to France, some of their members commenced in Aix-en-Provence on 5 May 1947.[91] The numerically most important of these simultaneous strivings towards new forms of apostolic missions within the industrial proletariat became the *Mission de France*.

Its seminary in Lisieux, Normandy, was officially called into existence by the French association of bishops in July 1941 and opened its doors in the fall of 1942. Not all French worker priests lived through the experience of Lisieux, but at the same time not all seminarians were French. In Lisieux, a town located in provincial Normandy at some distance from industrial France, seminarians were prepared for various apostolic missions amongst the working class, in the initial years none of them including full-time industrial labour. But to prepare for their spiritual practice in working class France, students were encouraged to read Marx and communist materials. Emphasis was placed on communal living; breakfast exercises included reflections on current events; and short-term apprenticeships in factories became the norm.[92]

Further stimulation regarding fundamental changes in the approach to missionary work amongst French blue collar workers was provided by the 1943 publication of the joint volume by Henri Godin and Yvan Daniel, *France, pays de mission?* This pathbreaking and highly influential study appeared in print at the right place and at the right time. It drew attention to the incontrovertible phenomenon of de-christianisation amongst the

---

90. On the origins and history of the Belgian worker priest movement, see Boland, *Dure percée*; Arnal, *Priests in Working-Class Blue*, 70-71; Poulat, *Naissance des prêtres-ouvriers*, 468-475; and, last but not least, De Greef, *Les prêtres-ouvriers en Belgique*, 1-23.
91. On the *Petits Frères*'s industrial mission, see Voillaume, *Charles de Foucauld*, particularly pp. 307-327, 338-353 and 423-434. It is perhaps of more than passing interest that, in the last decade of his life, none other than Jacques Maritain joined the order of the *Petits Frères*.
92. On the Lisieux think tank, see Poulat, *Naissance des prêtres ouvriers*, passim; Wattebled, *Stratégies catholiques en monde ouvrier*, particularly pp. 31-37; Arnal, *Priests in Working-Class Blue*, 25; but above all the biography of the head of the Lisieux seminary by Vinatier, *Le Père Augros*.

French industrial proletariat, and it provided a number of suggestions on how to turn this situation around.[93] Nowhere in this collaborative volume did Godin and Daniel suggest manual labour by priests, and the thought of engagement for working class self-liberation was equally far from their minds. And, indeed, their reflections on new forms of apostolic missions within working class France must be seen simultaneously as cause and effect of widespread ferment then affecting Catholic France, desperately trying to renew its link with a blue collar proletariat that had severed most ties with the Catholic world. Efforts to build new bridges took on manifold forms, including most notably reforms of sacerdotal and other practices in working class parishes.[94]

But in the process of opening up to the world of the working class poor, priests and parish activists experienced firsthand the pain and injustice of working class life at the same time that they received a taste of the particular solidarity and camaraderie of the workplace. The wish to do more for their flock than to aid them from the outside became increasingly strong and relevant. And while parish priests within France were beginning to consider going beyond the boundaries of traditional spiritual practice, many of their less fortunate colleagues were forced to share the daily misery of their fellow deportees in German labour camps and factories. In addition, by April 1943 the Archbishop of Paris, Cardinal Suhard, sanctioned the unprecedented practice of illegally sending volunteer priests to assist spiritually French labour draftees in Germany. At the same time other priests took part in all aspects of the military and/or civilian Resistance in occupied France. All these various experiments and experiences helped instill a deeply-felt belief in the necessity and utility of a more complete immersion within and exposure to the proletarian condition.[95]

By 1944 the first worker priest belonging to the *Mission de France* took up his post. By early 1947 the *Mission de France* counted five worker priests, and 1947 turned out to be the breakthrough year. At the end of that year, twenty-five French worker priests had taken up their appointment. "By their highpoint between 1952 and 1954, they numbered approximately one hundred, about eighty in the secular priesthood with the remainder in the Franciscan, Capuchin, Jesuit, Dominican, Pradosian and other religious orders".[96] At the same time, in Belgium the total number of worker priests, throughout the 1950s, never surpassed the ceiling of eight individuals at any one time.[97]

---

93. Godin and Daniel, *France, pays de mission?*, experiencing many reissues in subsequent decades. On Godin, the book, and the origins of the *Mission de France*, the standard reference work remains Poulat, *Naissance des prêtres ouvriers*, 36-114 and 378-414.
94. The most comprehensive survey of such gropings to reconnect with working class France are the first nine chapters in Wattebled, *Stratégies catholiques*, 13-170.
95. Again, the standard reference to these developments remains Poulat, *Naissance des prêtres ouvriers*, particularly pp. 180-375. For the impact of the resistance experience, see now above all Comte, *L'honneur et la conscience*, particularly pp. 113-283.
96. Arnal, *Priests in Working-Class Blue*, 68.
97. De Greef, *Les prêtres-ouvriers en Belgique*, table following p. 75.

The praxis of worker priest engagement fundamentally affected and transformed the lives of these men.[98] What originally was conceptualised as an exclusively apostolic mission, eventually became almost indistinguishable from a simultaneous social mission. Sharing all aspects of life of their co-workers soon meant participation in trade union work and, given the socio-political milieu of postwar industrial France, this most frequently entailed membership in the communist-dominated *Confédération Générale du Travail* (CGT). Some worker priests were chosen by their fellow workers for leadership posts in their union, and strike support work in oftentimes responsible positions became less the exception than the norm in then (as so often) strike-torn France.[99]

In short, in the eyes of the auxiliary bishop of Lyon, Alfred Ancel: "Instead of focusing above all on the light emanating from Christ via the Church", he wrote in a long letter to the worker priests of his diocese, "you have chosen to concentrate your efforts on the human beings you would like to save".[100] In the process, most traditional concepts of the meaning of priesthood and missionary work underwent a significant evolution, including sacerdotal practices. "Every major unprecedented step taken by these labouring clergy into the proletarian world brought with it a corresponding shift away from more orthodox perceptions of the priesthood. The standard notion of the priest as the holy and separate one, distinct from the people and the living embodiment of a higher, more spiritual world was challenged deeply by the worker-priests' plummet into the proletariat".[101]

In due course, the French and Belgian worker priests developed out of their own practice elements of a theology of labour, similar to the more deductive reflections by Marie-Dominique Chenu and Theo Pirker I cited above. Forced to justify their non-conformous activities, French priests began to invoke an "incarnational solidarity with the working class"[102], and, according to Arnal, the Belgian worker priests in particular, though few in numbers, came closest to systematising "an apologetic for the manual labour of priests".[103]

Indeed, this may be the moment to stress that, in general, a focus on the mere quantity of worker priests in Belgium and France would most definitely miss the mark. For the number of actively engaged, full-time industrial worker priests barely surpassed the one hundred mark. And, while the number of workers directly reached by worker priest apostolic missionary efforts cannot be asserted with any degree of certainty, those numbers, though incomparably higher, must have constituted a statistically equally

---

98. René Voillaume at several points in his voluminous study of the *Petits Frères de Jésus* refers to the experience of women, organised within the *Petites Soeurs de Jésus*, taking up full-time industrial work, e.g. pp. 323 and 352. This dimension of the "worker priest" phenomenon has apparently remained completely neglected in the literature to date.
99. Here I find Arnal, *Priests in Working-Class Blue*, passim, to be most informative.
100. Cited in Wattebled, *Stratégies catholiques*, 188.
101. Arnal, *Priests in Working-Class Blue*, 130.
102. This word play is Oscar L. Arnal's on p. 124 of his eminently readable volume.
103. Arnal, *Priests in Working-Class Blue*, 121. On this and other aspects of the worker priest phenomenon in Belgium and France, see now also Arnal's contribution to this volume.

insignificant segment of the respective industrial population of Wallonia and France. But a movement such as Left Catholicism, incorporating simultaneously party politics, theology/philosophy and apostolic/social missions, should never be measured by quantitative yardsticks alone.

The reverberations of these ideas and the repercussions of their praxis vastly exceed the limited reservoir of card-carrying party members, theologians or, in this case, active worker priests. The profound influence of these one hundred worker priests on their and subsequent generations of Catholic believers can perhaps be more adequately assessed by the recognition that all levels of the church hierarchy, including the Vatican, frequently debated the role and the usefulness of the worker priest experience in contemporaneous Catholicism. Perhaps the most convincing indicator of the long-range importance of the worker priest experience lies in their intellectual impact long after the Vatican terminated this particular apostolic experiment in 1954/5. Grégory Barrau, the historian of the French Catholic experience of "May 1968", has this to say about the worker priests' impact on French Catholicism in the late 1960s: "The mental and empirical horizon of the entire Catholic intellectual universe remained profoundly influenced, throughout the 1960s, by the dramatic episode of the worker priests".[104]

4.2. The Mouvement Populaire des Familles

The worker priest movement originated in the course of World War II and came into its own in 1947. Its spiritual origins, the intellectual and socio-political atmosphere which prepared its terrain, however, can be traced back all the way to the interwar period. The genesis of the MPF, a constituent part of this same wave of Left Catholicism arising in the 1940s, shows a roughly similar trajectory. The movements adopting the lable MPF (in France this name change occurred in 1941, in Belgium three years later) were founded in the mid-1930s within the larger fold of Catholic Action organisations. In France, the MPF was consciously conceived of as an organisation for former members of the JOC having come of age.[105]

Yet it was in the course of the Nazi-occupation of Belgium and France that the MPF began to develop its full range of activities aiming for concrete improvements in the daily life of its Catholic working class constituency, ultimately resulting, as was the case with the worker priests, in entirely new methods of community work unprecedented within Catholic social action at the very least. The occupation authorities' illegalisation of most independent social organisations, such as trade unions, Catholic or non-Catholic, stopped short of the church-hierarchy sponsored MPF and thus in a very real sense created the space for the social activities displayed by the rapidly growing numbers of MPF activists. Aiming to uplift working class families not only spiritually but also materially, the MPF helped coordinate the set-

---

104. Barrau, Le Mai 68 des catholiques, 18.
105. The organisational trajectory of the MPF is more than adequately covered for France by Debès, Naissance de l'Action Catholique Ouvrière. The most important signposts of the evolution of the Belgian MPF are traced in Pasture, Kerk, politiek en sociale actie, 62-71 and Zelis, "Les Équipes Populaires", 544-551.

ting up of soup kitchens, clothing exchanges, vacation trips, health services, heating assistance, aid to Prisoners of War, aid to families of Prisoners of War, eventually even setting up consumer cooperatives.[106] What may at first sight appear as the habitual work of social service organisations in any country in the world, soon began to take on highly militant and socially progressive overtones under the concrete conditions of occupied and later newly-liberated Europe.

In effect, already prior to Liberation the MPF in the francophone portions of Europe evolved into the quintessential Catholic social action group in industrial working class milieus, though organised around seemingly non-political issues. Yet problems such as housing, neighbourhood infrastructures or the lack of adequate nutrition almost immediately became highly political topics, both prior and subsequent to Liberation. In the course of its fearless defense of the social needs and rights of the urban poor, the MPF knew no taboos and confronted secular authorities of all political shades and variations, fired on by the voluntarist philosophical conviction characteristic of this Left Catholic milieu. Its uncompromising attitude shaped the MPF into one of the most dynamically expanding organisations at that time.

Its newspaper for France, *Voix ouvrières*, founded in early 1941, quickly gained a wide readership. In May 1941 it had a print-run of 45.000 copies; by September of that year it reached the figure of 80.000 copies. MPF membership rose dramatically in the post-Liberation winter of 1944/45. From close to 95.000 adherents at the end of 1944, it rose to 158.000 card-carrying members on 18 February 1945.[107] Small wonder that in 1944 many observers of Left Catholic activities may have regarded the MPF - and not the then still embryonic worker priest movement - as the most important concrete manifestation of the spirit evinced by the prophetic statements made in *France, pays de mission?*[108]

Total Belgian MPF membership figures were naturally lower than in France. Concrete figures have been hard to obtain, though its newspaper, *La Vie Populaire*, sold 11.000 copies shortly after Liberation.[109] In subsequent months the Belgian MPF in all likelihood underwent a similar expansion as was the case with its French homologue. At any rate, Joseph Cardijn, the founder and inspiration of the earliest and most influential of all Catholic Action groups set up in the interwar years, the JOC, addressed the first national study days of the Belgian MPF in the spring of 1945 with the following exuberant words: "The JOC by itself will not be able to save the working class. The JOC together with the MPF will secure the victory".[110]

---

106. References to these categories of social assistance effected by the MPF are in Debès, *Naissance de l'Action Catholique Ouvrière*, 39 and 69.
107. Debès, *Naissance de l'Action Catholique Ouvrière*, 39 and 73. Membership figures generally appear to have referred to the number of families supporting the MPF; at other times they refer to numbers of individuals.
108. Debès, *Naissance de l'Action Catholique Ouvrière*, 56.
109. Zelis, "Les Equipes Populaires", 548.
110. "Nous sommes prêts! La première Semaine d'Études du Mouvement Populaire des Familles", *La Vie Populaire*, 6-13 March 1945. Alhough the phrases reflect Cardijn's habitual optimism and exuberance, his statement is nevertheless a useful reminder of the centrality of the MPF within postwar Walloon Catholicism.

And it was in Belgium where the social action methods of the MPF found their most eloquent theoriser and defender in the Jesuit spiritual advisor of the MPF, Philippe De Soignie. His *Mystique Chrétienne et Ascension Ouvrière* is a passionate and convincing, if somewhat rhetorically overblown defense of the self-emancipation of its working class constituency: "*Mouvement Populaire des Familles*, the name alone may stand for its program. Movement, and not simply league or association. The point is to provoke unrest in our working class neighbourhoods, to impart an impulse, to generate massive energies which will carry the masses along with them". "Born out of the needs of the working class, led by the workers themselves, the MPF draws its program and its action from that powerful current of working class emancipation which is gripping the popular masses today". "In order to lead its educational and apostolic mission to a successful conclusion, the MPF must be a mass movement". "The MPF does not stop at gathering thousands of working class adherents, it spares no efforts to put them into motion on the road to concrete and fraternal results".[111]

The point of departure for MPF work would be an intense study of actual working class conditions: "To succeed, we must at first focus on the problems of daily life which affect the activists the most, which truly interest them: heating, food supply, clothing, neighbourhood issues, etc...." Then solutions must be imagined "with the active participation of the masses themselves", the latter statement indicating the true hallmark of MPF activism: "Being a mass movement, the MPF believes in the hidden resources of the masses". Priests and other religious supporters may initiate action, but their aim should always be to let working class members take over all directing activities as soon as possible. "The movement must be directed by the workers for the workers. That formula should be sufficiently well-known today to render it unnecessary to insist on this point".[112]

Similar visions of working class self-emancipation guided the actions of their French homologues, leading to the progressive removal of spiritual advisors from all leadership bodies of the French MPF, a process underway from 1943 onwards, soon leading to the virtual disappearance of all religious references in the pages of those publications not specifically geared to its spiritual advisors and overtly Christian members.[113] In the words of Joseph Debès, there rapidly emerged "a distorsion between the goal of social liberation, ... its working class character ... and its apostolic mission".[114] Originally constructed to surmount social class differences within the parish by means of stressing the unity of all believers, the parishes where the MPF was most active were soon becoming hotbeds of working class activism.[115] "From an apostolic movement, the movement could now become a workers' movement"[116], eventually breaking "the fragile equilibrium between

---

111. De Soignie, *Mystique chrétienne*, 66, 67, 109 and 78-79.
112. Ibid., 115, 68, 109 and 111.
113. The process of dechristianisation of the MPF can be followed in Debès, *Naissance de l'Action Catholique Ouvrière*, 50, 51, 83, 86 and 90. On the overall trajectory of the French MPF, see also the contribution by Bruno Duriez elsewhere in this volume.
114. Debès, *Naissance de l'Action Catholique Ouvrière*, 40-41.
115. Ibid., 184.
116. Ibid., 45.

social movement and apostolic movement, between social action and apostolic action".[117]

5. Conclusion

The apostolic/ideological/organisational itinerary of the French and Belgian MPF exemplifies some of the contradictory pathways entered into by some practitioners of Left Catholic ideology in the crucible of the mid-1940s. Created to re-ground Catholic spiritual beliefs in largely de-christianised blue collar working class milieus, the French MPF wound up becoming far more an organisational tool of a revitalised workers' movement than a mechanism for working class re-christianisation. Though perhaps the most extreme of the ideological trajectories of the Left Catholic milieus at the center of this essay, the MPF's evolution effectively underscores the promises and the perils of Left Catholicism in mid-century. Some of its extreme reticence against the forceful presence of priests, spiritual advisors and eventually even the employment of an openly religious language may in fact not only be due to the inner dynamic of a combination of apostolic and social missions but also due to the reaction of the Catholic hierarchy and others.

Soon after Liberation elements of the Catholic hierarchy, reflecting and promoting a growing sense of unease amongst a fraction of the MPF membership, began to voice doubts concerning the inner evolution of the MPF. At first in harmony with MPF spiritual advisors, many of them firm supporters of the general MPF course, separate circles of openly Christian MPF members began to gather across France, soon in effect evolving into a potential alternative to the increasingly laicised MPF. When a separate organisation was indeed set up in 1948, the *Action Catholique Ouvrière* (ACO), the latter was initially supported in full by the spiritual advisors of the far more powerful and numerous MPF, and peaceful coexistence of ACO and MPF seemed feasible. But a profound recomposition of the ACO leadership in 1950, masterminded by the Church hierarchy, soon streamlined the ACO and the latter became an open rival to the larger MPF.[118] The MPF continued its increasingly independent activities in various disguises, eventually forming one of the founding currents of the *Parti Socialiste Unifié*.

A somewhat similar picture, though with a different outcome, emerges from Belgium. Here, as early as 1947, the MPF witnessed the parallel buildup of *Équipes Populaires* (the functional equivalent to the French ACO), initially conceived of as a complement and not a threat to MPF activities. By the early 1950s, however, the *Équipes Populaires* were effectively utilised to

---

117. Debès, *Naissance de l'Action Catholique Ouvrière*, 13.
118. On the emergence and internal evolution of the ACO, see Debès, *Naissance de l'Action Catholique Ouvrière*, passim.

supplant and annex the few remaining structures of the MPF.[119] The rivalry between the Belgian MPF and the *Equipes Populaires* appears to have been caused by a similar, though less far-reaching process of secularisation, as was the case with the French MPF, and it was played out as an organisational feud between the Walloon Christian Labour Movement, the *Mouvement Ouvrier Chrétien*, and the Belgian MPF.

The worker priest phenomenon in both Belgium and France similarly suffered from a barrage of Church hierarchy sponsored attacks leading to its effective demise in 1954 (France) and 1955 (Belgium).[120] Likewise, some of the most forceful and eloquent theological defenders of Left Catholicism, such as Marie-Dominique Chenu, Yves Congar, and Henri de Lubac, endured frontal attacks by Church authorities, leading to the indexation of some of their works.[121] That Catholic fellow travellers experienced official disdain leading all the way to excommunication may hardly surprise.[122] But even the comparatively mild-mannered UDB had, earlier on and in a different political context, experienced the wrath of the Catholic hierarchy when Mechelen Archbishop Van Roey, the *primus inter pares* of Belgian Catholicism, called on Belgian Catholics to shun the UDB.[123]

As such, the similar fate, i.e. the demise of Left Catholicism in all of its manifestations sometime between the late 1940s and the mid-1950s, may in part be ascribed to the relative isolation of this intellectual current, increasingly viewed as a hostile element by church authorities, largely ignored by the non-Catholic Left, and oftentimes alienating - consciously or subconsciously - even its closest potential allies within the Catholic fold. Étienne Fouilloux, for instance, in an illuminating passage points out how the *Mission de France* had to overcome not only the frequently solidly conservative attitudes of important elements within the Church hierarchy but likewise faced opposition from reform-minded sections of the Catholic world who, having obtained certain gains in past struggles, soon became hostile to continued radical change.[124]

---

119. This picture of the history and evolution of the Belgian MPF and *Équipes Populaires* emerges from a wealth of documents I consulted in the archives of the *Equipes Populaires* in Namur and, above all, in several document collections in the Brussels' *Centre d'Animation et de Recherche en Histoire Ouvrière et Populaire* (here by far the richest single source is the *Fonds Victor Michel*). These documents also throw light on an apparent divergence of interpretations between Pasture and Zelis on this issue, referred to in Pasture, *Kerk, politiek en sociale actie*, 70.
120. The story of the forced ending of the worker priest movement is amply demonstrated for France above all in Leprieur, *Quand Rome condamne*, and the Belgian case, targeted in the wake of the successful closing down of the French experience, is described in De Greef, *Les prêtres-ouvriers en Belgique*, 53-71.
121. See, for instance, Guellny, "Les antécédents de l'encyclique 'Humani Generis'"; Fouilloux, *Une église en quête de liberté*, 279-300; and on the well-known case of Henri-Charles Desrochers' *Signification du marxisme*, see Pelletier, *Economie et humanisme*, 222-286.
122. The official condemnation of communist activities by Catholics on the part of the Holy See in 1949 is reprinted as Suprema sacra congregazione del Santo Offizio, "Scommunica dei comunisti," in Pombeni, *Socialismo e cristianesimo*, 301-306.
123. See Beerten, *Le rêve travailliste*, 119-121. Not all Left Catholic tendencies and factions suffered from similar attention by their spiritual superiors. For instance, the Dossetti group never faced a similar campaign of openly partisan disdain; on this see Pombeni, *Le 'Cronache Sociali'*, 224, note 83.
124. See Fouilloux, *Les chrétiens français entre crise et libération*, 151-152.

Yet ultimately the failure of Left Catholicism to survive as a current with a measurable influence must be located in the international political conjuncture characterising post-Liberation Europe. And it would have been indeed surprising had Left Catholicism suffered a different fate compared to its closest secular co-thinkers: the milieu of left socialist thinkers and activists located somewhere between social democracy and official communism. For this secular milieu, having likewise emerged in the course of the 1930s and reaching maturity and a certain public audience in the 1940s, equally foundered on the twin bedrocks of stalinism and atlanticism, coagulating out of this moment of opportunity and crisis in the 1940s and casting its petrified glow over the entirety of socio-political and cultural experiments after the open eruption of the Cold War. Where Lelio Basso, David Rousset and André Renard[125] failed, Guiseppe Dossetti, Maxime Hua[126] and Philippe De Soignie could not win.

As Left Catholicism declined, the commonality of purpose, which had formed an invisible bond between Left Catholic currents as diverse as, to give just one comparison, the *dossettiani*, operating on the higher levels of Italian national politics, and the worker priests, the latter having exchanged traditional priestly functions for daily toil in the steel mills of Belgium and France, tended to recede into the background. When Left Catholicism was in the ascendancy, differences between the various components were less significant than similarities. Thus, in the upward curve of Left Catholic influence and organisational capacity, the hostility or proximity to marxism or marxist political currents rarely prevented close cooperation between individuals or organisations belonging to the entire colourful spectrum of Left Catholics described and analysed in the above pages. In the downward phase of the movement, previously ignored or politely overlooked differences began to assume much larger importance, leading to internal splits and more easily exposing Left Catholics to repression from Church authorities.

Of course, this pattern of unity prevailing in moments of dynamic growth and, conversely, internal fracturing becoming more common in times of decline is a pattern all-too-familiar in other innovative movements challenging a given status quo. The student movements of the late 1960s and early 1970s are perhaps the most visible reminders of a similar process operating on a transnational scale twenty-some years later. As long as student activism expanded and seemingly controlled the streets and university lecture halls, pluralist organisations, such as the American and German SDS (in the US: Students for a Democratic Society; in Germany: Socialist German Student League), functioned relatively well without major internal rifts. When the movement declined, the various component parts of group-

---

125. All three political and/or trade union activists, hailing from, respectively Italy, France and Belgium, played important roles in their countries' war time and postwar political culture, though none of them became, for the most part, ever fully integrated into any of the mainstream socialist and/or communist parties existing at that time. Indeed, they agitated more often than not on the political margins of their countries' respective political Left, a tendency most pronounced in Lelio Basso and David Rousset, with André Renard eventually becoming the head of Belgium's socialist trade union federation and an activist in Walloon autonomist movements.
126. The spiritual advisor to the French MPF and close ally of leading worker priest advocates.

ings such as SDS splintered and formed the multitude of socialist and communist sects dominating the political landscape of the post-1968 European and North American Far Left.

Left Catholicism in the 1940s and early 1950s, of course, was very different from student activism in the 1960s and early 1970s. But, whatever their profound differences, both movements must be regarded as important social movements in their own right. And, qua social movements, they all benefited and suffered from the characteristic see-saw of the upward and downward cycles of such relatively amorphous, decentralised and largely uncoordinated social movements, with the attendant ebb and flow of openness and closure, relative imperviousness to repressive moves at one point and few effective barriers to repression at other moments.

Viewing Left Catholicism as a social movement may also explain its uneasy relationship to pre-existing Catholic organisations, be they political parties, trade unions or Catholic Action groups. As a new phenomenon, it was given a hostile or unfriendly reception by traditional organisations, including groupings that had only recently carried out major struggles to gain a place in the panoply of Catholic organisations themselves. Yet, as long as it experienced dynamic expansion in intellectual and/or organisational influence, such cold shoulder treatment mattered relatively little. In that very concrete sense, Left Catholicism, then, must be regarded as one of several social movements engendered by that particular moment of opportunity and crisis in the closing moments and the aftermath of World War Two I described in my opening paragraphs.

Yet, just like this moment of opportunity and crisis engendered theoretical and practical experiences in the secular sphere that disappeared in the late 1940s or early 1950s but eventually reemerged enriched with novel contributions from other socio-political and geographic contexts in the next transnational moment of crisis and opportunity during the late 1960s and early 1970s, so the socio-political and cultural imagination of Left Catholicism in the 1940s did not vanish without leaving a trace. To mention but two lines of continuity: First, the deliberations and decisions of Vatican II owe much to the ferment generated decades earlier by precisely this milieu of Left Catholicism I outlined above. Indeed, some of the most imaginative theologians of the 1940s directly influenced the proceedings of Vatican II as theological advisors to some of the Third World archbishops and others attending the gathering. Second, Latin American liberation theology of the late 1950s, 1960s and beyond traces many of its elements back to the elaborations and experiences of Western European Left Catholicism in the 1940s, and indeed some leading representatives of Latin American liberation theology have been very open about these lines of continuity.[127]

---

127. On these subsequent reverberations of Left Catholicism in the 1940s, see, amongst many other hints strewn throughout the literature, Kaufmann, "Ansätze einer Theologie der Befreiung in Europa?". The influence of Western European Catholic Action in the broader sense of that term on Latin American liberation theology can be gauged, for instance, in the "Préface" by Dom Helder Camara to Fievez and Meert, *Cardijn*, 7-10.

Far from being a brief interlude or footnote in the history of Catholicism, then, Western European Left Catholicism of the 1940s constitutes a central building block in the increasingly variegated spectrum of opinions characterising the Catholic experience at the dawn of the third millenium.

THE FRENCH CATHOLIC LEFT AND THE POLITICAL PARTIES

Jean-Claude Delbreil

The notion of left wing Catholicism lies, it seems, at the centre of certain rather important problems of definition and demarcation which require further clarification. This question should first be considered in relation to the notions of "right wing" and "left wing" as these notions have developed in the course of political history. However, the concepts and realities which these notions cover have themselves evolved in the course of history. This evolution has been due, in particular, to a more or less constant shift in left wing ideologies and politics towards the Right, and to the repeated emergence on the Left of new ideologies which shift existing ideologies toward the Right. This phenomenon can be seen to be true of all the great ideologies; it is also true of those connected with Christianity and Catholicism generally. It is, therefore, primarily in the general context of historical evolution that we should investigate left wing Catholicism in 20th-century Europe, in particular during the 1940s and 1950s. We should recall also that an ideology like "Catholic liberalism" began, in fact, in the centre Left; "liberal" Catholicism set itself up in opposition to "intransigent" Catholicism by merging with the left wing origins of liberalism. The problem is more complex for those currents of Social Catholicism and Christian Democracy whose principal origins in the most deeply rooted areas of intransigentism have been made evident and form the basis for Emile Poulat's[1] "triangular" diagram. This principal source does not, however, exclude the possibility of other sources further to the left; this is as true of the "first Christian Democracy" as of the "second Christian Democracy", emerging towards the end of the 19th century with its "Christian Workers' Conferences" and its workers' and trade union offshoots. This branch would have liked to progress further on social issues than the more traditional brand of social Catholicism. The complexities were also borne out in France in movements such as that of the *Sillon*, with Marc Sangnier at its centre, and in the *démocratie sillonniste*, which went further than an already socially and politically traditional Christian Democracy. This was particularly the case for the *plus grand Sillon*, which stood for a willingness to open up to left wing political powers, a willingness which was at the root of the 1910 condemnation.[2]

Here, we will primarily examine the relationship of the Catholic Left in France with the powers, parties and political tendencies in the period following the Second World War, while keeping in mind certain historical origins indispensable to the comprehension of the situation existing after 1945.

---

1. Poulat, *Une Eglise ébranlée*. See also Poulat, *Eglise contre bourgeoisie*. The "triangular diagram" or "triangular conflict" proposes a threefold distinction between liberalism, socialism and Catholicism, understood in the sense of "intransigent Catholicism". See also Tranvouez, *Catholiques d'abord*, 266.
2. Caron, *Le Sillon et la Démocratie chrétienne*.

Incidentally, it is also evident that other dimensions - intellectual, social or purely religious - should be included in order to furnish a complete analysis of the issue. However, an even closer examination, focussing on political actors only, seems to allow the formulation of some interesting conclusions straight away, in particular as far as Christian Democracy, its divisions and other possible forms of a "left wing Catholicism" are concerned.

1. Christian Democracy and the Catholic Left

These examples of the evolution of the ideological forms of French Catholicism immediately seem to demonstrate the hugely complex nature of any clear definition of this notion of "left wing Catholicism". It has been possible to classify, in turn, Catholic liberalism, social Catholicism and Christian Democracy, at a certain point in their history, as more or less left wing in their political and ideological configuration, in some tendencies at least, even without considering the various, and always very much minority, forms of "Christian socialism". However, up until the 20th century, all these currents were equally minor in comparison to the pre-eminence of a politically conservative Catholicism and an antirevolutionary fundamentalist Catholic Far Right. Even so, this right wing Catholicism, certain types of Christian socialism, as well as Christian Democracy and social Catholicism, may all have come from the same "intransigent" basis. It should also be noted that, at the beginning of the 20th century, these "Christian Democratic" tendencies had, generally speaking, already incorporated a section of social Catholicism and liberal Catholicism by virtue of being situated more or less to the left of "French political Catholicism". In this sense, there has always been a Catholicism on the Left or a Catholic left wing, represented for a time by Christian Democracy, as well as an extreme-left socialist Christian ultra-minority. The problem, firstly, is to ascertain whether this identification of left wing tendencies within Catholicism is, in itself, sufficient to situate these tendencies on the political Left. This had remained unclear before 1914, as Christian Democracy had not been successfully organised as a structured political party. As for the *plus grand Sillon*, the answer would seem to be that it might have tended towards a positioning on the Left, if it had emerged onto the electoral and parliamentary scene. At any rate, the question of the place of Christian Democracy within "Left Catholicism" as such is important as well. And it is a question which continued to be asked during subsequent stages, in particular during the 1940s. However, this question can, in fact, simply be addressed by looking at its historical origins, as the French situation itself illustrates. After the condemnation of the *Sillon*, the democratic Christian forces divided, resulting in two tendencies, whose mutual opposition sheds light on the origins of the problem in general. One section of the *démocrates sillonistes*, the *Jeune République* (JR), followed Marc Sangnier in a desire to move toward the Left, while another section joined the social and liberal Catholics in "democratic republican federations". This division between a left wing minority of Christian Democracy, which can broadly be classified as a left wing Catholicism, and a right wing majority, was perpetuated in the period between the wars after the failure of efforts to rally the two and the creation of an ephemeral *"ligue de la démocratie"*.

This situation led to the creation in 1924 of the *Parti Démocrate Populaire* (PDP), the first real democratic Christian party organised in France, but one which has stayed clearly to the centre Right of French politics, through the association of a left wing of social Catholicism and a right wing of Christian Democracy, with some liberal Catholic contributions.[3] However, another part of the Christian Democrats remained in *Jeune République* around Marc Sangnier; relations were never good between the two movements. The JR, despite its numerical weakness (5000 members, compared to 20.000 in the PDP), had wished to maintain contact with the other left wing parties, in particular the radicals and socialists, and it was included in the Popular Front coalition.[4] Such an example pre-dating 1940 would seem to prove that Christian Democracy, broadly speaking, cannot and should not be entirely assimilated into the Right or the Centre and that a "left wing Christian Democracy" can also exist, as examples in other countries have proved. However, the French situation tends to show that this branch of left wing Christian Democracy always stayed more or less in the minority, as a sort of "witness" to its left wing potentiality - though solely as a witness. In addition, in common with most *jeunes républicains*, Marc Sangnier rejected, as the *jeunes républicains* had done at the time of the *Sillon*, any sort of hasty or integral assimilation into Christian Democracy; they wished to reach beyond this Christian Democracy, sometimes even going as far as a form of socialism. And a certain kind of anticapitalism was officially propounded, in particular during the 1930s, during which time, on the international front, the JR and Marc Sangnier turned towards a "Christian pacifism". Although Marc Sangnier had left the JR in 1932 to devote himself solely to the struggle for peace, the JR continued to develop its doctrine in those directions, a development which became even more marked after 1945.

Even if the JR stood as living proof, if only by its existence, of the possibility of a left-oriented Christian Democracy, the simultaneous existence, by contrast, of the PDP seems to have demonstrated that the Christian Democratic majority inclined rather to the centre Right. The synthesis achieved by the PDP of several historical traditions indicated that such a confluence would almost naturally occur within the Centre or centre Right. A liberal Catholic influence seems to have been important enough to fix this first Christian Democratic party at the centre Right, rather than the Left, or even the centre Left. However, it should be stressed that, to a certain extent, the PDP also remained part of the left wing of French political Catholicism, some parts of it having moved further to the Left and crossed the political line between the Right and the Left. The PDP, already included by some observers on the Right together with the JR amongst what they called the "Christian Reds", remained at the left of the right wing, despite having dis-

---

3. Delbreil, *Centrisme et démocratie chrétienne en France*. See also Mayeur, *Des partis catholiques à la démocratie chrétienne* and Durand, *L'Europe de la démocratie chrétienne*.
4. Guerrier, *La Jeune République de 1912 à 1945*; Kesler, "La Jeune République"; Kesler, *De la Gauche dissidente au nouveau parti socialiste*.

tinguished itself in certain areas, such as in defending a form of social reformism which was rather daring for its time, or in following the path of a "Christian internationalism", which had laid the foundations of the future Christian Democratic Europe. The democratic Christians of the centre Right had emerged as a "Catholic left wing", relative to a conservative Catholicism embodied in a more powerful party, that of the *Fédération Républicaine* (FR). This would tend to prove also the relativity of what is called "left wing Catholicism". The Popular Democrats were thus on the Left, relatively speaking, of French Catholicism, while staying on the Right of the political scene, alongside the FR and opposed to the JR.

On the other hand, in the period between the two World Wars, the question of secularism remained one of the dividing lines between Right and Left, between a secular Left and a mostly Catholic Right which continued fundamentally to reject the Left. Nevertheless, the PDP had claimed in this matter to break down existing barriers and to go beyond the rift between Right and Left on the question of secularism. The distinctions now proclaimed to be of utmost importance regarded social questions in particular. The PDP had also developed a distinction between "secularism" in the sense of "neutrality", which was acceptable to Catholics, and intolerant "secularism", which was unacceptable. However, we should note that, further to the Left, JR was to defend on the Left those claims by Catholics which it considered legitimate, considering it necessary to act on this issue from within the left wing and its parties.

2. The Nuances and Splintering of the Catholic Left

Does this indicate that, from the period between the wars onwards, a series of fine distinctions should be developed, encompassing the relations between a Catholic Left, considered left wing in relationship to the conservative Right, beside a more authentic but more minoritarian Catholic Left, and an extreme-left wing, very much in the minority, represented by certain Christian socialists and communists and embodied at that time in the group surrounding *Terre Nouvelle*? If so, the problem of the "Catholic Left" in its expansion prior to 1940 would require clarification, even if it is clear that it was mostly after the Second World War that this term took on a new meaning, closer to a variant of the extreme Left and no longer merely a traditional Left. The problem would be, therefore, to discover whether, when one speaks of a "Catholic Left", this also includes left-of-centre tendencies within mainstream Catholicism, which would lead to an inclusion of political distinctions that could be characterised as belonging to the centre Right, as well as political tendencies situated on the Left, but in the context of a more or less moderate Left; or whether one understands "Catholic Left" primarily as referring to the period following the Second World War, i.e. as being close to the extreme Left and especially to the Communist Party, in the particular meaning of "progressivism" as understood in France after 1945. However, it seems necessary to affirm that one must make many fine distinctions within the overall "Catholic Left", which can extend from the centre Right to the extreme Left, or, if we exclude the centre Right, from a moderate Catholic Left to a more extreme Catholic Left which was able, for a time, to monopolise fully the meaning of this rather ambiguous term.

In any case, there is little doubt that it was mainly during the period after the Second World War, at the end of the 1940s and at the beginning of the 1950s, that the distinctions between the diverse nuances of this "Catholic Left" were clarified and that the large bodies which constituted it became more separate, whilst retaining lines of continuity, sometimes without realising it. In this way, Christian Democracy was reorganised around a new party which was much more powerful than its predecessors, the *Mouvement Républicain Populaire* (MRP). And it was with this party that the question of the integration of Christian Democracy into the Left imposed itself on a greater scale, particularly at the beginning of this party's history, though, subsequently, this problem was rapidly resolved in the negative. However, other tendencies were also then affirmed with more forcefulness than had been the case during the period between the wars, even going as far as what we might call a Catholic "extreme Left". We can therefore speak of a Catholic "centre Left" situated around Christian Democracy and the MRP, even if, and we will return to this, this centre Left was displaced more and more towards the centre Right of French politics; we can also speak of a "Catholic Left", which, though more authentic, remained in the minority. The latter would be dispersed into different parties: autonomous and distinctly Catholic parties, as *Jeune République* still was; new parties stemming from the Resistance, like the *Union Démocratique et Socialiste de la Résistance* (UDSR), in particular; and even the socialist SFIO (*Section Française de l'Internationale Ouvrière*). However, all of these "Catholics of the Left" can be said to have had a tendency to remain "independent" within the parties to which they adhered, showing preferences for a "dissident Left" or a sort of "new Left" which was in the process of searching for an identity and which was heralding the "second Left", of which we will speak further.[5] Finally, a certain minority came to constitute a very diverse extreme Left which gave rise to the problems of "Christian Progressivism", in constant interaction with progressivism in general, with communism, the Communist Party and even marxism as such. On the other hand, it must be asked whether this notion of a "Catholic left wing" should be limited simply to the political sense. It would indeed seem obvious that ideological and theological currents and apostolic and social movements should also be included in any discussion of such a notion. Not only must political dimensions be taken into account, but also intellectual, theological, spiritual and social ones. All of these movements and currents have always been connected by a sort of continuum, with almost constant interactions without which one cannot hope to understand them. Incidentally, as much as this is true of Christian Democracy as such, it is also true of the more "advanced" forms of Left Catholicism emerging after 1945.

5. The expressions "new Left" or "second Left" indicate those tendencies which originated in circles that were not originally on the Left, as with those who came from certain Catholic backgrounds and who were drawn progressively towards the Left. These left wing groups have often been distinguished from the "classic Left" by the absence of a tradition of "secularism", although they did finally accept this secularism in the sense of a "tolerant neutrality" in relation to all beliefs.

3. The Second World War, Ruptures and Consequences

Here, again, we need to reconstruct the left wing Catholic movement in the 1940s in its historical continuity as well as in its historical context, a context which changes with each period. It should be obvious by now that there were movements of this "left wing Catholicism" prior to the 1940s. They manifested themselves in a specific context, at the centre of which such forms of "left wing Catholicism" have always been in the minority and quite weak. However, these movements managed to lay the foundations for the new forms of this "Catholic left wing" which emerged after the end of the Second World War. The 1920s and 1930s were, without a doubt, decades during which foundations were laid and many essential steps taken, particularly in the French context and on the level of politics, affecting subsequent years during which the situation and circumstances were totally different, historically speaking. Nevertheless, one should take into account ruptures as well as continuities, and a distinct historical rupture undeniably occurred for "left wing" French Catholicism in the 1940s, even though the ground had already been prepared by certain political, intellectual and social developments. The circumstances and the conjuncture of the Second World War were at the root of these ruptures, though embedded in the context of certain continuities. What happened was a form of acceleration and a change of perspective of the entire set of problems and of the circumstances affecting those elements that could be regarded as the "Catholic Left". For example, the role played by the Catholics within the Resistance was in no way negligible and, in particular, that played by the centre right as well as the centre left Christian Democratic tendencies and by a certain "intellectual Catholicism". It would not be unreasonable to include Christian Democracy and a certain left wing Catholicism among the main currents of the Resistance. This was as true of the Popular Democrats in the *Liberté* movement, for example, as of the *jeunes républicains*, who were, proportionally, even more numerous in committing themselves to movements such as that of *Résistance*. The more the Catholics aligned themselves with the Left, the more numerous did they become as members of the Resistance, contrasting with the support given to Vichy by an important fraction of French Catholicism and of the Church. This was also the case for another Christian left wing tendency which took the form of such movements as *Témoignage Chrétien*. This part of the Left concurred with a Christian intellectual Left which had already emerged before the war and which had prepared the ground in a form of Christian "pre-resistance" to racism and fascism. Contacts made in the Resistance with communists and socialists, as an organic outgrowth of a more or less established "Resistance spirit" but also due to the position held by certain Christian Democrats in "official Resistance institutions", such as Georges Bidault, the president of the *Conseil National de la Résistance* (CNR) and a former popular democrat[6], played a relatively important part as well.

---

6. Duquesne, *Les Catholiques français sous l'occupation*.

4. The *Travailliste* Dream and the Birth of the *Mouvement Républicain Populaire* (MRP)

In this context, is it possible to speak of a movement towards the Left by most of the French Catholics involved in the Resistance, and in particular by the Christian Democrats? This also raises the question of the political direction of the new party, the MRP[7], which appeared between 1944 and 1945, in relation to the "Catholic left wing". Matters become rather complicated here, as they are marked simultaneously by elements of rupture and continuity, to the extent that it seems difficult, even when looking at the problem in a broader context, to fit this new party into a "Catholic left wing" category; at the very least, this must be done prudently and with reservations. Despite all this, the question arose of what was then called "French *travaillisme*" or the "dream of French *travaillisme*" in certain Christian Democratic milieus during the Occupation. This lies at the origin of the idea of an understanding between Catholics and socialists in postwar France. Between 1943 and 1944, the *Rue de Lille Group*[8], along with certain former Popular Democrats and Young Republicans, published the *Cahiers du travaillisme français*, based on the rather imprecisely defined idea of an alliance.[9] In 1944, *travaillisme* based on the British model was indeed an attractive idea for some. Thus, the British Labour Party became a model, as it was both reformist on social matters and non-anticlerical on religious matters, since it had many Catholic members. The necessity for practical, concrete solutions acceptable to all, Catholic or not, and independent of any and all denominations, was seriously considered. Apart from the group which had published the *Cahiers du travaillisme français*, led by Robert Buron, Georges Hourdin, Ernest Pezet, Emilien Amaury[10] and in which was evoked the "creation of French *travaillisme*" as a "Christian conception", other groups, such as that stemming from the *Confédération Française des Travailleurs Chrétiens* (CFTC), headed by men such as Robert Prigent or Marcel Poimboeuf (who was also a member of the PDP and then the MRP), also supported this idea. It can also be said that it was towards a sort of French *travaillisme* that individuals such as Claudius-Petit[11] or Henri Frenay[12] turned; after the failure of this attempt at French *travaillisme*,

---

7. Letamendia, *Le Mouvement Républicain Populaire*.
8. The "Rue de Lille Group" was a Resistance organisation whose objective was to provide facilities for editing, publishing and circulating booklets and newspapers available to Resistance movements. Many elements close to the PDP and JR collaborated in it.
9. Robert Cornilleau, a Popular Democrat, had, in 1927, already envisioned the possibility that, in the future, Catholics and socialists might collaborate; see his *Pourquoi pas? - Petit Democrate*, 23 January 1927, reissued in *"Pourquoi pas? Une politique réaliste"* (Paris, Valois, 1929).
10. These men had all been members of the PDP before the war and were close to Marc Sangnier.
11. Eugène Claudius-Petit (1907-1989), former member of JR, joined the UDSR and was Minister of Reconstruction from 1948 to 1953.
12. Henri Frenay, founder, along with many Christian Democrats from the PDP, of the newspaper and Resistance movement *Liberté*, which subsequently merged with *Combat*.

these elements moved toward the new UDSR. Gilbert Dru[13] was probably also in favour of the *"travailliste* idea".

In any case, we can ask what this temptation and this attempt in immediate postwar and post-liberation France meant. We can see in it the expression of a genuine upsurge toward the Left, at this juncture, of Christian Democracy and of a certain number of prewar Christian Democrats or Christian Democrats formerly active in the Resistance, a desire for a movement towards an understanding with a genuine left wing party such as that of the socialists, who were favoured over the Radical Party and Radicalism, to which the PDP had already drawn closer at the end of the period between the World Wars. However, the form assumed by this *travaillisme* was very vague. It could indicate either the fusion of a big Labour Party with the SFIO, or merely an understanding between a Christian Democratic Party and the Socialist Party. Moreover, these often confused propositions very soon came up against opposition from the principal leaders of the MRP. In fact, in 1944, this French *travailliste* temptation was only one of several potentialities and would turn out to be of minor importance. The others were the restoration of the prewar parties and the formation of a new Christian Democratic Party which would assemble the JR and the PDP in its first phase, thereby already showing an evolution toward the Left. The contacts established in the Resistance were not sufficient for the formation of a genuine *travailliste* force which would, in any case, have been unlikely to be a concept acceptable to the SFIO.

At the time of Liberation, at the centre of the PDP, in the federations which re-established contact with the former president, Champetier de Ribes, a majority was moving toward the formation of a "new Democratic Party" with the JR and other elements which had come out of the Resistance. Beside this majority, a minority preferred to uphold the former party, and a further minority seemed effectively to be moving more in the direction of the SFIO. Some federations or groups - for example, in the Haute-Garonne, in the Lyon region and in the Sarthe - turned towards the SFIO. The Marseille division claimed to aspire to a "great *travailliste* party", which the PDP, the JR, the MRP and the socialists would all join. Some former Popular Democrats moved towards the socialists, demonstrating in that case also the potential existence of a left wing current amongst the Christian Democrats; it is, however, difficult to determine the importance of this, for a majority of the former Popular Democrats turned towards the new MRP after it rejected the *"travailliste* option" when this was proposed by Marcel Poimboeuf, a former PDP leader. The constituent congress of the MRP marked the end of this *"travailliste* dream", a dream which had little chance of success in the political circumstances of postwar France. A large majority of the former Popular Democrats therefore accepted to join the new MRP, even though a minority rejoined parties further to the Left, such as the Socialist Party, or the UDSR at the centre Left.

---

13. A Catholic Resistance fighter from Lyon, executed in 1944. He supported various attempts to organise Christian Democratic tendencies at the same time that he promoted currents based on the "mystique of human rights".

5. *Jeune République* and Catholic Left

On the other hand, this was not the case with what already constituted the left wing of Christian Democracy before 1940, namely *Jeune République*, which was nevertheless divided vis-à-vis the important role played by the *jeunes républicains* in the Resistance and the "No" vote to Pétain's absolute powers expressed by the majority of its parliamentary members on 10 July 1940.[14] The question of the future of *Jeune République* and of its insertion into French political life after the war must be asked, as must the question of whether JR would move towards the formation of a more important political force around what was already a genuine "left wing Catholicism" before 1940. Divisions quickly became evident, as with the PDP during the same period. Some were seen to defend the idea of maintaining what was called "the common soul", according to an expression of Marc Sangnier's. Marc Sangnier had, incidentally, left JR, but he still remained the emblematic figure for a certain kind of historical "left wing Catholicism", in which Maurice Schumann[15], Guy Menant and others were also instrumental. However, the adversaries of such a fusion were also very numerous, among them Philippe Serre, Maurice Lacroix, Antoine Avinin, etc. Finally, alongside two mutually opposing motions, a third text was adopted by the party's National Council, proposing to uphold JR, of which Maurice Lacroix became the general secretary.[16] This option of the upholding of the autonomy of the JR largely arose from the fear that the newly formed MRP would move to the Right. Indeed, one of the aims of JR since the period between the wars had mainly been to somehow "bear witness to the Left"[17] and to stay linked to the Left as a branch of the Christian Democrats. It was in this way that JR would effectively remain a sort of witness-party, as it had always been and as it remained until its dissolution. Its founder, Marc Sangnier, on the other hand, adhered to the MRP, followed by Charles Serre[18] and a certain number of his friends, bringing about another split at the centre of the "left wing Catholics"; the presence of Marc Sangnier in the MRP seemed to guarantee that it would be anchored in the centre Left. Marc Sangnier became the honorary chairman of the MRP and Maurice Schumann became its first president. The problem of classifying "Christian Democracy" as belonging to the "Catholic Left" was therefore posed in different terms starting in 1944-45, in addition to the question of the distinction between the new MRP and the preserved JR.

14. Maréchal Pétain, the last president of the Council of the Third Republic, had demanded "absolute powers" at the National Assembly and at the Senate on 10 July 1940 in Vichy, in order that they yield constitutional powers to him. Only eighty parliamentary members voted against this measure, of which three were Popular Democrats and three (out of only five) "Young Republicans".
15. Maurice Schumann (1911-1948), formerly a member of JR, was the spokesman for Free France alongside General de Gaulle in London. He was the first president of the MRP, while wishing to remain faithful to de Gaulle and Gaullism. He was also the spiritual son of Marc Sangnier.
16. On this matter, see Guerrier, *La Jeune République de 1912 à 1945*, 746; Kesler, "La Jeune République"; Kesler, *De la Gauche dissidente au nouveau parti socialiste*.
17. This expression had been used by Marc Sangnier and certain leaders of JR.
18. Philippe Serre and Charles Serre were both members of *Jeune République*. Philippe Serre had been one of the 80 opposed to the absolute powers on 10 July 1940.

6. The History of the MRP and the Catholic Left

The disproportion, however, between the two organisations, i.e. between one of the first parties of Fourth Republic France and what can be termed an organisation whose primary role was that of being a "political witness" in the form of the JR, was even greater than it had been during the period between the wars. The biggest problem was that of the situation of the MRP in relation to the definition of "left wing Catholicism". First of all, there was a proportional change with respect to the PDP, as this Christian Democratic-inspired power went in one stroke from holding 3% of the votes to 25% after Liberation (during this time, it was the "foremost party in France"). This difference in the order of magnitude can be explained in the first place by the fact that one section of the traditional Catholic right wing electorate joined the party in 1945 when confronted with the dispersal of parties such as the *Fédération Républicaine*.[19] The paradox here was that with this electorate, further to the Right than that of the PDP, the MRP had, in the beginning at least, a more left wing bent and positioning. The question of the classification of the MRP "on the Left" in the years after the war must therefore be asked, as it forms part of an interesting problem; however, the response must be in the negative, despite some indications to the contrary. The MRP was, indeed, one of the parties which spoke quite clearly for a while of a "revolution" to be brought about in France at the moment of Liberation, but without specifying in its manifesto of November 1944 exactly what form this revolution should take, and saying only such things as, "we want a revolution", and issuing a "call to revolutionaries". Conversely, its leadership bodies stood further to the Left than those of the former PDP. It was marked by the arrival of former leaders of the JR as well as by that of the new 1930s generations, shaped by the *Association Catholique de la Jeunesse Française* (ACJF) in particular. It is also indisputable that the MRP created a relatively bold programme for social reforms between 1944 and 1945, which questioned capitalism itself, and which was remarkable, in the beginning, for the important place of Christian trade unionism in its framework. At its extreme, it stood for the replacement of the wage system with associations according to an ideal of social democracy which brought it closer to democratic socialism.

Could the MRP therefore be classified as being on the Left, despite everything, upon its foundation in 1944 and in the years immediately after the war? In a sense, it initially merited being placed on the centre Left, if one may judge by the positions it took up on social issues, in particular in relation to social reforms. It must be noted that the MRP was further to the Left on these issues at the time than a party such as the Radical Party - or what

---

19. The *Fédération Républicaine* (FR) had been one of the main parties of the "moderate Right" in the period between the wars, apart from the *Alliance Démocratique*. It had a more nationalistic and "Catholic" tone than the latter, and was directed towards the protection of Catholic claims. It was primarily, though not absolutely, a Catholic party, and the majority of Catholics of a "conservative" tendency continued to vote for it. The Federation (the majority of whose members had not been very active in the Resistance, in spite of the fact that the party had been represented on the National Resistance Council) dissolved despite an abortive attempt to re-form it in 1945 through newly constituted moderate parties such as the *Parti Républicain de la Liberté*.

was left of it - which remained ideologically positioned on the centre Left. The MRP was indeed in favour of a controlled economy and of economic planning; at the same time it was hostile to any attempts to make workers appendages of the state. It showed itself to be in favour of a certain type of self-management, where an association of workers would be concerned with management and company results. However, its social doctrine also included the resurgence of topics of professional organisation, which had arisen more or less from a previously existing form of social Catholic thought with traditionalist origins, besides topics much closer to a form of Christian Socialism which had also been inherited from the 19th century. In fact, leaving aside these apparent contradictions, the MRP achieved a sort of synthesis on social matters which led to a doctrine of social and economic democracy. Here, again, therefore, the problem is to determine whether this doctrine, which initially went beyond mere reformism, was sufficient to place the party on the Left of the political arena and to classify it as a part of the moderate variant of "left wing Catholicism". This might have been the case had there not been this traditional social doctrine to take into account. And, from the beginning, there were other political and ideological dimensions to contend with and in particular the issue of secularism, which quickly prevented any straightforward classification as being on the Left. Indeed, the MRP was often troubled by this question of secularism, as its predecessors had been, especially as it was in contact with such left wing parties as the socialist SFIO in the "Third Force" coalitions. This became an issue, most notably, regarding the question of freedom of choice in education. Also, the MRP's left-leaning social positions were rapidly toned down, despite the protestations and the resistance of an undeniable "social left wing" of the party.

It must be emphasised that the social and even socialist aspect of the new MRP in its beginnings was underscored by a fairly strong union presence originating in Christian trade unionism. It was thus that in 1945 a third of the members of the MRP national leadership came from the CFTC. And it is in this way that the question has arisen about a kind of "take-over", at the moment of Liberation, if only momentary and partial, by Christian trade unionism, linked closely to the MRP. A call to the "working elite" became indisputably a central part of the ideology of the party as well as that of the CFTC, including demands for a better organisation of the social welfare system, new labour legislation, and at least a partial assumption of methods of control over production and the exchange of goods. Union leaders emerged in key positions, such as Paul Bacon, Louis Beugniez, Jules Catoire and Robert Prigent. Recent studies looking at their role in the immediate postwar era have repeatedly raised the issue of the links between union activism and political action.[20] But, if Christian trade unionism was, at that time, more or less in positions of power within the MRP, it was not the only dominant current, just like the MRP itself, which was dominant in French national politics, was only dominant within the framework of the three-party system, together with the socialists and communists. However, it is

---

20. Béthouart, *Des syndicalistes chrétiens en politique* and Launay, *Syndicalisme chrétien en France*.

indisputable that this massive Christian trade union presence at the beginning of the party's history, in an MRP which was exercising political power in conjunction with left wing parties, influenced the character of a form of trade unionism which, until the period between the wars, had wished to remain very independent from the other unions, the latter then more or less associated with the secular political Left. The question of the beginning of a move to the Left by at least a section of Christian trade unionism must therefore also be asked in any discussion of left wing Catholics in the French political context. This question is intimately linked to the political dimension of the MRP in the postwar context and is of relevance for the subsequent history of the CFTC including its eventual breaking-up.

Also, on the level of national politics, from the beginning the MRP hoped for an understanding with the socialist SFIO, and it agreed, up until May 1947, to participate in the tripartite system, including the communists, before opting for the formula of the "Third Force"[21], which corresponded better with its ideal of a political and governmental coalition which would be more or less oriented towards the Centre. All of these positions situated it further to the Left than the former PDP, and socially more to the Left even than the Radicals. Ideologically, then, it could be classified in a conjunctural and relative way as centre Left, at least between 1944 and 1947. However, this situation was more or less the result of an optical illusion in the very particular case of postwar France. The change in circumstances with the beginning of the Cold War, the split with the communists, the pressure of a conservative electorate and perhaps also certain pressures in the Catholic world led quite rapidly to a context in which, from 1947 onwards and after some equivocations which were soon cleared up, it was no longer possible to speak of the MRP as being representative of the "Catholic Left". It more or less took over the role of the PDP "on the left of the right wing", at the centre Right, despite its positions on social issues and the Resistance to "conservative" tendencies, notably on the part of certain representatives of Christian trade unionism and of the Catholic social movement.

The general problem of the precise ideological and political signification of Christian Democracy, especially in France, can nevertheless be posed on the basis of the study of the MRP; the German and Italian cases would warrant a separate discussion. Is Christian Democracy a right wing tendency or is it something else? The answer would appear to have always been quite ambiguous. This is a result of the diverse origins, notably in France, of the form of Christian Democracy that resulted from the fusion of different ideological elements. In any case, Christian Democracy, even if it is not alone in this, also poses the problem of the Centre and of centrism, and even the question of the possibility of its existence as such. Should one speak, in relation to the Centre and centrism and notably in the case of the MRP in France after the Second World War, of the possible existence of a sort of

---

21. After the end of the three-party system in 1947, in which the Communist Party (PCF), SFIO and MRP participated, i.e. after the split with the PCF and the formation of the Gaullist RPF in the same year, the socialist and Christian Democratic parties were to constitute what was called the "Third Force" against the PCF and RPF, bringing together left wing forces such as the socialists and Radicals and right wing and centre forces such as the MRP or some moderate "independents".

"relative Left", in relation to other tendencies of "political Catholicism"? The difficulty here for the MRP resides in the fact that it attracted to itself, if only provisionally, one section of the conservative Catholic masses, as a result of the temporary collapse of the prewar "Republican Federation"-type traditional Right. However, this did not eschew the existence of left wing tendencies within the party, even if such tendencies were gradually marginalised or sometimes left the party. This would tend to prove that Christian Democracy is, and must be, something distinct from the various tendencies organised within traditional right wing parties. Whatever the case may be, it cannot be reduced merely to such tendencies, even if, on the other hand, one must not fall into the trap of speaking of it as "neither right nor left", which is, in and of itself, another problem.

The problem of the MRP in the postwar years must also be isolated from that of the MRP in the 1950s and even more so in the 1960s, as, during its first period and as opposed to inner-party developments in subsequent decades, the party showed evidence of a potential for evolution towards the Left, which formed the basis of the evolutions of some individuals towards a more firmly established Left. However, it should not be forgotten that, at least until 1946-1947, although the MRP was not the Gaullist party, it was, nevertheless, the party faithful to General de Gaulle. The relations between Gaullist and Christian Democratic tendencies in the MRP have always been complex. Indeed, it is possible to speak of a "Gaullist Christian Democratic tendency", one section of which joined the *Rassemblement du Peuple Français* (RPF) and the future Gaullist parties. Such an evolution puts any possibility of classifying the MRP and postwar Christian Democracy on the Left into perspective, even if the "Gaullist Christian Democrats" often embodied the distinction of "left wing" or "social Gaullism". As to the MRP's general political history, it too progresses more or less in this direction. The MRP was quickly affected by the consequences of its fundamental anticommunism, despite its temporary and forced alliance with the PCF. It was in this way that, from 1947 onwards, the MRP gradually became, not only one of the elements of the "Third Force", situated between the PCF and the RPF, but also one of the fundamental pillars of the Fourth Republic "system", as a result of which it quickly experienced the effects of an "erosion of power". Its initial social enthusiasm was quickly dulled in these circumstances, despite the pressure exerted by the "pro-working class Left" within the MRP and of some currents of the CFTC, which found the MRP's evolution toward the centre Right and Right to be excessive. Alternately, the MRP tried, at least until 1951, and partially even after that, not to cut itself off completely from the SFIO, and it pursued the idea of a "Third Force" which would include some left wing elements and in which it could act as the element of compromise. However, once again, this unwillingness to cut itself off entirely from the Left was not sufficient for it to be classified even at the centre Left; indeed, it could be considered that this drift to the centre Right, which cut it off from the "Catholic Left" in the strict sense of the term, was almost inevitable. Similarly, the decline of this party, whose initial success had been due to such specific circumstances, was no doubt inevitable, and this decline accelerated from the moment the party became one of many within the centre Right, be it in terms of membership figures or on the parliamentary level, as, from then on, it was in competition with the other "moderate" parties. The rift with the more genuine representatives of a "Catholic Left", which was itself quite varied, increased quickly; this was certainly the case for its relationship with the small JR, which continued to lead an independent existence.

7. *Jeune République* - Enduring Testimony to a Catholic Left

After 1944-1945, *Jeune République* indeed remained, as it had before the war, a witness to a left wing political Catholicism, very much in the minority despite being open to non-Catholics. Thus, in the October 1945 elections, the JR signed two agreements for a common initiative with certain Left and centre Left parties such as the SFIO and the UDSR. The UDSR's ambition was more or less to unite socialists of marxist and Christian inspiration around itself. Incidentally, some leaders of the JR, such as Claudius-Petit, soon left the JR in favour of the UDSR, although some movement in the opposite direction should be noted as well, such as that of Pierre Bourdan, who left the UDSR in order to join the JR and who became a minister in the Ramadier government. In any case, in the aftermath of the war, JR denounced the monopoly of the three biggest parties and thereby challenged the three-party system, while not situating itself to its Right and effectively acting as a representative of a sort of independent or "dissident Left". This original and courageous position meant, incidentally, that it was joined by a certain number of those who had formerly left it for the UDSR or the MRP. Although, in a sense, it had originally been situated to the right of the SFIO, the JR found itself positioned to the SFIO's left after the failure of the three-party system.

In matters of doctrine, *Jeune République* also attempted an original effort, which gradually led to the elaboration of what can be called "personalist socialism", in which references to Emmanuel Mounier were, of course, obvious.[22] It was under these circumstances also that a number of "progressive Christians" joined the JR, as well as a group headed by Georges Montaron of *Témoignage chrétien* and by activists of his journal and movement. However, even if contacts had been established with activists of *Terre nouvelle*, for example, a barrier had always existed against "Christian progressivism", which had always been considered too closely identified with the PCF and with marxism. On the other hand, although this small party managed to attract important personalities such as Léo Hamon, for a time, and, later, Jacques Delors, nevertheless it continued to experience the difficulties associated with a small political group. Some of its constituent elements were tempted into joining more important groups, such as the MRP, the SFIO or even, during the 1950s and 1960s, the *Parti Socialiste Autonome* (PSA), and later the *Parti Socialiste Unifié* (PSU), which eventual-

---

22. A manifesto of this form of Christian Socialism would later be published, in 1972, under the title "Manifesto of Bierville", in which the influence of Marc Sangnier's social doctrine also made itself felt, in the framework of an attempt to synthesise the thought of some of the principal protagonists of "left wing Catholicism" on intellectual and theological matters: see Delbreil, *Marc Sangnier*, and the testimony of Claude-Roland Souchet. Interview, 25 February 1994.

ly won over about half of JR's membership. This desire to bear witness to an "independent left wing Catholicism" was, therefore, not easy, and the JR always remained a small political formation which testified to the weakness of this form of genuinely left wing political Catholicism. Its ideological willingness to refuse both liberal individualism and state socialism demonstrated the difficulties of an autonomous path for those left wing Catholics who were more or less unclassifiable, and of whom other left wing parties tended to be wary. The JR subsequently also refused fusion into the new Socialist Party in 1971, finally ceasing all activity in 1983. Nevertheless, it can truly be said that it played a historic role, in particular in the immediate aftermath of the war, having a style quite close to certain socialist options, and going further than the MRP. It contributed to the preparation, in some cases, of a rupture, not only with the Right but also with the Centre, for a portion of French Catholics. In addition, certain "left wing Catholics" joined the centre Left UDSR.[23]

8. The Case of the Democratic and Socialist Union of the Resistance

The UDSR was another one of the new parties originating in the circumstances of Liberation, and, upon its creation in June 1945, it was intended to be the non-Communist Resistance Party, based on a federation of Resistance movements in which all the resistant groups, from Gaullists to socialists, including Christian Democrats, but with the exception of the communists, could come together. The UDSR also wanted to adopt a central position between the PCF and the Right, by presenting itself as *travailliste* and notably by wishing to go beyond the old divisions between believers and secular activists. However, it nevertheless intended to position itself on the Left favouring an alliance in which the SFIO would have been only one of the constituent blocks. The creation of this new party was meant, by its very nature, to attract a number of "democrats of Christian inspiration", who were, after the end of the war, seeking a non-denominational party, socially and politically further to the Left than previous similar formations. Actually, after the formation of the MRP and the failure of the *"travailliste dream"*, a number of these "Christian Democrats", such as Claudius-Petit, did join this organisation. On the other hand, the JR, after having refused to join the MRP, entered into an agreement for united action with the UDSR in 1945. One of the most illuminating examples was the case of René Pleven, a former leader of the ACJF, who, with Claudius-Petit and Antoine Avinin, was a founding member of the new UDSR and proposed to reform French political life by reaching beyond the traditional divides, beginning with the school question. However, Catholics only made up one section of the membership and leadership of the UDSR. Still, one might ask whether

---

23. Duhamel, *L'union démocratique et socialiste de la résistance*. The UDSR would remain a centre left "power broker" under the Fourth Republic, particularly under François Mitterand, who made the UDSR into one of the forces of resistance to Gaullist power at the beginning of the Fifth Republic, before it was dispersed into the *Convention des Institutions Républicaines*, then into the *Fédération de la Gauche Démocrate et Socialiste*, ultimately vanishing in 1965.

one is not dealing here with another type of "left wing Catholicism", situated this time clearly within the centre Left. In fact, it were the "independent Catholics" or "moderate Left Catholics", and not always the Christian Democrats, who joined the UDSR. It can be regarded as one of the symptoms of an evolution toward the Left of another fraction of postwar French Catholics. Other Catholics had joined the SFIO more discreetly, where they constituted a type of Christian minority which would always oppose anticlerical prejudices. These movements indicated a shift which began to manifest itself on the electoral level and which would merit further study, notably in certain Catholic areas, where the MRP electorate had not entirely passed over to the Right and to Gaullism.

9. The Catholic Left, Catholic Progressivism, and Emmanuel Mounier

In any case, it would be advisable to distinguish, during this period, the tendencies of a "Catholic Left" operating within the classical Left and within the centre Left from more extreme tendencies which proved to be more combative and, without a doubt, numerically more important than in the 1930s and which can be brought together under the term of "progressivism", even if this "progressivism" was ideological, intellectual and social rather than purely political. It should be situated on the extreme Left of French Catholicism in its historical evolution as well as in the context of the end of the 1940s, which facilitated the adoption of more extreme positions for a relatively important section of Catholics, though their importance should not be exaggerated. Taking into account the existence of this "progressivism" and this extreme Left vis-à-vis other political forces and vis-à-vis the majoritarian "Left Catholic" tendencies allows us to observe more clearly and to contrast the relative importance of the more mainstream Catholic "Left" compared to its more atypical and often more intellectual or social rather than purely political "progressivist" tendencies, which Yvon Tranvouez examines more closely in his contribution to this volume. However, here we should take note that this current did not lead to an organised political force, even if it sometimes linked up to already existing left and extreme left parties. This "progressivism" was, however, of greater relative influence than the "revolutionary Christians" had been in the period between the wars. The reasons for this temporary and relative success make up part of the general problematic of the "left wing Catholics", centred around movements as diverse as *L'Union des Chrétiens Progressistes, Jeunesse de l'Eglise, La Quinzaine, Vie Nouvelle, Economie et humanisme*, or, on the social level, the experience of the worker priests. The development of "progressivism" would not have been possible in the beginning without the ideological, theological and spiritual developments which had already emerged in the 1930s, and which had made possible the establishment of the duality of and separation between the spiritual and the temporal, the "separation of planes" which a philosopher such as Jacques Maritain had been among the first to express clearly, in particular in the context of the revival of Thomism.

In this context, although the influence of Emmanuel Mounier should not be underestimated, it should be seen in perspective, as it was not the only example of "Christian personalism", notably during the period between the wars, which witnessed also the "democratic personalism" of Paul Archambault[24], who stood more in the Augustinian tradition, and with whom Mounier was engaged in a controversy in 1934. Archambault's influence on Christian Democracy, in the strict sense of the word, was greater than that of Mounier, who was often very severe with regard to "Christian Democratism", its inadequacies and its dishonest compromises. Consequently, in *Esprit*, from the 1930s onwards, Mounier frequently referred to "revolution", while accusing the Christian Democrats of taking sides with "liberal established disorder". The case of Mounier and of the movement centred on *Esprit* seems, therefore, to merit a separate examination, as a practically autonomous current amongst the "Catholic Lefts", one which was close to finding a political outlet; at any rate, it had a precise historical significance. Mounier and *Esprit* stood incontestably further to the left than the Christian Democrats, as witnessed by his antiliberalism which sometimes bordered on antidemocratism.[25] An historian such as Sternhell[26] was able to classify him as one of the representatives of those ideologies which are neither of the Left nor of the Right and which lead to a form of "fascism". However, alongside of these more or less contestable similarities, the personalism of Mounier and of *Esprit* was closer to a form of "Left Catholicism", of which Mounier became one of the figureheads and one of the references subsequently used by Christian Democrats themselves. It was about separating the spiritual from the "established disorder", while dissociating necessary revolution from materialism. Mounier had rejected both fascism and stalinism and had sought a sort of "third way", economically and socially speaking, in common with some Christian Democrats, which explains the paradox that, after 1945, these Christian Democrats had a constant tendency to root themselves in his "personalism". In any case, this "personalism" constituted a barrier to any pure and simple adherence to marxism. Although with the new discovery of the working class after the war there continued talk of "revolution", and, although the Communist Party exerted an incontestable attraction in those years, marxism, as a philosophy, was rejected, and there was a rapid awareness of the crimes of stalinism. Under such conditions, Mounier and his movement turned towards a form of "new Left", which had a spiritual influence but was quite distant from progressivist commitments. If *Esprit* could have been momentarily classifiable as one of the PCF's "fellow travellers", this situation rapidly ceased. In this way, a new tendency, particular to the "Catholic Left", saw the light of day, next to the JR and the progressivist Catholics, and this tendency was for a while tempted to collaborate with Sartre's *Les Temps Modernes*. However, this rapprochement happened to coincide with the fail-

---

24. Paul Archambault was particularly connected to the PDP.
25. Winock, *Histoire politique de la revue "Esprit"*.
26. Sternhell, *Ni droite, ni gauche*.

ure of the *Rassemblement Démocratique Révolutionnaire* (RDR)[27], which Mounier had momentarily supported before his death in 1950, although the journal and movement were to continue.

10. In Lieu of a Conclusion

On another level, it can also hardly be contested that what can be termed the "antifascist reaction" exercised an important role in these evolutions from the period between the wars until the 1940s. It should be stressed that this tendency appeared very early within Christian Democratic milieus, generally speaking from the 1920s onwards, under the influence of exiled Italian Christian Democrats. Its evolution can be followed in numerous journals, such as *La Vie intellectuelle*, and allows a better understanding of Catholics' engagement in the Resistance from 1940 onwards. These activities resulted in a cumulative process through the contacts made in the Resistance by a large number of Catholics and of left wing Catholics in particular. This process, above all else, facilitated the participation in government of the Christian Democrats alongside the PCF and SFIO. For those who subsequently moved further to the Left, it facilitated commitments, if not within the PCF, then at least alongside it, in the various forms of progressivism, even after the outbreak of the Cold War. For it was then that the actual split occurred between the moderate wing of the "Left Catholics", generally speaking, who remained in the majority, and a more "advanced" wing which was to join the various manifestations of this "progressivism".

These evolutions always led, therefore, to internal diversifications of this "left wing Catholicism" and of its various distinctions, which can in no way be limited merely to the "progressivist" left wing in the aftermath of the Second World War. As much as "Left Catholics" had already constituted a network of tendencies before 1940, their diversity and expansion were further accentuated along with the discrepancies and consequences of a profound historical rupture in the political context of the aftermath of the Second World War. Indeed, initially it appeared as if those who were generally called the "Left Catholics" before 1940, i.e. the "Christian Democrats", who were qualified as "Christian Reds" by their right wing and extreme right wing adversaries, had suddenly won the majority with the triumph of the MRP, whose ambiguous significance with regard to the very notion of "left wing Catholicism", however, was quickly revealed. This ambiguity was further exaggerated by the continuation of an accelerated "drift to the Left" of other sections of French Catholicism. It seemed a very long time since the Christian Democrats, even those on the Left, had personified the "progressive" wing of French Catholicism. The continued existence of *Jeune République* and the entry of numerous Catholics into parties like the UDSR or the SFIO testified to the significance of this development. The explosion

---

27. The RDR was officially created in February 1948 and included Sartre, David Rousset, etc. It was supported by *Esprit*, but also by the JR. It was quickly weakened by the departure of Sartre in May 1949 and would decline from that year on. Theoretically, its aim was to bring together all the socialist forces not attracted by communism in order to construct a neutralist Europe independent of the two superpower factions.

of "Christian Progressivism", which could lead as far as open PCF membership, represented, of course, an extreme illustration of this phenomenon, but of a scope which had not been experienced in the past and which will, doubtless, not be found again. Even if a reversal of these developments occurred before long, matters would, in fact, never be as they were before. The dissociation of French Catholicism from the traditional Right subsequently seemed irreversible, and this has indeed remained the case. Catholicism showed that it could divide itself politically between a Right, a Centre, if such a notion exists, and the various distinctions of a "Catholic Left" as far as an extreme Left which experienced its finest hour in that post-war period. The question of "left wing Catholicism" must therefore be addressed in the broadest possible framework, from a historical perspective, and with regard to its political and ideological meaning, as well as in the context of its varied political, social, intellectual, cultural and, of course, religious and theological dimensions.

LEFT WING CATHOLICISM IN FRANCE. FROM CATHOLIC ACTION TO THE POLITICAL LEFT: THE *MOUVEMENT POPULAIRE DES FAMILLES*

Bruno Duriez

In a country like France, it seemed for a long time that to be Catholic and left wing was incongruous, and there were times when being in such a position made one an object of scandal in the view of some - the "good Christians" and the religious hierarchy - and an object of suspicion in the view of others, notably the political left wing. During the 1940s and 1950s, this matter was the subject of much, sometimes extremely violent conflict, associated with the historical upheaval of those years. At that time, the manner in which the Church defined its own relationship to politics became gradually modified, resulting in a form of political pluralism, i.e. the recognition and legimisation of the political diversity of Catholics and, in concrete terms, a situation whereby Catholics could declare themselves to be on the Left. The action and positions taken by "left wing Catholic" groups contributed to this change. Such transformations also came about as a result of the massive drop in the Church's influence on society as a whole. Religious decline in France contributed both to the liberation of some groups from traditional ties and to a pressure on the Church to practise greater openness. It is in this context that a form of left wing Catholicism was able to develop.

The religious socialisation of Catholics contributes to the manner in which they approach politics. In particular, it defines a certain manner of being on the Left.[1] However, there are many ways of living one's Catholic faith and of relating to the world. In so-called integralist models of repre-

---

1. In such an approach, it is important not to give in to nominalism. The question is not to ask if a certain organisation or individual is left wing or not. Political identity is, in itself, subject to representation and debate. Someone who believes her/himself to be on the Left may be dismissed by the person to whom (s)he speaks as being on the Right. Any position may be challenged or supported as a left- or right wing one. It is because of this that left wing Christians are often accused by left wing organisations of being on the Right and of disguising this, or, more simply, of not *really* being of the Left. On this and related issues, see also the contribution by Jean-Claude Delbreil elsewhere in this volume.

sentation of the world[2], religion is at the centre of all projects. The "revolutionary Christians" of *Terre nouvelle*, during the period between the wars, were "socialists because they were Christians"[3], like the "social because Catholic" members of the *Association Catholique de la Jeunesse Française* (ACJF) at the beginning of the century.[4] Conversely, others, whose religious conviction was just as strong, kept political positions distinctly separate. For these, one could be both socialist and Christian, but social position and religious conviction were not part of the same order of affairs. According to Jean-Marie Donegani, these models of action and of representation could be defined as marginalist.[5] There are, therefore, many ways to experience the relationship between religion and the other spheres of existence, in particular that of politics. There are many ways of being Catholic, and, equally, there are many ways of being a left wing Catholic.

The distinction between integralism and marginalism can be found again in the historical opposition of social Catholicism and liberal Catholicism.[6] The left wing Catholic organisations, as with those on the Right, placed themselves in one or the other of these two traditions: *le Sillon*, for example, fits into the first. Established in 1893 by Marc Sangnier, *le Sillon* was condemned by Pope Pius X on 25 October 1910 for mixing religion with democratic stances.[7] For its part, the *Syndicat Général de l'Education Nationale* (SGEN) of the *Confédération Française des Travailleurs chrétiens* (CFTC), created in November 1937, belongs in the second tradition. Despite being part of a Christian organisation, the SGEN defined itself as a secular association.[8] Its leaders participated in the creation of the movement *Reconstruction*, a tendency within the CFTC, whose influence in the confederation resulted, by 1964, in the secularisation of the CFTC.[9] The opposition between the two traditions, social and liberal,

2. We will call "integralist those systems of representation which proceed from a declaration of religious identity". (Donegani, "Identités religieuses et pluralité"). "This type of Catholicism calls itself integralist (...) because it longs for a form of Catholicism which can be applied to all the needs of contemporary society, while liberalism and socialism think that society itself possesses the means to resolve its problems and that religion should remain a private affair, a matter of conscience". (E. Poulat, *Encyclopaedia Universalis*, article on "Intégrisme", vol. 8.) See also Mayeur, "Catholicisme intransigeant, catholicisme social, démocratie chrétienne".
3. Rochefort-Turquin, *Front populaire*. The group (1935-1939) brought together Catholics and Protestants.
4. Molette, *L'ACJF (1886-1908)*.
5. Donegani, *La liberté de choisir*.
6. Mayeur, *Catholicisme social et démocratie chrétienne*; Maugenest, ed., *Le mouvement social catholique en France*.
7. Those responsible for *le Sillon* submitted to the papal decision. In July 1912, Marc Sangnier and the former *sillonistes* founded *Jeune République*, a non-denominational political organisation (Caron, *Le Sillon et la démocratie chrétienne*). This small organisation would play a part in the passage of some Catholics toward the political Left. With the *Mouvement de Libération du Peuple* (MLP) and other such movements, it would contribute in 1960 to the creation of the *Union de la Gauche socialiste* (1957), and subsequently of the *Parti socialiste unifié*.
8. This union brought together the teachers in the public school system. Singer, *Histoire du SGEN*. Those Catholics teaching in the public school system who were simultaneously defenders of that system were exposed to numerous difficulties in relation to the Church, in particular within the parishes.
9. Vignaux, *De la CFTC à la CFDT*; Georgi, *L'invention de la CFDT*.

marked the history of the beginning of the century and found expression in tensions even within Christian organisations. It continued throughout the 1940s and 1950s, including among those Catholics who affirmed their adherence to the political Left.

The history of the *Mouvement Populaire des Familles* (MPF) provides a privileged observation point for the tensions driving both French political life and the life of the Church during these two decades. It overlaps with the history of many other organisations and political and religious currents, for example the *Mouvement Républicain Populaire* (MRP), *Jeune République* (JR), Christian progressivism, the *Parti Communiste Français* (PCF), the *Mouvement de la Paix*, the CFTC, *Jeunesse de l'Eglise*, etc. Growing from within Specialised Catholic Action, the MPF belonged from the very outset to the tradition of integral Catholicism.[10] It was nevertheless beset by a tendency towards internal splits and fissures which was to result in its eventual break-up.

The militant members of the MPF, originally a movement for Catholic Action, continually attempted to articulate a Christian objective - a political objective as well as an objective for its social activism. This movement was to provide the basis for the creation of many other organisations in these different domains, at the heart of a unifying project. The movement was not immediately situated on the Left; it was only over time, following strong internal and external tensions, that a central position was created which attempted to unite Christian adherence with a left wing political stance. This movement was atypical in many ways. It was principally a Catholic working class one, in a country dominated by popular irreligiousness.[11] It brought together militants who affirmed themselves to be both Christian and left wing, in a country where Catholic adherence translated in massive numbers into right wing political stances. This doubly marginal situation allows an understanding of the modes of action privileged by it and the reactions which it provoked.

The two decades were marked by some particularly remarkable events. The Popular Front had just emerged when France entered the war. After the defeat came the Occupation and the Vichy regime. Liberation was rapidly followed by the conflicts associated with the Cold War. The political instability of the 1950s was brought to an end by the inauguration of the Fifth Republic (1958). The Church itself underwent great agitation during these years. The hopes raised during the period between the wars by Specialised Catholic Action were followed by the creation of new plans of action, such as that of the worker priests, who were guided by a consciousness of the necessity of their mission. The attempts to adapt the Church to the world and the theological reflection which accompanied those attempts, while not without internal conflict, led to the Second Vatican Council (1962-1965), which was their logical consequence, while at the same time ushering in a

---

10. In the 1930s, this current was not as intransigent in its attitudes to modern society as it had sometimes been at the end of the preceding century (Poulat, *Église contre bourgeoisie*). It accepted certain important aspects of that society. The Republic, notably, was no longer an issue for many Catholics. Nevertheless, Catholics in organisations such as the MPF continued to manifest a certain intransigence regarding politics and the compromises associated with politics.
11. Isambert, *Christianisme et classe ouvrière*.

new era. These new departures were mainly designed to find the means to bring the Church closer to the working classes. The MPF, which had originally been created as a movement of and by the Church, was one of the most important elements of this strategy.

The movement would encounter many metamorphoses during the 1940s and 1950s. Its history can be divided into several significant moments: its origins within Specialised Catholic Action, and in particular in the JOC; its clash with the Occupation situation and Vichy; political radicalisation; the break-up of the integralist model.[12]

1. Specialised Catholic Action: The Origin of a Manner of Existence in the World

The *Mouvement Populaire des Familles* was originally a Catholic Action movement, emanating directly from the *Jeunesse Ouvrière Chrétienne* (JOC). The organisation, and its militant members in particular, took from the latter a certain vision of the world and a method of analysis and action. It was these elements which would lead them into politics and, in the case of many of them, toward the Left.

The French JOC was created in the autumn of 1926 at the initiative of Father Georges Guérin, at Clichy, after an initial experiment at Tourcoing. This creation was directly inspired by Joseph Cardijn's Belgian JOC. The creation of the women's JOC followed shortly afterwards.[13]

"We will remake our brothers into Christians, through Jesus Christ we can do so", the Jocists sang. "It was this will to conquer and to preach to workers, by workers and for workers, which they first strove to inculcate".[14] The steps taken by the JOC are thus well summarised. Having had their origin in Church-sponsored youth associations, the Jocist sections soon distanced themselves from these: the problem was not to unite all the social groupings under a single umbrella organisation, such as the parish, but to define an activism specific to each social milieu. It was also important that any action should initially be led by people belonging to the same milieu: that workers should be evangelised by workers and young people by other young people. The slogan of the JOC, "for them, by them, among them", expresses this principal orientation of the JOC.[15] The specialisation of Catholic Action into "milieus" - the term preferred by the Church over the expression "social classes", which was judged to be too connotative of the

---

12. This article concentrates mainly on the collective work carried out by the *Groupement pour la Recherche sur les Mouvements Familiaux* (GRMF), which brought together researchers and former activist members of these movements. On the socio-historical methods used by this group, see Duriez and Chauvière, "Un dispositif de co-histoire".
13. Pierrard, Launay and Trempé, *La JOC*.
14. Georges Guérin, *L'Union*, (July 1927).
15. The affirmation of the priority of evangelisation based on milieus questioned the ACJF, created in 1886 by Albert de Mun, run by young students and organised along general, i.e. not milieu-specific lines. The JOC, supported by its chaplains and by the episcopacy, became a branch of the ACJF, but throughout their common history, tensions between the two movements were very present up until the crisis of 1956 which resulted in the demise of the ACJF.

class struggle and therefore of communism - did not come about without clashes with the so-called "general", i.e. cross-class movements, and with the parishes. Milieu specialisation was one of the determining elements of the manner in which the adult movements - for example the MPF - and their militant members saw not only their apostolic action and their place in the Church, but also their political analysis and action.

The Church's fears regarding socialism and the development of the workers' movement at the end of the 19th century and the beginning of the 20th century, which were already clearly expressed in *Rerum Novarum* (1891), were both confirmed and complicated by the Russian Revolution (1917) and the birth of the communist parties. In France, the Communist Party was born at the Conference of Tours (1920) as a result of a split in the *Section Française de l'Internationale Ouvrière* (SFIO). Historiography of the beginning of the JOC generally plays down this political context. Certainly, the JOC is solely defined as an apostolic movement. However, its target was also, more or less explicitly, to combat the hold of left wing organisations over the working class.[16] This is evident from testimonies by the Jocists and from the account of their clashes with street vendors of the rival press when distributing *Jeunesse Ouvrière*. From this came the conviction that the JOC, and thereby the Church, needed to defend its specific project for social transformation.

The formation by the JOC of an elite of leaders, as they were then called, within the working class youth milieu should have allowed the working class and the Church to draw progressively closer together. Considerable measures were put into place to this end: study groups, retreats, a press-office and numerous publications.[17] *Meneurs* became the title of the journal of the militant members of the adult movement which succeeded the JOC, the *Ligue Ouvrière Chrétienne*. The conviction that an active minority could lead the masses made its mark on militant members entirely committed to their cause.

Specific annual projects contributed to this training, but they were simultaneously lessons in activism. The procedure for what was later called the "revision of life" can be divided into three stages: "seeing, evaluating, acting". The first stage involved observation of life in the factory, life in the residential milieu and family life. The next stage involved an analysis of the factors determining the situation under scrutiny. The final stage involved specifying what overall action should be taken. This method, which was in part already the same as that of ACJF circles, broke with the methods which had been the customary practice in the Church until then. Action was not deduced from doctrinal teaching but was constructed through collective reflection. Education was not so much the acquisition of accumulated knowledge but instead based more on a pragmatic approach ("a gram of action is worth more than a ton of fine words" was another JOC slogan),

---

16. The attitude vis-à-vis the communist movement was sometimes expressed in a direct manner. Thus, in a JOC song, a clear contrast to "The International" was established: "You are not the 'damned of the earth' / You are not a 'prisoner of hunger' / You want to live and earn your bread / Through your work and wages. / Banish the hatred from your heart / Look to the future without fear / Thanks to Christ, the Divine Worker, / Your task is blessed". Extracts from *Sois fier ouvrier* (Worker, be proud).
17. Notably with the creation of *Éditions ouvrières*.

which, however, covered up the extent to which it was based on the internalisation of pre-given categories regarding the perception of reality. At any rate, this inductive approach to reality gave to those who shared it the conviction that they could define the direction of their own action.

The JOC established itself as a comprehensive movement for young Christian workers: "The JOC wants to be the guardian, protector and representative of working class youth. It is a school, a representative body and a collection of professional and social services".[18] The movement took charge of all aspects of the young worker's existence. This claim gave rise to tensions with the *Confédération Syndicale Chrétienne* and its *Equipes des Jeunesses Syndicalistes Chrétiennes*.[19] The JOC's plan was indeed both to change consciousness and to rechristianise the working classes and, furthermore, the whole of society.[20] In this sense, the movement can be comfortably placed in the perspective of integral Catholicism.[21]

The big conference organised in Paris in July 1937 for the tenth anniversary of the Jocist movement lived up to all expectations. The movement had grown considerably; it demonstrated not only what it had become but what its plans were for a regenerated society. The strikes of 1936 provided the Jocists with the opportunity to take on responsibilities in worker actions. They contributed to the reinforcement of the CFTC. Everything seemed possible.

Meanwhile, the JOC refused to confirm that it was a political organisation. It remained a movement of the Church, under the direct control of the hierarchy and its chaplains and had no distinct political position, on the one hand affirming its solidarity with working class defence movements, while at the same time opposing the communist project. The movement's, or its members' mode of action was that of "influence": "A militant member who influences the three areas of life (work, neighbourhood and leisure) in order to transform them - that is what the JOC is all about. It is in this way that we can say the JOC is powerful, because through its 20.000 French activists, it possesses this invisible means of conquest which can be called influence".[22] Changing lives by means of collective example made it possible to jointly experience the results of the actions carried out.

---

18. *Manuel de la JOC*, first French edition, Paris-Brussels, Les Éditions jocistes, 1930.
19. Belouet, "La JOC et les organisations syndicales".
20. As Father Guérin declared, "It is necessary, M. Cardijn explained, in order to give Church-sponsored youth associations an *integralist* Christian education, to cause the Christian principles concerning supernatural life to penetrate as far as the average workday and the 'everyday' life of apprentices and young workers: to make Church-sponsored youth associations have an impact on everyday life, instead of limiting it to action on Sundays and feast days". *L'Union*, July 1927, quoted by Debès and Poulat, *L'Appel de la JOC*, 226.
21. The direction taken by the movement obscures the role originally played by Father Jean Boulier, who was the editor of *l'Appel de la JOC*. Jean Boulier indeed represented Catholicism's liberal tendency (or, to use Émile Poulat's term, the "bourgeois" tendency), which explains his progressive disinvolvement from the movement. (On this, see Debès and Poulat, *L'Appel de la JOC*.) Much later, on 9 September 1950, following his active participation in the *Mouvement de la Paix*, Jean Boulier was to be stripped of his powers by the archbishop of Paris, Mgr. Feltin.
22. *Jocisme français, 1927-1939* (Paris, JOC and JOCF, 1939), quoted by Richou, *La Jeunesse ouvrière chrétienne*.

The insistence in Jocist theology on Christ as a person and on his human condition contributed to the overall vision of the movement: Christ too worked, as he was a carpenter. This particular emphasis enabled both manual work and the young worker to be regarded with more respect.[23] It forged a militant ethos in which the transformation of social relations was a part of God's work. As Aline Coutrot has shown, the JOC did not provide its members with a particular political direction, but educated them in an ethic of commitment and social responsibility.[24] The directions subsequently taken by the Jocists were varied and covered a wide political spectrum. Some of them became involved in left wing political formations which, when it occurred, was a brand new phenomenon. Education within the JOC had allowed those who had benefited from it to break with traditional political ties and rendered the possibility of a left wing political choice possible and legitimate in their eyes. However, at the beginning, the integralist vision of the movement led them to position themselves rather at a distance from political organisations and to define a political project specific to their movement.

These different aspects of the JOC procedure - action according to social milieu, education through inquiry, an integral vision of social change - were to mark the militant ethos of those who spent time in its ranks and who would go on to be constituent elements of the *Mouvement Populaire des Familles*. They were also to be the constituent elements of the subsequent political direction of that movement.

The creation of the *Ligue Ouvrière Chrétienne Féminine* in 1933, following the establishment of the group called *Aînés de la JOC* for men, guaranteed the continuation of the spirit of the JOC for the first Jocists to enter adulthood. The two movements soon fused (1935) to form a single movement, the *Ligue Ouvrière Chrétienne* (LOC) with two branches, one for women and one for men.[25] Like the JOC, the LOC defined itself as a "school, service and representative body". The primary objective was still the christianisation of the working classes. Some activities were common to both movements. This was true of many of their services, for example the service for the sick, ensuring the presence of the movements in sanatoria. The JOC provided the adult movement with most of its members. Full-time functionaries of the JOC immediately became full-time functionaries of the LOC. Strict endogamy within the JOC meant that any involvement in the LOC automatically constituted, for many, an involvement of an entire household. There was much continuity between the two movements.

The movement's objective was contained within the same overall, totalising perspective. This implied a reticence regarding the intervention of the state and the stress of the utility of intermediary bodies between the state and the individual. In defending the application of the principle of subsidiarity, the movement situated itself in line with the positions of the

---

23. "Worker, be proud and raise your eyes. You are not a slave to your machine".
24. "The hold of the JOC and of other similar organisations, such as the JAC, JEC and ACO, over its members on this point was more durable and more resistant than the ideological direction it gave them". Coutrot, *Élites et militants*.
25. Debès, *Naissance de l'Action catholique ouvrière*.

Church.26 The subtitle of the movement's mass circulation paper, *Monde ouvrier*, "the weekly of the family and of work"27, which was set up in March 1937, showed that the objective of the movement was to encompass all aspects of the existence of the families of workers. Nevertheless, the plan cherished by some, of a movement formed on the Belgian model of the *Mouvement Ouvrier Chrétien*, encompassing trade unions, social service organisations and other Catholic organisations geared towards the blue collar working class milieu, did not materialise. One reason for this was the presence of the CFTC and its permanent opposition to the MPF's claim to convey to its members the true meaning of their activism. The evolution of the movement, combined with the objections of the CFTC, made matters difficult for the integralist plans of the movement. However, during war and Occupation, hopes of realising this project remained high.

2. A Family-Centered Plan. Testing the Model: Vichy and Occupation

The Occupation and the Vichy regime, which followed the defeat of 1940, gave the MPF the opportunity to develop. As a movement sponsored by the Church, as opposed to the trade unions and political parties, it was not banned. Sales of *Monde ouvrier* increased considerably.

As for the JOC, it managed, certainly not without difficulty, to remain distinct from Vichy's efforts to create a single youth movement. The Church-sponsored pastoral youth option continued to dominate the youth movement. They kept up their work, even when this meant accompanying young people to Germany drafted in the framework of the *Service du Travail Obligatoire* (STO), while, by contrast, the STO remained officially unrecognised by the ACJF and the *Jeunesse Etudiante Chrétienne* (JEC). A "Jecist approach which was more national and civic, even 'political', and thus very close to that of the ACJF, can be contrasted with a more pastoral and social-activist oriented Jocist approach".28

---

26. "It is undeniable that this serious principle of social philosophy should neither be changed nor weakened; just as those actions which individuals are capable of discharging through their own initiative and means cannot be taken from them to be transferred to the community, so it would be to commit an injustice, as well as to disturb the social order in an extremely damaging manner, to take from groups of an inferior order those functions which they can themselves fulfill, in order to give them to a larger collectivity and to those of a more elevated rank. (...) Public authority should, therefore, leave affairs of lesser importance to groups of a lower rank, where the excess effort could be dispersed". Pius XI, *Quadragesimo Anno*, May 1931, no. 86-88.
27. GRMF, *Monde ouvrier, 1937-1957*.
28. Michel, *La JEC face au nazisme et à Vichy*, 265. Nevertheless, the JOC fully intended to continue with its activities and to brave certain prohibitions decreed by the occupier. It was for this reason that, in August 1943, the general secretariat of the movement, located on the Avenue Soeur Rosalie in Paris, was closed and its chaplain, Father Guérin, was imprisoned, officially for reasons of non-respect of the edict of August 1940 prohibiting the existence of all such movements (Bourdais, *La JOC sous l'occupation allemande*). Henri Bourdais was the national vice-president of the JOC at the time.

In the same way, the LOC continued to hold meetings and to act under the protection of the French episcopacy. With regard to the government, "the position of the LOC did not vary: it was that of the French Church".[29] The primary concern was, as for the JOC, to keep going and to maintain apostolic action: "As a movement for Catholic Action, the essential aim of the LOC is the rechristianisation of working class homes and of the world of work".[30] However, the directives announced by the French state also met with the approval of the bishops and the movement. "We find ourselves in a very favourable period for being able to step up the development of the LOC" (November 1940).

So it was with the pre-eminence accorded to the family: "For us, the family is the first of all natural societies. It constitutes the basic building block of society, and its rights predate those of the state. (...) As an essential element of society, the family must form the basis of the new order".[31] The general secretariat of the movement asked that "families of workers collaborate efficiently in the construction of a genuinely family-oriented social order" (November 1940).[32] Certainly, the LOC refused to reduce its action to the family question and to be assimilated into the "family movement", which had been first set up at the beginning of the century.[33] It meant, of course, to direct not only "family action", but also "worker action". Nevertheless, it seized the opportunity which it was given to portray lower class families as being at the centre of the committees for the coordination of family movements, created in 1941 by the Vichy Office for Family Affairs. From then on, the movement's plan for action would be structured around the family.[34]

In order to "penetrate the masses" more effectively, the LOC decided in August 1941 to change its name and became the *Mouvement Populaire des Familles*. By this, it meant explicitly to open itself up to the worker

---

29. National Council, Lyon, August 1941.
30. Fifth National Council of the LOC, Lyon, 30-31 August 1941, *Meneurs*, no. 75, part 2, October 1941.
31. Fourth National Council of the LOC, Lyon, November 1940.
32. "The [Vichy] *Charte du Travail* and peasant corporation testify to the fact that work, a profession, genuinely constitutes a major pillar of society. However, man is not simply a worker and does not simply belong to a professional organisation. There is another institution of which he naturally forms a part, and which takes first place in his concerns: the family. Next to the professional pillar, keeping in mind the differences existing between family and profession, the important matter was and is to build the family pillar". (Henri Maxime, *L'ordre familial en marche*, extract from the preface of a brochure edited in 1944 by the MPF and penned by Maxime Hua, the national chaplain of the movement) Already within the JOC, the family occupied a central position in the movement's objectives: "That the family is the first and most necessary of the institutions called for by the nature of man; that it is the first stone in the social edifice, and that its ruin brings about, sooner or later, that of society; that it is not only the source of life, but of all progress and of all civilisation. That the family of the worker, in particular, plays an essential role in humanity". Resolution of the conference at the occasion of the tenth anniversary of the JOC in 1937, quoted by Coco and Debès, *1937, L'élan jociste*. On this point, the JOC and the MPF came together in a position central to Catholic tradition, particularly social Catholicism. It was likewise a prominent and regular theme for discussion at the *Semaines Sociales*.
33. Talmy, *Histoire du mouvement familial en France*; Chauvière, "Mobilisation familiale et intérêts familiaux".
34. GRMF, *L'action familiale ouvrière et la politique de Vichy*.

"masses" without frightening those same masses with the Christian reference. It no doubt also intended, though less clearly, to affirm its presence in the realm of politics and to put pressure on Vichy's family policies. (In the same year, the *Ligue Agricole Catholique* became the *Mouvement Familial Rural*.) Even though the reaffirmed objective was that of "a great popular family movement which would lead the entire working class toward Christianity"[35], the choice to abandon the Christian label was not made without provoking internal resistance, notably in the North of France, where some complained about what they regarded as a decision to cancel all attempts at public affirmation of the Christian presence amongst the working class in the tradition of the JOC.[36] Militant members continued to analyse in small groups the situations they came across and to reflect on the Christian meaning of their action. It was the first stage in the secularisation of the movement, which would intensify in 1946, when the chaplains pulled out of the management teams. The movement then remained a movement of the Church; however, it was no longer "appointed" by the episcopacy, but "on a mission". The distinction demonstrates the uncertainty and the difficulty in maintaining a Church connection while simultaneously affirming the autonomy of the movement in the definition of its "temporal" directions, as they were then called.[37]

Faced with the difficulties of survival which families experienced in the years between 1940-1944 and notably the glaring food supply inadequacies in the cities, the members of the MPF established the *Service de l'Entraide Populaire* in their areas. This brought together various achievements and initiatives, particularly in supplying working class families and finding places in the countryside for children. It also sent parcels to prisoners, organised gardens for workers, etc. Organisations for aid and assistance, public and private, did exist, in particular *Secours National*, an official organisation of the Vichy government, and the Red Cross. The MPF members sometimes requested their support, notably financial, but wished to remain independent in the name of the principle inherited from the JOC: "among them, by them, for them". This was one of the essential traits of the movement: the concern to preserve their autonomy, in particular in relation to instances of state control, but also in relation to organisations independent of the state.

Close on the heels of the *Service d'Entraide Populaire* and in the same spirit, the MPF created the *Service des Aides Familiales*, to assist and relieve mothers of working class families: to this end, some form of aid for mothers already existed, but the service put in place by the MPF trained young working class girls it employed, and the mothers who used the service were involved in the administration of the service. In the same way, certain sections of the MPF established centres for working class families in their areas,

---

35. René Rollin, "L'organisation et l'administration de la LOC Mouvement populaire de familles", National Council, 1942, *Travaux* 43, 103 (*Travaux* is the publication of the proceedings of MPF National Conferences).
36. Vandenbussche, "Le mouvement familial"; Vandenbussche, "L'évolution de la Ligue ouvrière chrétienne dans la région du Nord".
37. Debès, *Naissance de l'Action catholique ouvrière*; GRMF, *De l'Action catholique au mouvement ouvrier*. In many dioceses, the MPF nevertheless continued to be "appointed" by the bishop.

distancing themselves in that way from the parish-run charitable houses.[38] At that time also, the service for the wives of MPF prisoners likewise affirmed the specific nature of the situation of working class families in relation to other associations for the wives of prisoners.[39] As with the other services, it was important again to be distinguishable from state-controlled organisations (*Maison de la famille, Maison du prisonnier*, etc.) and, in this way, to retain a means of influence. These services had a clear moralising intent: to support women living alone, far from their imprisoned husbands; to educate mothers of working class families along the lines of the training for regular members of the movement; to reconstruct family life in holiday homes, etc.

These multiple initiatives all over France, expressing the pragmatism of the movement, constructed an image of a movement of people in touch with concrete, material problems, embedded in working class communities. Members involved in these activities regularly recall that their objectives should not be reduced to the smooth functioning of services, but this repeated insistence only betrays the difficulty of counteracting the tendency to reduce the movement to these services alone.

Vichy and the plans of the National Revolution raised great hopes in the MPF, but the efforts of the French state to achieve hegemony, and in particular its efforts to unify these movements under its aegis, came up against the resistance of the Church and its organisations, notably the JOC and MPF. Just as the JOC refused the creation by the French state of a single youth movement, so too the MPF refused the creation of a single federation of local family associations in departmental unions and in a national union, as put forward in the *loi Gounot* in 1942. Faithful to the plan formed by the JOC, the members of the MPF defended the idea that working class families could only be represented by themselves and need not have recourse to notables or members of bourgeois families.[40] Concerned about its autonomy, the MPF showed its willingness to take charge by itself of all aspects of working class life. The political project of the MPF, centred on the defence of the working class family, took root here.[41]

As with other Christian movements, the proximity to some of the important political aspects of Vichy did not imply collaboration with the occupier. Without engaging their movement as a whole, members or teams of members here and there accomplished acts of resistance or participated in sheltering Jews. Leaders of the MPF joined the *Organisation Civile et Militaire* with Maxime Blocq-Mascart; the same held true of Paul Bacon and

---

38. See Nizey, "Naissance et développement du Mouvement populaire des familles (MPF) à Saint-Etienne".
39. GRMF, *Femmes, famille et action ouvrière*.
40. The *loi Gounot* only determined the reality of family associational structures in the latter's earliest stages. At the moment of Liberation, one of the members of the MPF, Robert Prigent, took charge of the foundation of the *Union Nationale des Associations Familiales* (UNAF). The unitary associations no longer existed, and the movements specialised by "milieus" were not represented as such at departmental and national levels. From then on, they would continue to assert the specific nature of the situation and the interests of working class families. (Chauvière, "Le baptême républicain de l'Union nationale").
41. Chauvière, "Une entrée en politique".

Robert Prigent, the national leaders of the MPF.[42] A large number of members ensured the circulation of the *Cahiers du Témoignage Chrétien*.[43] Moral resistance was easier for Christians to get involved in than armed struggle. This form of political involvement by Christians was to be seen again in following years, notably in those who were to become involved with the Left.

The position of the MPF with regard to Vichy became progressively more distant. In a report to the National Council in 1943, options for the movement and uncertainties were both summarised. The authors reaffirmed: "The MPF takes all its strength of character from the movement for Catholic Action. It proposes, above all, to win to Christ the entirety of workers and working class families. It pursues the apostolic action of the Church amongst the masses", the report claimed, "as there does not exist, strictly speaking, a position held by the Movement which formally obliges all its members, as well as all those who might become members, to apply themselves to it in a disciplined manner. (...) Faced with the *Charte du Travail* and the *loi Gounot*, we have never heard it said that we were for or against". The position of the movement with regard to politics was presented in the following terms: "1) The Movement can and must judge all problems raised by the organisation of society. No activity of the workers and working class families, whether economic, political, social or professional may escape its influence. However, judgements arrived at by the Movement must by their nature be of a moral and general nature. They will be dictated by our concern to defend the personal liberty and dignity of the worker, by our will to safeguard the rights and autonomy of the working class family, by our ardent desire to procure for workers every possible means of sanctification of which they have daily need. In formulating such judgements, we are contributing to the realisation of the fundamental unity of the working classes, a unity based on our Christian conception of life. 2) Having determined these general principles, the Movement leaves its members entirely free to choose between technical formulae and between economic, professional or political systems, on condition that these formulae and systems do not run counter to the general principles established by the Movement".[44] Such assertions were made with the object of cutting the ideological ties of members with Vichy, though certain qualms relative to this evolution could be heard within the MPF. The totalising objective of the movement and its refusal to engage directly in the game of politics, reduced to the level of confrontation with "technical" solutions, were both expressed in these lines. The way in which members would try to situate themselves in the upheaval following Liberation can already be anticipated.

---

42. Robert Prigent joined the Provisional Advisory Assembly in Algiers in 1943.
43. The national team of the MPF in Lyon participated in the *Témoignage Chrétien* network (Bédarida, *Les armes de l'esprit*).
44. *Travaux* 44, 19-20. The movement's doctrine was elaborated in a small circle. The role of Paul Bacon, who founded the paper *Monde ouvrier* before the war, was often a decisive one. His system of thought had its foundation amongst the non-marxist socialists of the 19th century and drew on contemporaneous authors such as Jacques Maritain.

At the end of the war, the movement was in a strong position above all because of its actions in the form of services. It continued to manifest a reticence with regard to political action[45], a sensitive issue for many leaders. The difficulties of the postwar period justified the maintenance and development of existing services and the creation of new ones. The movement's audience increased further. The paper *Monde ouvrier* benefited from the great movement for the development of the press in the immediate postwar period; its circulation figures surpassed 100.000. The MPF was to become involved in the social movements surrounding Liberation and their projects for a major overhaul of society. A new generation, principally stemming from the JOC, was to take responsibility for the movement. Confronted with the conflicts of the years from 1945-1950 and called upon to make choices during these years of turmoil, the leaders of the MPF found themselves taking up political positions, while refusing to call them by that name. In a few years, the MPF was to assert itself as a movement of the Left.

3. The Political Radicalisation of the MPF

The Liberation was an intense period of reclassification of political forces and of renewal of political personnel. The Resistance provided large numbers of recruits for the new political structures as well as senior civil service personnel. Catholics returned in force to the political scene.[46] They were particularly welcomed into the new *Mouvement Républicain Populaire* (MRP), which was glorified by the resistance of leaders such as Georges Bidault. The networks made up by their common prewar adherence to the ACJF worked to bring together people of different social origins. It was in this way that former Jocists and members of the MPF became involved in this party, particularly by the intermediary of the "worker teams" of the party, which continued the same JOC project for specifically working class representation. Paul Bacon, a former member of the leading LOC team and then of the MPF, chief editor of *Monde ouvrier*, as well as Robert Prigent, Simone Rollin and Fernand Bouxom, who were former national leaders of the MPF, represented this view, along with other former Jocists. Locally, in particular in the municipal councils chosen after Liberation, other members were also present. However, these groups were not always well-received within the MRP.[47] The origins and methods of these working class members

---

45. "Catholic Action, prepared by the social action of preceding generations, synthesises such social and spiritual action. We say social action and not trade union action, which is situated more on the level of official and openly political activity. We also do not target the social sphere institutionalised by professions and society. We mean that element of social being which is the actualisation of the fraternal, which is the actualisation of the divine". Paul Magand, "Le Mouvement populaire des familles", *Masses ouvrières*, no. 1, January 1944.
46. Fouilloux, *Les chrétiens français entre crise et libération*.
47. "If I founded these working class groups at the beginning, it was to allow new members and young people to make their voices heard and to promote their competence and mastery by means of precise actions. Everywhere that a Jocist could be placed, and particularly in posts of responsibility, it was done, and this was not always pleasing to older members, who constantly reminded us that everything had come from the CFTC". (Paul Bacon, quoted by Béthouart, *Des syndicalistes chrétiens en politique*, 104.)

were not always appreciated by other members of their party or by the electorate. Their adoption of a certain form of intransigence contributed to their political rejection. It also led a large number of them to refuse to become involved in a type of politics which represented, in their view, the need for compromise. Their pragmatism led them, instead, towards involvement in the sphere of social action.

A large number of members of the MPF refused to enter the MRP or rapidly withdrew from it. They felt out of place and unable to express their point of view in an organisation where they were in the minority. The alliances formed in the aftermath of Liberation (during the period of the tripartite government), but also the open welcome of members of former right wing parties, at that time generally discredited, into the MRP, caused these intransigent members to distance themselves. Still distinguishable by their rejection of the classical forms of political action, the *Mouvement Populaire des Familles* became the locus for their political expression, because of the impossibility of finding a place for themselves in unsatisfactory political organisations.

Interestingly, writings on the history of the MPF have tended to downplay the affinities of many of its members, even activists, with the MRP or at least with some of the so-called social-activist aspects of the party's orientations. In the French political scene of the period and subsequently of the 1950s, that party offered many of them the electoral option closest to their convictions. The radicalisation of the MPF's positions at the end of the 1940s alienated many of its members. However, this radicalisation did not prevent others from retaining their membership, thanks, in particular, to the latter's social service orientation. It is this many-sided position of the MPF, which makes it difficult to comprehend this phenomenon without resorting to over-simplification.

For the members of the MPF, the other major issue was that of trade union activism. The MPF clearly asserted its autonomy relative to the CFTC. It even intended to be the main locus of reflection and orientation for Christian workers involved in different domains of action, including that of industry. Another cause for tension between the MPF and CFTC was created in 1946 with the first elections to the governing boards of the Social Security administration (primarily in the areas of family allowance and health insurance). The management of the funds was shared between employers and employees, who were represented by elected members presented by their respective unions. The MPF intended, through the intermediary of its *Associations Familiales Ouvrières* (AFO), to ensure the representation of eligible parties, particularly mothers without salaries, in the administration of these funds. The CFTC opposed this move.[48]

---

48. The AFO list elected several representatives. On this subject, see Boucault, "La représentation des usagers dans les élections sociales".

Participating in the turmoil of Liberation, the MPF continued more than ever to push its overall objective, considering itself to be neither a trade union, nor a political party, nor a family association.[49] For the MPF, "apart from these activities, which are only partial, since they only touch the worker in one area of his life, there exists the idea of a totally new conception of man, a conception of a new dimension of life that should be made known and that should be lived. It is on this level that our MPF is situated. We consider that the worker is not just a citizen, a producer, or the head of a family; we consider that the head of the family is all of this together and that it is this entirety that constitutes his value as a man. We should say that we are the bearers of a conception of life, of an ideal, of a certain doctrine, and with all our strength we want to transmit this ideal and this doctrine into the lives of individuals, the lives within all human societies".[50]

The MPF's claim to operate in all domains of working class life can be seen in its choice of themes for the "annual campaigns" of the movement: "To build our houses destroyed by the war, but also to reconstruct and transform the living conditions of the working class family. To rebuild our factories and workshops but also to reconstruct and transform economic and occupational living and working conditions (December 1944)". "Production in the service of man" was the theme of the following year.[51] Exhibitions questioning the rights of the owners of industry to retain all power were organised as well.

The organisation of the movement and the extension of its domains of action made it similar to a political organisation, particularly as, at its centre, religious reflection was now confined to the spiritual activities groups which brought together isolated activists. Their journal, *Pages spirituelles,* dissociated itself in 1946 from *Meneurs,* the journal of the MPF leadership group. But the MPF still wished "the Christian activities of the entire workers movement"[52] to be assured within its ranks, creating an organisation to that effect based on the pre-existing spiritual activities groups and given the name of *Association Chrétienne du Mouvement Ouvrier* (ACMO), a cause of

---

49. "As to us, we made clear what we did not want to be. Not a trade union, since some already existed, nor a family organisation like those we knew. We did not want to be a political party. We wanted, probably unconsciously, to be everything at once. (...) It is true that we fit ourselves into the family slot for the simple reason that there was nobody in the working class milieu to do it. (...) We wanted to clear the MPF of a strictly family label in order to be able to ensure the participation of working class families in other areas of their daily life. (...) Let us say that what we were trying to do was to give the workers political training - we wanted to create a general movement". (Gaston Meynard, in GRMF, *Les Mouvements familiaux populaires et ruraux,* 41. Gaston Meynard was secretary general of the MPF after the war.)
50. "The spirit of the movement and the involvement of its militant members", a report given before the National Council of the MPF, 9-10 November 1944, quoted by Tamburini, *Une politique de l'agir*. It is interesting to note in passing that the central figure here is that of the "head of the family".
51. The choice of title demonstrates the connection with Jacques Maritain ("In order truly to put machines, industry and technology to work for man, they must be put to work for an ethic of the person, of love and of liberty" (Jacques Maritain, *L'humanisme intégral,* quoted by Paul Bacon three years earlier in a report for the MPF).
52. In November 1948 they issued the booklet, a special issue of *Témoinage, Pour l'Animation chrétienne du Mouvement ouvrier,* presenting the movement's overall objectives.

irritation to the leaders of the CFTC and of serious debates within the MPF itself where some members feared a reinforcement of clerical denomination.

The MPF itself progressively transferred its overarching religious objective onto its social and political activities. During the years following the war, the leaders of the movement searched for a way to encompass all the options of the different trade union and political organisations. It asserted itself as the "fermenting agent of total worker unity": "We will make the link between the various trade unions, we will be the initiators of trade union harmony on certain precise points, we will find the common ground which will permit common conversation, so that union leaders will no longer stay staring at each other but will feel that they have the same task to fulfill: to serve the working class".[53] Such a totalising claim could not be tolerated by the CFTC. The tensions between the two organisations became increasingly acute when the MPF indicated that Christians had a choice as to their professional trade union and that they could, without contradicting their principles, adhere to the CGT, dominated by the communists, and thereby "testify" even more to their Christian faith than as members in a Christian trade union. To complement activities of the AFO, created by the MPF in 1946, the movement launched the "groups of action at work". The MPF intended to ensure its presence in companies, in particular through the circulation of *Monde ouvrier*. However, the movement's plans were out of all proportion in relationship to its own numbers, and the trade unions would not accept these activists striving for "working class unity", except when they allowed them, here and there, to augment the balance of power in their favour, notably in the case of the CGT.

Rather than a precise political project, the MPF advocated an ethic of disinterested involvement: "Activists, who will remain or become again rank and file activists, will either emanate from the working class itself, sufficiently revolutionary to refuse welfare and personal liberty for themselves in favour of welfare and liberty of the working class as a whole, or there will never be a revolution. Only a blind belief in the working class will help us to be and to remain such militants in our factories and working class areas".[54] It was only by degrees, almost despite themselves, that the leaders of the MPF could be brought to involve themselves more radically in the political sphere. Activism around housing issues contributed to that evolution.

The question of housing was indeed one of the domains of action privileged by the movement. Post-war investigations showcased the extremely difficult housing situation in certain urban areas. The movement first made some proposals which contrasted little with those of the social reformers of the beginning of the century or which appeared during the contemporaneous period, for example on the necessity to build single-family homes. However, it was precisely because of that same pragmatism which made them hesitate to take part in political debates that militant members of the movement launched a series of squatting campaigns in Marseilles starting at the end of 1946.[55] They noted that many young couples could not find

---

53. Gaston Meynard at the National Conference in 1948 (*Travaux 49*, 78).
54. National Congress of 1948, *Travaux 49*.
55. GRMF, *La bataille des squatters et l'invention du droit au logement*.

housing - this was true of some of their own members - and that working class families lived in very poor housing conditions. The 1945 administrative ruling on the requisitioning of unoccupied housing was applied only rarely, if at all. They decided, therefore, to occupy empty buildings, chosen largely for symbolic reasons. For the most part, these were buildings which belonged to the Church or former brothels. The illegality of these practices, which were nevertheless absolutely necessary for the militants, marked by the JOC slogan: "Do it and it will be done", placed them in a situation of being forced to question the traditional positions of the Church both on the right to property and on the appropriate action to be taken to get things accomplished. Certain theologians and bishops (in particular Mgr. Chappoulie, bishop of Angers) justified the action taken. Some politicians, such as Eugène Claudius-Petit, minister for housing, used these actions to speed up the construction of new homes. In this instance too, as with other problems, the motivation of the militants was primarily moral: that "real justice" could run contrary to the law which protected property owners. The action was no longer explicitly justified by religious motivations; nevertheless, the militants gave it a religious sense.[56] The larger meaning of these actions by far surpassed their immediate results: finding housing for numerous families and a better application of the law. These actions made activists aware of the necessity for the development of more radical methods of action on these questions, as well as on other issues. It freed them from a deferential attitude towards the law and the established social order.

At the same time, the movement's leaders were challenged by all sorts of matters: economic difficulties, problems of subsistence (with rationing continuing for several years), the "deals" concluded by "profiteers", the political conjuncture of the 1947 and 1948 socio-political conflicts, the end of the tripartite government with the expulsion of communist ministers in May 1947, the split between the CGT-*Force Ouvrière* and the CGT in April 1948, the beginning of the Cold War. Intense reflection followed, as well as extreme internal tensions.

---

56. "Property is one of those words which a conscious Christian should pronounce only with secret terror. (...) How, in fact, can we, without betraying justice, "own" something while so many others "have nothing"? In order to have the right to command the ships, Christians should, like captains, be the last to abandon misery. Alas, we have not yet come to that. I often think of those "pious souls", solidly embedded in pampered, healthy bodies, who recite their "pater" daily in vast and sometimes historical lodgings. (...) The evil, dear "pious souls", (...) is that such souls do not speak with God of whom they are ignorant, because between them and him, there are so many people like you who make up a wall. (...) The evil is that because of you, these souls fall into temptation. And in order to relieve their burden at least to some extent, one day they will come with crowbars and picklocks and install themselves in what you call your "home". If you had opened the doors to them yourselves, you could have spoken to them of the Father. They might have understood. But you were absent, far from their misery, and because of that, the Reign of God began like a burglary. At nightfall, Justice came in by breaking and entering". (Etienne Cyprien, *Témoignage*, 14 January 1947).

The MPF now asserted more clearly than ever its adherence to the workers' movement.[57] Concerned to bring about working class unity, it participated in and even sought out the creation of coalitions of action with the CGT, the CFTC and the PCF. The criticism of capitalism and of the state, with which it was associated, became more agitated and radical. This led its leaders to raise the question of the relationship with the Communist Party, which, in their view, best embodied the working class movement tradition. At the same time, Christians in general were expressing a wish to understand marxism and its links to Christian doctrine and its hopes. It was during these years, for example, that Albert Bouche, a Dominican and the national chaplain of the JOC, published a series of articles on marxism in *Masses ouvrières*, the journal he had set up in 1944 for chaplains of the JOC and MPF. A book by another Dominican, Henri Desroches, *Signification du marxisme*, was published in 1949 by *Éditions ouvrières*, the JOC's publishers. But in the context of the period, these efforts were not all accepted by the Church's authorities. Henri Desroches' book was banned in 1951, and in the same year Albert Bouche was forced to abandon his administrative responsibilities in the JOC and the direction of *Masses ouvrières*.[58]

Some leaders of the MPF took part in the *Union des chrétiens progressistes* (1947). Some spoke at the *Mouvement de la Paix* demonstrations, and *Monde ouvrier*, the movement's paper, broadcast this fact. This placed them in a delicate position at a time when the Church was confronting this upheaval by reaffirming its condemnation of communism (in a decree by the Holy Office on 13 July 1949).[59]

In the newspaper *Monde ouvrier*, even more than in the programmatic texts of the movement, the phraseology changed. It was now the "capitalist system" which was denounced; participation in the "class struggle" was presented as necessary; the bourgeois classes were more and more clearly identified as the enemy. The miners' strike in 1948 was supported; the war in Indochina was questioned, etc. This radicalisation of the MPF's political discourse did not compromise the development of its services. However, these were justified by reasons other than the economic necessities of the moment: whether the question was one of consumption co-operatives or of holiday homes, to mention but two examples, they were presented as prefiguring a new society. In this regard, however, it is necessary to stress some increasingly apparent peculiarities. Reticence on matters openly political continued more or less directly to be expressed. One preferred instead to talk about "general problems" (a term also used during the same period in

---

57. "The MPF in the Workers' Movement" was a theme under discussion at the Montrouge National Conference in July 1947. "We must influence and even direct this evolution and transformation. The workers' movement is and must be the motor for this march forward of humanity towards a human, fraternal and classless society". Villeurbanne conference, July 1949, Orientation report (*Travaux 50*, 19).
58. Belouet and Viet-Depaule, "Albert Bouche ou l'itinéraire d'un frontalier". Henri Desroches and Albert Bouche subsequently both left the Dominican order and the priestly office.
59. Tranvouez, *Catholiques d'abord*.

the ACJF). For the MPF, the model for the coming society was not primarily based on the transformation of the state.[60]

At the same time, the division grew between the leaders of the MPF, who were aware of the workings of political action, and a mass of followers who benefited from their services. The gulf also grew between activists directly involved in politics and those who devoted most of their time to social service work. The latter found themselves regularly called to order: "Teams of militants at every stage... should be given the opportunity to come together and to reflect on working class life, with a view to acting efficiently and not only in regards to mutual aid; in hopes of having an impact on the working class condition and not simply in view of achieving a social goal with an often paternalistic character".[61] This division translated into strong internal tensions, not always made explicit as such, and this finally led to the break-up of the MPF.

Before it came to this, the choice to change the movement's name demonstrated a wish for a new direction. The principle decision was taken in July 1949 and, a year later, the MPF became the *Mouvement de Libération du Peuple* (MLP). This change resulted in a clearer distinction than previously aired between the action and reflection of the movement and those of its family associations. It indicated a wish to break with its image, which was that of a family movement, of devoted militants involved in multiple services. It wished to express the movement's approach to "general problems" - i.e. politics - and "action at work". However, for all that, "the *Mouvement de Libération du Peuple* does not wish to become a political party" but wished to become "a new working class force".[62] It understood itself to be the driving force of the entire workers' movement, outside of any individual party-political option.[63] This position recalled the "influence" which the JOC had intended to exercise on the lives and actions of workers.

Despite the importance of this movement and of its presence in the working class for the Church, the episcopacy could only follow the movement in the politicisation of its positions with difficulty, although it was connected to the latter by the mandate it had given it. The "mandate" signified

---

60. "If the desire to progress quickly is legitimate in a movement like ours, it also remains true that this desire is slowed by the necessity to take great care not to leave behind the masses too quickly (...). We do not wish to produce a revolution through effort and blood for that revolution merely to escape (us) (...), nor do we wish to find ourselves tomorrow in a society where the politicians will have taken over (...), nor do we want a system commanded by an elite of technicians and organisers (...), we want, in the society of the future, to play a role as free men". (François Picard, in a report given at the national conference at Issy-les-Moulineaux in July 1948 (*Travaux* 49)).
61. Marie Fraignier, in a report given at the conference at Issy-les-Moulineaux, whose main theme was "the uplifting of the working class".
62. *Monde ouvrier*, 24 October 1950. "We will address general problems outside of any spirit of partisan politics, independent of the influences of political parties and of electoral contingencies, with the sole aim of the total liberation of workers". (*Travaux* 50, 42).
63. "At the centre of a divided working class, at the centre of diverse unions and political organisations which divide the favours of the workers among themselves, our MPF is not just another organisation like the others. It wishes to unite and impel the whole workers' movement, in all its social and family, economic and political aspects, and to do so from within". (*Travaux* 50, 42).

that secular evangelism was seen as subordinate to the mission of the Catholic hierarchy. The movement manifested its autonomy too much by increasingly taking openly political positions, and the bishops could not accept that it engaged the Church on this ground.[64] Hostile lobbying efforts were carried out amongst the bishops, most notably by the CFTC, certain social secretariats and conservative organisations. The most violent accusations associated the MPF with the Communist Party. Some expressed a fear that the JOC would be dragged into it in turn.[65] In October 1949, the mandate for Catholic Action was definitively withdrawn from the *Mouvement Populaire des Familles* by the *Assemblée des Cardinaux et Archevêques* (ACA) in France, which took some of the leaders and chaplains of the movement, who were attempting to ensure the link with the episcopacy, by surprise.[66]

The French episcopacy's establishment in 1950 of a new movement, *Action Catholique Ouvrière* (ACO), marked both the episcopacy's taking control of Catholic Action and a rupture between so-called "temporal" and "spiritual" action, which the original project of the *Mouvement Populaire des Familles* had closely associated. Much more than the ACMO, which was an emanation of the MPF, the new ACO brought together adherents to and militants from the MLP and soon the MLO (about which below), from the CFTC but also other trade unions, members of the MRP, of the *Associations Familiales Ouvrières* and the *Associations Populaires Familiales*. Such political or trade union pluralism was not supposed to undermine religious unity.[67] The bishops were concerned that the ACO should not drift away in the same way as the MPF. The Catholic Action movement was to be the centre for reflection on past actions and, in the process of the "revision of life", become the locus of interpretation for collective action as the creator of anticipatory building blocks for the Kingdom of God. The final meaning of all activism was therefore certainly still religious, and religious faith was to inform all aspects of existence; however, the essence of the religious movement had to be personified by individuals, who were committed Christians, and no longer by a Christian organisation. This brought to an end an evolution which had already been initiated in preceding years with the removal of chaplains from positions of authority in the MPF (April 1946), the cre-

---

64. An extract from a letter by Cardinal Achille Liénart, then president of the *Assemblée des Cardinaux et Archevêques* (ACA), is quite explicit on this point: "In fact, this question has been asked in two ways: one which I had suspected from the beginning, concerning whether the liberty of temporal options when left, quite legitimately, to MPF adults, rendered it impossible for the Church to engage with them as it does ordinarily with militants of the Catholic Action movements, and the other, which only gradually became apparent, which is that, because of the freedom of options, an important number of workers refused to become involved in the MPF and therefore no longer had a Catholic Action movement at their disposal". (Letter of 31 October 1949, quoted by Debès, in *Naissance de l'Action catholique ouvrière*, 160.)
65. Joseph Debès, in GRMF, *De l'Action catholique au mouvement ouvrier*, 62.
66. "The Assembly states that the MPF has stepped outside of the proper domain for Catholic action". (Meeting of the ACA on 18-20 October 1949). Cardinal Emmanuel Suhard, archbishop of Paris and president of the ACA, from whom the movement had received great support, had died on 30 May 1949.
67. In the ACO groups, cohabitation was not always easily achieved. From 1951 onwards, the MLP's internal conflicts came out through the ACO. Political pluralism was, in reality, relatively limited within the ACO.

ation of the journal *Témoignage* in December 1946 and the separate organisation of the ACMO inside the MPF in the autumn of 1948.[68]

In order to avoid a drift toward temporal action, it was envisaged that membership in the ACO should be provisional on involvement in a non-religious organisation, whether association, party or trade union, and on participation in the "workers' movement". This was one of the reasons for the massive involvement of women without a profession in the family associations and in the area of social activism. This ethic of involvement in working class action, maintained by participation in the ACO, implied a desire for social change which, in the French political context, led towards left wing positions.

It is true that the political opening-up of the Church remained limited at the time. In the 1950s, it was only with difficulty that Church leaders, particularly the bishops, could envisage a left wing political orientation. The school question, and in particular the existence of private Catholic schools, continued to be one of the principal criteria for their electoral choices. Left wing militants were not well-accepted at Church assemblies. However, paradoxically, by actively supporting the ACO and the JOC, French bishops were sometimes accused in conservative milieus of "workerism", which also meant, in the context of the period, an accusation of indirect support to the Communist Party and the CGT.

Opposition to the ACO also came from those who refused to make a distinction between Christian action and social action, in particular from those attached to the denominational nature of the CFTC. Conversely, "the birth of the ACO contributed, despite its ambiguities, to progress in the distinction within the consciousness of Christian activists between organisations with a temporal vocation on the one hand and a spiritual one on the other".[69] It was in this way that the transformation in 1964 of the CFTC into the *Confédération Française Démocratique du Travail* (CFDT) was prepared within the ACO (in which activists of both CFTC and CGT were to be found).

During the same period the model of the ACJF, designed to continue linking Christian and social action, was questioned by the episcopacy.[70] This led to crisis and finally to the end of the ACJF in 1956. The ACO and the JOC came out of the crisis strengthened. They were considered to be the models for Catholic Action by the bishops. Nevertheless, the repeated con-

---

68. At about this time, the CFTC also took a step towards secularisation, which would come to fruition in 1964. In its 1947 statutes, it abandoned all explicit references to social encyclicals and replaced them with a more tenuous reference to the "Christian social ethic".
69. Georgi, *L'invention de la CFDT. 1957-1970*, 196.
70. "Catholic Action and social or civic action of Christian inspiration are distinct from one another. Both are necessary in their respective context. They need one another... (but) they must operate in distinct movements. (...) The ACJF was a singularly fertile social and civic action group and trained ardent followers up until the formation of Specialised Catholic Action". A doctrinal note on the ACJF and the youth movements by the ACA, *Documentation catholique*, 1956, no. 1238, col. 1426-1430, quoted by Régnier, "Les choix de Mgr Guerry", 79.) On account of his responsibilities in the Assembly of Cardinals and Archbishops, Mgr Émile Guerry played an essential role in dealing with these questions in the French episcopacy.

flicts between certain movements and the bishops regarding the application of the theology of the mandate of Catholic Action eventually resulted in the abandonment of the latter.[71]

From the end of 1949, the MPF, which became the MLP in 1950, was no longer a Catholic movement. It was marked by the tension, which it intended to overcome, between the "sense of history", based on historical materialism, and the "sense of man", not to be subordinated "to money and to the *raison d'Etat*", a tension which had its source in, and was justified by, its Catholic origins. In the political and social situation of the beginning of the 1950s, the movement would not succeed in managing this tension.

4. In Search of a New Left. The Break-Up of the Integral Model

In the course of years, the MPF had established an assortment of associations and specialised services: working class family associations, cooperatives, associations for family aid, etc. The initial evangelical plan of the movement depended on this plethora of activities. The political project set out more clearly between 1949 and 1950 by the MLP attempted to integrate these separate groupings.

In 1949, at the time of the MPF's national conference at Villeurbanne, the following activities, which, in fact, were largely carried out separately from one another, were noted. Three sectors were distinguished: a) the family sector (the working class family associations, the services, the representative functions); b) the economic sector (the teams for action at work, the cooperatives); c) the sector which "we could call the sector of 'general problems', which is the one touching all questions in which politics intervene". Actions were then noted which were carried out largely separately from each other. However, at the same time, the integral character of the movement's project was once again strongly reasserted: "The MPF is not just another organisation among the rest. It wishes to unite and impel the whole workers' movement, in all its social and family, economic and political aspects, from within". Nevertheless, despite repeated efforts, the movement had difficulty managing the tensions resulting from this internal division of tasks.

The accusations to which the movement was subjected, notably from other Christian organisations[72], and the difficulty in preventing the tendency towards the multiplication of factions created a crisis situation. Many events - the official cancellation of the mandate for Catholic Action (1949), the withdrawal of the UNAF from the MPF's family associations (1949), the fall in membership of the movement and the erosion of the number of sub-

---

71. Less than ten years after the ACJF conflict, the link between the lay apostolate and their doctrinal authorities was noticeably modified, if not in actual fact but certainly on the theological plane, by the Council of Vatican II. There existed then no longer any need for a mandate, since it was the collectivity of God's people which was charged with the apostolic mission *Lumen Gentium*, November 1964.
72. The MLP found support in *la Quinzaine*. However, *Témoignage chrétien* criticised the directions taken by the movement, judging it too apt to imitate the Communist Party. On these issues, see Tranvouez, *Catholiques et communistes* and his contribution elsewhere in this volume.

scriptions to *Monde ouvrier* caused uncertainty to grow.[73] This movement purporting to represent working class Christians had difficulties in obtaining recognition by the public. All of these elements in the context of a highly conflictual political situation serve to explain the crisis which came to a head in 1951 in a split within the movement. Some national leaders of the MLP established a new movement: the *Mouvement de Libération Ouvrière* (MLO).[74] From then on, two movements (the MLP and MLO) existed, each with a constellation of subsidiary associations (family associations[75], holiday homes, family aid, etc.).

Political affirmation remained more prominently present within the MLP. MLP militants were most often members of the CGT. For these Christians, the Communist Party was *the* working class party, the defender of the poor and the only force capable of changing the established order. In 1951, three leaders of the MLP travelled to the USSR. The MLP was campaigning in particular against the war in Korea, against the Atlantic Alliance, against the European Defence Community and against the first European initiatives. At the beginning of the 1950s, the MLP's positions were close to those of the Communist Party. This movement of Christian workers, taught self-restraint in relation to politics, by now took pains to define a distinctive political plan, while asserting the necessity of such designs. Some leaders joined the Communist Party in 1953.

Such positions could not avoid causing tension between those who resisted the communist influence and those who accused the former of yielding to anticommunist propaganda. The movement's press gave a voice to those concerned about the movement's proximity to the Communist Party. From 1953 onwards, and with the death of Stalin, these positions evolved into a critique of Soviet communism. The Krushchev report of February 1956 and the events in Budapest in the same year contributed to this new sensivity. The Algerian War also provided access to political action for other Christians. The MLP mobilised in favour of decolonisation. Several militants were persecuted and sometimes imprisoned for these actions. This was also the moment when some young students and intellectuals joined the MLP, notably in Lyon, Paris and Grenoble.

It was not without some hesitation on the part of the activists that the movement continued to refuse to consider itself as a political party. Nevertheless, in January 1956, MLP militants presented themselves at legislative elections with the movement's label. In the same year, advances were made to other organisations united by a common critical attitude to the Communist Party, the SFIO and right wing parties. These culminated in the creation of the *Union de la Gauche Socialiste* (UGS) in December 1957 by the MLP, *La Nouvelle Gauche, Jeune République, l'Action Socialiste* and the

---

73. In 1949, just over 36.000 members were registered after a highpoint of 97.500 in 1946. After the split, in 1951, the MLP claimed 13.000 members. In November 1952, at the conference of Tours, the movement hoped to number 7000 in 1953 (of whom 1100 were to be considered activists).
74. GRMF, *Une communauté brisée*.
75. The MLO's working class family associations took the name of *Association Populaire Familiale* (APF) in 1952.

Groupes d'Unité Socialiste.⁷⁶ This was the end of the *Mouvement de Libération du Peuple*. *Tribune du peuple* took over from *Monde ouvrier*. MLP Christians found themselves in a party where they were in the minority and dominated by other tendencies. In 1960, new advances were made and a new fusion occurred with the UGS, the *Parti Socialiste Autonome*, which brought together dissidents from the SFIO, and *Tribune du Communisme*, made up of former members of the PCF, a fusion which produced the *Parti Socialiste Unifié* (PSU). In this new group, the working class Christians of the MLP found little opportunity to voice their opinions. In addition, within the PSU, Christian militants were often suspected of not respecting secular principles.⁷⁷ Some MLP members had refused to become involved in the UGS and when the PSU came into being, other former members of the MLP refused to join it. Still others left the party quite quickly.

During this time, the family associations continued their neighbourhood actions and the services continued to develop as well. Formal links with the MLP were forcefully asserted, all the more so because, in fact, they were weakening. There was increasing criticism of the manner in which the services removed militants from political action. With the creation of the UGS, the working class family associations assumed their independence. Those who refused to participate in the creation of the UGS and PSU withdrew unto themselves. The claims to a "global nature", which were still in the tradition of the now non-denominational movement, were now expressed within the domestic associations which subsequently became the *Confédération Syndicale des Familles* (CSF).

It was this same comprehensive plan which was also expressed by the MLO, which also defined itself as a "movement of synthesis".⁷⁸ The MLO advertised itself primarily as a movement for the uplifting of the working class. Like the MLP, it developed activities designed for civic or cultural training. On the Algerian War, its positions were close to those of the MLP, and both quickly defended Algerian independence. As was the case with the MLP, the MLO took pains to maintain its links with the *Associations Populaires Familiales* (APF) and the service associations. The umbrella movements, whether that of the MLP or MLO, survived only with difficulty as the subsidiary associations developed.

Former members of the MLP were to discover MLO militants in the PSU. The MLO militants were to discover even later former MLP members gathered at the *Centre de Culture Ouvrière* (CCO) in order to establish a cultural and educational movement, *Culture et Liberté*⁷⁹, in 1971. Many found

76. Kesler, *De la Gauche dissidente au nouveau Parti socialiste*.
77. As the following extract indicated: "There are many of us in the Rhône area who wish to leave (the PSU) if a verdict is not reached as to the incompatibility of simultaneous adherence to the PSU and membership in the JOC, ACO, and, more generally, all forms of Catholic militancy". (A letter to the *Comité Politique Nationale* from a federal leader in the Rhône in May 1961, obviously hostile to any sort of Catholic influence.) In the same letter, he says that the *Confédération Syndicale des Familles* (CSF) [about which below] "is under indirect Church control" and that "it is not new to sell one's merchandise under a false outward appearance" (quoted by Kesler, *De la Gauche dissidente*, 301).
78. According to the title of a brochure which it published in 1959, *Action ouvrière et mouvement de synthèse*.
79. Tétard and Lefeuvre, *Culture et Liberté*.

themselves in the new Socialist Party in the 1970s, particularly after the *Assises pour le Socialisme* in 1974, at which the APF and leaders of the CFDT and PSU participated at the invitation of the Socialist Party. These different paths led Christian militants towards the Left, either directly, by means of an increasingly close association of their organisation to others, or indirectly, through individual adhesion encouraged by adherence to a Christian movement, such as the ACO, or one of Christian origin, such as the MLO. The MLP's working class family associations, which became the CSF in 1959, and the APF, which became the *Confédération Syndicale du Cadre de Vie* (CSCV)[80] in 1975, were part of this current as well, while simultaneously affirming their adherence to the workers' movement, to the political Left, and to their overall plan of action focussed on the family, neighbourhood or the quality of life.

The Christian plan for social change concluded with the disappearance of the movement which embodied it. The MPF's integral project, reasserted by the MLP and MLO, dissolved into a series of specialised activities, autonomous in relation to one another. A series of organisations remained who, at least on the leadership level, situated themselves within, if anywhere, the left wing political sphere. By now, no Left Catholic organisations existed, or no longer existed, only Catholics who were involved in left wing organisations. These organisations, however, remained influenced by their Christian origins, and this continued to characterise their manner of approaching politics. Their distrust of the actions of the state and, more generally, the game of politics resulted in, most notably, their participation in the activities of the current oriented towards self-management in the 1960s and 1970s.

5. Conclusion

The MPF and its metamorphoses represented one current of the Christian social movement which grew out of integral Catholicism. The melting-pot of this current was Specialised Catholic Action. The latter catalysed young people into action and, above all, shaped their representations of a world waiting to be constructed. This represented a break from a position of respect for an established order and for its corollary, patronage, i.e. the duty of those in superior positions (lords, princes, benefactors, employers, etc.) to take care of those inferior to them. Consciousness was raised as to the responsibility of each individual toward the common good. The command to action as a means of constructing God's kingdom on earth provided the driving force for many initiatives. The JOC caused young people, who, for the most part, had already been prepared for this by their previous religious education, to feel legitimised in leading such action. It was in this manner that they inserted themselves into the political sphere. "The reintegration of Catholics into a democratic society is one of the major occur-

---

80. Those opposed to this transformation, which voided itself of any reference to the family, established the *Associations Populaires Familiales Syndicales* (APFS). The CSCV eventually became *Consommation, Logement et Cadre de Vie* (CLCV), while the APFS rejoined the CSF.

rences in the social and political evolution of France in the 20th century".[81] However, for Catholics, there was not an immediate acceptance of republican individualism. The political project was formed on the basis of a rejection of the all-powerful intervention of the state. The defence of the family played a central role in this. More fundamentally, the project was initially one of a Christian transformation of society. The secularisation of the MPF and other Catholic movements dissipated this project, which would be replaced by an affirmation of the "global" objective of the movement. However, the multiplication by division of the different member organisations progressively reduced this totalising objective.

The formation of the political discourse of the "Christian Reds", as they were sometimes called, had its roots in this project. However, in the situation of the postwar years and at the beginning of the 1950s, it took pains to distinguish itself from that of communism, then at the height of its legitimacy based on its involvement in working class struggles and the Resistance. It was very difficult for militant Christians of working class origins to formulate a project, simultaneously distinct from that of the MRP and from that of the Communist Party. Out of this difficulty arose the hesitations, the internal tensions, the conflicts with the religious hierarchy and with other Christian movements, and, finally, the internal crisis and the transference of their global objective outside of politics proper. These circumstances may also explain their lack of influence on the organisations of the New Left which were formed during the 1950s.

From then on, firmly placed within ACO as their religious anchor, these Catholics joined left wing political organisations. Although political choice was a matter for the individual alone, the motivation for involvement remained a religious one. The model for action was therefore still integralist. From the JOC to the MPF and its numerous metamorphoses, there existed, despite important changes, many lines of continuity. The massive participation of these militant Catholics in certain organisations, such as the CSF and CSCV, gave to the latter their political complexion and explains some of their internal tensions. This can equally be seen in the case of the CFDT.[82] These organisations, which found their principal political outlet within the Socialist Party, currently play an important role in French political and social life, particularly in regions where the influence of the working class population and the Catholic tradition are both important.

These organisations allowed Catholics to become involved within the Left, in a country where to be Catholic usually signified right wing sympathies. They contributed progressively, at the price of sometimes violent conflicts with the Church, to the recognition of political pluralism within the Church and to the relative acceptance by the Church of the presence within it of openly left wing individuals. However, in the course of this evolution, it now became the turn of the integralist model for social change to

---

81. Prost, "Changer le siècle", 21.
82. Certain militant Christians also occupied eminent positions in the CGT or PCF, but they only amounted to a small number. The access of activists, particularly by members of the ACO or former members of the JOC, to high positions of responsibility elsewhere, was one of the aspects of the strategy for openness of these organisations. See in particular Andolfatto, "Attitudes religieuses et implications syndicales".

undergo questioning. Supporters of the integralist model could not accept such political pluralism - neither those of the Right, for whom it was evident that a Christian could not adhere to the Left, nor those on the Left (the *Chrétiens pour le Socialisme*, for example, for whom reading the Bible could only lead to a left wing political option), although all rejected certain extreme positions, particularly that of the extreme Right.[83] What was at stake in these debates was a model of social and political action, but likewise a certain view of the Church and a certain theology.[84]

---

83. However, it must be noted that strong attachment to Catholicism conserves the options of the extreme Right. Michelat and Simon, "Niveau d'intégration au catholicisme et vote".
84. Donegani, *La liberté de choisir*. See also Bréchon and Denni, *Attitudes religieuses et politiques des catholiques pratiquants*.

LEFT CATHOLICISM AND CHRISTIAN PROGRESSIVISM IN FRANCE (1945-1955)

Yvon Tranvouez

The concept of "Left Catholicism", suggested by Gerd-Rainer Horn, deals with three distinct phenomena concerning political involvement, theological reflection and apostolic zeal. Can these three developments of the 1940s and 1950s be regarded as closely related phenomena on a European scale? Having repeatedly tried to do so, I am still not convinced. Yet I believe that the various experiences he mentions have something in common. Indeed the anxiety, vigilance, reprobation and even sanction by the Catholic hierarchy are evidence that these concepts may be approached together, at least in respect of their common experience of victimisation by the hierarchy. But is this a coincidence or a convergence? To me, this question gets to the heart of the matter. In order to clarify this problematic from a French point of view, and considering that Bruno Duriez has already written the essentials regarding specialised Catholic Action, let me concentrate on three reflections.

The first will deal with Left Catholics in France from a strictly political point of view. The second will concern what is to me a specifically French phenomenon, Christian progressivism. In Christian progressivism between 1950 and 1955, two logics, a political and a religious one, intersect and even fully merge. Their synergy explains the repressive measures decided on by the hierarchy at different levels. Finally, I will look back at some of the questions Gerd-Rainer Horn suggested, so as to underline what seems to be, in my opinion, a difficulty in the underlying problematic.

1. **Categories of Analysis**

The topic of Left Catholicism in France's postwar period is quite ill-definable. To clarify the problem, we must be aware of the specific constraints of the nation's political life, before suggesting a typology of Left Catholicism and before interrogating it on the basis of other parameters.

Three main elements illustrate the political situation in France at that time. The first concerns the Vichy syndrome.[1] Amongst the countries targeted by the workshop generating this anthology, France is the only nation which experienced a government that had surrendered to the conditions of the enemy during the experience of the Nazi-occupation and which thereby obtained a relative independence before engaging on the path towards total

---

1. See Rousso, *Le Syndrome de Vichy*, focussing on the role of memory after the Second World War in France.

dependency and collaboration. After Liberation, this situation resulted in two significant consequences. On the one hand, the parties of the political Right lost their legitimacy. The voters, deprived of their usual representatives, became somewhat forced to vote for the Left. On the other hand, the *Parti Communiste Français* (PCF), reinforced by its role in the Resistance, now had the advantage of a prestige that ensured a dominant position amongst the Left.

Second element: the question of Church-state relations. If the Fourth Republic refers constitutionally to a secular state, it is only because the word "secular" became the object of a subtle exegesis in which the Assembly of French Cardinals and Archbishops distinguished four different meanings, two of which acceptable to this body.[2] From then on, the Christian Democrats could accept a definition that their partners within the tripartite government - socialists and communists - definitely did not understand in the same way. The apparent agreement on the principles could never erase the patent disagreement on the facts. The attitude towards Catholic schools, very much present in many regions of the country, remained one of the discriminating criteria between the Right and the Left. The last element to take into consideration is the colonial problem. As early as 1946, the war in Indochina created a new gulf between the defenders of the French Empire and the partisans of the emancipation of indigenous peoples.

Regarding all these elements, it seems to me that three different categories of Left Catholics can be distinguished in postwar France. The first concerns the Christian Democratic trend. Already the choice of its party's name, the *Mouvement Républicain Populaire* (MRP), indicates a refusal of the traditional parties' policies and the experience of the French state. Anchored within Resistance ideology, the MRP founding programme has most assuredly a revolutionary dimension, which situates it on the Left. However, this initial political orientation barely survives the first elections. As early as 1945, the influence of its conservative electorate contributes to this disillusionment. From then on, everything will move the MRP further away from its original perspectives: the competition from the Gaullist trend (the *Rassemblement du Peuple Français*, RPF); the experience of the colonial wars; the resurgence of the school question with lawsuits against the principles of Catholic schools, who refuse to pay taxes on the proceeds raised by fundraising activities; later, the projects for a European Defense Community.[3] However, an extremely critical left wing remains within the MRP, which plays a similar role to that of Dossettism in Italy, albeit much less influential. As evidence, it is worth considering the involvement of the former Resistance activist and unwavering anticolonialist, Claude Gérard, at the beginning of the 1950s on the editorial board of the fortnightly paper *La Quinzaine*, originating in the *progressiste* milieu. These *progressistes* form a second type of Left Catholics, choosing to become closely allied with the PCF. They create their own organisation, the *Union des Chrétiens Progressistes* (UCP). Their manifesto is published in December 1947, aiming

---

2. See Poulat, *Liberté, laïcité*.
3. On the MRP, the standard reference remains Letamendia, *Le Mouvement Républicain Populaire*. But see also the contribution by Jean-Claude Delbreil elsewhere in this volume.

above all to struggle against the widespread anticommunism in Catholic circles, rather than to develop an original political line. Their existence as a specific movement comes to an end in 1951[4], destabilised by the Vatican's decree of July 1949 prohibiting all collaboration of Catholics with communists and having chosen to regroup within the wider framework of the *Mouvement de la Paix*.

Between these two poles, Christian democracy and *progressisme*, we clearly notice a third type of Left Catholics, at the same time nondenominational, anticolonialist and anticommunist, in variable proportions and with variable nuances. Indeed, from an historian's point of view, they do not constitute a distinctive organisation but instead they are linked by similar oppositional sentiments. Within such a framework we can distinguish the following tendencies: a political formation, such as *Jeune République* (JR), in a direct line of continuity with the heritage of Marc Sangnier's *Sillon*; a trade union movement such as the group *Reconstruction* within the *Confédération Française des Travailleurs Chrétiens* (CFTC); a social movement like the *Mouvement Populaire des Familles* (MPF) and its much more overtly political successor, the *Mouvement de Libération du Peuple* (MLP); periodicals as influential as the weekly *Témoignage chrétien*, a Catholic weekly stemming from the Resistance, as well as *Esprit* magazine, founded by Emmanuel Mounier in 1932, or, for instance, highly influential research centers, such as *Economie et Humanisme*, established in 1941 by the Dominican Father Louis-Joseph Lebret, appealing to a communitarian Christian revolution.[5] On the whole, it is a social and moral Left, which is more focussed on advocacy and critique than on the seizure of power. We have to wait until the mid-1950s before some of them take part at different levels in the construction of a "New Left", thus undertaking the first step towards a reformed socialism.[6]

Christian democracy, *progressisme*, New Left: this threefold distinction is more convenient than satisfactory. Indeed, it should be relativised for two reasons. The first is due to the chronological gap it tends to ignore. In its Christian Democratic version, Left Catholicism exists solely in the Liberation period. In its *progressiste* configuration, it really only starts to exist in the late 1940s. As a "New Left" phenomenon it only emerges in the early 1950s. Indeed, due to this lack of chronological overlap, some individual paths could cross all three trends. Jean Verlhac, one of the key members of the UCP, had been initially attracted and then rapidly disappointed by the MRP; he would then play a role in helping a portion of Catholic *progressistes* evolve towards the New Left.[7] Yet there is another reason to mistrust such a rigid classification, in that it obscures the articulation patterns of political involvement and religious membership. Some are Left Catholics because they are Christians, sometimes pushing to the limits the realities of an integral Catholicism. By continuously claiming that faith has demands but no solutions, Father Marie-Dominique Chenu, being close to the *progressistes* Christians and the spiritual advisor of *La Quinzaine*, relativises the

---

4. See Rouxel's *thèse*, *Les Chrétiens Progressistes*.
5. On the latter, see above all Pelletier, *Economie et Humanisme*.
6. See in particular Kesler, *De la Gauche dissidente au nouveau Parti socialiste*.
7. See Verlhac's account, "La jeune génération catholique en 1944 et le Parti communiste".

Church's social doctrine and legitimates Christian political pluralism; yet he does not consent for all that to the total separation of the spiritual and the temporal planes. Some others deliberately adopted this separation, claiming to be members of the Left and also Christian, according to the liberal penchant for declaring faith a private matter. For instance, the historian and trade unionist, Paul Vignaux, together with his friends in *Reconstruction*, keep warning against a left wing clericalism that seems to endure amongst the *progressistes* Christians. We must be aware that this religious division into integralists and liberals cuts across the political divisions I have tried to define. A two-dimensional diagram, consisting of a political and a religious vector, would therefore showcase not just three but six potential types of Left Catholics.

Even when focussing solely on the political dimension, the concept of Left Catholicism covers very diverse realities. But things become even more difficult, for in France the mutations of the *progressiste* movement intersect with the evolution of the workers' apostolate, crystallising into what was called Christian progressivism.[8]

2. French Exceptionalism

Within Left Catholicism, Christian progressivism should be considered a manifestation *sui generis*. In effect, it constitutes a specifically French phenomenon resulting from a gradual convergence (from 1950 onwards) between the moderate wing of the *progressistes* Christians and the most advanced elements of the apostolic missionary movement amongst the French working class. Such a convergence between a political phenomenon - the *progressistes* Christians - and a religious phenomenon - the industrial missionary movement - marks the beginning of what its adversaries called "Christian progressivism", a redoubtable phrase in which Christianity is used as an adjective, a concept that progressivist Christians would always refuse due to their insistence on the separation of the spiritual and temporal planes. Yet it is undeniable that a certain synergy occurs here. And its consequences become so destabilising that the Catholic hierarchy intercedes at different intervals to end this experience.[9]

Regarding the panorama of Left Catholicism portrayed by Gerd-Rainer Horn, one may have noticed that France is the only nation to showcase innovations that may be called "of the Left" in the political, theological and apostolic domains. The comparison with Italy, on the one hand, and Belgium, on the other, is quite revealing. Deeply marked by *progressisme*, Italy does not experience any phenomena similar to the worker priests. Even milieu-oriented specialised Catholic Action organisations do not really exist, for Italian Catholicism remains fundamentally attached to the model of unitary Catholic Action, grouped into four branches (men, women, young men,

---

8. Translator's note: The author uses the same French term, *"progressisme"*, to denote two distinct tendencies that are closely intertwined but not identical. For the English text, I have chosen to use two different expressions to facilitate the distinction between those two meanings.
9. See Tranvouez, *Catholiques et communistes*.

young women). On the contrary, Belgium develops apostolic initiatives towards the working class world, which are somewhat similar to those observable in France. Yet, as communism does not play a major part in Belgium, at least on a national scale, *progressisme* barely emerges, except here and there in Wallonia. France is the only nation where an important *progressiste* current coexists side-by-side with a developed missionary movement. It is again in France that the most significant intellectual developments can be observed. Gerd-Rainer Horn is right in insisting on the relevance of the written works of Maritain, Mounier or Chenu. Yet, in the late 1940s, we must also consider the determining influence of the publications of *Jeunesse de l'Eglise*, a community led since 1936 by the Dominican Father Maurice Montuclard, works that developed an increasingly detailed critique of actually existing models of Christianity.[10]

After their own respective evolutions, these diverse components of French Catholicism's vanguard merge in 1950. The *progressistes* Christians no longer have any reason to maintain their separate organisation. Condemned by the Catholic hierarchy, they are no longer of any use for the new PCF strategy of friendly cooperation with Catholics in their struggle for peace. Within the UCP, the gap widens between a left wing, which intends simply to join the PCF or its satellite organisations, and a moderate wing which desires to work towards a reorientation of the Church in order better to contribute towards separating the various Christian milieus from their conservative roots. At the very same time, as mentioned by Bruno Duriez, the MPF completes the process of deconfessionalisation and politicisation, which makes this former Catholic Action movement evolve into the *Mouvement de Libération du Peuple*. Developing a logic of work within industrial factories, the worker priests are able to gauge the influence of the PCF and the *Confédération Générale du Travail* on the working class. And they dissociate themselves from the confessional organisations. *Jeunesse de l'Eglise* radicalises its reflections and moves the working class question to the forefront of theological analysis. Some of them identify with the campaign for the signature of the Stockholm Appeal and lend their support to the manifesto, "Christians Against the Atomic Bomb", authored by Father Henri Desroches, together with a group of Christians from the 13th *arrondissement* of Paris. This public statement, resulting in condemnation by the entire Catholic press, including *Témoignage chrétien*, reveals their isolation and leads to the creation of their own platform, *La Quinzaine*, the first issue of which is published in November 1950.[11]

---

10. Regarding this intellectual movement, Thierry Keck's forthcoming dissertation will be of great value. In the meantime, see his article, "Le père Montuclard, l'Action catholique et la mission". Also note the contribution to this theme by Moulier-Boutang, *Louis Althusser*, I, *La formation du mythe*. The papers of Father Montuclard and *Jeunesse de l'Eglise* are now available on the World Wide Web: <www.moulin-a-vent.univ-lyon2.fr>
11. See Tranvouez, *Catholiques d'abord*.

Editoral board of *La Quinzaine*

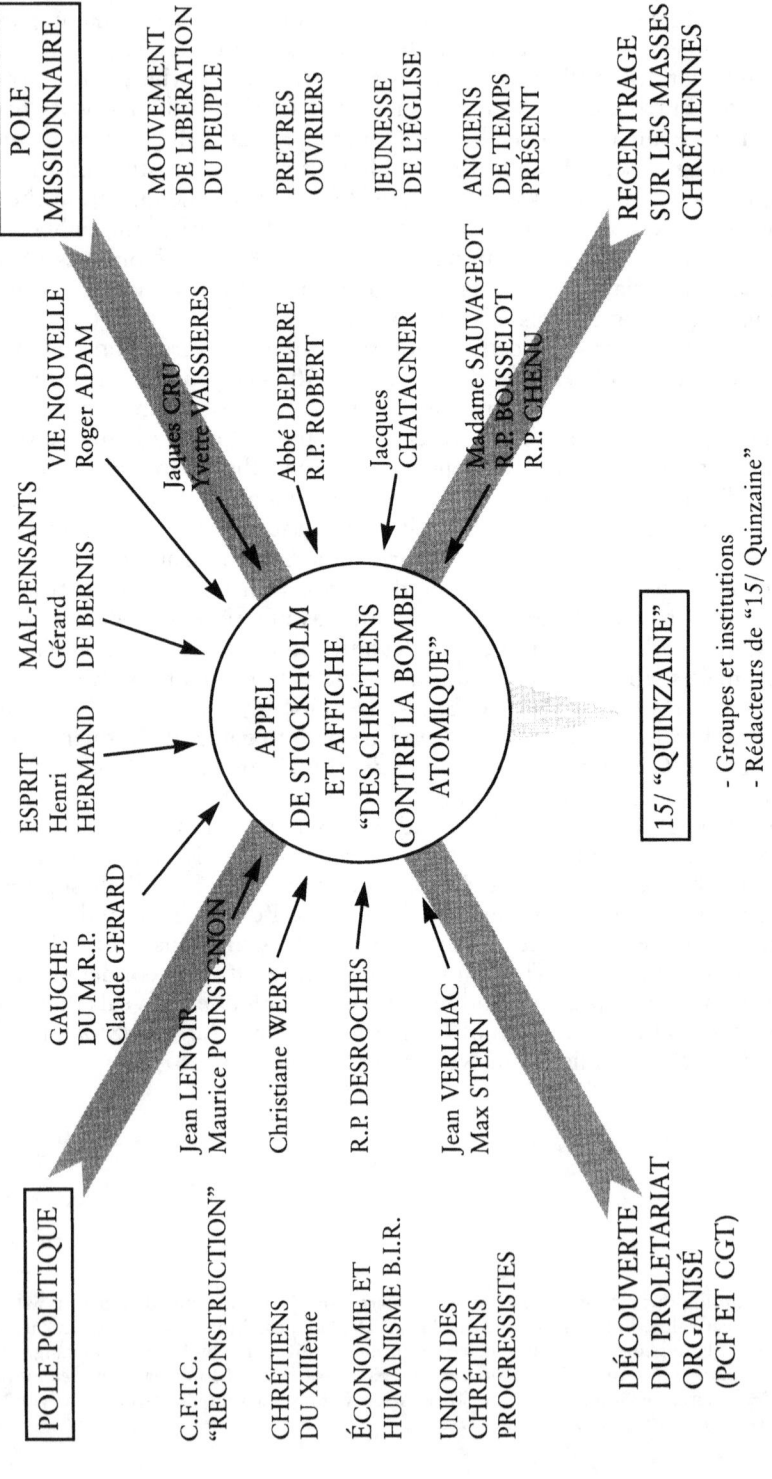

Nothing reveals better the origins of Christian progressivism than a close look at the editorial board of *La Quinzaine* at its very beginnings. In order to underscore the underlying logic of this situation, it will be useful to draw a representational picture, even if this approach has the disadvantage of ignoring multiple and overlapping memberships. Max Stern is simultaneously a leader of the UCP and a lay member of the *Mission de Paris*; Christiane Wéry is also deeply involved in the UCP; Gérard de Bernis was at one point the national leader of the *Jeunesse Etudiante Chrétienne* (JEC); and the list could go on. This group of individuals is not so much a distinct coalition than a very vague grouping where networking plays an essential part. This being said, we observe that *La Quinzaine*'s collaborators come from organisations or publications which clearly originate amongst the new Catholic vanguard, like the UCP or *Jeunesse de l'Eglise*, or from the fringes of older or more traditional structures, such as the MRP and the CFTC. The oppositionist journal, *Les Mal Pensants*, first published in 1949 on the margins of the youth movements belonging to specialised Catholic Action, and the BIR, the short-lived *Bulletin d'Information et de Recherche*, established in 1950 by Father Desroches, close to the Parisian branch of *Economie et Humanisme* and based on the militant experiences of the Christians of the 13th *arrondissement*, are perfect examples of this confluence which immediately threatened the Catholic hierarchy. Indeed, through *La Quinzaine*, some highly controversial positions, challenging on account of their political audacity or their missionary zeal, could find an echo within parishes or Catholic Action movements.

It is thus easy to understand why the movement could not survive for very long. The condemnation of *Jeunesse de l'Eglise* by the Assembly of French Cardinals and Archbishops in 1953 is followed by the ending of the worker priest experience in February 1954 and the condemnation of *La Quinzaine* by the Holy See in February 1955. *Jeunesse de l'Eglise* was blamed for a dangerous theology, substituting a logic of assumption with a logic of incarnation, which appeared to make the modern world a mandatory and insurmountable frame of reference and the proletarian revolution a precondition for evangelisation. Its influence on the worker priests was particularly feared; the latter, by means of their contacts with the *progressistes* milieus were already suspected to have undergone a marxist indoctrination prejudicial to their mission. Calling into question the traditional conception of the priesthood and relativising the specialised Catholic Action models did the rest and justified, according to Rome, the injunction made to the French bishops to end this experiment. As for the direct intervention by the Holy Office in the case of *La Quinzaine*, on one level this was probably due to the fact that the paper had welcomed contributions by some former members of *Jeunesse de l'Eglise* and that it had appeared to express, in its last months of existence, the point of view of those worker priests who refused to comply with the Vatican demand to give up full-time industrial labour. Yet this hostile intervention can more fruitfully be explained by the international context, primarily by the demise of religious freedoms in

Eastern Europe and the corresponding condemnation of several Christian *progressistes* organisations and leaders by Rome.[12]

Thus, in relation to Gerd-Rainer Horn's hypotheses, the analysis of Christian progressivism has an ambivalent meaning. On the one hand, it confirms that political, theological and apostolic developments that one may roughly qualify to be "of the Left", could, in the aftermath of World War II, be closely linked. Yet, on the other hand, the analysis reveals that this meeting of the minds, based on far left positions, is directly linked to the peculiarity of the French apostolic missionary outlook as well as to the conjuncture of the Cold War.

3. Geography, Chronology and Geometry

Therefore, insisting on this French peculiarity, I would like to revisit briefly three aspects of the problematic raised by Gerd-Rainer Horn: What is the geography of Left Catholicism? What is its chronology? What is its geometry?

Its geography has never been determined *a priori*. The framework of Western Europe may not be the most relevant when considering the phenomena under review in these pages. The focus on Western Europe is certainly well-adapted to the analysis of Christian Democracies, which used this region as a home base from which to develop a unique international strategy.[13] We know that the combined efforts of Konrad Adenauer, Robert Schuman and Alcide De Gasperi gave rise to a certain anxiety amongst other political forces, thus sustaining the myth of the "Vatican Europe".[14] Yet, likewise, the leaders of the MRP were criticised by their own left wing, the latter hostile to Atlanticism.[15] The international horizon of Christian progressivism is a bit different. Up to 1950, tropisms are quite evident. Christian *progressistes* are close to Franco Rodano and to the current emerging from the Italian Christian Left. The missionary movement shares the concerns and experiences of Belgian Catholicism. On the contrary, after 1950, Christian progressivists and the missionary movement become increasingly interested in the people's democracies, whose experiences seem to prefigure the future. The editorial board of *La Quinzaine* entertains close relations with the Polish Catholics of *Pax* and *Dzis i Jutro* and translates for its French readers several theoretical articles in which Boleslaw Piasecki, Wojciech Ketrzynski and others try to reflect on the situation of Christianity in marxist societies. To a lesser degree, the reflections of Pastor Hromadka in Czechoslovakia and those of Martin Niemöller in East Germany are also entering the discourse of Christian progressivists. These political and religious alliances outlive the condemnation of *La Quinzaine* and continue at least until the events in Budapest in the fall of 1956, which will lead to harrowing revisions. Thus Left Catholicism should be studied as a phenomenon

---

12. Thus, in 1955, Christian progressistes in Poland, Hungary, Czechoslovakia and China incur condemnation.
13. See Durand, *L'Europe de la démocratie chrétienne*.
14. See Chenaux, *Une Europe Vaticane?*
15. See Berstein et al., eds., *Le MRP et la construction européenne*.

affecting all of Europe, though it may also be useful to take into consideration its American equivalents, such as the movement associated with Dorothy Day and the *Catholic Worker*, to mention but one example.

As much as I defend a more all-inclusive geographical approach, I am equally in favour of a more restricted chronology. Gerd-Rainer Horn is undoubtedly justified in highlighting Jacques Maritain's precocious and enduring influence, particularly his *Humanisme intégral*, generally considered to be the Bible of the new generation of Christian Democrats. He is also right to find therein some evidence to link post-1945 Left Catholicism to its beginnings in the interwar period. Likewise, by relativising the relevance of the Church's traditional social doctrine, it is obvious that the nonconformists of the 1930s, and more particularly Mounier and the journal *Esprit*, played an important role in the emergence of a "second Left" of Christian origin in France, along with the historical socialist or communist Left.[16] It is no less obvious that the progressivist current itself owes much to the heritage of the weeklies *Sept* (1934-1937) and *Temps présent* (1937-1940 and 1944-1947) and therefore to the passage to the Left and then far Left of a certain portion of social Catholicism at that time. Despite all this, it seems to me that the most important new element of the postwar period, that is the involvement of a fraction of the Catholic vanguard on the side of the PCF, is above all a generational phenomenon. This does not mean that the French Catholics discovered marxism only then. David Curtis has ably demonstrated the attention they had been paying to it, as well as their reflections on it, as early as the 1930s.[17] Yet during the war the new Catholic generation experienced communism as a central element of the French Resistance and after 1945 its dominant influence on the working class. It is this dual concrete experience which resulted in Christian progressivism, rather than the utopian quest for a theoretical synthesis between marxism and Christianity. *La Quinzaine*'s editors do not stand in a direct line of continuity with *Terre Nouvelle* (1935-1939), a periodical which gathered Protestants and Catholics of the far Left during the period of the Popular Front. Christian progressivists are not the heirs of the "revolutionary Christians", as the militants of *Terre Nouvelle* used to call themselves.[18]

Finally, if we intend to preserve the concept of Left Catholicism in order to comprehend the entirety of the phenomena presented here, I need to insist on Left Catholicism's variable geometry. There are undoubtedly three political Catholic left wing tendencies, each of them, as I suggested above, internally divided by the fracture line between integralism and liberalism. There are also two apostolic left wing tendencies, if we take into consideration the differences, mutual inabilities to understand each other, and even conflicts opposing apostolic missionary movements to specialised Catholic Action. The intellectual Catholic Left is no less fractured. The *nouvelle théologie*, searching for its own identity in the Jesuit seminary of La

---

16. The expression was used vis-à-vis the *Confédération Française Démocratique du Travail* (CFDT) by Hamon and Rotman in their *La Deuxième Gauche*. Much additional information on this topic can be found in the special issue of *Esprit*, *Les militants d'origine chrétienne*, April-May 1977.
17. Curtis, *The French Popular Front*.
18. See Rochefort-Turquin, *Front Populaire: Socialistes parce que chrétiens*.

Fourvière, is very different from the "open" Thomism propagated by Jacques Maritain and Father Chenu, and the theoretical universe of *Jeunesse de l'Eglise* and its epigones is again distinct.[19] Yet - and here Gerd-Rainer Horn's attempt proves to be wholly justified - it is true that, in the most dramatic moments, all these different tendencies which were on occasion deeply divided, stuck together in the face of adversity. Indeed, Left Catholicism exists. It is that tendency which Rome condemns or which Rome has the French bishops condemn.[20] This solidarity can be observed in the refusal to suppress the Catholic *progressistes* in the wake of the Vatican's 1949 decree. Again, it can be noticed in the reactions to *Humani Generis* in 1950. But it is particularly obvious in the emotions aroused by the end of the worker priest experience in 1954. But this closing of the ranks is not long-lasting. As an example, I merely wish to mention the polemic debate opened in December 1954 by an article published in *L'Express*, in which François Mauriac calls on the "Christian Left" to support the Mendès-France government. The text merits extensive quotation.

"Today there exists a Christian Left. Today there exists an efficiently organised Christian trade unionism. If some of the MRP leaders seem to have forgotten the ideals they held when they were young, rest assured that, along with the recently excluded MPs, thousands of Christian Democrats are ready to regroup. The church of the CFTC and the worker priests, the church of the *Mission de France* and the *Fraternités* of Father de Foucauld, the church of *Témoignage chrétien* does not resemble the church which, in Dreyfus' time, remained overly attentive to the commands of the extreme Right and the antisemitic Leagues. (...) How could our bishops not wish for the entire young Catholic generation, together with the Christian trade unionists, to become one of the centerpieces of this new, liberal and antimarxist Left that is being reconstructed at this very moment?"[21]

"Elegant nonsense", *La Quinzaine* replies in an unambiguous editorial: "Faced with the myth of Christian civilisation, employed by the established order and by the Catholic Right from Jean de Fabrègues to the MRP, today Mauriac presents another myth, that of the Christian Left. (...) Why such an odd association between the CFTC and the worker priests? Why link the worker priests to this current, although François Mauriac probably knows that they have truly nothing in common with this liberal and antimarxist Left? Is Mauriac not just wishing to use for his own purpose the emotional shock felt by numerous Catholics in the wake of the worker priest affair? (...) There are better things to do today than to drag Catholics into a new political adventure by playing with their hearts and feelings, than to pinpoint some whipping boys and to make them think that politics is the fight of Good versus Evil. This backwards integralism is a dangerous temptation".[22]

---

19. See Fouilloux, *Une Eglise en quête de liberté*.
20. To show the breadth of the emotion aroused by the worker priest affair is precisely the intent of Leprieur, *Quand Rome condamne*.
21. *L'Express*, (25 Dec. 1954).
22. *La Quinzaine*, 96 (15 Jan. 1955).

To me, this hostile exchange less than one year after the banning of the worker priests is the best evidence to underscore the limits of the applicability of an overarching concept of Left Catholicism to France. These elements of differentiation I have just now drawn attention to make the scene a bit more complex. It nevertheless remains a fact that, in the long run, all these Left Catholics, whose divergences I have highlighted, contributed objectively to the recomposition of socialism and to the evolution of the Church.

These are a few remarks, though probably too short and too schematic, in order to contribute to the discussion Gerd-Rainer Horn initiated. In the late 1940s and early 1950s, it is obvious that Left Catholicism in France can only be understood in its interaction with two phenomena: on the one hand the influence of the PCF on national political life and, on the other, the acute awareness of working class dechristianisation. None of these phenomena is unique. The first can be observed in Italy, the second in Belgium. But the conjunction of the two only occurs in France, and it is this peculiarity that provokes the phenomenon of Christian progressivism, which is unparalleled anywhere else. From this point of view, the French case is an exception. On other matters, one may have noticed that I am more sensitive to the diversity of Left Catholicism than to its unity which, to me, remains relative and, when it exists, remains purely defensive in view of the interventions of the Church hierarchy. But I know that by dint of marking the differences and peculiarities, one runs the risk of obscuring the global stakes and to preclude an overall comprehension of the entirety of the above phenomena.

THE MILIEU OF LEFT CATHOLICS IN BELGIUM (1940s-1950s)

Jean-Louis Jadoulle

When applied to Belgium of the 1940s and 1950s, the expression Left Catholicism raises many difficulties and questions. First, there is the question of the term itself. When the expression is only used occasionally[1], the term "Left" indicates the liberal, socialist and communist parties of the time.[2] When used in Catholic circles, the term parties or government of the Left stresses their common denominator: anticlericalism. Consequently, it is understandable that the term Left Catholics is used with reservations.[3]

The next question is one of delimitation. If a Left Catholicism exists, what are its boundaries? From the *Confédération des Syndicats Chrétiens* (CSC) to the Christian Democratic fringes of the *Parti Social Chrétien* (PSC), including progressive circles within the university milieu, within the clergy and within Catholic intellectual journals, whether secular or ecclesiastical but in favour of a reform of society and of the Church, there existed many Catholic milieus potentially on the Left in the Belgium of the 1940s and 1950s. How can such diversity be comprehended? What common emphases can be identified to justify the common term of Left Catholics?

---

1. In often very different ways, however. See, above all, on the milieus which are the subject of this study: "Qu'est-ce qu'un catholique de gauche?", La Relève, 5 (26.02.1949) 8, 4-5; M. Laloire, "Le Pape parle aux patrons catholiques", La Revue Nouvelle, 5 (15.09.1949) 10, 196; "A la rencontre de Jeunes Sociaux-Chrétiens", La Relève, 7 (20.01.1951) 3, 1; Eversharp, "Droite ou gauche?", La Relève, 8 (13.09.1952) 37, 2; "L'avenir du PSC", La Relève, 20 (15.05. 1954) 8. For La Revue Nouvelle, see in particular R. Aubert, "Le malaise des catholiques français et les leçons de l'histoire", La Revue Nouvelle, 8 (15.06.1952) 15, no 6, 631. For the Belgian groups around the journal Esprit, see Archives du Monde Catholique (ARCA), Université Catholique de Louvain-la-Neuve (UCL), Papiers Jean Van Lierde, no. 76.02, a circular by Élie Baussart, Jean Cordier, Fernand Heuse, Paul Leburton, Yvonne Leloux, Charles Leroy, Marie-José Masson, Marguerite Ruelle, André Schreurs and Jean Van Lierde (written in late 1955 or early 1956).
2. Gerard, "Christian Democracy in Belgium", 69, note 13. J. Gérard-Libois also speaks "of the three parties which a derisive vocabulary classifies under the 'Left' label" (J. Gérard-Libois, "Comment les Belges ont voté le 1er juin 1958", La Revue Nouvelle, 14 (15.07.1958) 28, no 7, 51). See also "A gauche... Et à droite", La Relève, 6 (18.11.1950) 45, 4.
3. There are a number of them. See, in particular, for the milieus studied below: Meunier, "Réflexions sur la gauche et la droite", La Revue Nouvelle, 7 (15.06.1948) 7, no 6, 570-580; A. Molitor, "Une histoire qu'on ne sait plus", La Revue Nouvelle, 10 (15.12.1954) 20, no 12, 495, and "Catholiques de droite? Catholiques de gauche?", La Revue Nouvelle, 13 (15.03.1957) 25, no 3, 315-316. For the Belgian page of Témoignage Chrétien, see in particular P. Lovry, "Chrétiens de gauche ou chrétiens de droite", Témoignage Chrétien. Edition belge, (11.03.1949) 244, 3, and "Gauche, droite...!", Témoignage Chrétien. Edition belge, (25.12.1953) 494, B. For La Relève, see in particular "Ou sont les hommes de bonne volonté?", La Relève, 4 (25.12.1948) 51, 1, and Eversharp, "La peur de l'électeur?", La Relève, 7 (07.07.1951) 27, 1.

Finally, there is the question of meaning. Conceived in the context of the French Revolution, adopted to indicate constantly mutating political tendencies before eventually moving out of the context of politics proper, the Left-Right conceptual pair is hampered by the lack of precision. What meaning should be given to the Left label, if not that of progressive provenance? A guarantee of openness to change and of a certain daring with regard to the future? At what stage can such a reformist spirit be situated on the Left?

Thus, rather than studying Left Catholicism in Belgium in the 1940s and 1950s, we have chosen to deal with the history of four Catholic intellectual milieus which were active in francophone Belgium and classically situated to the left of Belgian Catholicism. These four milieus are *La Revue Nouvelle*, *La Relève*, the Belgian team of *Témoignage Chrétien* and the Catholics involved in the *Esprit* groups in Belgium.[4] Such a study has, at the outset, allowed for a clear delineation of the kind of *progressisme* attributed to them. It also suggests a method for approaching Left Catholic milieus which can be effected by the constant comparison of their positions with those normally operating within other Belgian and Roman Catholic spheres. It also allows one to de-emphasise the question of the relevance of gauchisme and *progressisme*[5] for these milieus and to pose the question of their modernity.

1. Four Progressive Catholic Milieus

Founded in 1945 and inheritor of *La Cité Chrétienne*, directed by Canon Jacques Leclercq, *La Revue Nouvelle* was manifestly Catholic in profile. The "demands of the times"[6] indeed made it necessary, according to those promoting the new periodical, to reconnect with an "integrally Christian conception of life".[7] This concern to bring to light the secular implications of the Catholic faith remained constant at least until the end of the 1950s. Anchored to the objective for which it was initially founded, the Christian identity of *La Revue Nouvelle* explains the editorial choice to keep a large place "for the direct study of religious problems and related philosophical questions".[8] However, this did not make the periodical a religious or theological journal. Its editor, Jean Delfosse, often shared with contributors his fear that the journal might take on the "appearance of something halfway between a diocesan and a theological journal. The vast majority of the fine texts which I have for this year were written by ecclesiastics on theological and moral subjects or by secular writers, also on those sub-

---

4. On these different milieus, the circumstances of their foundation, their actors and achievements, see Jadoulle, *Chrétiens modernes?*, 76-334.
5. The term "progressisme" is used in this article in a different sense compared to the meaning of that term in the French context. As explained below, the Catholic intellectual milieus at the center of this investigation explicitly delimited themselves from the French milieus of *chrétiens progressistes* whom they accused of being too close to marxist positions.
6. "Départ", *La Revue Nouvelle*, 1 (01.02.1945) 1, no 1, 2.
7. Ibid.
8. Ibid., 7.

jects. I would like, while retaining the feeling of the journal, to place a greater emphasis on its role as a secular journal, written for secular people and filled, as far as possible, by articles written by them".[9]

This concern primarily to address secular individuals and to provide them with the spiritual nourishment necessary for their secular activities was reflected in the direction and organisation of the journal. This was carried out by two laymen, André Molitor and Jean Delfosse. Many ecclesiastics (Jean Jadot, Roger Aubert, Jean Vieujean, Charles Moeller...) nevertheless played an important role, nourishing the young journal by means of their articles and their ideas.

La Relève came into being during the Occupation. In the course of the year 1941, Father Beda Rigaux, founder and organiser of the Centre for Christian Culture, which was frequented by a number of well-known Brussels Catholics, took the step of bringing together the youngest of these and created a group which he thereafter named *La Relève*. Reminding them that they represented the young generation which, in the future, would have to rebuild the country from a Christian perspective, he urged them to anticipate the postwar problems. This group held regular meetings over many months. Their exchanges centred on the reconstruction of the country and the problems of public life in general.

After Liberation, the principal promoters of the group, and in particular Jean Michiels and Arthur Gilson, decided to annex it to the developing PSC. What would quickly become the "central team of *La Relève*"[10] counted on several teams, similar to that which had been active during the Occupation.[11] They constituted the first links in the movement of *La Relève* which emerged at the end of 1944 or at the beginning of 1945. It defined itself at that time both as a movement for the education of citizens in public matters and in the responsibilities - not merely political - which should be exercised in society at large, and as a pressure-group which would attempt to influence the development of the new PSC and to attract new candidates to their lists. From 1945 onwards, the groups were invited to support the electoral campaign of the PSC, while members who wished to embark on a political career were invited to sign up for the new party. In the elections of February 1946, many members of *La Relève*, such as Arthur Gilson, Pierre Harmel and Raymond Scheyven were elected. However, after the ballot, the leaders of *La Relève* decided to shut down the movement, refusing to see their movement become a sort of party within the party, the

---

9. Groupe d'Études des Historiens de l'Europe contemporaine (GEHEC), UCL, Archives de *La Revue Nouvelle*, no. 190, Jean Delfosse to Léopold Genicot, (Brussels), 29.01.1954. See also no. 184, Jean Delfosse to Jean Vieujean (Brussels), 16.01.1952, and no. 187, Jean Delfosse to H.-M. Oger (Brussels), 4.02.1953.
10. Ibid.
11. La Relève. *Mouvement d'étude et d'action politique. Le sens d'une politique. Position de principe. Statuts du mouvement*, Brussels, [March 1945], 9.

PSC. The *La Relève* group emerged subsequently as the "progressive wing"[12] or "progressive stimulus"[13] of the PSC.

The existence of the Belgian team of *Témoignage Chrétien* has been documented since March 1947.[14] Already active for several months, it was made up of a nucleus of four people: Jules Gérard-Libois, Father Paul Bourgy, Hubert Dewez and Father Damien Reumont. From September 1948, they formed the first editorial committee of the Belgian section of *Témoignage Chrétien*.[15] They circulated the French paper, *Témoignage Chrétien*, supplemented by one or two Belgian pages, in Belgium for ten years.

The promoters of this new periodical immediately showed themselves to be very sensitive to the "missionary problem, and more precisely to the problem of the Church within the proletarian milieus".[16] From November 1948, the editorial committee announced its decision to produce a journal that would openly take sides and which would support "all great movements for human liberation and apostolic mission".[17] Opposed to every attempt to look inwards and to any attempt at rejection of the contemporary world, the Belgian team of *Témoignage Chrétien* chose to devote their efforts to discover a new presence in the world for Christians and to search for a new "Christian vision of the world in which God asks us to be His witnesses".[18] For "the Church must, in the coming decades, enter resolutely into the movement of the modern world in order to take it on and thus to save it".[19] If this missionary preoccupation focussed on the working class in particular, attention to the condition of this class went beyond bridging the gap separating it from the Church. It was equally important to draw attention to "the problem of a reform of social, economic and political structures. Just as the *Ancien Régime* was brought down by the rise of the middle classes, we think that the middle-class system is challenged by the working-class movement".[20] This reform-oriented position took on a distinctly anticapitalist tone.

12. "Étienne de la Vallée Poussin nous parle du rôle de 'La Relève' dans le P.S.C.", *La Relève*, 1 (09.12.1945) 18, 1+3.
13. C. Van Der Bruggen, "Pourquoi un bureau d'études politiques", *La Relève*, 2 (17.03.1946) 11, 6. See also "'La Relève' n'est pas un stand", *La Relève*, 2 (24.03.1946) 12, 1, and P. Lion, "Journal d'un lecteur", *La Relève*, 6 (3.06.1950) 22, 9. Arthur Gilson, Pierre Merten and Charles Roger confirmed this role of "progressive stimulus" and agreed on the expression: see the interview by J.-L. Jadoulle with Arthur Gilson, Lasne, 7.04.1999; with Pierre Merten, Brussels, 16.04.1999, and with Charles Roger, Brussels, 18.05.1999.
14. ARCA, Papiers Paul Leburton, Andrée and Jules Gérard-Libois to Paul Leburton, Brussels, 1.03.1947. This is the oldest document with the heading *Témoignage Chrétien, Équipe belge*, which we have found.
15. Centre d'Action et de Recherche en Histoire ouvrière et populaire (CARHOP), Brussels, Papiers Hubert Dewez, an account of the meeting of the *Équipe belge de Témoignage Chrétien* in Brussels, 21.09.1948, s.l., s.a.
16. CARHOP, Papiers Hubert Dewez, Jules Gérard to Mme Hubert Dewez, Brussels, 10.09.1947.
17. "Homme parmi les hommes. Notre témoignage", *Témoignage Chrétien. Édition belge*, (26.11.1948) 229, 3.
18. Ibid.
19. Ibid.
20. "TC belge présente son bilan anniversaire", *Témoignage Chrétien. Édition belge*, (18.11.1949) 280, 3.

Established in 1932 by Emmanuel Mounier and Georges Izard, the French journal *Esprit* attracted a certain number of well-known Belgians. From the period between the wars, *Esprit* groups appeared in Brussels, Liège and Louvain. They were swept from the scene by the upheaval of the Second World War. In the aftermath of the conflict, groups formed again, first in Brussels and then at Louvain, Liège, Verviers, Seraing, Charleroi, Mons, La Louvière, Namur, Arlon and Gembloux. Contrary to the three other intellectual milieus already mentioned, they did not have a press apart from a small bulletin for strictly internal use; they defined themselves primarily as discussion groups and as centers promoting personal growth. Above all, the personalism[21] from which they more or less drew their inspiration constituted a platform which allowed well-known people from Catholic backgrounds as much as from socialist, free-thinking Protestant or Jewish ones, to come together around a common ideal. The pluralism inherent in the *Esprit* groups made them a novel milieu. An important number of well-known Catholics, who were deeply involved in the editorial team, or the larger circle of contributors to *La Revue Nouvelle*, *La Relève* or the Belgian edition of *Témoignage Chrétien*, frequented these groups, for example Élie Baussart, Hubert Dewez, Claude Josz, Jean Ladrière, Paul Leburton, François Persoons, Robert van der Gucht, Jean Van Lierde and Yves de Wasseige. Some, like Jules Gérard-Libois, a member of the Brussels *Esprit* group and editor-in-chief of the Belgian page of *Témoignage Chrétien*, were even a driving force.

These four intellectual milieus therefore presented a relatively similar profile. Apart from the *Esprit* groups, they drew on a strong Christian inspiration. This marked Christian inspiration did not, however, make their journals specifically religious or theological ones; they publicised themselves rather as journals of general interest, widely open to topical political, economic and social events. Their interest in international affairs was also evident, as well as their concern to keep readers informed of the evolution of intellectual currents and of different forms of cultural expression.

The executive posts and principal responsibilities, as far as the direction of these various periodicals was concerned, were in the hands of laypersons. All three milieus were therefore good examples for the progressive rise to the foreground within Church life of a certain number of secular intellectuals. This determining role for laypersons should not, however, eclipse the essential contributions of many ecclesiastics, such as Father Jadot and Canon Aubert to *La Revue Nouvelle* or Father Paul Bourgy in the editing of the Belgian edition of *Témoignage Chrétien*. The *Esprit* groups were also largely made up of lay-people.

Similar by virtue of the profile of the periodicals they edited and by the roles they conferred on lay members, these milieus also deserve to be described as "intellectual". Whether through their training, their profes-

---

21. On the personalism of Emmanuel Mounier, see in particular Winock, "*Esprit*". On his influence in the Belgian Catholic world before and after the Second World War, see the comments by Gerard, "Du parti catholique au P.S.C.- C.V.P.", 26-28; Gerard, "Christian Democracy in Belgium", 68; Pasture, "Redressement et expansion", 273-275; Jadoulle, "L'évolution du programme du Parti Social Chrétien", 361-362; Lamberts, "Du personnalisme au social-personnalisme", 366; Lamberts, "L'influence de la Démocratie chrétienne en Belgique", 254; Sauvage, *La Cité Chrétienne*, 98-99.

sional itinerary, their interests or the demands of the publications which they helped to edit, most of the members of the different milieus were distinguishable by a marked "intellectual" profile. Their objective to influence the course of society and of the Church and to summon these to their faith in order to suggest reforms which they deemed necessary also meant that they were authentic "Catholic intellectuals". Whether, therefore, we take this term in its contemporary or sociological[22] sense, or whether we interpret it according to the meaning it had when the expression was first coined, i.e. the time of the Dreyfus affair, when an intellectual became defined as one who, basing himself on a certain expertise and/or notoriety, becomes involved in society[23], the milieus who are at the center of this study deserve the qualification of "intellectual".

The study of these different milieus, the people who ran them and the relationships which they developed, justifies the notion, expressed by former participants, of a far-reaching affinity between the four groups. Determining the members of these four milieus or of readers of one of these three periodicals, who were simultaneously taking on the role of contributor, reader or member in one or several of these other milieus, it is clear that a relatively important number of people was involved in two or three of these groups. The presence of these people in several groups, along with the numerous instances of close cooperation and near-identical thinking amongst the editorial teams of the three periodicals, who often read and approved each other, indicates the existence of a veritable network of intellectual sociability.[24]

A close observation of this intellectual cross-fertilisation, however, also reveals that the greatest proximity existed, on the one hand, between *La Revue Nouvelle* and *Témoignage Chrétien* and, on the other hand, between the *Esprit* groups and the latter two milieus. The number of people who were members of the *La Relève* group and of an *Esprit* group or who were also contributors to or readers of the Belgian page of *Témoignage Chrétien* was very low. The circle of contributors to *La Revue Nouvelle* occupied a position which, although close to that of *La Relève* and of *Témoignage Chrétien*, can be described as occupying a middle position.

The relative position of these milieus vis-à-vis each other, insofar as it has been described above, is corroborated by a study of the socio-professional profile of the members of or contributors to the different groups.[25] Contributors to *La Revue Nouvelle* and members of the editorial staff of *Témoignage Chrétien* included a relatively large proportion of ecclesiastics. The readership of *Témoignage Chrétien* - the only readership about which we have sufficient information - also included a large number of priests. By contrast, apart from Father Beda Rigaux, whose activities soon distanced

---

22. This is the definition chosen by Sirinelli, ed., *Dictionnaire historique de la vie politique en France*, 524: "intellectuals are those who participate in cultural creation or in the progress of scientific knowledge, as well as those who contribute to spreading and popularising the concrete gains of this creation and knowledge" [J.-F. Sirinelli].
23. See in particular Julliard and Winock, eds., *Dictionnaire des intellectuels français*, 12; Ory and Sirinelli, *Les intellectuels en France*, 9.
24. See Jadoulle, *Chrétiens modernes?*, II, 328-334.
25. Ibid., 76ff.

him from the group, the team of *La Relève* did not include a single ecclesiastic.

The socio-professional profile of secular contributors to or readers of the three periodicals also differed. The circle of contributors to *La Revue Nouvelle* was primarily made up of persons who had come from the world of the press and of publishing houses as well as universities. The executive and editorial committees and the principal contributors also included many highly-placed civil servants. The profile of members of the *La Relève* group was very different: senior officials, senior advisors and political office holders, company directors, bankers and lawyers were the most numerous. Although many held important posts at a university during the period between 1945-1958, academics and journalists only occupied a marginal position. As with *La Revue Nouvelle*, the influence of people holding positions of authority in Christian trade union circles appears quite weak. Blue collar workers, white collar employees or professionals were totally absent. Contributors to *Témoignage Chrétien* came from a relatively similar milieu compared to that of *La Revue Nouvelle*, although they did include a higher proportion of union leaders and laypersons active in Catholic Action movements. These two latter categories made up a large proportion of the journal's readership. However, civil servants, who made up a large number of the main organisers of *La Revue Nouvelle*, were present only in negligible quantities among contributors to *Témoignage Chrétien*.

As for the *Esprit* groups, they brought together well-known people principally from the teaching profession and particularly from universities. Journalists and members of the liberal professions, union leaders, priests and ministers and, especially, civil servants, industrialists, financiers and political office holders constituted a small minority. Apart from Seraing, workers were absent from the groups. This was also true of the members of *La Relève* and the contributors to *La Revue Nouvelle*. The Belgian edition of *Témoignage Chrétien* could only count nine workers among its subscribers.

A study of the positions adopted by the different milieus confirms this greater affinity between the *La Revue Nouvelle* team and the editors of the Belgian edition of *Témoignage Chrétien*, particularly with regard to religious matters. The space devoted to religious matters, to the evolution of Christian thought and to the life of the Church by the editors of *La Revue Nouvelle*, *La Relève* and the Belgian edition of *Témoignage Chrétien* differed widely. Religious questions were the subject of very few debates in the columns of *La Relève*. Its promoters gave priority to political, economic and social questions. They clearly differed in this way from the shapers of the editorial policy of *La Revue Nouvelle* and the Belgian edition of *Témoignage Chrétien*, where religious questions, in one way or another, were the subject of marked interest. In accordance with their original project, the editors of *La Revue Nouvelle* and *Témoignage Chrétien* dedicated many articles to exploring the paths of a renewed presence of Christians in the world. The first were nevertheless distinguished by a more pronounced attention to the evolution of religious thought and of spirituality, as well as to the Church's position in the world. Conversely, missionary unease when confronted with the gulf separating the Church and the working classes was more evident in the columns of the Belgian page of *Témoignage Chrétien*.[26]

On secular matters, the promoters of *La Revue Nouvelle,* of *La Relève* and of the Belgian page of *Témoignage Chrétien* initially shared a number of fundamental positions, particularly on economic and social matters. The editors of the three periodicals, critical of the capitalist regime, called for a society which would give workers a greater role to play in the management of the economy and the sharing-out of wealth. They also agreed in their demand for a growing intervention of the state in economic activity. Halfway between a market economy and marxist state socialism, the institution of a regulated economy had to go hand-in-hand with the installation of structural reforms[27] and the consolidation of the social security system. This economic and social democracy had to be supplemented by the demand for access to secondary and higher education for the greatest possible number of people. The realisation of this vast programme ideally necessitated a bringing together of all progressive forces. An attempt to secularise political life, making it possible to forge associations regardless of religious difference, was therefore necessary.

It is important to underline the boldness of these common demands. The editors of the three periodicals shared the most reform-oriented positions advocated by the PSC and the CSC. They also appropriated the most daring points of view that could then be found within the Church's social doctrine.

This common progressivism nevertheless concealed certain important divergences. Those involved in *Témoignage Chrétien* showed a keen sensibility to the problems of the working class. If they refused, like their counterparts in *La Revue Nouvelle* and *La Relève*, to follow French *chrétiens progressistes*[28] into an alliance with the communists, they showed themselves to be less uneasy when faced with the question of the compatibility of Christian and marxist beliefs. They also appeared more critical of the capitalist system and more favourable to the nationalisation of some sectors of the economy. Their disappointment in relation to the details of structural reforms implemented in postwar years was likewise more pronounced. They were also opposed to the plans for reform of the social security system, whose object was to restrict the areas covered by compulsory insurance to major risk areas only.

On political matters, the *Témoignage Chrétien* group criticised the plans of those who had believed in the possibility of reforming the PSC from the inside. *La Relève's* choice to attach itself to the PSC was therefore

---

26. On these religious questions, see Jadoulle, *Chrétiens modernes?*, 3, 342-471.
27. This expression indicated reforms whose objective was to set up a dialogue between employers and workers at every level - national, industry-wide and local.
28. This polemical title strove to compromise several different movements which should, nevertheless, not be confused: the *Union des Chrétiens Progressistes* (1947-1951); *La Quinzaine* (1950-1955); becoming *Le Bulletin* (1955-1957) and subsequently *La Lettre* (1957-); *Jeunesse de l'Église* (1943-1953); and *Économie et Humanisme* (1941-1966). On the question of Christian *progressisme* in France, see Tranvouez, "Mission et communisme"; Tranvouez, *Catholiques et communistes*. On the rejection of the orientation of French *progressistes* Christians by the Catholic milieus studied here, see Jadoulle, *Chrétiens modernes?*, IV, 507ff.

implicitly condemned, and the path which the *Union Démocratique Belge* (UDB)[29] had attempted to follow was justified *a posteriori*. The editorial committee pleaded incessantly for a coalition between the PSC and the *Parti Socialiste Belge* (PSB). Its reserve in the royal question[30] - it was necessary to await the conclusion of the affair before the Belgian team of *Témoignage Chrétien* made its fundamental position explicitly known - demonstrated its conviction that the question should remain an open one for all Christians. It also betrayed the hope that the king would withdraw, as the division of the country rendered his return to the throne politically impossible. The repeated questioning of the efficacy of Catholic schools by some organisers of *Témoignage Chrétien* and the stress on the value of the experiences of Christians active in public education likewise demonstrated a distinct unease as to the slogans mobilising the Catholic world. It cannot be denied that a certain number of contributors to the journal, notably among the members of the *Esprit* groups, expressed a preference for non-denominational schooling.

The editorial team of *La Relève* defended positions very different from those of the Belgian team of *Témoignage Chrétien* on several questions. More convinced of the effectiveness of a market economy, more nervous regarding the spectre of a strong state, it refused to become involved on the issue of nationalisations. Not content with the manner in which structural reforms were being put in place, it advocated realism and patience. It regularly reminded readers of the necessity to take into account the imperatives of economic profitability. The presence in the group of an important number of company managers and bankers surely explains this attitude. For them, the project for the reform of the social security system, by restricting the grounds for obligatory insurance to major risk areas only, showcased both a justified fear of a strong state and the hope, expressed by the editorial team, of handing to each person his proper sense of responsibility. The divergences between the organisers of *La Relève* and *Témoignage Chrétien* regarding structural reforms and health and disability insurance reproduced the existing tension regarding these two matters between the PSC and CSC. On political matters, if it shared a common interest in the secularisation of public life with the Belgian team of *Témoignage Chrétien*, the editorial team of *La Relève* instantly distanced itself from the UDB. It also ceased quite quickly to support programmatically a coalition between Social Christians and socialists and pleaded for the constitution of homogenous PSC governments, the problem being the opposition of left wing parties to the king's return and their advocacy of equal support to public and Catholic school systems. Like the PSC, the *La Relève* group thereby became active in

---

29. On the beginnings of the UDB and its history, see Willame, "L'Union démocratique belge" and especially Beerten, *Le rêve travailliste en Belgique*. See also Pirard's testimony, "Un météore dans la vie politique et intellectuelle de la Wallonie".
30. The attitude of the king, Léopold III, in May 1940 and during the Second World War divided Belgians after Liberation. While the PSC called for the king's return to the throne, the PSB and the liberals were, in the majority, opposed to this. The royal question did not come to a conclusion until August 1950, when Léopold III delegated his powers to his son, Prince Baudouin. On this royal question, see in particular Gérard-Libois and Gotovitch, *Léopold III*; Stengers, *Léopold III et le gouvernement* and Theunissen, *1950, le dénouement de la question royale*.

demanding a popular consultation on the royal question and, after the inconclusive outcome of the referendum, demanded the king's return, and it likewise became involved in the campaign for the defence of Catholic schools from the *législation Collard*.[31]

Closer to the Belgian team of *Témoignage Chrétien* in its attention to religious questions and in the profile of its contributors, the editors of *La Revue Nouvelle*, who benefited from the collaboration of a certain number of contributors held in common with *La Relève*, showed a number of affinities with the position of *Témoignage Chrétien*. The two editorial teams seemed to share an equally severe critical view of the abuses of the capitalist system. They came together in their unfailing support of an alliance between the PSC and PSB, through the expedient of a governmental coalition. The favourable attitude of organisers of *La Revue Nouvelle* vis-à-vis the UDB should not be forgotten either. They also shared with the promoters of *Témoignage Chrétien* the conviction that the division of the country rendered the king's return politically impossible. Whether Léopold III's attitudes in May 1940 and under the Occupation could be positively assessed nevertheless divided the editorial teams; *Revue Nouvelle* appeared less inclined to demand the sovereign's abdication. It also shared the unease of the organisers of *Témoignage Chrétien* regarding the return of confessional divisions, particularly in the field of education.

The reservations emanating from their Christian faith regarding cooperation with communists and their fear of a strong state nevertheless found the editors of *La Revue Nouvelle* and *La Relève* in relative proximity on certain issues. Both rejected the path of nationalisations and called for a reform of the system of health and disability insurance giving beneficiaries some individual responsibility. The editorial team of *La Revue Nouvelle* was also more inclined to advocate patience when confronted with the slowness and insufficiencies of structural reforms. With a sense of fatalism, it joined its forces to the formidable effort for the mobilisation of Catholics in favour of non-denominational schooling.

The study of the positions defended by the three periodicals therefore confirms the greater affinity of the Belgian team of *Témoignage Chrétien* and that of *La Revue Nouvelle* and the intermediary position of the latter. The *Esprit* groups likewise were the venue of debates and discussions that were linked in more ways than one to the columns of *La Revue Nouvelle*, *La Relève* or *Témoignage Chrétien*. The desire for a deconfessionalisation of Belgian politics and for close cooperation between Christians and socialists, posed in sharp terms but frequently disappointed, was therefore patently obvious in all four milieus at the center of this article. Criticism of the capitalist regime united them just as much.

---

31. From June 1950 to April 1954, Belgium was led by a homogenous PSC government. The Christian Social minister for state education, Pierre Harmel, put into place the political objective of ensuring continued subsidies for Catholic instruction. However, in April 1954, the PSC majority was replaced by a liberal-socialist majority. The new minister for state education, the socialist Léo Collard, undertook to dismantle the legislation put in place by his predecessor. The Collard legislation provoked much defensiveness in Catholic circles. On this "war of the schools", see in particular Haagdorens, "De mobilisatie van de katholieke zuil", and Tyssens, *Guerre et paix scolaires*.

The *Esprit* groups were nevertheless also a locus for the adoption of more daring positions. Very critical regarding the PSC, a number of members of the groups, including some Catholics, seemed more inclined to trust the PSB. One after the other, they rejected the objections to the idea of a regular collaboration with marxists traditionally raised in Catholic milieus. On the school question, a number of protagonists from the *Esprit* groups advocated the establishment of a unified, non-denominational school system.

A study of the positions defended in the columns of *La Revue Nouvelle*, *La Relève* and the Belgian edition of *Témoignage Chrétien* therefore allows these three milieus to be situated on the fringes of political Catholicism, within its most progressive wing. *La Relève's* choices to support the new PSC and to assure its fidelity to the 1945 Christmas Programme placed it on the PSC's left flank. Marked by a concern for the secularisation of political life and the reform of society, its positions were nevertheless often clearly distinct from those defended by the *Témoignage Chrétien* team. The latter appeared the most daring in challenging the slogans meant to comfort the Catholic community - particularly on the royal question and the school question - as well as by criticising the actually existing social and economic system. The editorial team of *La Revue Nouvelle* occupied an intermediary position on both issues. Many Catholics involved in the *Esprit* groups shared *Témoignage Chrétien's* positions, if indeed not defending even more daring ones.

2. From Progressivism to Modernity

When approached in that fashion, the question of the progressiveness of these milieus, classically situated to the left of Belgian Catholicism, seems to lack perspective. It seems that the question of progressiveness within the contemporary Catholic world cannot be examined without reference to the works that have contributed to the revelation of the intransigent origins of contemporary Catholicism, to which currents as diverse as Christian Democracy and antimodernist integralism were indebted.[32]

This intransigent Catholicism first defined itself, in the 19th century, by a complete rejection of liberalism, its antecedents, the Reformation and its offshoots, marxism and socialism. The latter two were in effect regarded as merely having pushed the capital errors of liberalism to extremes. Against this array of ideologies, intransigent Catholics proclaimed their "no", more concretely: their intransigence.

This rejection was based on the firm belief that Christianity contained the fundamental truth, the sole possible key to man's and society's happiness. This integralism was justified in two ways. First, a parallel was established between the emergence of the social question and the progressive

---

32. The essential works are those of Jean-Marie Mayeur and Émile Poulat. See Mayeur, "Catholicisme intransigeant"; Poulat, "Pour une nouvelle compréhension de la démocratie chrétienne"; Poulat, *Catholicisme, démocratie et socialisme*; Poulat, *Église contre bourgeoisie*. On these works and the Italian historiography on which they draw, see Jadoulle, *Chrétiens modernes?*, V, 709-721.

retreat of Christianity in the 18th and 19th centuries. The intransigent Catholics also nursed a very idealised vision of the Middle Ages, which were perceived as having been a time of social harmony and especially of Christian unanimity. These two observations gave rise to the conviction that Christianity held the key to a resolution of the social problem.

Intransigent Catholicism thus motivated the adoption of a whole series of reform-oriented positions, particularly in the leadership bodies of Christian Democracy. The defence of workers' rights necessitated a Christian overhaul of society, and the involvement of intransigent Catholics in the resolution of the social question therefore assumed a highly tactical value for the Church. The rule of Leo XIII, beginning in 1878, would lead the Church progressively to adopt this new and very dynamic posture.[33] The politics of the *Ralliement* and the new political theology of Leo XIII[34], the restoration of Thomism as the official Christian philosophy[35] and the support for attempts to improve the position of the working class were all part of the project marked with the seal of intransigentism. Noting the irreversibility of the political systems brought about by the revolutions at the end of the 18th and in the course of the 19th centuries, Leo XIII "shifted (...) the efforts of the papacy in order to find the means to influence society, politics and social issues".[36] It was also the dynamics of intransigentism which seems to have led Leo XIII to sanction the second generation of Christian Democrats, that of Romolo Murri and of Father Lemire, in his encyclical *Graves de Communi* (1901).[37] This papal intervention, which intended to remove any liberal connotations from Christian Democracy, confirmed the antiliberalism inherent in intransigentism which inspired the Vatican's politics. The history of intransigent Catholicism, as it has been uncovered by E. Poulat, in the end experienced one last metamorphosis in the integralist response. Called into existence by the research of so-called modernist theologians, integralists targeted the second generation Christian

33. See in particular Aubert, "Léon XIII", 205-206; Giovanni, "Sull'integralismo cattolico", 167, Poulat, *Catholicisme, démocratie et socialisme*, 65-66.
34. Initiated by the encyclical *Au milieu des sollicitudes* (1892), the politics of the *Ralliement* marked Leo XIII's acceptance - faced with the inability to change the course of history - of the Republican constitutional system which prevailed in France.
This went hand-in-hand with the restoration of Thomism (see the encyclical *Aeterni Patris* from 1879; see note 35 below) and notably of the political theology of Saint Thomas who, while distinguishing spiritual and temporal planes, accorded the former supremacy over the latter. See in particular Latreille, "La pensée catholique sur l'État"; Thibault, *Savoir et pouvoir*.
35. See in particular *Atti dell'VIII Congresso Tomistico Internazionale*; Aubert, "Aspects divers du néo-thomisme"; Aubert, "Le contexte historique et les motivations doctrinales de l'encyclique 'Aeterni Patris'".
36. Poulat, *Église contre bourgeoisie*, 120.
37. This second Christian Democratic generation became known particularly by its desire to engage itself on the level of parliamentary politics and, if necessary, to create new political organisations in the process. In 1896, in France, Father Lemire thus established an ephemeral *Parti Démocrate Chrétien*. In Italy, Father Murri founded in 1905 the National Democratic League. These initiatives divided Catholics politically and were therefore judged to be unacceptable by Leo XIII and then by Pius X. On this second generation and its principal protagonists, see Jadoulle, *La pensée de l'abbé Pottier*, 37-38. On Father Lemire, see Mayeur, *Un prêtre démocrate chrétien*. On Romolo Murri, see Traniello and Campanini, eds., *Dizionario storico del movimento cattolico in Italia*, II, 414-422 (M. Guasco).

Democrats, accused of betraying the intransigentism which the integralists proudly proclaimed to publicly defend.[38]

The concept of intransigentism sits uneasily with the idea of a liberal origin of Christian Democracy, which is one of the currents of Catholicism traditionally recognised as being among the more progressive. It also indicates the deep ties connecting currents as opposed to one another as Christian Democracy and integralism, or politics as different as those of Pius IX, Leo XIII or Pius X. If the progressive positions on secular matters held by the Christian Democrats cannot screen or mask the basic intransigentism which they share with those who accused them of social modernism, the historian can only note the limits of categories like progressivism and conservatism - and left and right versions thereof. The triangular diagram - liberalism, socialism, Christianity - proposed by E. Poulat and the revelation of the unanimous refusal, by all Catholic currents operating at the end of the 19th century and at the beginning of the 20th century, of the first two ideologies constitute, therefore, an effort to take into account in an improved fashion the complexity of that key period of the history of the Church. It profoundly subverted such categories as "Left-Right" or "progressivism-conservatism".

The question of progressivism in the Catholic world brings with it the question of the fundamental intransigentism of contemporary Catholicism. If progressivism initially had to measure itself against the positions and conceptions commonly accepted at the time, the question must be asked to what extent the progressive or Left Catholic intellectual milieus examined in the course of this study broke with the intransigentism which appears to be one of the motivating forces of contemporary Catholicism. It seems that the question of the progressivism of the milieus examined should be extended to include an investigation of the abandonment of intransigentism occurring within the orbit of precisely these milieus.

For a definitive response, the question of the end of intransigentism would require much more research. It most notably would require a precise characterisation of intransigentism. We have limited ourselves to one feature only, the most fundamental one in our view: that of antiliberalism. Contrary to the commonly accepted notion that sees the Church and faith as the ally and instrument of the middle classes against marxist revolution, the intransigent mentality is marked by a fundamental antiliberalism. The example of Christan Democracy is, again, revelatory: the accommodation to the liberal or middle-class system occurring from the first Christian Democratic generation onwards in no way signified any adherence to the fundamental principles of economic, political or philosophical liberalism. The openness or progressive attitude vis-à-vis many of the questions involving the organisation of society went together with a certain conception of faith and a certain method of involvement in society, making no concessions to new ideas and particularly to liberal philosophy.

It is nevertheless important to draw a precise picture of this antiliberalism. What did Catholics – and which Catholics? - object to in liberalism? We have attempted to provide an answer, partially in response to this question,

---

38. On the intransigent origins of Catholic integralism, see Poulat, "Intégrisme et catholicisme intégral"; Poulat, "L'intégrisme", 32-36.

by examining a vast corpus of papal documents, from Pius VI to Pius XII, in order to discover the principal objections to liberalism.[39] Seen from Rome, antiliberalism was seen as a rejection of three of the essential postulates of political and philosophical liberalism, namely the idea of the social contract, the separation of Church and state and liberty of conscience. This three-fold rejection served as a basis of analysis in order to examine the attitude of the milieus studied here in relation to liberalism and therefore to judge the mechanism of their eventual separation from intransigentism.

Contrary to the church authorities, the progressivist Catholic milieus which we have examined were united by their recognition of the solid foundations of the liberal democratic system. Their hope of a clearer distinction between the secular and religious spheres led them to call for a form of separation between Church and state. The process of the secularisation and autonomisation of temporal realities was considered to be beneficial. The organisers of these different milieus concurred in their recognition of the non-confessional nature of the state and called for the institution of a system of religious freedom. However, the liberal claim that religion is a private affair was strongly rejected: the Christian in no way ceased to be a Christian outside of the space of his conscience.

The prominence of this fundamentally different conception in relation to antiliberalism, prevailing in Roman Catholic circles in the 1940s and 1950s at the very least, seems to indicate a positive response to the question of an abandonment of intransigentism. Far from effecting an unconditional - intransigent - rejection, the progressive Catholic milieus examined in this study in fact established a compromise with liberalism. It is obvious that a compromise was pursued. The liberal claim that religion was limited to the confined space of individual consciences was unacceptable to Christians concerned to live their faith in every aspect of life and was plainly rejected. Compromise could not lead to the abandonment of principled positions. However, many essential premises of political and philosophical liberalism, to which the Church continued to be opposed, at least until Pius XII, were directly admitted. The compromise which thus came about seems sufficiently profound to indicate a decisive break with the intransigent mentality.

The initial project to validate the label of progressive which was often attached to the French-speaking Belgian Catholic milieus examined in this study leads therefore to an interpretative hypothesis which identifies an initial effort by these groups, in the aftermath of the Second World War, to distinguish themselves from Catholicism's fundamental antiliberalism. The compromise which thereby came about with liberalism seems sufficiently significant, and antiliberalism seems sufficiently part of Catholic intransigentism, to mark a rupture with the foundations of contemporary Catholicism as they existed, up to and including at least the first decades of the 20th century.

Meanwhile, the question of an abandonment of intransigentism leads to one final question. If the compromise which came about with liberalism signified an abandonment of intransigentism, did it mark the entry of Catholics into modernity? The adaptation to the modern world of the Church and of

---

39. See Jadoulle, *Chrétiens modernes?*, V, 770-784.

the Christian method of existence stood at the centre of the progressive Catholic milieus' project. The recognition of the unavoidable novelty of the contemporary age was obvious: Christianity had become outdated. The question of modernity and of the adaptation to the modern world was also an important one in the intransigent mentality. Fundamentally reactive, intransigentism owed some of its success to the scale of the disaster it painted if modern man persisted in his negation of God. However, while the milieus which are the subject of this study chose to compromise in this respect in order to give faith a space in which it could blossom, the others would not budge from an intransigent rejection of the modern world.

The question of modernity, of its origins, the compromises it necessitated and the resistances called forth by it, lies at the centre of any history of contemporary Catholicism. However, we are still lacking studies offering a more differentiated portrayal of this modern world, as seen through the eyes of Catholics. Modernity likewise constitutes a category of analysis used by a number of theologians and sociologists, and less frequently by historians, to demonstrate the break effected by Enlightenment philosophy and subsequently by liberalism in Western societies. In fact, the portrayal of modernity by some theologians and sociologists of Christianity, and the view of liberalism as it has appeared in the texts of the Church authorities, converge in a surprising manner, to the extent that the question of the abandonment of the residual antiliberalism of Catholicism, in the context of the milieus examined here, leads to the question of the latter's orientation vis-à-vis modernity. To what extent did the compromise made with liberalism, considered here as the spearhead of modernity, cause progressive Catholics to enter into modernity?

The debates surrounding the idea of liberty of conscience have permitted us to identify what could be regarded as a locus of resistance to one of the basic requirements of modernity. If the confrontation with the modern ideal of the individual subject led to an acceptance of secularisation and the separation of Church and state, as well as to a position favouring freedom of religion, the stress on the autonomous nature of the sphere pertaining to matters of conscience is closely related to the upholding of the principle of the uniqueness of the True, which may appear as a faint echo of the integralism central to the underlying intransigentism of contemporary Catholicism. Anticipating the terms of the declaration *Dignitatis Humanae*[40], the recognition of liberty of conscience in fact is linked to the recognition of religious freedom. On the level of its innermost conscience,

---

40. In affirming that "human beings have a right to religious freedom", the declaration *Dignitatis Humanae* (1965) marked a fundamental change of attitude for the Church. Breaking with the litany of condemnations which had prevailed up until then, the Church now based the principle of religious freedom on the dignity of mankind. This religious freedom was defined by the exclusion of all constraints. The recognition of religious freedom was therefore situated *ab extra* and not *ab intra*: the Church's essential intention was to preserve the faith from any exterior constraint and to guarantee its unconstrained practice in civil society. *Ab intra*, humanity remained constrained by the Truth. Thus, if the declaration *Dignitatis Humanae* certainly manifested a recognition of religious freedom, it nevertheless did not imply a full and absolute recognition of liberty of conscience. See Jadoulle, *Chrétiens modernes?*, VI, 793-796.

however, humanity remains constrained by a truth which can only be conceived of as unique. If the different milieus which are the object of this study therefore afforded a genuine opening in the sphere of relationships between Church and state, the relationship between humanity and Truth remains unaltered. Assent to religious liberty in the domain of civil society does not go hand in hand with the rejection of the existence of an integral truth, a rejection to which the open recognition of liberty of conscience could have led.

Progressive on a number of secular and religious questions, the four Catholic intellectual milieus which we have attempted to understand therefore carried out a major compromise with political and philosophical liberalism. They proceeded in this way toward a significant rupture with the constituent antiliberalism of Catholic intransigentism. Their project of adapting faith and Church to the modern world nevertheless was linked to a particular understanding of the question of liberty of conscience. The persistence of the conception of man as a naturally religious being and of religious truth as fundamentally unchanging and unique can be regarded as constituting the outlines of an integralist mentality persisting despite the rupture with intransigentism.

The study of Left Catholicism therefore requires a twofold examination. The historian must first remember that he cannot demand of "a dedicated Catholic of the last century [to reason] like a man who already shared our preoccupations".[41] *Progressisme* or *gauchisme* can only be measured against what was thinkable and conceivable in the Catholic world towards the end of the 1940s and during the 1950s. Underscoring the fundamental intransigentism of contemporary Catholicism should nevertheless lead the historian to reformulate the question of progressivism as that of the abandonment of intransigentism which may have occurred by means of and within Left Catholic milieus. If carried out by way of studying the precise character of the compromise with liberalism achieved by these milieus, this approach leads one to place Left Catholicism in the context of liberal modernity, with which intransigent Catholicism had refused to make its peace.

---

41. Poulat, *Église contre bourgeoisie*, 243.

THE *TÉMOIGNAGE* OF THE WORKER PRIESTS. CONTEXTUAL LAYERS OF THE PIONEER EPOCH (1941- 1955)

Oscar Cole-Arnal

With the arrival of the early 1950s the worker priest witness had caught the public eye. By that time approximately one hundred Catholic priests in France and Belgium had entered the full-time work force by mandate of their bishops or their religious orders. What began as a case-by-case trickle in the early 1940s had grown into a small movement which emerged full force into public consciousness as a *cause célèbre* by 1953 and 1954. Mostly an unknown *présence*, save in the proletarian ghettos and within Catholic circles, the experience erupted into the wider public with sensationalist newspaper articles (1949). From that time, and especially in the early 1950s, popular and analytical articles appeared with growing frequency. As well, the noted author Gilbert Cesbron wrote a best-selling novel, *Les Saints vont en enfer* (1952), which paid tribute to the worker priests. His was only the most well-known among a number of novels and plays on the subject. Indeed, this publicity proved to be the catalyst which triggered the hierarchy's defensive reaction against the experiment that they had launched piece-by-piece in the early 1940s.

Interest in the worker priest experience could not be contained in spite of the hierarchy's attempt to circumscribe the movement. Sympathetic bishops, Left Catholic allies, and worker priests who obeyed their official church in the condemnation of 1954 found ways to work around the limitations expected by the Vatican. This state of limbo persisted until the Second Vatican Council, under Paul VI, legitimised this form of ministry as *prêtres au travail*. In spite of the new name given to labouring priests, the old popular jargon "worker priests" (or *"p-o"*, *prêtres-ouvriers* in French-speaking areas) remains the name of choice over the more official title. The movement has spread since the mid-1960s, and the 1980s and 1990s have witnessed the emergence of numerous works, both personal and scholarly, related to the subject. Fascination with the worker priests remains a reality within academia and the wider public.[1]

---

1. Most of the data for this chapter I have retrieved from my earlier book *Priests in Working-Class Blue*, as well as from my collected research files gathered in the preparation of this earlier work. At the same time more recent scholarly works have emerged on the subject. For examples, see de Berranger, *Alfred Ancel*; Leprieur, *Quand Rome condamne*; Moine, *René Boudot*; Benoît et al., *Le Ciel était Rouge*; Pierrard, *L'Église et les ouvriers en France*, 188-208 and 271-280; Huret and Combe, *Fidèle insoumission*; Jacquet and Ancel, *Un militant ouvrier dialogue avec un évêque*, and Olhagaray, *Ce mur il faut l'abattre*. Nonetheless, the standard reference in the field remains Poulat's, *Naissance des prêtres ouvriers* and his more recent update *Les prêtres-ouvriers*.

1. The Context of Worker Priest Birth

Although priests began to undertake full-time manual labour only in the early 1940s, their experience and model of ministry grew out of an extended history of Catholic concern with the ever-growing industrial proletariat. Officially, this evolving commitment emerged with Pope Leo XIII's pioneer encyclical *Rerum Novarum* (1891) and came to be known as the "social doctrine of the Church" or more colloquially social Catholicism. Belgium and especially France proved to be the laboratory for social Catholic experiments, from the social paternalistic work of Count Albert de Mun and the Christian Democratic radicalism of Marc Sangnier's *Sillon* before the Great War to the interwar grass-roots efforts of specialised Catholic Action. In fact, the latter 1920s and 1930s generated a vast network of Catholic social justice groups, many of them concentrating on specific missionary experiments to the industrial work force.[2]

Much of the old Church-state battles had softened with the re-establishment of a Vatican embassy and with the condemnation of the right wing *Action Française* (December 1926), thus allowing Catholic progressives to concentrate on working class issues. During the 1930s the two major Catholic forces dedicated to this mission were the confessional trade unions and the specialised Catholic Action movement known as the *Jeunesse Ouvrière Chrétienne* (JOC). This latter group, founded by the Belgian priest Joseph Cardijn with the patronage of Pius XI, spread quickly to France where it became the most influential youth movement that emerged from the working class itself. In fact, the JOC dedicated itself to a model of working from within, "like ministering to like". Young Catholic labourers bore a living and present witness to their comrades both in the neighbourhoods and at the factory. This model of social Catholicism provided both direct and indirect grist for the mill that would turn out the worker priests in the 1940s.[3]

More immediately the worker priests came to birth out of crisis and a series of loosely related activities. At a macro level the experiment emerged when French Catholicism reeled under the emergency conditions of war and Occupation (1940-1944). Although virtually all French Catholics of note welcomed Marshal Pétain's leadership in the collaborationist Vichy regime at the outset (1940-1941), the Church's clerical leaders and its dominant right wing expressions, such as the daily *La Croix* and the *Fédération*

---

2. I use the term "Christian Democratic radicalism" for Marc Sangnier's pre-World War I *Sillon* because of its grass-roots character, its openness to the most leftist sectors of French politics and trade unionism, as well as its position on the far Left of the social Catholicism of its time. Even in the interwar period, Sangnier's *Jeune République* positioned itself on the far Left of French Christian Democracy, as exemplified by its alliance with the Popular Front coalition of the 1930s. For details, see Arnal, *Ambivalent Alliance*, 9, 107-108, 147, 156-157 and 159.
3. For descriptions of this Catholic interwar pluralism, consult Arnal, *Ambivalent Alliance*; Paul, *The Second Ralliement*; Hellman, *Emmanuel Mounier*; Rémond, *Les Catholiques, le communisme et les crises*; Murphy, *Communists and Catholics in France*; Christophe, *1936, les catholiques et le front populaire,* and Laudouze, *Dominicains français et Action Française*. For specific details on the JOC, see *La Jeunesse Ouvrière Chrétienne: Wallonie Bruxelles, 1912-1957*, I-II; Pierrard, et al., *La J.O.C.*, and Cole-Arnal, "Shaping Young Proletarians into Militant Christians".

Nationale Catholique of Phillipe Henriot, continued to back Vichy and even the Nazi occupation as preferable to communism or even the resistance of Charles De Gaulle. In fact, the interwar Catholic Left had buckled under a right wing Catholic resurgence in France in the latter 1930s. At the same time the crises of the early 1940s resurrected the disparate Catholic Leftists who rose in the fires of the Resistance movement. De Gaulle himself was a practicing Catholic, and after the martyrdom of Jean Moulin, the interwar Christian Democrat Georges Bidault assumed the leadership of the Gaullist resistance umbrella, the *Conseil National de la Résistance*. Other Christian Democrats, the Catholic unions, the clandestine review *Témoignage Chrétien*, and numerous clergy, especially at the grass-roots, joined the French communists to liberate *la Patrie*. This division between collaborationist Catholic rightists and *résistants* Catholic Leftists, followed by the Allied victory, gave to French Catholic progressives the power and influence to recreate both France and their church after their own progressive vision.[4]

In this multiple crisis of occupation, collaboration, resistance, liberation and internal power shift, social Catholics concentrating on working class missions found the space to reshape older models and create new ones in the industrial worlds of France and Belgium. The forced labour requisition imposed on Vichy by Germany, the *Service du Travail Obligatoire* (STO), operational by February 1943, served as a turning point for the JOC which had welcomed the Pétain regime with scarcely concealed joy. However, the STO forced many *Jocistes* into German labour camps. Some hid, others joined the Resistance and still others became radicalised by the harsh reality of their forced labour status. Even a few prelates, such as cardinals Achille Liénart and Emmanuel Suhard, sought to undermine this act of aggression in spite of their support of the Vichy government.[5]

Within the crisis of this broader context emerged some key personalities, programs and events which gave birth directly, at a micro level, to the initial worker priest experiments. At the centre of these specific activities was the reigning cardinal archbishop of Paris Emmanuel Suhard, who had a direct hand in virtually every creative effort of the French church to cross the wall between the faithful and the industrial proletariat. His early career coincided with the Church-state troubles at the turn of the century, events which intensified his royalism and drew his sympathies toward the *Action Française*. However, his devotion to Leo XIII pressed him in the direction of social Catholicism and helped him break with the monarchist cause in the mid-1920s. While archbishop in the ancient see at Reims (1931-1940) he won his cardinal's hat and received his domestic sense of mission through patronisation of the JOC. Upon the death of Jean Verdier, Suhard received the papal call to serve as archbishop of Paris, France's prime see (May 1940).

---

4. For overviews of French Catholic divisions during the war years, consult Halls, *Politics, Society and Christianity in Vichy France*; Christophe, *1939-1940: les catholiques devant la guerre*; Allen, "Resistance and the Catholic Church in France"; Duquesne, *Les Catholiques français sous l'occupation*; Cole-Arnal, "Roman Catholic Church in France".
   Two excellent more specialised works are Hellman, *The Knight-Monks of Vichy France*, and Bédarida, *Les Armes de l'Esprit*.
5. For specific material on the STO and Catholic response to it, see the appropriate sections in Halls, *Politics, Society and Christianity*, and Duquesne, *Catholiques français sous l'occupation*.

Immediately thereafter the Germans arrived in Paris beginning a four-year occupation. Suhard supported Maréchal Pétain's Vichy regime throughout its brief existence, and it remains one of history's ironies that this conservative collaborationist cardinal ended his career as the most important patron of the French Catholic "Pentecost" which would lead Catholicism to the chambers of Vatican II.[6]

During the dark days of the Occupation Cardinal Suhard set in motion a number of initiatives which led directly to the birth of the worker priest experience. Convinced that France had abandoned its religious heritage for various forms of secularism, the cardinal directed his vocation almost exclusively to creative domestic missionary endeavours. Shortly after the German occupation of the capital, Suhard convinced the French hierarchy to set up a seminary at Lisieux dedicated to training priests exclusively for missionary work in those sections of France, both rural and urban, that Catholic sociologists had demonstrated as virtually devoid of religious practice. Its doors opened in the Fall of 1942, and over the next decade it would train no less than 25% of the nation's worker priests. In addition, its pedagogical spirit, its retreat conferences and its controversial apprenticeships (*stages*) in manual labour, all begun during the war years, served in a broader way to authenticate the worker priests' mission.[7]

More directly related to the worker priest mission was the sociological study by two *Jociste* chaplains Henri Godin and Yvan Daniel, *La France pays de mission?*, commissioned by Suhard and appearing in September 1943. Through the use of stark statistics and crisp analysis the two priests demonstrated that the Parisian working class resided outside the influence and impact of the Church and that the recovery of the proletariat to faith demanded direct and collective mission work via a total plunge into the labouring milieu. No worker priest ministry was called for, but the small community, the *Mission de Paris*, which emerged from this work and Suhard's direction (December 1943- January 1944), came to serve as the heart and brains of the worker priest experience.[8] The STO (1943-1945)

---

6. For details on the life and impact of Suhard, consult the definitive *Le cardinal Suhard* by Vinatier. In English, Arnal's *Priests in Working-Class Blue* contains some useful material on the role of Suhard in the creation and support of these missions. See also the relevant material in Poulat's massive works cited in footnote 1. Interestingly enough, Poulat himself was a worker priest prior to his distinguished career as one of his nation's foremost academics.

7. A description of the pioneer phase of the *Mission de France* seminary can be found in Arnal, "Beyond the Walls of Christendom". For more detail consult Six, *Cheminements de la Mission de France*, 11-85; Faupin, *La Mission de France*, and the work of the seminary's first superior Louis Augros, *De l'église d'hier à l'Église de demain*. Jean Vinatier describes and analyses the role of Cardinal Achille Liénart in the troubled period of the seminary in *Le cardinal Liénart et la Mission de France*. Interviews of leading figures during the *Mission de France*'s early epoch include: Louis Augros, St. Symphorien-de-Lay (4 July 1979); Jean Vinatier, *Mission de France* priest and writer, Fontenay-sous-Bois (7 June 1980); and Daniel Perrot, *Mission de France* seminary professor (10 May 1979).

8. Godin and Daniel, *La France pays de mission?* See also the relevant sections in Poulat, *Naissance* and Arnal, *Priests*. The author learned interesting details of this effort through interviews with Yvan Daniel, Paris (14 May 1979), and Father Jacques Hollande, director of the *Mission de Paris*, Paris (28 May 1979). Other sociological studies by Catholics on religious practice in the same epoch include LeBras, *Introduction à*

provided the occasion for priests to taste the direct reality of grueling manual labour. In order to insure the spiritual welfare of young men force-requisitioned into German factories, Cardinal Suhard called upon Father Jean Rodhain to send clandestine chaplains into these same factories to work side by side with those forced into labour at German munitions plants (March 1943). Some died from the experience, such as the Jesuit Victor Dillard, but not before writing his memoirs of factory life. Others returned fired with the spirit of a new form of incarnate priesthood. Their factory experience inspired writings and testimonies which gave birth directly to worker priest initiatives. Most famous of these memoires was Henri Perrin's *Journal d'un prêtre-ouvrier en Allemagne*.[9]

Meanwhile, in southern France independent of Cardinal Suhard emerged a worker priest experiment created by some avant-garde Dominicans grouped into a team called *Économie et Humanisme*. Based in Marseille this équipe issued from the inspiration of Father Louis-Joseph Lebret, a Dominican who had been practicing a form of participatory sociology since 1929. In that year he helped organise among Breton fishers the specialised Catholic Action movement called the *Jeunesse Maritime Chrétienne*. He dreamed of creating a team of Catholic sociologists prepared to employ their craft in mission and social transformation in the Marseille area. Thus was born *Économie et Humanisme* in 1941, and out of this context the Dominican Father Jacques Loew was mandated both to research a hands-on study of the workers of the city's port, published as *Les Dockers de Marseille*, and to labour as a docker himself. Hence in 1941 Loew became the first full-time worker priest.[10]

As a result of the direct input of Cardinal Suhard and the various initiatives he supported, the worker priests of France became a reality even before Paris was liberated in August 1944. At the same time these clerics were individual human beings, who entered the world of manual labour from very personal contexts of their own. In age, they ranged from Auguste Rosi (58 years old in 1950) to a few, such as Bernard Cagne and Albert Guichard, who were 26 years old in 1950. A handful were born in the early 1900s, but individuals from the two largest groups saw the light of day during the Great War or the early 1920s. Hence most entered the work force

---

l'histoire de la pratique religieuse en France, and Boulard, *Problèmes missionaires de la France rurale*. In contradistinction to the *Mission de France*, the *Mission de Paris* was not a seminary, nor was it viewed as a training institution for mission priests in general. Instead it contained a team of priests which concentrated on relevant, mobile and creative ministries to the industrial proletariat in the Parisian area.

9. Details can be found in the appropriate sections of Poulat, *Naissance* and Arnal, *Priests*. Three examples of this literature are: Perrin, *Journal*; Victor Dillard, *Suprême Témoignage*; and Hadrien Bousquet, *Hors des barbelés*. Father Rodhain himself described this experience to an interviewer in *Une charité inventive*.

10. Louisette Blanquart, former member of *Économie et Humanisme*, interview (22 June 1979); "Manifeste d'Économie et Humanisme", *Économie et Humanisme* (février-mars, 1952), 3- 52; Lebret, *Les Professions maritimes à la recherche du bien commun*. The definitive study of Father Lebret's career is Pelletier's, *Économie et Humanisme*. My data for Jacques Loew's role in the early 1940s include chiefly an interview with him, Fribourg, Switzerland (14 May 1980); and his three works: *Les Dockers de Marseille*; *Journal d'une mission ouvrièr*; and Pamela Carswell's translation of *En mission prolétarienne* called *Mission to the Poorest*.

from their mid-20s to their mid-30s. Of the 38 worker priests I interviewed from the pioneer group, 13 came from religiously-divided families (practicing Catholic and lapsed Catholic, often anticlerical), and 2 came from totally non-religious families. The remaining 23 grew up in families where both parents practiced their faiths regularly. In several of these, the parents were intense traditionalists, even royalist. Finally, in terms of their religious training, about 25 of the roughly one hundred original worker priests came from various monastic orders, the Dominicans alone numbering 12 with the remaining religious scattered among the Jesuits, Capuchins, *Fils de la Charité* and the Prado community. The other 75 served as secular priests within the French Catholic diocesan system. As well, about 25% received training at the *Mission de France* seminary either before or after ordination.[11]

2. The Belgian Worker Priest Experience

The entry of Belgian priests into industrial toil proved more focused than the here-and-there French experience, which only coalesced with time. Although this ministry came to fruition in lock step with the *Mission de Paris*, it had fueled the dreams of Belgian priest Charles Boland since the early 1920s. A contemporary of Joseph Cardijn, Boland shared the prophetic vision of avant-garde church missions to the proletariat with the JOC founder. For over twenty years he met resistance from the dominating milieu of classical Catholicism and was denied a worker priesthood by the bishop of Liège on several occasions. Nevertheless he persisted by spending his vacation periods in the midst of working class life. By the early 1930s Father Boland began to articulate to his hierarchy a theology of the worker priesthood which French worker priests would embrace in the 1940s. He spoke of the need for missionaries to the industrial toilers "living their life" and added his conviction that priests for the workers must be workers themselves. Boland insisted that priests at the factory embodied both the scandal of the cross and the bodily incarnation of Christ, especially in those hidden years when Jesus toiled as a carpenter. Throughout the 1930s Father Boland sustained his courage and vision through a spirituality focused on Mary, "the virgin of the poor". Continuous setbacks did not deter him from the conviction that effective witness to workers compelled priests to "return to the

---

11. Poulat, *Naissance*, 444-465; Leprieur, *Quand Rome*, 321; "Équipe des Prêtres de la Mission de Paris" (1951) 12 pp., in the *Mission de Paris* Papers (1951), hereafter referred to as MDP. To my knowledge the *Mission de Paris* Papers are not in any public archives. Originally they were in the possession of Father Jacques Hollande, who in turn gave them to Father Joseph Debès of St. Denis, a co-author with Émile Poulat on the subject of specialised working class Catholic Action. Since my use of these almost twenty years ago I do not know exactly the whereabouts of the papers. However, I do retain in my possession photocopies of this entire material: "Prêtres-Ouvriers"(List of location & religious communities), 12 pp., in MDP (1953); similar hand-written list (untitled), 9 pp. (lists 99 worker priests), in MDP (1954). For data on births, religious practice of families, I tallied my own interviews with worker priests into the process, in particular: Bernard Cagne, Paris (21 June 1979); Albert Guichard, Paris (21 June 1983); Bernard Lacroix, Fils de la Charité, Grenoble (15 June 1983); R.P. Césaire Dillaye, Capuchin, Paris (14 May 1979); and Jean Tarby, Chartres (13 June 1983).

workplace... to render Christ to the workers". By the early 1940s his persistence paid off, and with the permission of his bishop, he entered a factory in 1942 there to cut tubes for a living. Thus, at the very moment when the Dominicans had sent Father Jacques Loew to the Marseille docks, Charles Boland had emerged in Belgium as its first worker priest and father figure to those who followed in his wake.[12]

Joining with Father Damien Reumont, a long-term Capuchin friend who had spent time in a German labour camp, and a militant *Jociste*, Hector Cools, Boland created a community called the *Fraternité des Ouvriers de la Vièrge des Pauvres* (OVP) in Liège. By 1946 the city's bishop Mgr. Kerkhofs had authorised this missionary endeavour, and two other priests had joined as well, one a Capuchin, the other a Josephite. Soon thereafter ill health forced Father Boland to leave his plant. However, Boland continued to serve his OVP through the dark nights of the French experience and the final restitution of the worker priest mode of sacerdoce by the Second Vatican Council.[13]

The OVP and its leadership stand out as the most prominent contribution that the Belgians made to the French-speaking worker priest movement. Father Boland had paved the way virtually by himself in the interwar years. His apprenticeship laid the groundwork both theologically and with the Church hierarchy. Although innovation and expansion would pass to the French by the mid-1940s, Fathers Boland and Reumont continued to provide the entire movement with a credible and sophisticated theology backed by their factory experiences. Boland contributed to his worker priest brothers a developed theology of Christ's presence among the workers as a worker, as well as a solidly based spirituality of work itself. As for Reumont, he used his talents to sustain communication with the *Mission de Paris* and proved to be a skilled apologist for the worker priests when they sustained serious and protracted opposition.[14]

Indeed, Boland and the OVP kept abreast of the rise of the French worker priests and maintained occasional contact throughout the years. As well, younger Belgian priests and seminarians responded enthusiastically to Godin's *La France, pays de Mission?* and several became students at the *Mission de France* seminary, including Liège worker priests Louis Flagothier and Albert Courtoy. At least one Flemish priest in Belgium picked up on the enthusiasm of his French-speaking comrades. Thus, from the moment of the first factory entries (early 1940s) until the condemnation of the French

---

12   Poulat, *Naissance*, 188-196; Boland, *Dure Percée*, 27-28, 30-34, 44, 48-52, 61 and 63.
13. Poulat, *Naissance*, 470-474 and 477; Boland, *Dure Percée*, 60-75; "Fraternité des O.V.P.", (15 June 1947) 4- 6 and 18, and Père Damien Reumont, "Fraternité des Ouvriers de la Vièrge des Pauvres", (1947) 2- 3, both in MDP (1947).
14. Boland, *Dure Percée*; Boland, "Prêtres en milieu du travail", 438-452 and "Position actuelle du Prêtre en milieu du travail", 552-566, both in *Évangéliser*, mars & mai 1947 respectively, found in MDP (1947); Boland, "Travail d'usine et vie spirituelle", 4pp., in MDP (1953); Damien Reumont, *Fraternité des Ouvriers de la Vièrge des Pauvres*, 4pp., in MDP (1947); and Père Damien, "Enquêtes dans les Centres de Mission Ouvrière en France", 13 juin 1947, 1-19, in MDP (1947).

movement by the hierarchy in 1954, Belgian and French worker priests sustained a solidarity of sporadic and pragmatic contact.[15]

3. The Context of "Worker Priest" Naturalisation

The creation of the *Mission de Paris* and the entry into the workforce of a number of Belgian and French priests with the permission of their bishops or monastic orders emerged out of the history and crises sketched above, but this earlier context describes only the soil out of which the experience grew. The phenomenon of their actual *témoignage* blossomed from the proletarian world they entered. Forty worker priests alone toiled in Paris and its industrial suburbs. Most of the remainder were scattered throughout France in major industrial centers, eleven in the Lyon area, five each in Marseille, Limoges and Toulouse, eight from Belgium's industrial centers, two from Nice, two from Montceau-les-Mines, three from Bordeaux, one from Tours, three from the Lorraine region, three from the Le Havre area, nine from the textile basins of the Nord (Lille) and Jean Volot who toiled on the high seas. Add the ten who worked in public works construction (mostly vast hydro-electric dams), and we reach a total of 108.[16] To be sure, there was some advanced experience of that for those priests and seminarians who had either participated as clandestine chaplains in Germany or lived a *stage* through the *Mission de France* seminary. Father Hadrien Bousquet, a Franciscan with some previous working experience, discovered, as a labouring chaplain, the need for the Church to identify with the working class and its aspirations, and the martyred Jesuit Victor Dillard claimed that his toil in a German factory moved him to criticise the Church's attachment "to a bourgeois civilisation" and to call for priests who "would live as completely as possible the working class life".[17]

As well, many of the worker priests grew up in poverty within working class or peasant families, families which often found parents divided in their religious values. By way of example, André Depierre, a *Mission de Paris*

---

15. Poulat, *Naissance*, 18, 401, 405 and 474; Boland, *Dure Percée*, 60-64; Louis Flagothier and Albert Courtoy, interviews granted to the author at Liège (8 June 1983); Liège worker priests, "Les Signes de l"Évangile dans le monde ouvrier" n.d., 10pp., in Louis Flagothier personal papers; "un Curé houilleur", a newspaper piece on a Flemish worker priest miner who was a member of the O.V.P., in MDP (1946); A. Wankenne, s.j., "Prêtres-ouvriers", (Jan., 1953), in a Belgian review, 411-421, in MDP (1953); and Gabriel Ringlet, "Les prêtres-ouvriers liégeois-qui sont-ils? Que disent-ils?", *La Wallonie*, (30 mars 1983) 1, 10. At the time of the worker priest shutdown there were eight French-speaking worker priests in Belgium (Boland, *Dure Percée*, 64).
16. Leprieur, *Quand Rome*, 321. The discrepancy between 99/100 worker priests and this total is explained by the fact that some worker priests worked in more than one place during these years, i.e. Henri Perrin (Paris and the Isère). Interview with Joseph Robert, friend and co-worker of Perrin, Paris (27 June 1979); interview with Jean Volot, sailor at the *Mission de la Mer*, an international apostolate linked directly to Rome (19 May 1980). See also Perrin, *Priest and Worker*, 99- 130 and 171-225; Boland, *Dure Percée*, 64.
17. On the clandestine priests, consult Poulat, *Naissance*, 196-201; Bousquet, *Hors des barbelés*, 20, 27, 48, 60, 63-64, 70, 73-75, 80-81 and 111-116; and Dillard, *Suprême Témoignage*, 5-6, 17, 32, 34, 36-39, 41-42 and 46.

worker priest, recalled that his impoverished parents had no voice in their parish, driving him toward giving "responsibility to the poor within the church". Father Jo Gouttebarge, a St. Etienne metallurgist, remembered the grinding poverty of his childhood and the hardships of his widowed mother trying to raise her three children. He called himself "a companion of this misery", a misery he took into his priestly vocation in the slums and factories of St. Etienne. The Lille Dominican worker priest Joseph Robert recalled his working class family and the suffering of that life. That's why, he told the author, "I grew up with a working class consciousness".[18]

Other worker priests, usually from the same class background, found that the necessity of working before they entered the priesthood provided its own vital training ground for a worker priest life. In some instances, worker priests from privileged backgrounds found that such a position did not shield them from the pain lived daily by the proletariat. The Dominican Father Jacques Screppel told the author of his childhood days when his mother walked him through labouring class ghettos to his private school: "I was struck by the contrast... between the very beautiful house of my parents... and the very miserable houses [of the workers].... I decided at that moment that the fortune of my parents came from their [labourers'] work and that I had a debt to these workers who provided my parents' fortune".[19]

Nonetheless, this remembrance of the hard life of work and poverty, did not protect the worker priest movement itself from the profound *choc* to these roughly one hundred priests when plunged fully into working class life. In the brief period of this pioneering venture (roughly from the mid-1940s to 1954), the working priests found their lives and values changed so radically that they would become alien to the very Church which had sent them there in the first place. This new reality of ghetto and factory changed priests to worker priests in a manner that transcended ideology, giving these pioneers a radically new way to understand their Christian faith and life. An examination of three facets of this transformation proves instructive: entry, daily existence and militancy. These three points of focus delineate roughly the evolution of their brief journey within working class life: 1) Their initial adaptation, entry and daily existence (1942-1948) and 2) their exposure to public scrutiny through their increasing working class militancy (1948-1954), terminating with the hierarchical condemnation of the French movement (1953-1954). The shutdown of its Belgian counterpart followed soon thereafter (1955).

---

18. Personal interviews granted to the author: André Depierre, Montreuil (20 June 1979); Joseph Sanguedolce, *Joseph Gouttebarge* in Robert Pacalet private papers, 3 and 17; and Père Robert, "Rapport sur mon engagement", Paris (22 Jan. 1949), in MDP (1949).
19. Charles Pautet, "Le Père Charles...", (7 Aug. 1947) 1; Jean-Marie Petit, report, Paris 20th arrondissement(Oct. 1949) 1; and Roger Deliat, report Boulogne-Billancourt (1949) 1, all in MDP (1949). Deliat, *Vingt Ans chez Renault*, 15 and 17. Interviews: Jacques Screppel, Hellemes (9 June 1983); Henri Barreau, Gagny (16 May 1979); Bernard Cagne, Paris (21 June 1979); and Jean Volot.

3.1. Entry

For the most part these priests entered the working world *incognito*, yet invariably their identities were discovered. At that point their baptism of fire began, especially on the factory floor. Their life as workers commenced in the often painful reality of looking for a job in order to feed themselves. To understand more easily the reality of toil at the Marseilles docks, the Dominican order sent Jacques Loew to experience life there. Quickly he learned that men had to look for docking jobs by standing in line every morning to get hired. Just as rapidly he discovered that he would be fired if he could not keep up the work cadence determined by the bosses. Jesuit Henri Perrin faced despair when his initial optimism fell with his inability to find work in the south of Paris.[20]

However, in the postwar prosperity finding a job did not prove difficult for long. The *choc* of entry came chiefly at the shop floor in the midst of their toil. By far, most of the worker priests sought to conceal their priestly identity in order to become fully a worker among other workers and to avoid the deeply rooted anticlericalism found among the labouring classes. At the same time, they decided to be open about their priesthood when the occasion demanded it. In such incidents, most of the worker priests experienced their conscious entry into the proletariat. Two such examples illustrate the point: In his memoirs, Roger Deliat describes the conversation that led to his discovery. A work comrade asked him if he was married, to which Deliat replied negatively. "Why not, divorced?" said his persistent comrade. "Ah, you don't make love to women?" "That's right," replied Deliat. Finally, after having ascertained that Deliat was neither impotent nor turned off by women, the worker blurted out, "My word, surely you're not a priest?" "Yes, I am", responded Deliat. Stunned, his frustrated companion said, "You're pulling my leg, old buddy; I don't believe it. I've never seen a priest at the factory. Maybe you're defrocked?" "No", Deliat replied tersely. The conversation closed with these words of confusion from his comrade: "Tell me! I have the impression that you're fuckin' me over. You're pokin' fun at me, you know?" No wonder it took several days before the other toilers believed Deliat.[21]

Jacques Loew's work entry proved more typical, a blend of incredulity, hostility and suspicion giving way to trust and solidarity. During one of his lunch breaks, he heard some of his work comrades describe priests as "human pigs who exploit others". To an anarchist beside him called Mustache, who spoke of a particular priest as "a fat pig", he posed a question. "Hey Mustache, do you know the priest at Cabucelle?" After Mustache's negative reply, Loew stated, "Well, I'm that Cabucelle priest". That caught everybody's attention, and immediately the worker lunch group gathered around Loew and pumped him with questions. The worker priest explained that this entry to daily toil was prompted by the desire to "share the suffering of poor people just like Christ has done".[22]

---

20. Interview with Jacques Loew, Fribourg, Switzerland (14 May 1980); Loew, *Mission to the Poorest*, 21-22 and 28; Perrin, *Itinéraire d'Henri Perrin*, 157 and 159.
21. Deliat, *Vingt ans chez Renault*, 22.
22. Marseille report to Mgr. Delay (1948), 21- 23, in MDP (1949).

Again and again these priests told of a clandestine entry followed by the discovery that they were priests. Usually, the workers felt that the priests spied for the bosses or wanted to convince them to become active Catholics, but such suspicion lasted only briefly. Michel Bordet, worker priest at Longwy in the Lorraine area of France, recalled the words of one assembly line comrade: "You preach well at Mass; at the church you make good sermons. But the day when you came into the factory with us, that moment was the natural moment for the right to speak. Before you didn't have the right to speak". These experiences of Deliat, Loew and Bordet reflected the entries into the work place of virtually every worker priest. Their naturalisation into the proletariat had begun.[23] In a very short time the worker priests won the support and admiration of their factory comrades. They had passed their baptism of fire, but their vocation to be one with their comrades required accepting and living the day-to-day experience of factory toil and the grimness of the proletarian ghettos.

3.2. Daily Existence

Again and again the worker priests spoke of the dehumanising conditions discovered in the rhythms of relentless toil and human privation. Although their particular jobs ranged across the entire spectrum of blue collar toil, they expressed unanimity in their conviction that this work was unjust, brutal and alienating. Such experience was echoed again and again by virtually every worker priest.[24]

Father Jean Wernier reported how shift work became for him a rediscovery of the "great pain of a suffering humanity and of Christ's body torn apart by sin". In the Lorraine "Bobby" Pfaff and Michel Bordet remembered the awful heat generated by the molten steel of their factory, and André Piet of Marseille spoke of the physical numbing produced by endless standing at the assembly line. This relentless slavery to the machine's cadence proved to be the constant refrain of these working clerics. "We are one of the factory wheels", said one. "It keeps turning; we must turn with the rhythm which

23. Interview with Michel Bordet, Simian-la-Rotonde (27 May 1983). For more details on Father Bordet's entry experiences, see Benoit, *Le Ciel*, 52-56. The author unearthed parallel experiences from the following sources: Interviews with: Gabriel Genthial, Bernard Striffling and Jacques Vivez at Courbevoie (11 June 1979); Henri Barreau at Gagny; Louis Bouyer at Colombes (21 May 1979); Jean Olhagary at Paris (13 June 1979); Jean Legendre at Plateaud-Assy (6 June 1983); and Jean Cottin at Paris (17 June 1980); "Problème missionnaire", Limoges report (1950) 21, in MDP (1950); "Quelques points acquis" (1 Sept. 1948), in René Boudot private papers (1948); Olhagary, *Ce Mur*, 62-67; and Boudot, *René Boudot*, 76-78.
24. The following description expressed the almost universal sentiment of the worker priests: "Projet de Déclaration", 2, in Henri Barreau's private papers. "We had experienced the factory atmosphere, the continual persecution, the lack of liberty, initiative and confidence, the scornful and condescending smiles of the foreman, the hush-money of the management, the penalties, the arbitrary firings, the lay-offs. We have experienced everything that hides behind the language of production needs: the sending away of those who are no longer young enough or lively enough and for others, infernal work, the cadence, the incessant march against the clock, the physical and nerve-wracking exhaustion, the nightmares while sleeping and the habitual deception on payday of ridiculously low wages".

has been imposed upon us, neither faster nor slower". Still another reflected about his slavery to "physical fatigue, tedium, discouragement": "I was nothing else than an anonymous particle doing a job.... Produce and shut up".[25] Beyond this dehumanising tedium lay the constant health hazards and dangerous conditions so endemic to the factory system. The Dominican Father Jean Legendre entered a priest retirement community in the French Alps because of the silicosis he contracted during his textile labour as a worker priest, while others remain convinced that the premature deaths of Jo Gouttebarge and Jo Lafontaine resulted directly from the unhealthy conditions where they toiled. Still others recalled again and again work comrades mutilated and killed by virtue of unsafe machinery. Most graphically the worker priests joined the list of labour martyrs in the person of Father Michel Favreau who was crushed to death on the docks of Bordeaux.[26]

Brought face to face daily by such realities, it did not take long for the worker priests to awaken to the profound injustices of the industrial system. They raged against the habitually stingy wages received by workers, against the constant fear of lay-offs, the threats both subtle and direct, especially against active trade unionists and the firings. Yet during this painful journey they discovered as well the powerful solidarity and camaraderie characteristic of this labouring class. André Piet called this "one of the most beautiful things I have known". At Limoges Father Georges Baudry told of a worker who laboured voluntarily with a tubercular comrade so that his ailing brother wouldn't lose his job. "No one wants to work with him", said the volunteer, "but just the same, he's got to work to eat". No wonder Father Baudry responded to this sacrificial act: "For me the factory was a meeting place with God. I truly found God's presence in the reactions and attitudes of my comrades".[27]

Although the work place came to define worker priest life increasingly, their reality outside the circle of work mirrored what they experienced on the factory floor. Most frequently, they lived in one room in the squalor of tenement apartment buildings. They spoke of isolation, bare essentials and the high cost of renting even for a minimum of facilities. Jacques Loew offered poignant descriptions in his *En Mission prolétarienne*: "Smell, sight, touch, constantly irritated by parasites; hearing continually assaulted by sudden outbreaks of quarreling and children crying: the senses are put on severe trial. But can a house be certified as unsanitary on these grounds? Alas, no! Unsanitary - that which causes illness, fire, ten times more quickly than elsewhere, but what statistics can convey the sound of these early

---

25. Jean Wernier in "Témoignages des prêtres ayant été au travail", 115, in *Cahiers de la Mission de Paris* (1955); G. B. , "Simples Réflexions" (Oct. 1948- July 1950) 1-2, in MDP (1954); André Deléage, "Réflexions sur mon stage", 4, in MDP (1954); Interviews with Bordet, Piet, Robert Pfaff, Paris (10 June 1983); and the Belgian worker priests Louis Flagothier and Albert Courtoy; *Joseph Lafontaine*, 3, in Jacques Jaudon private papers; Benoit, *Le Ciel*, 56.
26. Interviews with Flagothier, Courtoy, Legendre, Francis Vico, Montluçon (24 May 1980), and Robert Pacalet, Lyon (5 July 1979); Deliat, *Vingt ans*, 33-39; "Conclusions des journées de prêtres-ouvriers", (16-17 Feb. 1952) 2, in MDP (1954); "La Fin d'un apôtre moderne" (1951), in MDP (1951); Sanguedolce, *Joseph Gouttebarge*; *Joseph Lafontaine*; Père Jacques, "A la memoire de nos camarades", *Eveil Syndical* (June 1950) in Jacques Screppel private papers; Olhagary, *Ce Mur*, 67.
27. Piet, Laval, Flagothier, Courtoy and Robert interviews; G. B., "Simples...".

catarrhal or tubercular coughs". No wonder Loew was enraged by the slum landlord system which he called "an institution akin to that of ancient slavery". At the same time the worker priests discovered that their incarnation of grim lodging served to intensify solidarity they had found with their factory comrades. As one worker told his Marseille worker priest friend: "Because you live in the same kind of housing that we do, you are everybody's friend".[28] As well, food, clothing and leisure for the worker priests mirrored that of the working class with whom they had become an integral part.[29]

This day-to-day proletarian rhythm reshaped their faith and its articulation in significant ways. The traditional notion of incarnation, God's direct identification with humanity through the person of Jesus Christ, provided a natural focus for their experience, and frequently they used that word or others which substituted for this more traditional concept. Phrases such as *"être avec"* ("to be with"), *"partager"* ("to share"), *"vivre la même vie"* ("live the same life"), *"dedans"* ("from the inside"), *"présence"* ("presence") and *"communauté de destin"* ("community of destiny") were the most frequently used examples of the latter. Henri Barreau called his worker priest life "the recommencement of Christ's incarnation", and the Belgian Damien Reumont stated forthrightly that he undertook factory work "just as Christ himself became a man in order to save others". Alfred Ancel, France's pioneer worker-bishop, described his incarnation as being "a worker like the others" in order to mirror Christ who "for thirty years became a man like others".[30]

This description of worker priest life as the embodiment of Christ's earthly existence was painted in numerous instances with poignancy. Indeed many of these clerics articulated this incarnation of Christ in terms of their

---

28. Interviews with worker priests Pfaff, Cottin, Bordet, Laval, Legendre, Barreau and Bouyer; Jean Gray, Auxerre (11 June 1983); Émile Poulat, Paris (20 May 1983); Bernard Chauveau, Boulogne-Billancourt (11 May 1979); Bernard Tiberghien, Dunkerque (12 June 1980); Jean Tarby; Philbert Talé, Antony (1 June 1983); and Maurice Combe, Lyon (14 June 1979). Other interviews: Hollande and Maxime Hua, priest in adult specialised Catholic Action, Paris (9 May 1979). Sanguedolce, *Joseph Gouttebarge*, 17-18, 22 and 30; Loew, *Mission*, 26 and 29-35; "Marseille Reports", 31; Olhagary, *Ce Mur*, 70-73.
29. Although I learned these things in great detail from my interviews, I cite simply a few of my written sources: "Journée des religieux missionnaires", (6 Feb. 1949) 2-3, in MDP (1949); Henri Perrin, "Note sur les 2 articles", (15 July 1949), in MDP (1949); A. D., report (July 1945) 13, in MDP (1945); Sanguedolce, *Joseph Gouttebarge*, 46-48; André Depierre, "Ce témoignage persévérant de Dieu", *Esprit* (Dec. 1950) 906; and Perrin, *Itinéraire*, 182-183.
30. Interviews with worker priests Vidal, Robert, Combe, Gray, Loew, Screppel, Barreau and Dillaye; André Chavanneau and Yves Garnier, Limoges (31 May 1983), and Alfred Ancel, Lyon (14 June 1979). Interviews with Dominican theologians Yves Congar and Marie-Dominique Chenu, Paris (15 May 1979). "Problème missionnaire", Limoges Report, 28, in MDP (1950); A. D., report (July 1945) 13, in MDP (1945); P. Besnard, report, Paris 18th (1949) 2, in MDP (1949); Robert Pacalet, letter to Hollande (28 Dec. 1948) 1, in MDP (1948); Loew, *Mission*, 90; and Pierre Riche, report, Paris 20th (Oct. 1949) 2, in MDP (1949). Quoted material in order: Barreau interview; Père Damien Reumont, "Fraternité des Ouvriers de la Vièrge des Pauvres", (1947) 2-3, in MDP (1947), and Ancel interview.

daily cadence as workers.³¹ However it was the worker priests of the Belgian OVP who articulated most clearly the incarnational notion on manual toil by clergy. This apologetic was developed in the face of conservative Catholic polemics challenging the legitimacy of a priest as worker and proved prescient in light of opposition which reached a groundswell in 1953 and 1954. Father Charles Boland began to articulate such notions of worker priesthood as early as 1929 in a brief report entitled *Quelques Principes relatifs à l'apostolat sacerdotal à l'usine*. He observed that "to convert them [workers] to Christ, we must have missionary workers just like them, living their lives". Shouldn't their priests, he added, "also live these factory lives?" He spells out the logic of this priest worker incarnation by pointing to the life of Jesus and his family in Nazareth: "Before all else, this would be a certain means, in the name of the church and above all its priestly body, to render homage to the longer part of Jesus' and Mary's lives: labour in obscurity in Nazareth. In effect, the life of manual labour aligns itself quite well to Christian mortification and prayer, just like the life of our most fervent religious orders throughout the ages".³²

In the years to follow Boland expanded upon this basic theology, especially in short writings designed for his *Fraternité des OVP*. His own entry into work served to intensify this incarnational spirituality of work, as exemplified by this poignant utterance: "With the incarnate Word, I attained the redemption of the world through the sufferings of my work by fatigue, by cold and by heat, by monotony, by filth, by wounds, by coarseness, by the injustices of the foremen and the scorn of their bosses and by mockery and calumny which brings all the rest of these together. In sum, I find that which is most valuable: *the Cross* [emphasis in the original]. Yes, this is surely the only mystique acceptable for a 'worker priest': the redemptive cross of the working class milieu, and its liberating cross as well".³³

Occasionally poetry proved a chosen medium to portray the profound poignancy of working class existence as demonstrated by the verse of Jo Gouttebarge.³⁴ Equally original was the form of vocational vow utilised by Henri Barreau in his personal journal, an expression of incarnational faith shared in common with his *Mission de Paris* brothers: "I commit my life and offer all that I am... to become and to be a true worker while, at the same time, a priest among the workers, just as you have been a man, God among

---

31. Letter, Saint-Brieuc (4 March 1954) and "Raisons d'être des prêtres-ouvriers", 5, in J.O.C. Dossier on the worker priests, Paris, in MDP (1954): "When we aren't hired, when our body is broken with fatigue, we are with Christ, who could have been a prince or doctor, but who chose, until he was thirty years old, this working class life and who continues to be humiliated, exploited and who suffers in his very flesh which is that of the poor and exploited construction workers.... The priest who endures this world fulfills in his body that which marks the suffering of Christ. Christ's witness can not be the word only but also blood. We live the passion of Christ with our worker brothers".
32. Boland, *Dure Percée*, 28-30.
33. Ibid., 54. Similar values are articulated in detail by another member of the O.V.P. *équipe*, Père Damien Reumont, 'Fraternité des O.V.P.", (15 June 1947) 1-19. See also C. F. Boland, "Prêtres en Milieu de Travail", *Evangéliser* (mars & mai 1947) 438-452 and 552-566, for a fuller development of his worker priest apologetics.
34. For an example, see Joseph Gouttebarge, "Cafard" (1950), 18-21 in Sanguedolce, *Joseph Gouttebarge*.

others. To take up and carry in my priestly heart their entire life, work, poverty, struggles, sufferings and hopes, the humiliation of their most base conditions..., their temptations, just as you took up our flesh and carried our sins".[35]

3.3. Militancy

Barreau's mention of "struggle" in his understanding of incarnation underscores the most important watershed in the worker priest journey. With their turning toward activism, the labouring priests drew increasing fire from earlier critics. As the worker priests entered deeper and deeper into their proletarian incarnation, they concluded that *"présence"*, *"partager"* and *"être avec"* involved total identification with their toiling comrades. Consequently they became active militants in the working class movement. A logical first step in this direction meant joining the trade union at their work place. Jacques Loew called his union membership paper "my identity card, my passport into the workers' world", and Henri Barreau defended his entry into a metallurgical union with these words: "Because the proletariat is exploited, I am in solidarity with it for better or worse. Also, as a consequence of being a Christian, I am committed to take every means which I consider appropriate in this action of liberation.... These are my reasons... for joining the CGT".[36]

Indeed, the vast majority of worker priests joined the communist-dominated *Confédération Générale du Travail* (CGT). In spite of the initial hostility they encountered with anticlerical members, they found that the CGT was the union of choice for most workers and that it defended its constituents much more vigorously than the reformist confessional unions (CFTC). Even those few who entered the Christian federation linked up with its left wing in the hopes of radicalising the CFTC. In the French *Nord* and Belgium the bishops forbade their worker priest from entering the more radical leftist unions, whether the communist-oriented CGT or the leftist Belgian *Fédération Générale du Travail de Belgique* (FGTB), controlled by socialists. Both unions represented the large majority of workers in their regions. Faced with this dilemma, worker priests like the French Dominicans Screppel and Legendre and the Belgians Flagothier and Courtoy entered no unions but joined their leftist brothers when struggles erupted at the work place.[37]

---

35. Henri Barreau, "Tu es pour eux un démon", 13-14, in Henri Barreau's private papers.
36. Loew interview; H. Barreau (c. 1949) 1, in MDP (1949).
37. Interviews with worker priests Cottin, Bordet, Depierre, Genthial, Combe, Bouyer, Barreau, Olhagary, Chaveau, Pacalet, Dillaye, Loew, Talé, Pfaff, Poulat, Laval, Poulat, Gray, Tarby, Screppel, Legendre, Flagothier, Courtoy and Cagne; Paul Guilbert, Venissieux (16 May 1983); Jacques Jaudon, Grenoble (15 June 1983); Albert Guichard, Paris (21 June 1983); Bernard Lacroix, Grenoble (15 June 1983); Bernard Striffling and Jacques Vivez, both at Courbevoie (11 June 1979). Also Perrin, *Itinéraire*, 163; Sanguedolce, *Joseph Gouttebarge*, 26; Jean Olhagary, report, Paris 20th (Oct., 1949) 3-4, in MDP (1949); *Jeunesse Ouvrière*, II, 301-303.

Certainly the nature of worker priest militancy within the union movement (*engagement* was their term of choice) varied according to both the personalities and contexts of each toiling cleric. The form of Belgian worker priest relations with the union movement is a case in point. Most worker priests remained grass-roots militants and relatively anonymous save in their own local union. Michel Bordet, André Depierre and Jacques Loew maintained such a stance with resolute intention, even when approached by their comrades to accept leadership positions. Others found themselves drawn reluctantly into local struggles. François Vidal became a union delegate under such friendly pressure, and at a Lille textile plant Father Bernard Tiberghien helped organise a CGT local in the midst of the plant management's effort to lay off workers.[38]

Others proved less reluctant and although they refused to push themselves forward, they responded readily to their comrades' requests. Most of these were elected as rank-and-file delegates for their locals. Among these a number rose to higher union posts, such as Jo Lafontaine, priest-docker at Le Havre. He became his union's secretary, first at the work place and then for the entire city. At Limoges Francis Vico, first a local delegate, advanced to the secretariat of the CGT for his entire trade.[39] Quite likely the two most prominent labour leaders among the worker priests proved to be Jo Gouttebarge and Henri Barreau.

Toward the end of 1952 Gouttebarge was elected as a CGT delegate by his steel plant comrades. While at this post he fought relentlessly against paternalism in the roll-shop, defending especially the North Africans who toiled there. In another instance he took up the gauntlet for eighty laid off workers. As well, he tackled the editorship of his local's newspaper and used its pages both to protest injustices and to promote trade union unity. He stood at the avant garde of the union being one of the first to advocate an end of French rule in North Africa. At the point of the Church's condemnation of the worker priests Gouttebarge was named secretary of the CGT's regional *comités d'entreprise*.[40]

Mission de Paris' Henri Barreau was one of the first worker priests to become an active *cégétiste*. By the latter 1940s he held a prominent post in his Montrouge local and proved so popular that his comrades pushed his candidacy for the post of full-time secretary of the *UST de la Seine*, the largest and most militant of CGT metallurgical federations in France. So unprecedented was this choice that it created ripples in both the highest levels of the Catholic Church and French communism. "A priest at the head of a CGT section" posed a serious problem "at the level of the central committee of the Communist Party". However, Barreau's grass-roots support prevailed, pressing *le Parti* to live with this anomaly. On the ecclesiastical side there were tremors as well. Even progressives debated the wisdom of

---

38. Interviews with worker priests Depierre, Loew, Bordet, Vidal and Tiberghien. See also Benoit, *Le Ciel*, 65.
39. Interviews with worker priests Combe, Pacalet, Talé, Gray, Garnier, Chavanneau and Vico. See also Ch. Monier, "Formation d'une section syndicale", (Sept.- Oct. 1953) 2, in MDP (1953) and *Joseph Lafontaine*, 13.
40. Sanguedolce, *Joseph Gouttebarge*, 24, 26, 28, 39 and 44-45; Joseph Gouttebarge, letter to Cardinal Gerlier (14 March 1954) 2, in MDP (1954).

this. Some felt this act grew out of "a normal evolution of priestly witness", whereas others believed that union posts belonged exclusively to the laity. Even the worker priests themselves debated the issue. Finally, upon the insistence of Father Barreau's *Mission de Paris* brothers, Father Hollande convinced higher Church authorities to accept the move.[41]

Even greater difficulties emerged for the institutional Church when these newly unionised priests participated actively in strike actions with their toiling brothers and sisters. Once again, the worker priests believed that incarnation necessitated a total involvement in working class life, an involvement which included solidarity on the picket lines. Virtually all of these clergy stood with their union's strike actions. In some instances this militancy included criticism of the confessional unions when they refused to support such work stoppages. Even though the Dominicans of the Nord and the Belgian priests could not join the unions of their choice, they participated readily in the strikes of these anathematised unions. Father Screppel even delivered speeches at strike rallies, and along with Father Legendre he collected food and other provisions for striking families.[42]

A few examples demonstrate clearly different manifestations of such involvement. At Longwy Father Michel Bordet felt uncomfortable at the thought of a priest on strike and was prepared to cross a picket line at his plant. He recalled: "At the factory gate, I encountered the strike pickets which stopped me and caused me to reflect upon the reasons why they were on strike". The very next day, he mused, "I was a striker with them". Both Jo Gouttebarge and Henri Perrin took more active leadership roles. During the great strike waves of August 1953 Gouttebarge, at St. Etienne, managed to organise work stoppage solidarity of all three major trade union federations for a full eight days. One comrade recalled how "Jo" managed to hide about 200 workers in a church crypt while they were being hunted by the police. In his memoirs Henri Perrin described his leadership role at Tignes where huge hydroelectric dams underwent construction. Low wages, dangerous conditions and substandard housing combined to generate the 42 day strike wave of 1952. Perrin was selected as secretary of the union's organising committee and member of its strike solidarity commission. He crafted bulletins and daily memos of the strike's progress, as well as coordinating the picketing, creating discussion groups, soliciting provisions for striking families, setting up strike offices and publishing leaflets. These efforts proved effective enough for the union to gain a collective agreement with gains in wages, safer conditions and better housing.[43] Metallurgical

---

41. Interviews with Barreau and Hollande; Secrétariat d'information, "Notes confidentielles du 1er et 8 juin 1951", 1 p., in MDP (1954); "Conclusions des journées de prêtres-ouvriers" (16-17 Feb. 1952) 2, in MDP (1952).
42. Interviews with worker priests Loew, Chauveau, Screppel, Cottin, Flagothier, Courtoy, Legendre and Tiberghien. "Des prêtres-ouvriers de Limoges" 1p., in MDP (1954); Jacques Screppel, handwritten notes, "Historique grève Fives-Lille" (1950) 1-4, in Screppel private papers.
43. Bordet interview; Sanguedolce, *Joseph Gouttebarge*, 37-38 and 41-42; Perrin, *Itinéraire*, 262, 265, 271, 273-276, 278-280, 283-286, 291, 295-298 and 301.

worker priest "Bobby" Pfaff defended his militancy and that of his clerical comrades by arguing that justice for the workers demanded strike actions.[44]

Pfaff's more inclusive notion of worker militancy asserted that any and every question that affected worker life and consciousness demanded worker priest *engagement*, whether locally or nationally. The most publicised of these commitments proved to be worker priest entry into the *Mouvement de la Paix*. Although its organisational muscle and the largest sector of its membership was communist, the Peace Movement flourished as a non-partisan pluralistic effort to ban nuclear weapons and remove NATO from Europe. Its public leader Father Jean Boulier inspired Francis Vico to join up, and Jo Gouttebarge's critiques of the armaments industry prompted him to organise public events to recruit members for *le Mouvement*. However, it was the arrest of two *Mission de Paris* vicars Louis Bouyer and Bernard Cagne that became a *cause célèbre*. On 28 May 1952 a massive demonstration occurred in Paris to protest the arrival of the American general Matthew B. Ridgeway as commander-in-chief of NATO. The police were out in force, and pitched battles followed. In the melee many were wounded and others arrested including the two priests. This incarceration of two clergy produced a media event and much shock and embarrassment within the institutional Church. Until this moment open publicity on the worker priests in the mainstream media was virtually non-existent. The arrest of Fathers Cagne and Bouyer changed that.[45] The spotlight turned on the worker priests, providing the grist their enemies could use against them.

4. The Context of Worker Priest Church Conflict

Although the anti-Ridgeway protest catapulted the worker priests into the public eye, thus embarrassing their church and infuriating their ecclesiastical enemies, opposition within the Church had been brewing from the beginning. As early as 1946 Fathers Hollande and Augros visited Rome to

---

44. Robert Pfaff, "Quelques Réflexions...", 6-8, in René Boudot private papers: "Another reason for struggle is this certitude that the working class cannot obtain any improvement whatsoever in its living conditions save by a strike, thus by violence. The great dates are strike dates. That's also a shame, but that has been their experience. Only the strike succeeds.... I no longer wish that we separate politics from professional demands in order to determine a strike's legitimacy". Official social Catholicism took the position that "political" strikes were unacceptable and demanded that workers participate only in those strikes that were clearly for exclusively work-related ("professional") issues.
45. Interviews with worker priests Legendre, Screppel, Laval, Talé, Gray, Vidal, Pfaff, Guichard, Chaveau, Combe, Pacalet, Cottin, Robert, Barreau, Tarby, Vico, Jaudon, Piet, Bouyer and Cagne. Also Jacques Screppel, "Premières intuitions", 4, in Screppel papers; Deliat, *Vingt Ans*, 31; "Un prêtre-ouvrier de Donzère-Mondragon", *Marseillaise*, (29 Oct. 1952) 1; "Les Prêtres-Ouvriers du Rhône et de la Loire", Lyon (4 March 1953) 1-2; Équipe de Marseille (1953) 1-4; Mgr. Raymond Touvet, letter to Jacques Hollande (11 May 1953), all in MDP (1953); Albert Gauche, "Aux ouvriers chrétiens" (1954) 1-4, in MDP (1954); H.-M. Féret, "Explication de vote" (1950), 1-8, in MDP (1950); G.B., "Simples Réflexions" (Oct. 1948- July 1950) 10, in MDP (1954); Sanguedolce, *Joseph Gouttebarge*, 22-23 and 80; Henri Barreau, "Projet de Déclaration", 3, in Barreau papers; and L. Bouyer and B. Cagne, "Pour ceux qui ne pourront jamais parler et qu'on ne voudra pas croire", *Colombes* (30 May 1952) 1-4, in MDP (1952).

allay suspicion with respect to their avant garde missions. Although they were received supportively by the future Paul VI, Mgr. Montini, other prelates remained aloof and suspicious. The Pontiff himself, Pius XII, demonstrated caution in his audience with the two men. He appealed for prudence which worked effectively as long as the worker priests kept a low profile. However, the year 1949 proved to be a critical turning point for their ministry due to a series of events beyond their control. In that year the popular press printed a number of sensationalist stories which promoted the worker priests. Especially controversial were the articles which appeared in *France Soir* and *Paris-Presse-Intransigeant* (July). Father Hollande felt compelled to defend his *Mission de Paris* to the growing number of suspicious bishops. Roughly two months before the press articles appeared, cardinal Suhard, the worker priests' most significant patron, lay in state while working class Paris mourned his passing.[46]

Finally, that summer the Holy See published a decree against communism and Catholic collaboration with communists in any form. This had immediate repercussions on the worker priests. After all their plunge into working class life in all its fullness made contact and camaraderie with communists a fact of life. Even the antimarxist Father Loew had many communist friends as well as being active in the communist-led CGT. From their point of entry at the workplace to their *engagement* in strike action and other forms of militancy they encountered, worked with, found friendship among and shared struggles with active members of *le Parti*. However, it was this CGT contact and worker priest militancy that prompted them to reassess the Church's traditional anticommunism. Their on-the-ground solidarity with CGT militants, and the overwhelming entry of worker priests into the more militant communist-led federation led them to cast an increasingly critical eye at the more timid confessional unions. A lived solidarity, far more than ideology, cemented worker priest friendship with grass-roots communists. Certainly a number of ex-worker priests after their official condemnation (1954) joined the Communist Party, and perhaps a few before the Church's shutdown of the experiment. However, party membership and aligning with high-level communist officials proved to be more a fear-driven myth of right wing Catholics rather than the reality itself. Worker-priest experience, friendship and solidarity with communists was a "grass-roots" phenomenon that grew up among rank-and-file communists on the factory floor, in the bistros and in the ghetto neighbourhoods. In fact, the worker priests praised these communist militants as the avant-garde of the toiling classes, even while they remained critical of elements within the marxist world view.[47]

---

46. S.-E. Mgr. Montini, 8-9; Mgr. Tardini (28 Nov. 1946), 7; Mgr. Ottaviani (29 Nov. 1946); "Audience de Sa Sainteté Pie XII (27 Nov. 1946); Augros, Hollande, Laporte let ter (1 Dec. 1946), all in MDP (1946). For the controversial press letters and other publications about the worker priests in the wider public arena, see *France-Soir*, (15-18, 20-21 and 23 July 1949); *Paris- Presse- Intransigeant*, (16-20 and 22-26 July) 1949; Cesbron, *Les Saints vont en enfer*; and the examples cited in Arnal, *Priests*, 167. Hollande letters to Mgr. Ancel (6 Aug. 1949) 1-2 and Mgr. Chappoulie (8 Aug. 1949) 1, both in MDP (1949); Vinatier, *Cardinal Suhard*, 423-430.
47. For details and sources with respect to the relationship between the worker priests and French communists, consult Arnal, "A Missionary *Main Tendue* Toward French Communists".

This is not to say that the worker priests did not wrestle with the more philosophical questions surrounding Christian-marxist dialogue and collaboration, although this activity did not consume their reflections. Indeed, the worker priests criticised the hierarchy's condemnation of communism as an impractical abstraction. Instead, the more philosophical of the worker priests were inclined to defend collaboration with French communists and the CGT on the basis of missionary stances found throughout Church history. Both Joseph Gouttebarge and Henri Perrin reminded conservative Catholics that the Church had converted the barbarians by incarnating itself into their culture. In this way, they argued, the Church was able to embrace a civilisation, baptise it and then transform it. While repudiating marxist materialism and atheism, these worker priests insisted that their stance of *présence* and solidarity was a necessary missionary strategy in this world outside the Church.[48]

Consequently, the Vatican's universal condemnation of communism and all collaboration with it came as a devastating blow to the worker priests. At one level, powerful and sympathetic sectors of the French hierarchy sought to mitigate the effects of this blanket anathema by publishing their own slightly softer version on the same subject and by producing a written *Directoire* to define the parameters of worker priest ministry. These efforts, rather than building bridges, exacerbated growing tensions between the worker priests and their bishops. Attempts by the future worker-bishop Alfred Ancel to ease the growing gap served to drive the wedge deeper between the two parties. His arguments circumscribing priestly manual labour and criticising militancy in the communist-led unions enraged the various worker priest *équipes* (teams). There the conflict simmered and widened slowly until May 1952 when Fathers Bouyer and Cagne were arrested in the massive anti-Ridgeway protest in Paris. The wide publicity given to these arrests provided the catalyst that rendered virtually inevitable the ecclesiastical condemnation of the worker priests.[49]

Within a year a concerted attack was leveled by the Vatican against various progressive sectors of the French church. The worker priests found themselves at the center of these assaults. From 1952 to the late summer of 1953 both the Vatican and Cardinal Liénart of Lille circumscribed the progressive elements at the *Mission de France* seminary as a prelude to closing it down and reorganising it. The worker priests were next. Step by step the hierarchy undercut their ministry. Official social Catholic bodies began to complain, the *Mission de France* was not permitted to train its seminarians for a worker priest ministry, and the bishop of Marseille ordered the work-

---

48. Ibid., 549-554.
49. "Sur le Décret du Saint Office et la Déclaration des 4 cardinaux français" (Oct. 1949) 1-11, in MDP (1949); "Projet de Directoire pour les prêtres travaillant en usine", (May 1951); Alfred Ancel, "... aux prêtres-ouvriers du diocèse de Lyon", (22 Sept. 1951) 2-13; Jacques Hollande, letter (All Saints 1951) 1- 2, all in MDP (1951); Robert Pfaff, "Quelques Réflexions sur et à propos du Directoire...", 1-2, 5-7, in Boudot papers; Interviews with worker priests Bouyer and Cagne; "Pour ce qui...", Etienne Borne, "Polémiques et Dialogues", *Terre Humaine* (July-August 1952) 123-128; "Deux prêtres passés à tabac", *Vie Intellectuelle* (July 1952) 1-6; and "Prêtres et Partisans", *La Quinzaine* [no date, 1952] 13, in MDP (1952).

er priests in his dioceses to lay down their tools. The situation grew from bad to worse. Meetings between worker priests and the bishops proved fractious, and polarisation grew. In spite of the desire of France's highest ranking prelates to save the worker priest experiment, the Vatican had decided already to close it down. Cardinals Feltin of Paris, Liénart of Lille and Gerlier of Lyon were summoned to Rome in November 1953. There Pius XII commanded them to carry back and enforce the decrees he gave them. 1) Each worker priest must be directly under the control of his local bishop (thus undermining the worker priest network that had emerged since the late 1940s). 2) All these clergy were expected to undergo special doctrinal and spiritual supervision under the tutelage of their bishops. 3) The extent of their manual labour was to be limited to protect "their priestly state", and 4) They were commanded to drop all "temporal *engagement*", including "trade union and all other responsibilities". In spite of pleas and carefully crafted defenses by both the worker priests and their supporters, the French episcopate passed on the papal ultimatum and gave the worker priests until 1 March 1954 to comply. The outcry of the general public, the national press, working class organisations, leftist Catholics and influential theologians against the condemnation availed for nothing. In fact, some noted Catholic supporters, especially among the Dominicans, fell under a variety of censures for such open support. The month of March 1954 passed rather quietly. Roughly half the worker priests complied with their bishops' orders while the other half disobeyed and remained at the work place and in their unions.[50]

Though granted a reprieve for slightly over a year, the Belgian worker priests fell victim to a similar fate. Reflecting upon the debacle of his French priestly comrades, Father Boland sought to prevent a similar action against the Belgian labouring clergy by encouraging official representations to the Holy See to convince Pius XII to retain the Belgian experience. These efforts proved unsuccessful. Shortly after the French condemnation the patron bishop of Belgian worker priests forbade further training in this model for seminarians. Within a few months, under Roman pressure, the bishop called upon the Belgian worker priests to lay down their tools. Although deeply

---

50. Siefer, *The Church and Industrial Society*, 319-323. For the story of the trials of the *Mission de France* seminary, see the earlier cited works on the subject; "Regard sur notre histoire", *Lettre aux Communautés* (Nov. 1954) 4-16; interview with working *Mission de France* seminarian Aldo Bardini, Bagnolet (10 May 1980), and in English Arnal, "Beyond the walls...", 44-45. Deliat, *Vingt Ans*, 125-127, 130 and 133-135; Mgr. Delay to Comité diocésain d'ACO de Marseille (4 May 1953) 1-3; Piet, Monnier, Gauche letter to Mgr. Delay (5 May 1953) 1; Mgr. Delay letter (27 May 1953) 1-2; Cardinal Feltin letter (23 July 1953), all in MDP (1953). Also "Équipe de Marseille" (1953), in both Piet and Vidal private papers; "Déclaration (Nov. 1953) 1, in MDP (1953); interviews with worker priests Dillaye, Olhagary, Barreau, Tiberghien and Pacalet. See also Petrie, ed., *The Worker Priests*, 147-204 (these pages carry the major public documents in the last stages of the conflict). The Dominican brother François Leprieur's *Quand Rome condamne* is an exhaustive and scholary work which details the condemnation of those Dominicans involved in and supportive of worker priest ministries. For other particular views on the conflict from 1952-1954, consult Berranger, *Alfred Ancel*, 167-183; Olhagary, *Ce Mur*, 148-168; Benoit, *Le Ciel*, 99-149; Moine, *René Boudot*, 80-85; and Arnal, "Theology and Commitment: Marie-Dominique Chenu".

distressed they obeyed without exception, but in their joint statement they explained their submission in these words: "We can only work for the reconciliation of the Church and the working class in the midst of the Church".[51]

The subsequent story of others who re-entered the Church, of bishops who sought creative ways to save the experiment and of the return of a labouring priest ministry through a decree of the Second Vatican Council carries us beyond this pioneer phase. All that remains is to suggest the contexts of this condemnation that explain why it occurred and why it occurred when it did. As indicated above, the worker priests had enemies within the Church from the beginning of their ministries in the 1940s. Ultraconservatives and integrists were realities in France and Rome since the First Vatican Council of 1870. Perhaps even more important were the cautious skeptics, especially those within the episcopacy and including the pope himself. Indeed, both the *Mission de France* and the various worker priest *équipes* produced a nervousness among more traditional Catholics, even among those habitually labeled as progressives. Hence, when the public spotlight fell upon the worker priest movement, the more cautious supporters, especially the French bishops, tried to contain worker priest militancy in a form of ecclesiastical damage control.[52]

At the macro level the worker priests fell victim to the changing geopolitical scene. Created during the dark hours of collaboration and Resistance and entering the bright light of day in the euphoria of victory and hope, the worker priests blossomed quietly in a context of Soviet-American-British "friendship", experienced as *tripartisme* in France. The two pariahs of the Third Republic, Christian Democrats and communists emerged from the war with heroic *Résistance* credentials, while more conservative Catholics and the episcopate were tarred with the brush of collaboration. The Fourth Republic came to life in an alliance of socialists, communists and Christian Democrats (*Mouvement Républicain Populaire*, MRP), and the two chief labour federations, the Christian CFTC and the communist-led CGT, entered the postwar period working together. Communist and progressive Catholic bodies moved from hostility toward cautious alliances. In such an atmosphere leftist Catholic experiments and writings flourished. However, by 1949 the Cold War was in full force in France and elsewhere. The Iron Curtain stood between Eastern and Western Europe; both sides had the bomb; and NATO stood as a military bastion against the Eastern Bloc countries. The Vatican welcomed the Cold War as one means of liberating Pius XII from the stain of collaboration with the Nazis and Italian fascists. From his days as a nuncio to Germany Eugenio Pacelli (Pius XII from 1939) pursued his powerful obsession against all forms of marxism. The arrival of the

---

51. Boland, *Dure Percée*, 63-64.
52. For an overview of this left (progressive)/right (integrist) strife within French Catholicism and at the Vatican, consult the following works: Ravitch, *The Catholic Church and the French Nation*, 51-152; Arnal, *Ambivalent Alliance*; Paul, *Second Ralliement*; Rémond, *Les Catholiques*; Murphy, *Communists and Catholics*; and Christophe, *1936, les catholiques et le Front populaire*. See also the works cited earlier with respect to the war period (1939-1945). For this push-pull relationship of bishops and the worker priests, consult Petrie, *The Worker Priests*.

Cold War and various "Red Scares" freed him to pursue a resolute campaign against leftists both without and within the Church. In addition, his particularly authoritarian style of rule insured that there would be no negotiations around the curtailing of the worker priests. Cardinals Feltin, Liénart and Gerlier experienced that during their Roman visit of November 1953. The demotion of Giovanni Montini, the only high-level Vatican prelate to defend the worker priests, to an archepiscopal post in Milan underscored the reality of a pope who would tolerate no opposition.[53]

At the micro level the worker priests found they faced increasingly mounting resistance from the more rightward drifting MRP, both in local and national conflicts. As well, the highest levels of specialised Catholic Action joined the ranks of worker priest critics. Even the most friendly bishops not only distanced themselves from specific support of the worker priests, but they also questioned the very notion of such a priesthood. "To be a priest and to be a worker are two functions, two different states of life", asserted Cardinal Liénart, "and it is not possible to unite them in the same person without altering the notion of the priesthood". Meanwhile the worker priests themselves, deeply altered by their proletarian experiences and several years of joint consciousness-raising, had reached opposite conclusions, often in the heat of much debate among them.[54] They insisted that the very integrity of their priesthood demanded a life-long incarnation into proletarian life, and they begged their bishops to uphold them.[55]

Under direct instruction from the pope and deeply troubled by a form of priesthood structurally more and more independent of hierarchy control, the bishops opted for the traditional model of decree from on high and demanded obedience to the same. The lengthy letter of Bishop de Provenchères to his clergy (February 1954) spells out in detail this more conservative notion of the nature of the priesthood and hierarchical authority. He asserted that the Church does send priests to the working class but not "to work in a factory or to carry on the activities of working class militants". Indeed, in traditional fashion, his position was non-negotiable: "The

---

53. Leprieur, *Quand Rome condamne*, 340-347; Vinatier, *Les Prêtres Ouvriers*, 69-104; Benoit, *Le Ciel*, 99-107. For a portrait of Pius XII, see the controversial but well-documented work by Cornwell, *Hitler's Pope*.
54. "Vous êtes des ouvriers, vous n'êtes plus des prêtes", (Dec. 1952) 2-7, in MDP (1952); Petrie, *Worker Priests*, 68-69; Interview with Georges Bidault, leader in the MRP, Paris (18 May 1979); "Document vert", *Prêtres Ouvriers*, 225-242; "Rapport Jean Gray", in MDP (1953) and in Vidal private papers; "Déclaration de travailleurs chrétiens sur les grèves d'Août 1953", 1-4, in MDP (1953); "Cause Tessier-Barreau", (24 April 1953) 1-4, and "Procès Verbal d'audience", 7-13, both in Barreau; R. Salanne, "Réflexions sur les décisions concernant les prêtres-ouvriers", *Lettre aux Fédéraux* (March 1954) 1, 3 and 10; Secrétariat Général JOC, "Circulaire aux Fédérations" (9 Feb. 1954), 1p., in Dossier on Worker-Priests, JOC Archives, Paris, Avenue Soeur Rosalie. Interviews at Lyon with Christian trade unionist Jacques Jacquet (14 June 1979); at Paris with Louisette Blanquart (22 June 1979); and at Longuyon with René Boudot (4 June 1980). For the Liénart quote, see "La Déclaration du Cardinal Liénart", *Semaine Religieuse de Lille* (10 Jan. 1954), in *Documentation Catholique* (7 Feb. 1954).
55. Petrie, *Worker Priests*, 201: "We have been told that a mission means setting forth without possibility of return.... We believed in what we were asked for, and have lived accordingly. We do not ask you to live the life you have asked of us.... We do ask you to respect the roots we have grown. We do ask you not to stifle in us Christ's call to share the lot of our brethren in labour".

Bishops, with their responsibility for the government of the Church, have the duty of passing judgment on the experiment and, if necessary, of correcting deviations".[56]

Appropriately and in fairness, the drama of this polarisation between the worker priests and the French hierarchy, which sealed the doom of the pioneer phase of the experience, proved less a tale of angels and demons than a portrait akin to a Greek tragedy. Both France's high-ranking cardinals and the worker priests were torn in two just as they were torn apart from each other. Cardinal Liénart, long a supporter of working class justice, found ways to follow the papal "letter of the law" while retaining as much of the worker priest model that he could manage. Indeed, he proved to be the leading prelate in convincing the Second Vatican Council to legitimise the form of labouring priest. In Lyon, some worker priests remember Cardinal Gerlier bursting into tears at the Roman judgment. For his part, Cardinal Feltin created new forms of mission to workers by expanding and reshaping existing models. And the worker priests, torn by their "two fidelities" (worker and priest), were forced to choose between the two, and so they did, but not without deep sorrow. Perhaps, the chief context underscoring this tragedy, was expressed by the patron of the worker priests years earlier, Cardinal Suhard himself: *"Il y a un mur qui sépare l'Église de la masse"*/ "There is a wall between the Church and the masses". The worker priests breached that wall only to find that their Church institution had not come with them.[57]

---

56. Ibid., 149 and 151.
57. Again, the primary documents that reveal the content and poignancy of the split between worker priests and hierarchy can be found in Petrie, ed., *Worker-Priests*, 147-202. Interviews with worker priests Ancel, Pacalet, Screppel, Tiberghien, Robert and Volot provided the personal stories of the pain experienced by some of the cardinals. Interview with Mgr. Robert Frossard, Paris (2 July 1979); "Rencontre entre les prêtres-ouvriers ayant quitté le travail et NN. SS. Le cardinal Feltin, de Bazelaire, Lallier" (16 July 1954) 2-7, in MDP (1954); "Entretien avec les évéques", (18 July 1954) 1-12, in Boudot papers; Suhard quote in *Les Prêtres Ouvriers*, 34.

CHRISTIAN MOVEMENTS AND PARTIES OF THE LEFT IN ITALY (1938-1958)

Antonio Parisella

1. General Terms, Concepts and Criteria[1]

The expression *cattolicesimo di sinistra*, i.e. the Italian translation of *Left Catholicism*, is not used in Italy. Its use emphasizes confessional, rather than historical and political, affiliation: persons or groups are defined in relation to their Catholic credentials, of which the ecclesiastical authority is judge, rather than their political identification with the Left, which is the result of the believer's free choice. Historically, the decision of individuals or organised groups to become active in movements and parties of the Left has also led to conflicts with the political stance of the ecclesiastical hierarchy, which has, in general, opposed them, and adopted doctrinal and/or disciplinary measures against them, thus opening the way to confusions between levels – ecclesial and political – and between responsibilities which have persisted in time. Those Italian Catholics who have opted for the Left have not been concerned to motivate their political choices with needs of religious type or to indicate them as the only possible options, but have claimed the right to make them with the same legitimacy with which others have made theirs. They have affirmed that the political terrain was one in which the laity, and not the doctrinal and disciplinary power of the Church's hierarchy, enjoyed responsible autonomy.

The term *sinistra cattolica* (Catholic Left) has, on the other hand, been used by some to emphasise confessional affiliation, as an essential characteristic of social or theological or cultural experiences within particular ecclesial situations or Catholic associations distinguished by more marked social involvement or social participation. Some have also used this term to indicate different experiences either within organisations or independent of

---

1. See Bedeschi, *La Sinistra cristiana*; Bedeschi, *Cattolici e comunisti*; Tramontin, *Sinistre cattoliche di ieri e di oggi*; Giura Longo, *La sinistra cattolica in Italia*; Bedeschi et al., *I cristiani nella sinistra dalla Resistenza a oggi*; Pombeni, *Socialismo e cristianesimo*; Brena and Pirola, *Movimenti cristiani di sinistra*. For the ideological contexts of political Catholicism in particular, see Traniello, "Cattolicesimo e società moderna"; Scoppola, "La democrazia nel pensiero politico cattolico"; Baget Bozzo, "Il fascismo e l'evoluzione del pensiero politico cattolico"; Brezzi, *Il cattolicesimo politico in Italia*; Campanini, *Cristianesimo e democrazia*. For the attitudes towards Catholics of the various components of the Italian Left, see Zunino, *La questione cattolica*; Portelli, *Gramsci e la questione religiosa*; Botti, *Religione, questione cattolica*. For the historical and ideological problems of the period as a whole, see Campanini and Traniello, eds., *Dizionario storico del movimento cattolico in Italia*; Malgeri, ed., *Storia del movimento cattolico in Italia*; Berti and Campanini, eds., *Dizionario delle idee politiche*. For the history of Italy during the period I refer the reader to Vecchio, Saresella and Trionfini, *Storia dell'Italia contemporanea*.

them: Catholics were considered as a sociological or political reality, who unified different things together as a force of the "Left".

With greater precision the term *"sinistra cristiana"* (Christian Left) has been used to denote the ethical or religious inspiration of persons or movements firmly placed in the spectrum of the political Left: the term had been historically used to denote a specific organised political experience. The cognate term *cristiani di sinistra* (Christians of the Left) has also been used in common parlance with the same meaning, but to emphasise the personal choice of individual intellectuals, exponents of the clergy, or lay organisations whose political stance on the Left was well known. The term *cristiani nella sinistra* (Christians in the Left), on the other hand, is preferred to denote the organised experience of groups, movements and parties characterised by an explicit political (and also ideological) program of the Left. Lastly, the term *sinistra democristiana* (Christian Democratic Left) is used to denote those political currents placed towards the left of the spectrum within the *Democrazia Cristiana* (DC).

The following criteria will be used to identify the experiences of the Christian of the Left discussed below. The first is political independence from the ecclesiastical hierarchy. It involves two consequences: namely, that the persons and groups to which we refer did not intend to involve the ecclesiastical hierarchy's responsibilities in their own political initiatives; instead, they claimed the right as laymen to make their own independent political decisions and the positive value of exercising their own responsibility by responding to the need to realise Christian values and by adopting the means historically most appropriate for doing so. The second criterion is that their activities have given rise to a political identity independent of the DC, given that the DC, by its very inter-class nature, would have been unable to carry out but a moderate and conservative policy due to the predominance in it of those representing particularly strong economic and social interests. The third refers to their decision to have identified the trade union federation and the parties of the Left as privileged interlocutors for a policy of the Left. The fourth refers to their decision to have considered political democracy and social progress, even in their most radical forms, as primary values that are inseparably linked and that need to be realised together: a policy of the Left, in fact, would not be characterised as such merely by paternalistically considering popular classes and sections of society as its passive beneficiaries, but only by promoting their active involvement as political protagonists in their own right.

These criteria are met, and these characteristics found, in the political experiences of, on the one hand, the *Movimento dei Cattolici Comunisti* and its heir, the *Partito della Sinistra Cristiana*, and, on the other, the *Movimento* (later *Partito*) *Cristiano-Sociale*, which was a rival of the former movement and offered an alternative to it. We will also discuss *Cronache sociali*, a progressive current within the DC (whose exponents were also called *dossettiani* after the name of the group's leader Giuseppe Dossetti): it originated, in part, from impulses similar to those that had given rise to the former movements, but also, at a precise moment, from the political hypothesis of using the party to implement them. But, before directly tackling the analysis of all of these experiences, some general components of the Italian "case" need to be briefly recalled. This will enable us to understand the existence of longer-term problems that still persisted in the 1940s and 1950s.

In the history of the Catholic movement in Italy the moderate or conservative majority currents were opposed by minority currents which may be considered either as "Left Catholic" or "Left Christian". Antisocialism, originally the dominant motive, had been for some the main driving force leading them to socially and politically radical positions in order to oppose socialism on its own terrain, accusing socialists of collusion with bourgeois and Masonic circles. Nor were there lacking those who considered democracy as the terrain for the supercession of the liberal state, and who had proposed collaboration with radicals and socialists as a necessary channel for its realisation. This had happened in the early years of the 20th century. It had happened in the years immediately following the First World War during the experience of the *Partito Popolare Italiano* (PPI). And it had happened in the opposition to the rise of fascism, when the problem of collaboration with the communists had been posed for the first time, and in the struggle against fascism once it had become a regime.

During the fascist period, however, significant new developments had taken place. The best known was the *ralliement* of the Church of Pius XI towards the regime, with the objective of reconquering society through the institutional safeguard of the Church's activities. This had led to the Church winning an area protected from the direct influence, or interference, of fascism, both in the educational institutions for the young and in the organisations of *Azione Cattolica*, which were placed directly under the authority of the bishops. In this context, moreover, a strong influence was exerted by a markedly hierarchical conception of the relations between laity, clergy and bishops founded on the theology of the *Corpus Mysticum*, according to which the Catholic laity acts *in temporalibus* not according to its own designs, but in response to a mandate of the bishops, whose hierarchical apostolate it was called to assist. But, at the cultural level, we should also recall the strong reaffirmation of Thomism as the foundation of Catholic culture in opposition to the idealism of Giovanni Gentile, the most influential philosopher of fascism. This also meant the fundamental distinction between the natural and the supernatural: according to an evolutionary interpretation, this would have meant that the supernatural was the field of theology and the teaching of the bishops, whereas the natural was the field of science, including that of the social and political sciences, and also the field of the activity of the laity.

During the fascist period, a kind of interruption took place in the political memory of Catholics with regard to the tradition of the Catholic movement and of the PPI. The result was that the new generations of Catholic youth sought new cultures for inspiration, and this took place in a context in which the objective was more that of correcting totalitarianism than of building a democracy which was unfamiliar to them and which seemed unattainable in the 1930s. The opposition of those Catholics who were also antifascists was thus characterised, above all, as moral and cultural opposition. It was motivated more by confessional reasons (against what was perceived as anti-Christian) than by political reasons (against what was perceived as antidemocratic): the majority of militant Catholics thus sought the foundations of a social rather than a political culture.[2]

This may be exemplified by the characteristics of some experiences of Catholic intellectuals. As early as the 1920s, Gerardo Bruni, former militant of the PPI and philosopher with a special interest in scholasticism, had begun to conduct research and to publish studies on the relations between politics and philosophy, and between politics and society, that had found corroboration in the writings of Jacques Maritain.[3] In the course of the 1930s Igino Giordani, he too a former exponent of the PPI, had, in a series of books and articles, sought in patristics the foundations of a form of political action inspired by Christianity.[4] In 1939 Giorgio La Pira founded the review *Principi* in Florence. At its basis was a "return to the clarifying light of principles".[5] In 1943 the so-called "Code of Camaldoli" was drawn up by members of the *Istituto Cattolico di Attività Sociali* and exponents of the Movement of Catholic Graduates. Entitled *Per la comunità cristiana. Principi dell'ordinamento sociale a cura di un gruppo di amici di Camaldoli* (For the Christian Community. Principles of the Social Order Drawn Up by a Group of Friends of Camaldoli), it was not published till 1945 but was already circulating in the underground: it represented a *summa* of thought on society, on the economy and on the state in the light of Catholic doctrine.[6] In 1944 Father Roberto Angeli gave a series of lectures to young university students in Livorno, with the title *Appunti di dottrina sociale cristiana* (Notes on Christian social doctrine)[7]: other similar lectures were being given elsewhere in Italy. Between 1942 and 1944, members of the DC in many places were formulating programs for the reorganisation of society a good deal more radical that those of the *Idee ricostruttive della DC*, drawn up and circulated by De Gasperi in 1943.[8]

All these different experiences had a common denominator, one that was typical of Catholic culture, but that also represented its limitation: that of seeking a model for an ideal society faithful to the principles by which Christianity is inspired, but that was little rooted in the concrete analysis of the dynamics of the classes and social groups and the real conditions of political and institutional life. Paying attention only, or mainly, to cultural formulations and to theoretical aspects may have its interest, but without a search for corresponding forms of social and political behaviour it may lead to errors in perspective. We may thus find the affirmation of programs that, in a personalist perspective[9], supported the intervention of the state in the economy, or the mixed economy as the "third way" between capitalism and state socialism, or a decentralised, almost federalist state organisation, based on strong local autonomy, etc. But what was needed, apart from this theo-

---

2. See Parisella, "Il laicato cattolico"; Vecchio, "Il laicato cattolico di fronte alla guerra".
3. See Parisella, "Bruni Gerardo".
4. See Sorgi, ed., *Igino Giordani*.
5. See *La Pira o gli anni di "Principi"*.
6. Falciatore, ed., *Il Codice di Camaldoli*.
7. See Merli, *Le lezioni in Santa Giulia di don Roberto Angeli*.
8. See Varnier, ed., *Idee e programmi della DC nella Resistenza*.
9. Social personalism is the current of thought which argues that the values of the person and the rights of the person should become the main criteria for the evaluation of political and institutional life; see Rigobello, "Persona".

retical input, was to ascertain how persons and groups were concretely involved in the existing social and political dynamics. With the Resistance to the Nazi occupation and to the fascism of the *Repubblica Sociale Italiana* (RSI), an important shift did in fact take place in the direction of realism: it led to the adoption of political options that had as their content the effectiveness of the struggle for liberation. It was necessary to seek other partners who would enable that struggle to be conducted in as efficient a manner as possible and to seek agreement with them, even if that meant overcoming mutual mistrust and particularly strong ideological contrasts. This was possible for the experiences that gave rise to parties and movements, but was less characteristic of social experiences. One of the main reasons for this was that, during the years of fascism, a powerful control over the activities of the laity had been developed by the bishops, and this persisted also in the immediate postwar period. Organisations such as the *Confederazione delle Cooperative Italiane* (CCI) or the *Associazioni Cristiane dei Lavoratori Italiani* (ACLI) and others had been promoted by the *Istituto Cattolico di Attività Sociali* (ICAS)[10], while an agreement between FIAT and the *Opera Nazionale per Assistenza Religiosa e Morale agli Operai* (ONARMO) for the provision of pastoral care in factories had already been in operation since 1940. The agreement stipulated the terms for the provision of pastoral care in factories, and regulated the activities of industrial chaplains: it would later be extended to other firms through an agreement with the manufacturers' federation, the *Confederazione Generale dell'Industria Italiana* (Confindustria).

2. Communist Catholics and the Christian Left (1937-1945)[11]

In 1937 a group of members of the youth movement of *Azione Cattolica* in the popular neighbourhoods in South Rome issued a brief document with the title *I nostri doveri oggi* (Our Duties Today). In the space of a few lines they summed up convictions and commitments that expressed opposition to fascist dictatorship and the wish to combat it:

"1) *Azione Cattolica* may represent since 1931 [in 1931 fascist attacks had been mounted against Catholic youth clubs – A.P.] the one mass organisation capable of educating Catholics in antifascism; 2) it is necessary, however, to descend from the level of moral protest to that of political struggle; 3) the underground political struggle conducted with all means and with all its risks (prison, etc.) may save us as Catholics from dramatic responsibili-

---

10. ICAS had been founded in 1925 with the aim of maintaining the teachings of Catholic social thought alive within economic organisations which, in order to survive, had become incorporated in the fascist apparatus. It had become a specialised technical agency of *Azione Cattolica* by 1943, and after Liberation was given the task of promoting the reorganisation of various Catholic associations of social and professional groups. See Maggi, "L'Istituto cattolico di attività sociale".
11. Bedeschi, *La Sinistra cristiana e il dialogo con i comunisti*; Bedeschi, *Cattolici e comunisti*; Casula, *Cattolici-comunisti e Sinistra cristiana*; Cocchi and Montesi, eds., *Per una storia della Sinistra cristiana*; Antonetti, *L'ideologia della Sinistra cristiana*; Parisella, "I cattolici-comunisti e la sinistra cristiana"; Ruggieri and Albani, *Cattolici comunisti?*; Malgeri, *La Sinistra cristiana*; Papini, *Tra storia e profezia*.

ties (racism, war) and set in motion the one thing to be done: destroying fascism; 4) to achieve this, while not breaking with the past (*Partito Popolare*), we need to distinguish ourselves from it due to the split that it in fact represents in the unity of the popular forces (save for a few exceptions) and due to the party's resistance to passing from moral protest to the political protest of active daily struggle; 5) we need in this viciously fought struggle to explode the myth of the political unity of all Catholics, exploited and exploiters alike, by promoting a movement of the Christian Left".[12]

It should be stressed in the first place, that the issuing of this document was an act committed by young lay people, who thus expressed their determination to act independently of the Church hierarchy, because they felt themselves responsible for the conduct of the entire Catholic world towards fascism. In the second place, it should be pointed out that the document's judgment on the political experience of Catholics and the identification of present and future commitments were based on realistic non-ideological analyses.

In the course of the following year, the group, to which the blanket name *Cattolici antifascisti* (anti-Fascist Catholics) was given, and whose main exponents were Paolo Pecoraro (who drafted the document and was ordained priest in 1940) and Adriano Ossicini (son of a former exponent of the PPI[13]), tried to get other youth groups, representing both students and workers, in Rome and in other towns of central Italy, to merge with it: particularly important was the meeting with other middle-class youth from secondary schools and associations of central Rome. They included Franco Rodano, later to become cultural leader of the group and one of the most important intellectuals of the Italian Left.

In a phase in which the underground activity consisted especially in the diffusion of propaganda materials and meetings for the education of activists, the contribution of Franco Rodano was essential for the group's theoretical production.[14] It is to him, in essence, that the drafting of two documents is due: the first - written jointly with Adriano Ossicini and Paolo Pecoraro - with the title *Manifesto del Partito cooperativista sinarchico*, issued in 1941; and the second with the title *La proprietà*, in 1942.

From 1942 on, the links with the communist youth of Rome, the nucleus of the future leadership group of the Communist Party in the capital, became closer. At the same time the group changed its name to *Partito Comunista Cristiano* (PCC). Its program was drafted by Franco Rodano in 1942 and accompanied, in the early months of 1943, by two sets of directives: the *Direttive per l'attività politica del militante nell'ambiente borghese* (Directives for the Political Activity of the Activist in the Middle-Class Environment) and *Dal gruppetto clandestino al lavoro di massa* (From the Underground Grouplet to Work Amongst the Masses). In the party's first

---

12. For the text of the document: Cocchi and Montesi, eds., *Per una storia della Sinistra cristiana*, 14.
13. Of the numerous autobiographical writings by Adriano Ossicini, see for instance Declich, ed., *Cristiani non democristiani*; Ossicini, *Il cristiano e la politica*; Ossicini, *L'isola in mezzo al fiume*.
14. On Franco Rodano, apart from Del Noce, *Il cattolico comunista*, see Mustè, *Franco Rodano*; Papini, "La formazione di un giovane cattolico". See also Possenti, *Cattolicesimo modernità*.

documents the main concern was to strike the right balance between ideological and political decisions. Critiques were mounted at once against forms of fascism and bourgeois democracy, and against the tradition of Catholic social culture (rights to property, anti-state mentality, co-operatives, etc.). At the same time, they indulged in speculation on the ideal model of society. But now the struggle against fascism became the central concern and was set in a historical and political context in which the value of the class struggle, the destruction of the bourgeois state, the dictatorship of the proletariat and the historic role of the *Partito Communista Italiano* (PCI), of the USSR and of the Third International, were recognized. Even if its absolute independence from them – as also from the Church – was proclaimed, the party nonetheless expressed its willingness to collaborate with them on the basis of specific agreements. The organisational independence from the PCI derived from the atheist premise that the Communist Party still maintained.

In 1941 and in 1942 the members of the group, or *comunisti cristiani*, had already suffered arrests and repression. On Easter Sunday 1943, together with their companions in the PCI, they held a demonstration for peace in the Piazza San Pietro, on the occasion of the Pope's blessing: following this event, they suffered a massive number of arrests and almost disappeared from the scene until the collapse of fascism (25 July 1943). During the 45 days of the Badoglio government that preceded the military defeat of 8 September 1943 and the Nazi occupation of Italy[15], the group's exponents were freed from detention and for a short time called themselves *Sinistra Giovanile Cattolica* (Catholic Youth Left). Then, once their underground struggle had resumed, they established the armed formation of the *Movimento dei Cattolici Comunisti* (MCC), the third in numerical size of those operating in Rome. From the political point of view, attempts at entering into partnership with other groups of Catholic inspiration had failed during the brief intermission of political freedom; the groups in question then entered either the DC or the *Movimento Cristiano Sociale* (about which see below). This turn of events led to closer relations with the communists, while the adoption of the name "movement" in the group's title also implied a recognition of the strategy and political platform of the PCI, from which only the religious question continued to separate it.

At the ideological level, the clarification contained in the pamphlet *Il comunismo e i cattolici* dates to this period. It was written by Fedele D'Amico, on the basis of opinions shared and principles enunciated by Franco Rodano and Adriano Ossicini, with whom the philosopher Felice Balbo had also associated himself. The key element of the document is a dual distinction, both on the Catholic and the marxist side: the distinction

---

15. On the night of 24-25 July 1943 the *Gran Consiglio del fascismo* asked the King to resume the military command. Vittorio Emanuele III, in response, dismissed Mussolini and ordered his arrest. He appointed Pietro Badoglio, *maresciallo d'Italia*, to head the government. Badoglio began secret negotiations with the Allies for a separate peace: the armistice, including an unconditional surrender, was announced on 8 September. The government and the King moved from Rome to Brindisi, while the Germans occupied Italy, leaving the nation in a situation of chaos and the armed forces in disarray. During these same critical days the antifascist parties formed the *Comitato di Liberazione Nazionale*: under its political guidance the Resistance began.

between religion and politics, between ends (supernatural, theological, the responsibility of the authorities of the Church) and means (historical, social, technical, the responsibility of the laity), on the one hand; and the distinction between dialectical materialism (as general view of the world and philosophy of history) and historical materialism (as historico-critical analysis of economic and social dynamics, and hence as sphere of social and political science), on the other. The result was the affirmation that it was possible to reconcile a religious view of the world with a social and political practice based on marxist analysis. Another salient point lay in the distinction between the Church as religious reality and as historical reality: it was affirmed that the antireligious premise of communism could be overcome, because religion could be presented as not necessarily counter-revolutionary, while the historical and material organisation of the churches – as in Russia and Spain – could be admitted as an obstacle to revolution, precisely because it generated anticlericalism. As regards the attitude of the Catholic Church to fascism and Nazism, a distinction could be drawn between the acts of self-preservation, such as the policy of the Concordat, and the acts of dissociation and condemnation based on the fundamental incompatibility between the two, in just the same way as, in the struggle then in progress, the conduct of the laity and antifascist priests might have seemed to contradict that of the bishops and priests more tolerant to the Nazi occupying forces and the fascists. This theme was to be examined and elucidated by D'Amico himself, by Rodano and by Balbo, especially in the columns of *Voce operaia*, the paper of the Movement both in its underground phase and later in its legal phase following the liberation of Rome (4 June 1944).[16]

Having emerged from the underground and entered the broad daylight of public life, the exponents of the Movement, the *cattolici comunisti*, made an important politico-strategic choice. They rejected, in the first place, the idea of seeking support among the rural population (the *contadini*) because they rejected the traditional canons of the communist idea (Lenin, Gramsci) on the propaedeutic value of Christianity, understood as the ideology of the most backward sectors of the popular classes, in contrast to atheist socialism and communism (dialectical materialism), understood as the ideology of the working class. But this meant abandoning a terrain for mass action and leaving the field free to the activity of the DC among the rural population. Criticised and rebuked by the *Osservatore romano*, the *cattolici comunisti* avoided developing the polemic at the ecclesial level or adopting the two solutions proposed to them: that of ceasing their activity as an organised movement, and that of individually joining either the DC or the PCI. In the summer of 1944 they decided instead to promote a new political formation, the *Partito della Sinistra Cristiana* (PSC). In establishing this new party they were joined by a part of the leadership group of the *Movimento Cristiano Sociale* (MCS) and also by exponents of Catholic associations and of the

---

16. See Malgeri, *"Voce Operaia". Dei cattolicicommunisti alla Sinistra cristiana*.

Christian Democratic Left around *Politica d'oggi*, which had been defeated in the congress of their party in Naples.17

From the ideological point of view, the decision to establish the new party may seem an entrenchment in positions that seemed to privilege political confessionalism at the expense of class affiliation. Yet the coherence with which its theoretical and political views were reiterated in the party's documents showed how firm its rootedness in the strategy and tactics of the political Left and especially of the PCI really was. In line with the policies of the latter and with those of the other two parties of the Left – the *Partito d'Azione* (PDA) and the *Partito Socialista Italiano di Unità Proletaria* (PSIUP) – the PSC endorsed the proposal of "progressive democracy", i.e. the overcoming of representative democracy through forms of decentralised participation, spread throughout the national territory, and based on the role of the parties and national unions and associations, such as the General Confederation of Italian Trade Unions (CGIL), the *Unione delle Donne Italiane* (UDI, the Union of Italian Women), the youth organisation *Fronte della Gioventù*, the National Partisans' Association of Italy (ANPI), etc. These types of organisation would, in the view of the new party, have permitted the main economic and social problems to be tackled, in the sense of the struggle against privileges and the correction of inequalities. More than to ideal programs, the PSC had recourse to feasible options vis-à-vis the *de facto* relations then in the process of being established. In this way – as in the case of the PDA – the experience of the Resistance and of the *Comitati di Liberazione Nazionale* (CLN) as new protagonists of political and institutional life were in some sense projected into the postwar period.18

Despite the understandable opposition in Catholic circles and obstacles raised by exponents of the DC, the life of the PSC – also thanks to the particular ability of its cadres and leaders – enjoyed a degree of organisational success in many liberated provinces, especially in central Italy. Cadres and militants of the PSC were present in the local administrations and in the mass organisations formed after Liberation. In those in northern Italy, where the partisan struggle continued, there was an active campaign against Nazis and fascists by groups and by individuals who supported the *Movimento dei Lavoratori Cristiani* (MLC, the Christian Workers' Movement), with its

17. *Politica d'oggi* was the title of a review published in Rome between 1944 and 1948. Its editor Domenico Ravaioli had been an exponent of the *Democrazia Cristiana* of Romolo Murri and then of the PPI of Luigi Sturzo. This review - like the contemporary *Politica sociale* edited by Giovanni Gronchi, another exponent of the first *Democrazia Cristiana* and the PPI, and secretary of the Catholic Italian Trade Union Federation - played a role of internal opposition on the left wing of the DC of De Gasperi, supporting the implementation of a program favourable to the Republic, to trade union unity and to unity with the parties of the Left. Associated with the review were, among others, the jurist Costantino Mortati (one of the "fathers" of the Constitution of the Italian Republic), the journalist Quinto Tosatti, and the sociologist and economist Alberto Canaletti Gaudenti, who published in its pages the research he carried out when he was a companion of Gerardo Bruni in the *Movimento Cristiano Sociale*. Ravaioli also published another short-lived periodical, *Tendenza* (1946), in support of the campaign in favour of the Republic in the institutional referendum of 2 June 1946. His most important documents are the appeal *Parole chiare di un gruppo di democratici cristiani* (1944) and the booklet *Politica di sinistra nella Democrazia cristiana* (1945). On *Politica d'oggi* see, in particular Boffi, "Domenico Ravaioli".
18. On this in particular, see Malgeri, "I programmi dei cattolici comunisti".

periodical *La voce del lavoratore*, and who, after the Liberation of Italy (25 April 1945), would join the PSC.[19] Attempts were made in vain to involve in the life of the party Guido Miglioli, the former leader (prior to fascism) of the Catholic peasant movement in the Val Padana and leader of the Left within the PPI.[20]

But, paradoxically, it was precisely the political phase marked by the reinforcement of the PSC and the qualified success of its political initiative that was characterised by a change in the general context that jeopardised the very hypothesis on which the party had been founded. In fact, in the autumn of 1945 the government of Ferruccio Parri – the resistance leader of the PDA appointed Prime Minister after Liberation – collapsed, and with it the partnership between the six parties of the CLN. It was succeeded by a government led by the Christian Democrat leader Alcide De Gasperi and supported by a coalition between the DC, PCI and PSIUP. In these circumstances the destiny of "progressive democracy" seemed to be reduced to the formulation of conditions for defining the form of the state – by the referendum of 2 June 1946 – and for electing the Constituent Assembly that very same day. It was the DC that, in the strategy of the Left and of the PCI, was recognised as interlocutor, since it represented the broad mass of the Catholic population; and the results of the election would confirm this role.

Two possible ways ahead lay open to the PSC: either that of remaining alive as a combative minority political group, with a role more of witness than as creator of political initiatives; or that of winding itself up and allowing its cadres and political leaders – who brought with them considerable experience, rapidly amassed in the underground struggle – to amalgamate themselves with the major political forces. The choice between these two options divided the leadership and the party's first congress, held in December 1945: the former option was favoured by Adriano Ossicini, Mario Montesi, the former members of the *Movimento Cristiano Sociale* and the more recently established organisations; the latter by the *cattolici comunisti*, headed by Franco Rodano. Albeit by a small margin, it was the latter option that won the day, with the result that – a rare event in political life – the party declared its own dissolution.

3. The Movimento and Partito Cristiano-Sociale (1938-1953)[21]

The experience of the *Movimento Cristiano Sociale* (MCS) took place almost concurrently with that of the *cattolici comunisti*. The two groups shared the aspiration to establish a political formation of Christians of the Left, but differed in their political and ideological views and in their plat-

---

19. The geography of the PSC is analytically reconstructed by Malgeri, *La Sinistra cristiana*, on the basis of the maps of the party's organisation office now in the archives of the Istituto Luigi Sturzo, Rome (Archivio Gabriele De Rosa).
20. See Leonori, ed., *La figura e l'opera di Guido Miglioli*; Casula, *Guido Miglioli*; Parisella, "Guido Miglioli".
21. See Tramontin, "Partito cristiano-sociale"; Parisella, "Il Partito cristiano-sociale"; Parisella, "Unità proletaria o Democrazia cristiana?"; Parisella, ed., *Gerardo Bruni e i cristiano-sociali*; Parisella, "I programmi dei cristiano-sociali italiani"; Merli, *Le lezioni di Santa Giulia di don Roberto Angeli*.

form. The platform of the MCS was more consonant with the cultural tradition of the Catholic movement. The movement's inspiration ultimately derived from the social encyclicals and the teachings of Luigi Sturzo, reviewed in the light of innovative developments in philosophy, political science and sociology made in France during the 1920s and 1930s: Nicolaj Berdiaev, Georges Gurvitch, Jacques Maritain, Boris Mirkine Guetzevitch and Emmanuel Mounier.

The movement's first document was a mimeographed handbill with the title *Biblioteca di studi cristiano sociali*, distributed in Catholic intellectual circles in 1939. Under the guise of a network of libraries of social studies, the objective was pursued of linking official or spontaneous groups or associations around a project initially cultural and educational in aim, but with a longer-term goal of formulating social and indirectly political programs and measures. Couched in the ambiguous language of a document calculated to deceive the fascist censorship, it explicitly enunciated the project "of creating a huge educational movement that would penetrate all of society, with the creation of reciprocal and profound knowledge concerning the various social environments and promoting exchanges of experiences and points of view in such a way that the formulation, examination and proposed solutions of the various problems be as well-adapted to the complex reality as possible". Somewhat more clearly defined was the type of protagonists to be involved in the enterprise: "a large number of scholars of proven ability", "an extensive network of objective informers", "a wider circle of sympathisers who, once seriously informed of the various problems, would diffuse a knowledge of them especially among the working class, peasant, student and white-collar masses". Privileged sectors of intervention were the "education of the person", the family, the world of work and social relations.

The promoter of the project was Gerardo Bruni, former young militant of the PPI and closely associated with Luigi Sturzo. After the advent of fascism, he was employed by the Vatican Apostolic Library together with Igino Giordani. Later he became closely associated with Alcide De Gasperi. A philosopher, Gerardo Bruni had been a protagonist of the international movement for the renewal of scholasticism during the 1920s and 1930s: his *Riflessioni sulla scolastica* (Rome: Bardi, 1927) had at first been reviewed by Monsignor Francesco Olgiati in the *Rivista di filosofia neoscolastica* (September/October 1928), the journal of the Università Cattolica in Milan and by James H. Ryan in *The New Scholasticism* (January 1928), the journal of the Catholic University of Washington; subsequently it was published in an expanded English edition with the title *Progressive Scholasticism* (St. Louis-London: Herder, 1929), translated and introduced by John S. Zybura. Bruni had also published studies and articles on political and moral philosophy in a number of authoritative Catholic academic journals (*Vita e pensiero, Rivista internazionale di scienze sociali, Rivista di morale e di diritto, Bollettino filosofico* of the Pontifical Lateran University, *Studium, Fides*) and in the Vatican newspaper itself, the *Osservatore romano*. From the study of general problems of the relation between theology, philosophy and politics, Bruni had, in the course of time, progressed to the problem of the relation between state and citizen and between state and civil society and, finally, to the more positive aspects – echoing Maritain, but in a fairly independent way – of the "new humanism" and the "new order".[22] Apart from Igino Giordani and Alcide De Gasperi, he was also in close contact with other men particularly influential in the culture of the new generations of Catholics, such as Guido Gonella and Giorgio La Pira. Moreover, he had maintained links with other exponents of pre-fascist Christian populism and syndicalism and had developed new relations with young intellectuals of the *Federazione degli Universitari Cattolici* (FUCI) and the Movement of Catholic Graduates: they included, in particular, Paolo Emilio Taviani, an economist and social scientist, then a young secondary-school teacher in Pisa and lecturer at the University of Genoa, and later leading exponent of the Resistance in Genoa, member of the Constituent Assembly, member of parliament and government minister in the ranks of the DC.[23] The idea of promoting the formation of active and socially committed "cadres" in a new movement of Christian inspiration, ultimately aimed at political action, had been developed together with Anna Maria Enriques. She was a young Jewish medieval historian and archivist who had decided to convert to Catholicism, but who – after the racial laws issued by the Fascist regime in 1938 – had decided to share the fate of her own family and had therefore refused the baptism that would have saved her from discrimination. On losing her state job, she too was taken onto the staff of the Vatican Library, where she became friends with Ada Alessandrini, another young scholar who was subsequently to play a role in the movements of the Christian Left (about which see below). Active in the Resistance in Florence, Anna Maria Enriques was executed by a Nazi firing squad at Cercina (Florence) in 1944.

To clarify the sources of the Christian-social ideas that lay behind the *Movimento Cristiano Sociale* we may refer to two texts written by Gerardo Bruni in the same period. Published in two journals of philosophic and religious culture destined for a specialised public, and hence exempted from rigid control by the fascist censorship, they were distributed as offprints. The first, with the title *Odierni indirizzi della filosofia sociale*, was the text of a lecture given by Bruni in Rome and published by the *Bollettino filosofico* in early 1940; the second, published in the journal *Fides* with the title *L'ordine nuovo nel pensiero di S. S. Pio XII*, was a comment on an address given by Pope Pius XII for Pentecost 1941, on the occasion of the tenth anniversary of *Quadragesimo Anno* and the fiftieth anniversary of *Rerum Novarum*. The point of departure in both these papers is a fundamental critique of nationalist and racist regimes which are founded not on the primacy of the person, but on that of a collective and abstract subject – the nation, the race – on which the absolute power of the state is based. Historically such regimes were the expression of the reaction by the European ruling classes who, after the First World War, and in response to the advent of the masses, had rejected the policies and solutions proposed by the reform-oriented movements and parties. A mere return to liberal regimes was, in Bruni's view, inconceivable, because they were based on an "economistic"

---

22. The numerous studies of Gerardo Bruni in part precede and in part were published contemporaneously with the works of the French philosopher, whose inspiration and method they share.
23. See Brizzolari, *Un archivio della Resistenza genovese*; Bartolozzi Batignani, *Dai progetti cristiano-sociali alla Costituente*.

and individualistic conception of man: a conception that had produced gross concentrations of wealth and curbed the very liberties it proclaimed, thus giving rise to inequalities and to conflicts, both domestic and international. Nor was a communist perspective desirable, because in it economism and statism not only suppressed freedom, but were also combined with atheism. So what Bruni called "new order" ought to have as its basis the humanism of the person. And the objective of this ought to be the dismantling of inequalities and the struggle against poverty by the action of the public authorities to regulate the use of property and its diffusion, through a political regime based on support and consensus freely expressed and on the guarantee of the rights of the person and of intermediate social groups. At the international level, a supranational authority would have to regulate political and economic relations and prevent conflicts.

Between 1941 and 1942 the movement's search for relations and contacts with local groups continued. But as a result of military conscription, such contacts were established mainly with representatives of the older generations or with the very young: particularly effective were those established in the regions of central Italy, in the Veneto and in Liguria. It was also significant that the young members of the *Partito Cooperativista Sinarchico* should have tried to reach an agreement with Bruni: in fact he met with Adriano Ossicini, Paolo Pecoraro and Franco Rodano. Though their differences in terms of their historical and social analysis and their conception of property were not inconsiderable, they could be clarified and overcome. But what was for Bruni an insurmountable obstacle, and what was for the members of the *Partito Cooperativista Sinarchico* an unrelinquishable condition, was the strategic choice of the communists as privileged interlocutor. Gerardo Bruni also had meetings and discussions with Alcide De Gasperi – who in mid 1942 was also seeking relations with various groups in order to absorb them into the DC – and was invited to the meetings that former members of the PPI held in the house of the lawyer Giuseppe Spataro in Rome to formulate a joint program. To these meetings, however, he was no longer invited due to his radical positions on matters of property and the non-confessional character of the state.

On 27 and 28 March 1943 Gerardo Bruni gathered together various representatives of local groups of the MCS for its first underground "national congress": it was held in a convent for nuns. Some of the delegates, former militants of the PPI and Catholic trade unionism, subsequently entered the DC; others abandoned Bruni for De Gasperi at the time of the congress. They included Alberto Canaletti Gaudenti, sociologist and economist, who had drawn up the economic guidelines for the MCS program. Approved at the congress, though only diffused in August, the program identified statism, nationalism, racism and capitalism as the mortal enemies of freedom and social justice. At the top of the program's agenda were the rights of the person, the freedoms of association, of the press, of teaching and of religion, and the independence of social groups. The Constituent Assembly would have the job of deciding on the form of the state, which ought to be founded on active employment as the condition to enjoy political rights. As far as economic organisation was concerned, the program did make some provision for a sector of state-run nationalised enterprises (banks, insurance houses, transport, strategic industrial sectors), as well as a sector of free competition, with forms of profit-sharing and worker participation in management, and a sector of free ownership for artisans and peasants. On the international level the program called for the overcoming of forms of nationalism and conflicts in the framework of a federal organisation of Europe and an organisation of relations between states based on disarmament, free trade, and free access to raw materials.

During the summer of 1943 the numerous contacts aimed at promoting a union between the MCS and the DC failed to bear fruit, though the DC continued to attract individual exponents of the movement (such as Paolo Emilio Taviani) and hence reinforced its internal tendencies favorable to a Republic and to a more radical social program. After the Nazi occupation, the members of the MCS fought – armed and unarmed – in the Resistance, both in their own formations (Rome), and in joint formations commanded by others (Tuscany, Umbria, Veneto). They signed alliances pledging unity of action with the PSIUP in Rome and with the PDA in Florence. But then these parties decided that the right to politically represent Catholics should be granted exclusively to the DC, which opposed the admission of members of the MCS to the central *Comitato di Liberazione Nazionale* (CLN) (they were present in some of the local CLNs). The ranks of the MCS were not only thinned by defections, but also by wartime atrocities: the victims included Anna Maria Enriques and Dante Lenci. Others were deported to concentration camps, some of whom, like Father Roberto Angeli, had taken part in some important military engagements against the Nazis in central Italy (Collalto Sabino, in the province of Rieti, and Monticchiello, in the province of Siena) and helped some underground military operations (Livorno).

After the liberation of Rome the *cristiano-sociali* decided to change their name from *Movimento* to *Partito*, but went through a very difficult period: on the one hand the DC, strengthened by the support of the clergy and of the Catholic organisations but also by the recognition of its role by the parties of the Left, won the allegiance of Catholic militants in the various liberated provinces; on the other, Christian Social activists rejected the attempt of the *cattolici comunisti* to absorb them into the PSC, considering the latter too close to the strategy of the PCI. Within the party there was a change in membership, with new recruits replacing older ones. This determined the need to produce educational materials of an ideological nature for the new members. Thus, while the party began to engage with domestic and international politics in the pages of *Azione sociale*, its pamphlets *Chi siamo, Il nostro impegno, I presupposti storico-dottrinali, Noi e il comunismo* and *Noi lavoratori* offered its critique of contemporary society on the one hand and of communism on the other. These critiques closely reflected the teachings of Jacques Maritain (with whom, on his arrival in Rome as French ambassador to the Holy See, Bruni was to have frequent meetings). In the course of the following year, when the elections for the Constituent Assembly were approaching, the party updated its program. It was important that the question of the non-confessional nature of the state and the equal freedom of all religious confessions should be emphasised. In the same way, it was significant that support should be given to the rights to life, to work and to the use of property, understood as freedom from need, and, together with these rights, those that completed the rights of the person, such as freedom of teaching, the right to free primary education and the right to have access to secondary schooling. These were the conditions to realize the "classic" freedoms of association, press and political activity. But equally important, in the party's new program, was the need to combat the abuses of the administration and the system of justice by reasserting the freedoms of the individual vis-à-vis the state and those of the intermediate social entities. According to the principles of social and juridical pluralism, the state ought to give them and local institutions – municipalities, provinces, regions – the opportunity to satisfy the needs of the citizens directly in a decentralized manner. At the apex of the pyramid of power ought to be a bicameral parliament, a head of state other than the head of the government, and a supreme court guaranteeing constitutional rights. In its economic and social part, the program contained no innovations: it essentially recycled the policies already contained in the former programs of the MCS. From the political point of view, after the failure of the attempt to establish relations with Guido Miglioli, the PCS could for a certain period count on the support of Adriano Olivetti, industrialist, publisher and intellectual who was inspired by the communitarian ideas of Emmanuel Mounier, but this contact too was later broken off in a painful manner.

In the elections to the Constituent Assembly the PCS performed poorly, obtaining just slightly more than 50.000 votes, but it did at least succeed in getting its leader elected as a deputy. He took part in the assembly's work, with some interventions of considerable intellectual stature. In some he tackled the most dramatic problems of the nation's social and economic situation. He urged the three mass parties to show a greater commitment to combining a short-term economic policy, based on the business cycle (wages, prices, food), with a policy of full employment and reform (currency exchange; agrarian reform; nationalisation of banks, insurance houses and hydro-electrical industries). In other speeches, he expounded the thought of the PCS on some problems of vital importance for the organisation of the state. First, he argued against any incorporation of the provisions of the Lateran Pacts of 11 February 1929 in the Constitution, not only because they had been stipulated by the fascist regime, but because the policy of the Concordat was in contradiction to full democracy. Second, he declared himself favorable to freedom of education, understood both as freedom to teach and freedom to choose the form of teaching, but at the same time he supported an integrated school system comprising a mix of public and private schools, placed on a level of equality and accorded equal finance, but socialised in their management. Third, he expounded the ideas, developed with Olivetti, on the organisation of political power at the local level, on the basis of which the "community" ought to be the local subject of politico-administrative integration at the territorial and economic level. Lastly, after the second half of 1947, he dedicated some interventions to the division of Europe and the impact that the difficulties within the DC – due to its inter-class structure – were having on the political system.

Following the failure of its attempt to give rise to a "third force" with what remained of the PDA, with the two Socialist parties and with the *cristiano-sociali*, at the end of 1947 the PCS joined the Popular Front, the *Fronte Democratico Popolare*, but then rejected the idea of its transformation into an electoral alliance.[24] It participated with its own independent lists in the elections of 18 April 1948: it considerably increased its overall votes (73.064), obtaining support where it had not been present before, but, as a result of the new electoral law, failed to get any of its candidates elected as *deputati*. The experience of the party as an organised national force ended: all that remained were the local groups and individual exponents in the left wing administrations of *comuni* and provinces or as leaders of trade union organisations. After various abortive attempts to resurrect the movement in various ways, Gerardo Bruni continued to be a point of reference to them right up to his death in 1975.[25]

4. The Role of *Cronache sociali* (1947-1951)[26]

The first number of the fortnightly review *Cronache sociali* was published in Rome on 30 May 1947. Its promoters were Giuseppe Dossetti, Amintore Fanfani, Giorgio La Pira and Giuseppe Lazzati: i.e. four exponents of the DC, elected to the Constituent Assembly on 2 June 1946. Dossetti and Lazzati were also members of the party's National Council, within which they had expressed positions contrary to the centrist and moderate line of the party's leader Alcide De Gasperi. Dossetti had participated in the Resistance as chairman of the CLN in the province of Reggio Emilia, while Lazzati, as an officer drafted into military service, had, after 8 September 1943, been interned in a German concentration camp: he was one of the approximately 700.000 troops who had refused to support Mussolini's *Repubblica Sociale Italiana*. During the German occupation, Fanfani, in turn, had emigrated to Switzerland, while La Pira, a long-standing antifascist, had lived in the underground. The four had participated actively in the party's electoral campaign; Dossetti and Fanfani had directed the DC's propaganda machine.

The emergence of the review coincided with the political crisis preceded in January by the split of the Socialist Party (PSIUP) into two parts (the PSI and the PSLI, later the PSDI). At the end of May this led to the expulsion of the socialists and communists from the government and to the formation of the fourth De Gasperi government, a single-party DC government with the support of some Liberal "technicians". During the same period, a Catholic industrialist, Angelo Costa, became president of the Italian Manufacturers' Federation, the Confindustria. However, it should be

---

24. The *Fronte Democratico Popolare* was established in Rome on 28 December 1947 as a coalition between different forces - trade union, social and political - that opposed government policy. On the model of the French, Spanish and Chilean experiences in the 1930s, it was then transformed into an electoral alliance in response to the pressure exerted by the PSI. The alliance rested on the hypothesis that, if united, the parties of the Left could at least hold the relative majority in the balance of power and thus, after the elections, claim the right to form the new government.
25. Subsequently, the heir of Gerardo Bruni, Lidia Giancola, deposited his archive, which also includes the papers of the *Movimento* (and *Partito*) *Cristiano-Sociale*, at the *Fondazione Lelio e Lisli Basso* in Rome.
26. Galli and Facchi, *La sinistra democristiana*; Glisenti and Elia, eds., "*Cronache sociali*"; Campanini, *Fede e politica*; Pombeni, *Le "Cronache sociali" di Dossetti*; Pombeni, *Il gruppo dossettiano*.

recalled that the promoters of the new review had long set up an association of Catholic laity, called *Civitas Humana*, of which Giuseppe Dossetti was president, and which was aimed at the development of culture and spirituality so that its members might bear a coherent Christian witness in civil society and in public life.

The review declared truth as its method, i.e. to aim for a detailed and documented knowledge of the problems of social and civil life at a time when the nature of the political struggle was prompting others to glorify the aspects of ideological identity and party membership. Its role was thus aimed not at providing a partisan mouthpiece for a particular current within the DC, but at the identification in the international and Italian context of a program of responses to the most urgent problems posed for the development of the human condition.

The fact of operating in a country liberated from fascism, a country in which a true democracy was in the process of being built up and its economic life and social relations reconstructed, determined a choice of interlocutors and methods aimed more at giving rise to a genuine political movement than of furnishing general guidelines to public opinion. Those chosen as privileged interlocutors of the review were those directly involved in political and social activities and fully conscious of their responsibilities. Subsequently the sociological characteristics of the intended recipients of the review's message were defined with greater precision. Apart from central and regional leaders of the DC and of the trade union movement, they also included central and local exponents of the clergy and of Catholic organisations and persons who had responsibility in economic and administrative activities. A particular invitation was addressed to them, urging them to become the protagonists of the educational or cultural activity, or of the social and political role, that the review wished to promote, and to forge relations of collaboration with its board of directors and editorial staff. This inner core of privileged interlocutors was to be combined with a wider area of persons coming from the same backgrounds, but not necessarily in leadership roles. The persons in question ought to have enthusiasm for and willingness to engage in an activist commitment, as well as organisational ability to permit the review to reach its readership, i.e. a wider periphery of people coming from the same backgrounds, in whom the review could generate interest, or of particular places where it might be read: libraries, associations, parishes.

As for the review's method, its effort was explicitly concentrated on the gathering of information and the analysis of the facts and concrete data in which social, political and economic action was manifested. It wanted, above all, to avoid two types of approach which it clearly believed were present in other initiatives of political culture during the same period: on the one hand, the tendency, a fairly typical one, to tackle problems in their general terms and to discuss them almost exclusively according to questions of principle; on the other, the tendency to subordinate evaluations and interpretations of the existing situation to mere questions of tactics or actions aimed at concrete objectives of immediate intervention. The effort seemed to be that of trying to understand, and allowing others to understand, the mid-term processes in which social, political and economic action ought to be rooted, if possible according to a longer-term strategic design.

To this end, invitations to participate were addressed to those who were directly involved in the activities of associations and in economic and administrative life. Such an invitation was significant for two reasons: in the first place, because, in the Italy of the 1940s, the development of social research was fairly limited: therefore having a network of qualified observers represented an enviable cultural and intellectual resource. In the second place, because asking those daily involved in concrete action to furnish analyses of tendencies and conjunctures encouraged them to enhance and qualify their degree of understanding, to assume more conscious roles and to make more appropriate decisions: in other words, to prepare themselves to perform leading functions in society.

The need to form a political leadership group within the complex Catholic social and cultural world, already present before the conflict with the closely allied socialists and communists in 1948, seemed all the more pressing after the landslide electoral victory of the DC. It was a victory to which sectors of the ruling classes in the economy, in finance, in the civil service had contributed. To prevent the party from being conditioned by the nature of its elitist support, it was therefore essential that it should now assume a more decidedly popular character, as the tool of a mass democracy that was not exhausted in the mere exercise of the right to vote. And in this respect – according to the constitutional scheme elaborated in the Constituent Assembly and promoted most authoritatively by the Catholic jurist Costantino Mortati – the major national parties, those with mass appeal, presented themselves as the means for the democratic involvement of the popular masses in the life of the state, an issue that in the aftermath of the First World War had been the central problem of the crisis of the liberal state and that fascism had resolved by means of the totalitarian state.[27]

The founders of *Cronache Sociali* believed that the active participation of citizens in the life of the party should play a role of primary importance in the formulation of a program of social measures compatible with the objectives of the reform of the structures of society that the Constitution of the Republic – which came into force on 1 January 1948 – had indicated as essential for the project of a democratic state. Its most significant difference from the liberal state ought to consist in the promotion of real levels of justice and equality. But a party supported by the active and militant participation of its members and electors ought to perform two other functions: first, to control and ascertain that the conduct of the elites present in the decision-making centers of the state were compatible with the aims enunciated by the Constitution and by the programs of the parliamentary majority that interpreted and implemented it; second, to ensure that the conduct of the party itself, though taking due account of the interests of the social groups and bodies to which its electors and members belonged, were independent of any direct pressure exerted by them. The precondition to enable both these functions to be exercised was that the party should have a leadership that would be, if not homogeneous, then at least cohesive and consensual

---

27. See Ruffilli, ed., *Cultura politica e partiti nell'età della Costituente. I. L'area liberal-democratica*; Elia, "La Commissione dei 75"; Franceschini, Guerrieri and Monina, eds., *Le idee costituzionali della Resistenza*; Antonetti, De Siervo and Malgeri, eds., *I cattolici democratici e la Costituzione*.

and that it should collectively support programs of economic, social and state action that would indicate goals sufficiently precise and comprehensible both to the elector and to the militant to mobilise their consent and participation. The internal struggle between the various currents was to be regarded as a contribution to achieving an internal organisation that would not disguise differences in outlooks, ideals and interests, inevitable in a party that crossed class barriers and that was based on the political unity of Catholics: the latter, in fact, could not be postulated as an absolute principle, but could be accepted only as a state of necessity determined by the exceptional political situation that the nation was going through.[28]

In vindicating its own autonomous role, with its own distinctive social and ideological character, within the political unity of Catholics, the founding fathers of the review were also expressing a precise ecclesial view. Giuseppe Dossetti, Giorgio La Pira and Giuseppe Lazzati were not only militant Christian laymen in politics, but also – as Giorgio Campanini has pointed out – "Christian thinkers": the first, Professor of Canon and Ecclesiastical Law, paid special attention to the dimensions of family life and intermediate social groups; the second, Professor of Roman Law and specialist in Thomist philosophy, was particularly concerned by issues involving the person; while the third, Professor of ancient Christian literature and leader of *Azione cattolica*, had developed the specific theme of the role of the laity in the Church.

As in the case of the *cattolici comunisti* and the *cristiano-sociali*, the theoretical foundation was traditional and Thomist: it was based on the distinction between the natural and supernatural, from which derived the various spheres of faith and science, and hence of politics as the science of earthly reality, the privileged interpreters of which are the laity. All three had developed a conception of the autonomous and responsible role of the laity as interpreters of Christian inspiration in earthly realities, firmly referring to the doctrine of the Church, but not subordinated to it in their action. What emerge from their writings are a series of interpretations of the presence of the Christian in history; these interpretations are deduced from a theology of incarnation which is compatible with a plurality of free and responsible social and political options. They therefore dissociated themselves from a conception which was then prevalent in ecclesiology, and especially in the *Azione cattolica* headed by Luigi Gedda; according to this conception, political unity was almost an earthly projection of the mystical body of Jesus, understood as a juridical and organisational unity structured according to hierarchical principles.

The unity of Catholics understood as political necessity was the consequence of the change in the political situation. The modification of the relations between the former Allies in the international struggle against Nazism and fascism had eroded the collaboration between the different forces that had found expression in the *Comitati di Liberazione Nazionale*, even before it had had an opportunity to produce all its effects. The first postwar government, led by Alcide De Gasperi, and based (from the end of 1945) on a coalition between Christian Democrats, socialists and communists, had begun the reconstruction of the country, and the coalition between the same

---

28. See Guizzardi, *L'unità dei cattolici in Italia*.

parties in the Constituent Assembly had permitted the construction of the institutional framework of democracy. After the expulsion of the socialists and the communists from the government (Spring 1947) and its electoral victory on 18 April 1948, the DC was faced by a historically significant task, that of bringing popular solidarity as an essential element within the government's activity, in such a way as to transform the anticommunist bloc, on which its support was based, into a progressive bloc.

The opposition to communism, necessary for the defense of freedom, ought not to have the conservative character of the defense of the existing social order, but the alternative character of the realisation of a more just social order. It was therefore the task of the more coherent and committed Catholics to assume this mission, because the Socialist movement in Italy was fragmented and made impotent by its recent split into two branches. Anticommunism, however, was not only a political necessity, but also an ideological battle. Like Gerardo Bruni and Jacques Maritain, but in contrast to Franco Rodano and the *cattolici comunisti*, the men of *Cronache Sociali* regarded as impossible any ideological and cultural dialogue with the communists. The marxist philosophy of the communists, in their view, remained imprisoned by a metaphysic alternative to, and incompatible with, that of those who had a religious view of life; and the diametrically opposed values by which it was sustained meant that the value of the state was regarded as absolute, since it was the expression of a reality, that of class, that was regarded as superior to the person.

Initially, articles on economic and social policy had been mainly focused on general themes of Christian social doctrine. But then more specific attention was devoted to particular aspects of the problems and the search for appropriate solutions. From the very first number of the review, with an article by Amintore Fanfani, the need to combat inflation had been accepted as an essential prerequisite to prevent the costs of reconstruction, due to the spiraling prices, from further aggravating the burdens of a population already suffering hardship, and leading to a further reduction in consumption, which for many people had already been reduced to the barest subsistence levels. The new phase, following the stabilisation of prices achieved towards the end of 1947, was to be marked by the overcoming of the distinction between short-term policy, i.e. provisions aimed at tackling the most urgent problems, and structural reform policy, i.e. measures aimed at resolving more deeply rooted problems in the country, such as unemployment, poverty, low pay, lack of essential services, economic dualism. In contrast to the economic policy of De Gasperi, who had hitherto, in agreement with the Catholic president of the Confindustria, Angelo Costa, assumed a more markedly liberal (or free market) character, *Cronache Sociali* began, from 1948, to support the need for a more decisive state intervention. The need was also affirmed both to undertake the reform of individual sectors, such as the agrarian reform[29], and to act according to a precise economic and social program.

The group's most important publications in the area of social and economic thought were Amintore Fanfani's *Colloqui con i poveri* (1941; new edition Milan: Vita e pensiero, 1950) and *Persona, beni, società in una rin-*

---

29. See Istituto nazionale di sociologia rurale, ed., *La riforma fondiaria: trent'anni dopo*.

novata civiltà cristiana (Milan: Giuffré, 1945), and Giorgio La Pira's *L'attesa della povera gente and Difesa della povera gente* (published in 1950 in, respectively, numbers 1 and 3 of the review, which were among those most widely distributed). In 1951 Fanfani and La Pira both contributed to a book on works of mercy, published in Turin with the title *Ama il prossimo tuo*. In these texts the authors enunciated the principles by which they were inspired. But for specific prescriptions aimed at tackling the real problems of social and economic policy we need to refer to the many articles published in the review. In them we may note an effort to draw on the same sources of what seemed at the time the most advanced points of the social thought of the Western Left, i.e. the policy of the Labour government in Great Britain and the legacy of the reformist culture of the Democratic Party of the period of Roosevelt in the USA[30]: close attention was paid to the Beveridge Plan, and the idea was canvassed that it was possible to combine the interventions of the Marshall Plan with provisions for the development of "depressed areas", such as an agrarian reform and the *Cassa per il Mezzogiorno* (the Development Fund for the South of Italy).

In a country, like Italy, characterised by a surplus of population and a shortage of capital, it was not possible to rely solely on emigration to restore a balance between the need to work and the lack of productive activities to satisfy it. International aid and state support could be usefully focused in a selective manner on those economic sectors that were able to respond to productivity criteria (growth of goods produced, lower prices, and increased employment). Moreover, public investments in the "depressed areas" could, it was argued, create the direct demand for goods and services and revitalise local economies and societies, creating added demand through the widening of a market that poverty had rendered stagnant.

The group's reformist commitment was not limited to the battle of ideas, but would be directly expressed in the action of Amintore Fanfani, Minister of Labour in the fourth De Gasperi government, with Giorgio La Pira as Under-Secretary of State. Given the conditions in which he was forced to operate, Fanfani failed to perform in full the role he had envisaged of being a minister for the economic defense of the most disadvantaged classes. Yet he did succeed in pushing through a provision of great social significance, which, like his other measures, was directly supported by *Cronache sociali* and strongly indicative of the group's reformist philosophy. The provision in question was a plan for the construction of *case popolari* (public housing), financed in part by a modest deduction from wages. Its implementation was entrusted to the *Istituto Nazionale delle Assicurazioni*, the state-run agency for national insurance, to which public housing projects had already been entrusted during the Fascist period. It was a social policy measure aimed at satisfying a widespread collective need: numerous families were, as a result of congenital poverty or war-time destruction, still having to share housing or live in otherwise makeshift or provisional accommodation. The provision had other positive effects, both direct and indirect: it directly generated work in the building industry, while the spin-off effects of

---

30. See Roggi, *Riviste cattoliche e politica economica*; Roggi, "Il mondo cattolico e i 'grandi temi'".

the investment helped to regenerate connected sectors and the economies of the towns and provinces directly involved.

After the Korean War, the stance of *Cronache Sociali* and its exponents came into conflict with the policy of the government which, in common with that of other Western nations, supported the need for rearmament. They had hitherto supported the Western line and had criticised pacifism and those tendencies within the Catholic world favouring a dialogue with the communists on peace. But they were not entirely supportive of the Atlantic Pact, preferring bilateral relations that would have lent greater emphasis to the role of the European countries.[31] These problems and different viewpoints accentuated friction within the DC and within the government.

In the course of 1949 and in early 1950 the situation deteriorated. Social protests among workers and peasants often degenerated into bloody conflicts between demonstrators and the police: several were killed or seriously injured. In this situation Giuseppe Dossetti campaigned for the government to implement a more courageous and coherent social policy. The De Gasperi government had, in the meantime, been weakened by defections: it had lost first its Social Democratic, then its Liberal ministers, and then the exponents of *Cronache Sociali*. The President of the Chamber of Deputies, Giovanni Gronchi, was also highly critical of De Gasperi's leadership. Giuseppe Dossetti, however, at the time threw in his support for De Gasperi, hoping to exert influence on him. He became one of the national vice-secretaries of the DC. This support was, he thought, indispensable to campaign effectively against all those – both inside and outside the DC, and not only on the Right – who opposed the reforms that were being prepared and, more generally, state invervention in the economy. After the municipal and provincial elections of 1951, due to a loss of consensus on the part of the DC, especially on its right, the position of *Cronache Sociali* became particularly difficult, both inside and outside the party. Giorgio La Pira had been elected Mayor of Florence. Amintore Fanfani chose to follow his own political path, as also did some of the younger contributors to the review (Achille Ardigò, Giovanni Galloni). During the government crisis of July 1951, Fanfani negotiated directly and separately with De Gasperi: this effectively spelled the end of the experience of *Cronache Sociali*, even though some members of the group entered the government (Ezio Vanoni in charge of major economic policy, Fanfani of agriculture).

The leadership of the group thus passed into Fanfani's hands: Dossetti summoned his staff and contributors to the castle of Rossena, in the Emilian Appennines, to announce his departure from political activity.[32] This was – in effect – virtually a declaration of the failure of the ideas that had inspired the birth of *Cronache Sociali* four years earlier. Continuing the policy of opposing De Gasperi would only have played into the hands of those who

---

31. On all these aspects, see, in particular: Pacetti, Papini and Saracinelli, eds., *La cultura della pace*; Vecchio, *Pacifisti e obiettori negli anni di De Gasperi*; Formigoni, *La democrazia cristiana*.
32. On the experience of some members who, after the end of *Cronache Sociali*, attempted a new political project based on the initiative of a new generation, see Tassani, *La Terza Generazione*.

– whether in the Catholic world or outside it – did not accept the model of democracy of which De Gasperi was the guarantor: in other words, the opposite ends of the political spectrum, the Right or the PCI. That was why it was necessary to close ranks around the Christian Democrat leader: not to construct a state according to the Christian view, but to incorporate Catholics in practice as decisive elements in the construction of democracy. The proposal of plans for the future thus gave way to the defense of the *status quo*. The crisis also derived from the fact that the cultural (and religious) presuppositions were lacking in the Catholic world to make it a spearhead and protagonist of the radical renewal of society and of the state. Dossetti therefore expressed the hope that the best intellectual energies that had gathered around *Cronache Sociali* would now be concentrated on an educational action and on research aimed at the formulation and implementation of a new political culture, as presupposition for future action.

5. Scattered Political Fragments of the Christian Left (1948-1953)

Already on the occasion of the expulsion of the parties of the Left from the government, in May 1947, some exponents of the Left of the DC, Christian trade unionists from the CGIL (General Confederation of Italian Trade Unions) and former members of the PSC had set up a *Movimento dei Lavoratori Cristiani di Unità Sindacale e Politica* (Movement of Christian Workers of Trade Union and Political Unity). Then, in the electoral campaign of 1948, apart from the PCS, which despite supporting the Popular Front had not participated in the electoral alliance that followed it, another Christian formation of the Left had appeared: on 7 March 1948 the only number ever to appear of the journal *La Pace* published the *Manifesto del Movimento Cristiano per la Pace* (MCP).[33] The movement in question was not the Italian section of the international movement of the same name, which still exists to this day, but an Italian political movement formed around Guido Miglioli. Miglioli had at first formed a so-called *Corrente Cristiana per la Pace*. Only later did he establish the new movement, having obtained the support of former exponents of the Christian Democrat Left associated with *Politica d'oggi* (such as Ada Alessandrini and Mario Montesi), former members of the MCS and later of the PSC (such as Pio Montesi), of the MCC and later of the PSC (such as Franco Leonori), of the MCS and of the PCS (such as Silvio Zorzi and Otello Sacchetti), and others. The aim of the movement was to recompose in the Popular Front the unity of the popular forces realised by the Resistance: a unity which had been undermined by the pro-Western stance of the DC, identified as the party of war. The electoral campaign was conducted on these issues and on that of the unity of workers, with direct reference to the Christian values affirmed by the Gospel. The weakness of its political positions, the slenderness of its

---

33. See Montesi, "Di qua, di là dal Tevere"; Alessandrini, "Guido Miglioli e il Movimento cristiano per la pace"; Alessandrini, "Incontri e scontri con Gerardo Bruni"; Urettini, "I cristiano-sociali di Treviso"; Casula, *Guido Miglioli*; Vecchio, *Pacifisti e obiettori nell'Italia di De Gasperi*, 40-48. See also the contribution by Giorgio Vecchio to this volume.

financial support, the attacks mounted against its members, combined with the internal struggle for supremacy within the Front between socialists and communists, concurred, however, to render the movement marginal. It performed poorly in the elections; none of its candidates was elected. In spite of that, the movement expressed itself against the dissolution of the Front and in favour of the development of a unified platform of the Christian Left.

But the problem of how to give a coherent voice to the scattered fragments of the Christians of the Left persisted. A meeting of members of the MCP, of the MCS and of a so-called *Movimento dei Cristiani Indipendenti* (MCI), of which nothing is known, was held in Florence on 19 December 1948. They decided to set up yet another movement, the *Movimento Unitario dei Cristiani Progressisti* (MUCP)[34], whose platform did not significantly differ from that of the movements that had preceded it: the need to guarantee all the democratic rights upheld by the Constitution; opposition to the errors of centrism; identification of the cause of democracy with the cause of peace; anticapitalism in the name of democracy and Christianity. Trade union unity and a government formed by all mass-based parties remained the main political objectives. However, the fact that a movement with a similar name existed in France and the direct involvement of its exponents in the *Partigiani della Pace* (Partisans of peace) and in the campaign against the Atlantic Pact led, first, to the *Osservatore romano* mounting a polemical attack against the movement on 27 January 1949, and then, in July, to the ecclesiastical authorities issuing canonical provisions for the exclusion of the Italian *cristiani progressisti* from the sacraments, in application of the decree of the Holy Office of 1 July 1949 on the excommunication of communists.[35]

Shortly after the defeat of the Front, Italy had been shaken by a near-insurrection in July 1948, following the attempted assassination of the leader of the PCI, Palmiro Togliatti, by a young right wing militant. In the confused situation that had followed, the Christian trade unionists of the CGIL had split into two and a rival federation was set up: the so-called *Libera Cgil*, from which both the *Confederazione Italiana dei Sindacati dei Lavoratori* (CISL, a non-confessional trade union organisation of Catholic workers), and the *Unione Italiana del Lavoro* (UIL, trade union organisation of Social Democratic and Republican workers) would be born in 1950. But a nucleus of Christian trade unionists had remained in the unitary federation, giving rise to the *Corrente Sindacale Cristiana Unitaria* (CSCU); its existence was endorsed at the CGIL Congress in 1949, when 1% of the

---

34. See A. Alessandrini, "Un cattolico espone le ragioni dei cristiani progressisti", *Rinascita*, (April 1949) 162-168; A. Alessandrini, "Cristiani progressisti e cristiani conservatori", *Mondo operaio*, 5 February 1949, "Les chrétiens progressistes dans le front de la paix aux côtés des communistes et des socialistes", *Voix Ouvrière* (Geneva), 7 April 1949; "La frattura", *Il Paese*, (3 August 1949); "Di fronte all'offensiva clericale. I cristiani progressisti in difesa della netta divisione tra sacro e profano", *Il Paese*, (21 August 1949); Montesi, "Di qua, di là dal Tevere".
35. It should be noted that the French Progressive Christians, admonished by Cardinal Suhard at the beginning of the same year, dissociated themselves from their Italian counterparts in July: they argued that since they themselves were not communists, no canonical sanctions could be applied against them; *Le Monde*, 16 July 1949. See the contribution by Yvon Tranvouez elsewhere in this volume and also Tranvouez, *Catholiques et communistes*.

votes, equivalent to approximatively100.000, was granted to it.[36] It was headed by Federico Rossi, one of the federal secretaries of the CGIL. Rossi had been the closest associate of the Christian trade union leader Achille Grandi, who had died in 1946. Grandi had been active before the rise of fascism and had signed the pact of trade union unity of June 1944 on behalf of the *corrente sociale cristiana*. In the documents marking the establishment of the CSCU the reasons for trade union unity are reaffirmed: it was considered a Christian duty towards the exploited. At the same time the ideological motives from which the split in the federation had derived its justification were rejected: division could only reduce the bargaining power of the trade union movement. As for the internal life of the federation, full freedom of opinion was vindicated, combined with the disciplined acceptance of the legitimate resolutions of the federal decision-making bodies. As regards the methods of political struggle, the validity and the legitimacy of the general strike and of non-collaboration (so long as it did not degenerate into sabotage) and the value of solidarity across different categories of workers and support for the claims and rights of invalid and pensioned workers were reaffirmed. In the attempt to give strength and political representativeness to its own trade union role, the trade unionists of the CSCU took part in the meeting held in Florence from 9 to 10 December 1950 for the unification of the Christian forces of the Left and became the cornerstone for the establishment of the *Movimento Cristiano del Lavoro* (MCL) in early January 1951.[37] The documents marking its foundation contain nothing new, other than the traditional affirmations of principle of the Christians of the Left on the moral incompatibility between capitalistic egoism and the human values whose affirmation had been prevented by the division of society into classes: a consequence of this position was an acceptance of the class struggle as means of defense and the need for structural reform. Each political program ought to have peace simultaneously as its condition and as its objective, in order to realise concretely, in freedom and democracy, those Christian values that are a source of vitality of a just society.[38]

The national meeting of the *Avanguardie Cristiane* and the groups of the review *Adesso*, promoted by Father Primo Mazzolari and his associates,

---

36. The CSCU survived until 1963, when - according to some of its exponents - it was sacrificed in the bid to heal the rift between the CGIL and CISL and restore unity between them. According to some observers, it had, by this time, been reduced to almost a fiction. But it cannot have been so at the beginning, given the high number of intermediate cadres who formed part of it and who, according to the proceedings of the trade union congresses, held posts as leaders of trade unions, intersectoral workers' associations and *camere del lavoro* (local general worker's associations).
37. See M. Pini Accurti, "Caratteristiche e linee d'azione del Movimento cristiano del lavoro", *Nuovo Corriere*, (6 January 1951); Montesi, "Di qua, di là dal Tevere".
38. What became of Federico Rossi's archive after his death remains a mystery, nor is there any explicit trace of the CSCU as such in the historical archive of the CGIL: the references given here are taken from handbills and pamphlets preserved in the archives of the *Fondazione Lelio e Lisli Basso* in Rome and the archives of Ada Alessandrini and Marco Palmerini; other documents are also to be found in the Archive of Gerardo Bruni in the same *Fondazione*.

was held in Modena at much the same time.[39] It was an opportunity to engage in a dialogue entered into some time ago to find – beyond anticommunism – points of convergence even with those on the opposite side of the political spectrum on issues of poverty and peace. It was also a way of giving visibility and a mouthpiece to the variegated world of Catholic associations and groups that was being formed outside the official circuit by those who shared neither the moderatism prevalent in the party, nor the particular activism of *Azione Cattolica*. But, in spite of the great enthusiasm aroused by the meeting, its result was somewhat disappointing and devoid of any further consequences. Jeers and protests were reserved for these Christians of the Left.[40]

In the local government elections of 1951 the parties of the majority (DC, Liberals, Republicans and Social Democrats) suffered a defeat, especially as a result of efforts by the monarchist and neofascist Right. The social reforms of centrism had shown no positive short-term results: they frightened away the conservative strata without enlarging the support of the popular strata. On the other hand, the parties of the Left continued ceaselessly to mobilise the masses on the most acutely felt issues of the day: the development of the South, trade union and political rights on the shop-floor and elsewhere, the struggle for peace, the campaign against the Atlantic Pact, the Labour Plan of the CGIL. Faced with this dwindling support, the parliamentary majority considered correcting the electoral law for the election of the Chamber of Deputies based on proportional representation: the party or the coalition of parties that reached a total of 50%+1 of the valid votes would be given a majority premium that would raise the number of deputies to 380 out of 589, i.e. approximately two thirds.

This situation prompted the opposition of both the Right and the Left to mobilise itself against the centrist coalition. The electoral campaign was as bitterly fought as that of 1948. The Christians of the Left contributed to the campaign within some minor formations that in the end did not win any seats, yet with the effect of subtracting votes from the centrist coalition. The PCS backed the list of candidates of the *Unione dei Socialisti Indipendenti* (USI), headed by the two *deputati* Valdo Cucchi and Aldo Magnani, who had resigned from the PCI (the USI polled 225.495 votes). Some *cristiano-sociali* and Adriano Ossicini supported the list of *Unità Popolare*, promoted by former exponents of the PDA who had later joined the *Partito Repubblicano Italiano* (Ferruccio Parri) and the PSDI (Piero Calamandrei) (*Unità Popolare* polled a total of 171.071 votes). Other Christians of the Left, including Mario Montesi, had joined the *Alleanza Democratica Nazionale*, led by the economist and former Liberal minister Epicarmo Corbino (the *Alleanza* polled 120.950 votes). Others, including Ada

39. See Bedeschi, *La sinistra cristiana*; Lusi, "Un esempio di non conformismo"; Bedeschi, *L'ultima battaglia di don Mazzolari*; Tassani, "Le 'Avanguardie cristiane' a convegno"; Campanini and Truffelli, eds., *Mazzolari e "Adesso"*. See also the contribution by Giorgio Vecchio elsewhere in this volume.
40. The *Communist daily* spoke of a "fruitful meeting", see "Un incontro fruttuoso", *l'Unità*, (13 January 1951), while the review of the Christian Democratic Left criticised its "lack of political qualification" and failure to arouse the attention of the political organisations; see F. Pecci, "Il primo incontro delle Avanguardie cristiane", *Cronache sociali*, (15 January 1951).

Alessandrini, Silvio Zorzi and Otello Sacchetti, backed the list of the *Movimento Socialista Cristiano* (MSC), which once again proposed the symbol and the program of the *cristiano-sociali* and which polled barely 2749 votes in the few electoral colleges at which it presented itself.

6. Conclusion

The elections of 1953 marked the defeat of Alcide De Gasperi and the beginning of a period of considerable political difficulty. The Christian Democrat leader died in the following year, bequeathing the leadership of his party to Amintore Fanfani. Fanfani pledged himself to the construction of a mass political organisation capable – within a neocapitalist development – of formulating and managing a state policy of intervention in the economy and in society, of the type conceived by the neovoluntaristic school from which he came. What remained of the experience of *Cronache Sociali* was combined with the various positions within the DC and produced a mixture that became the policy of the party and its alliances. The new currents of the Left within the DC, in turn, became the interpreters in various ways of the needs for social reform and for the necessary adjustments to make the institutions of the state conform to the provisions of the Constitution. From within the DC itself proposals were advanced for an "opening to the Left" according to various perspectives: political and programmatic attention to what the political and social Left, as a whole, represented; attention to the events that were developing and the prospects being shaped in the socialist movement, especially after the death of Stalin (1953) and after the 20th Congress of the Soviet Communist Party and the Soviet invasion of Hungary (1956).

Outside the DC, the road of "dialogue with the Catholics" was chosen by the socialists. According to their leader Pietro Nenni, this was a political project and, hence, tended to be carried out with their most numerous political representatives, i.e. with the DC. As far as the communists were concerned, the strategy of their secretary Palmiro Togliatti to reinforce the PCI as an integral part of a bourgeois democratic state led to a recognition of the powers that operated within it: they included the institutional reality of the Catholic Church and the political reality of the DC. Rejecting any support for movements that claimed to challenge the party's hegemonic role in the working class, the PCI supported those who tended to create the conditions for future dialogue: hence, the politico-cultural reviews of the *cattolici comunisti* of past and present. The most important of these was *Il dibattito politico*, published since 1955 by two former Christian Democrat members of the Chamber of Deputies, Mario Melloni and Ugo Bartesaghi, both of them expelled by Fanfani from the DC for having voted against Italian membership of the Western European Union (WEU).[41]

Tensions and ferments continued to agitate the ecclesiastical world, Catholic intellectuals and associations throughout the 1950s. They were caused by antipathy to the policy of the DC, by the social consequences of the economic transformations, by the problems of international solidarity

---

41. See Tassani, *Alle origini del compromesso storico*.

posed by the anticolonial struggles, and by the influence exerted by innovative international cultural and theological currents. Alongside long-standing motives for various grievances, new ones also emerged, but for some time the conditions were not such as to allow the ferments or tensions to be expressed in a combined and coordinated manner. Up to the end of the 1960s such dissent was expressed by the so-called "spontaneous groups of believers and non-believers for a new Left"[42], and in the course of the 1970s and 1980s by the *Movimento Politico dei Lavoratori* (MPL) promoted by Livio Labor, former president of the ACLI, then by the "Catholic independents" in the parliamentary group of the Independent Left[43] and by the *Cristiani per il Socialismo*, the Italian branch of an international movement.[44]

Such persistence in time would seem to confirm an observation made by the philosopher Felice Balbo, former protagonist of the *Partito della Sinistra Cristiana*, apropos the phenomenon of the Christian Left in general: "By Christian Left I mean the political movements that to a greater or lesser degree, and with greater or lesser maturity, emerged in the aftermath of the Second World War, especially in Europe (Italy, France, Poland, Czechoslovakia, etc.), but not only in Europe (Vietnam, Algeria, etc.), with the aim of emancipating Catholics from so-called bourgeois politics. These movements always remained minorities. But the ideological position of currents of the Christian Left, in a more or less conscious and dogmatic form, is far more widespread than might appear from the groups explicitly qualified as such. If we do not want to reduce the Christian Left in the broad and historically profound sense to para-communist phenomena, I believe we must agree that its existence originated from the impossibility either of rejecting the 'denunciation' or accepting the 'solution' of communism".[45]

To better define the interpretational field of the social, political and cultural phenomena we have been considering, this observation may be combined with that of another philosopher, Giulio Girardi, protagonist of another movement, the *Cristiani per il Socialismo*, who wrote: "The revolutionary potentialities, even if repressed, of many Christian needs cannot be ignored. Albeit within reformist and anticommunist limitations, they contest the established order: for example in the various forms of social Christian activism and – limited to particular sectors and periods – in the Christian Democracies (…) Of course, in evaluating preconciliar anticommunism, and its significance in a revolutionary history, due account must be

42. See Rotelli, ed., *I gruppi spontanei e il ruolo politico della contestazione*; Rositi, ed., *La politica dei gruppi*; Nesti, "I gruppi minoritari cattolici"; Sidoti, "'Questitalia' e la polemica sui temi dell'organizzazione politica"; Rotelli, "I gruppi spontanei del '68".
43. See Sircana, "L'origine della Sinistra indipendente"; Gozzini, *Oltre gli steccati*; Zanuttini, "Gli archivi dei gruppi parlamentari"; see also Ossicini, *Il cristiano e la politica*.
44. Paci, "I Cristiani per il socialismo"; Milanesi, "Identità religiosa e impegno politico"; Girardi, *Cristiani per il socialismo: perché ?*; Ramos Regidor and Gecchelin, *Cristiani per il socialismo*; Jervolino, *Questione cattolica e politica di classe*; Parisella, "Memoria di parte sull'esperienza italiana", Parisella, "Cristiani per il socialismo"; Cuminetti, *Il dissenso cattolico in Italia*.
45. Balbo, "La sfida storica del comunismo al cristianesimo". The role of Felice Balbo in the theoretical formulation of the Christian Left was pointed out, in particular, by Antonetti, *L'ideologia della Sinistra cristiana*.

taken of the ideological context of Constantinian Christianity on the one hand and stalinist marxism on the other, as also the economic and political context of the Cold War. In particular, the character assumed by marxism, both on the theoretical and on the practical level, in the stalinist period, prevents us from unhesitatingly qualifying all forms of anticommunism as counter-revolutionary".[46]

---

46. Girardi, *Cristiani per il socialismo: perché?*, 79-81.

CHRISTIAN MOVEMENTS AND PARTIES OF THE LEFT IN ITALY

From *Movimento di Sinistra Cristiana* to *Partito della Sinistra Cristiana*: Evolution of One Political Party

1.1 The Various Names

Movimento di Sinistra Cristiana	1937
Cattolici Antifascisti or Cattolici di Sinistra	1938
Partito Cooperativista Sinarchico	1941
Partito Comunista Cristiano	1942-Summer 1943
Sinistra Giovanile Cattolica	Summer 1943
Movimento dei Cattolici Comunisti	September 1943-November 1944 (Central and Southern Italy)
Movimento dei Lavoratori Cristiani	September 1943-April 1945 (Northern Italy)
Partito della Sinistra Cristiana	September 1944-December 1945

1.2 The members

The list of members has been drawn up on the basis of information and references contained in the specialized literature on the subject: some names are those of persons who played an important role in the movement and in the party in the underground phase and then in the phase immediately after the end of the war, but who played no significant role in Republican Italy; others played a significant role in Republican Italy, although they had only been relatively unimportant rank-and-file members prior to Liberation.

Acchiappati, Fr. Giuseppe
Anfossi, Simonetta
Balbo, Felice
Barca, Luciano
Benedetti, Tullio
Bianchi, Fr. Stefano
Bontadini, Gustavo
Boringhieri, Paolo
Brezzi, Paolo
Califano, Elio
Ceriani Sebregondi, Giorgio
Chiesa, Romualdo
Ciarletta, Nicola
Cinciari Rodano, Marisa
Cocchi, Mario
Coccia, Amedeo
Corti, Lucia
D'Amico, Fedele
Del Noce, Augusto
De Piaz, Fr. Camillo
De Rosa, Gabriele
Dessanay, Sebastiano
Emiliani, Vincenzo
Ferrarotti, Franco
Gaggero, Fr. Andrea
Galizia, Mario
Garroni, Laura
Garroni, Silvia
Giunti, Aldo
Leonori, Franco
Lombardini, Siro
Massimi, Filippo
Migliori, Tullio
Mira, Giuseppe
Montesi, Pio
Moruzzi, Paolo
Motta, Mario
Orlandi, Silvio
Ossicini, Adriano
Ossicini, Agnese
Ossicini, Isabella
Ossicini, Teresa
Passerin D'Entreves, Ettore
Pecoraro, Fr. Paolo
Pediconi, Luigi
Pintor, Silvia
Rinaldini, Antonio
Rodano, Franco
Romanò, Angelo
Romano, Vincenzo
Saba, Vincenzo
Sacconi, Filippo
Saraceno, Pasquale
Scassellati, Ubaldo
Sella, Guido (Giulio)
Tatò, Antonio
Tedesco Tatò, Giglia
Tranquilli, Vittorio
Turoldo, Fr. Davide Maria
Zapelloni, Roberto
Zapelloni, Sandro

Members of the *Movimento* and *Partito Cristiano-Sociale*

The list has been drawn up on the basis of information and references contained in the specialized literature on the subject, of the electoral lists for the Constituent Assembly and the list of the correspondents of Gerardo Bruni: some names belong to persons who played an important role in the movement and in the party in the underground or in the phase immediately after the end of the war, but who then played no major role in Republican Italy; others played roles of major importance in Republican Italy, although they had only been relatively unimportant rank-and-file members prior to Liberation.

Agnoletto, Arduino
Angeli, Emilio
Antiochia, Corrado
Archetti, Italo
Bellotti, Antonio
Bertoli, Raffaele
Bo, Giorgio
Bozzini, Lidio
Bracci, Lucangelo
Bruni, Gerardo
Canaletti, Gaudenti Alberto
Cappellotto, Italico Corradino
Cavaceppi, Vittorio
Cremoni, Erminia
Da Pavullo, Fr. Placido
De Rosa, Gabriele
De Simone, Renato
Enriques Agnoletti, Anna Maria
Fabbri, Daniele
Ferrari, Giorgio Emanuele
Figara, Aroldo
Francescaglia, Francesco
Guidotti, Mario
Lapponi, Lorenzo
Lenci, Dante
Loi, Giuseppe
Mascagni, Luigi
Merlini, Luciano
Montesi, Pio
Olivetti, Adriano
Orlandini, Renato
Palmerini, Marco
Piazza, Leonida
Piccagli, Italo
Pini, Renato
Pizzinato, Urbano
Poggiolini, Danilo
Rosini, Ennio
Rosini, Ezio
Rossi, Federico
Rovero, Giuseppe
Sacchetti, Otello
Scalone, Gaetano
Sesini, Silvestra Tea
Solina, Achille
Spada, Aldo
Taviani, Paolo Emilio
Tisei, Felice
Tosatti, Quinto
Vigli, Marcello
Virzi, Antonio
Zanoni, Anna Maria
Zappa, Francesco
Zatterin, Ugo
Zorzi, Silvio

Members of the *Cronache Sociali* group

The list has been drawn up on the basis of names that figure among the list of supporters of *Civitas Humana* and of the lists of the review's promoters, distributors, editors and contributors.

Albonetti, Achille
Ambrico, Gaetano
Amorth, Antonio
Ardigò, Achille
Baget Bozzo, Gianni
Barbi, Paolo
Bianchini, Laura
Boiardi, Franco
Briatico, Franco
Caffè, Federico
Carraro, Luigi
Cavallaro, Giovan Battista
Ceccacci, Glisenti Marcella
Cialdea, Basilio
Ciccardini, Bartolo
Cossiga, Francesco
Costa, Don Franco
Criconia, Giuseppe
Dal Falco, Luciano
Di Rovasenda, Fr. Enrico
De Biase Gaiotti, Paola
De Cesaris, Benedetto
Del Noce, Augusto
Dossetti, Giuseppe
Dossetti, Ermanno
Elia, Leopoldo
Fanfani, Amintore
Fogolari, Giulia
Forlani, Arnaldo
Forcella, Enzo
Gaiotti, Angelo
Galloni, Giovanni
Geremia, Giusto
Glisenti, Giuseppe
Golzio, Silvio
Gorrieri, Ermanno
Grassini, Franco
Guala, Filiberto
Guano, Don Emilio
Gui, Luigi
Guidotti, Mario
Jannaco, Carmine
Jannaco, Giorgio
La Pira, Giorgio
Lazzati, Giuseppe
Lombardini, Siro
Malfatti, Franco Maria
Massaccesi, Ettore
Meucci, Gampaolo
Minoli, Eugenio
Montanari, Fausto
Moro, Aldo
Mortati, Costantino
Pastore, Giulio
Pecci, Egisto
Pecci, Franco
Romani, Mario
Romanò, Angelo
Sabatini, Armando
Sala, Rino
Scoppola, Pietro
Turoldo, Fr. David Maria

"LEFT CATHOLICISM" AND THE EXPERIENCES "ON THE FRONTIER" OF THE CHURCH AND ITALIAN SOCIETY (1939-1958)

Giorgio Vecchio

1. Introduction

Italian historians rarely use the expression "Left Catholicism". In the thousands of titles dedicated to the history of the Italian Catholic movement from its origins to 1945, only in a few cases have the authors chosen to discuss "Left Catholics", and this happened in reference to the experiences of the Christian Democratic Party of Romolo Murri at the end of the 19th century.[1] One obvious exception to this tendency is found in the studies dedicated to the specific events of the *Movimento dei Cattolici Comunisti* (later the *Partito della Sinistra Cristiana*), operating from the end of the 1930s to 1945 on a strictly ideological and political level, many of its members having strong links with the underground of Catholic Action, especially in Rome. Only one author, Silvio Tramontin, has entitled his book *Sinistra cattolica di ieri e di oggi* (The Catholic Left of Yesterday and Today), but the coverage is episodic, perhaps a result dictated by editorial requirements.[2] In fact, the narration covers both the official Catholic organisations of the early 20th century, as well as all the social and trade union experiences, and, further, those of the Popular Party, antifascism, the *Assoziazioni Cristiano dei Lavoratori Italiani* (ACLI), and the left wing of the Christian Democrats, etc. Also, with regards to the Italian Republic period, the definition "Left Catholicism" had a markedly political meaning: from time to time and without a precise or fixed meaning, it came to refer to the Left within the DC (the Dossetti group, the *corrente della Base*, etc.), critical believers opposed to the idea of political unity among Catholics, and it further applied to the militant Catholics who were members of the left parties, such as the *Partito Socialista Italiano* (PSI) and the *Partito Comunista Italiano* (PCI) or the extreme left parties formed after the fallout of 1968.[3]

---

1. The reference is to the works of G. Cappelli and C. Pelosi: see Archivio per la storia del movimento sociale cattolico in Italia, Fumasi, ed., *Mezzo secolo di ricerca storiografica sul movimento cattolico in Italia*. This volume describes and examines some 4392 titles, including books and articles.
2. Tramontin, *Sinistra cattolica di ieri e di oggi*.
3. See the contribution of Antonio Parisella in this volume for coverage of all of these topics.

At the social and ecclesiastical levels, there operated even less of a single definition to cover all the individuals and groups that had tried to impress upon the Church the need for renewal, contesting in various ways the persistence of traditional mentalities or authoritarian practices. These reformers addressed the daunting problems of freedoms within the Church, including a dialogue with non-believers (especially communists), while attempting to reform the social structure, and to attack both poverty and social injustices. Therefore it was possible - depending on the time period - to speak of "Progressive Catholics" or "Democratic Catholics" or "disobedient" Catholics, as well as "prophets", or, after 1965, of "council Catholics", a reference to the influence of the Second Vatican Council. The decision to include in the title of this chapter "Left Catholicism" and "the experiences on the frontier", always within quotation marks, expresses the general difficulty this implies. The term is used here to indicate the overall experience of those Catholics who, outside of politics, had worked towards a profound and decisive reform of the ideas and the behaviours of the Church in its confrontations with the problems of society.

2. The Heritage of the Resistance

During the Second World War the Catholic Church played an increasingly important role, especially between 1943 and 1945, when Italy was divided under the dual Allied and German military occupation. As Italy intervened in the war (10 June 1940), bishops and priests took a prudent position, distancing themselves from the propaganda and the slogans of the regime. They above all returned to the concept of war as "God's punishment", similar to the Great Flood, where war was to punish men for their sins and lead them to conversion. The faithful, therefore, were invited to obey the established authorities and thus prove their patriotism. After the fall of fascism (25 July 1943) and the collapse of the state (8 September 1943), bishops and priests found themselves having to assume many civil powers and responsibilities, becoming representatives and protectors of all of those entrusted to them. In the south they were the interlocutors for the Americans and the English; in the zones with the majority of combats they attempted to prevent further destruction and to make their own cities "open cities"; in the areas controlled by the Germans and the fascists, they shared right until the end the suffering of victims of Allied bombing or of the reprisals and deportations carried out by the Germans. The large majority of bishops and priests worked to save the greatest possible number of human lives (including Jews, partisans and antifascists, and escaped Allied prisoners). All of which contributed to the creation of particularly strong ties between the Italian people and the Church, which in turn established the groundwork for the electoral victories of the Christian Democrats.

The war also profoundly changed the internal life of the Church. The parishes had to transform themselves in order to survive, to adapt themselves to circumstances. They also had to celebrate mass outside of the church, among the evacuees or in precarious circumstances. Priests were often forced into closer contact with their flock than they had previously experienced, and thus lost their sacredness along with the custom of respectful distance between themselves and the lay population, in particular from women. In the cities, they spent their days in bomb shelters or attending to evacuees; in the countryside or mountain regions, they had to adapt themselves to sudden escapes from enemy soldiers or search parties; in the prisons or camps they shared in the suffering and the discomforts of all the prisoners. In fact, many Italian Catholic priests experienced grave difficulties during the war: nearly 200 of them lost their lives, killed by the Nazis, others were tortured, still others were deported to Dachau having been charged with aiding Jews or partisans. Of particular note among such priests is Father Pietro Pappagallo, shot at the Fosse Ardeatine in Rome, who inspired the priest protagonist in the masterpiece of Italian neorealism, the film *Roma città aperta*, directed by Roberto Rossellini. Other examples include Father Aldo Mei, who prior to being shot in Lucca left a testimony of the highest spirituality; and Father Elio Monari, from Emilia-Romagna, shot in Florence because he had protected partisans as well as communists. In many cases - as in the Marzabotto commune (Bologna) at the beginning of autumn 1944 - the parish priests were killed together with their followers inside the same church.

The laity - especially youth and men - experienced in a more direct manner the necessity to come to terms with their own conscience all by themselves. Faced with dramatic choices (Go with the partisans? Accept the authority of the Italian Social Republic? Search for some way to avoid making such a choice, or go into hiding?), they found themselves without the points of reference that they were previously accustomed to after 20 years of fascist dictatorship. Only in part could the clerics give direction and counsel, while officially the Church made no pronouncements. There was therefore a compelling appeal to personal responsibility and consciousness; what is more the parish priests were forced to overcome their own attitude toward respecting authority, instilled as it was over many years of education and propaganda, in order to make the necessary choices that went against the law, such as the matter of when to take up arms, when to give them up, or how to accommodate a search party.[4]

The collapse of 1943 imposed on all Catholics the need to once again reckon with politics and democracy, especially given the opening made by the Pope with his wartime Christmas radio messages. The history of the Catholic movement, especially its more democratic and antifascist components, was unknown to the younger generation and the very concept of democracy was completely new to them. Names such as those of Father Luigi Sturzo were only remembered by the older generation, while De Gasperi was still unknown to most people. Moreover, the conditions at that time required all Catholics to compare themselves with completely new persons and experiences, as they had opportunities to meet foreign soldiers, including Lutherans, Anglicans, Muslims, Hindus, as well as to have direct relations with Jews and communists. The parish priests often found them-

---

4. See Vecchio, "Il laicato cattolico italiano".

selves having to deal with and even accommodate those "different" from themselves.[5]

The idea of an imminent radical turning point in Italian society was widespread. The Pope himself indirectly referred to it each time he spoke of the need to build a "Christian civilisation". But this idea turned out to be particularly strong among those Catholics that had shared in the struggle and the ideals of the Resistance. In the pages of *Il Ribelle and Quaderni del Ribelle*, clandestine papers that expressed the views of the partisan group around Teresio Olivelli[6] (1916-1945), it is possible to read very strongly worded passages on the necessity of the state to intervene in the economy in order to limit social inequalities. Together with Carlo Bianchi (1912-1944) from Milan, Olivelli also elaborated, between 1943 and 1944, a theoretical discussion of informative principles for a new social order, which was based on the following premise: "The world is in crisis: something has died in the convulsions of our times: something, with sadness and with force, is looking to come to light. Dead is the epoch of high finance, the era of capitalism that generated infinite riches and infinite misery. An organisation without a soul permits greater poverty, the anarchy of production, the exploitation of man by man, steeped in the cult of violence, in state despotism and the self-consumption of war. Emerging from this is a workers' society, more free, more just, with greater solidarity, and more Christian".[7]

In 1944, Paolo Emilio Taviani of Genoa, who was then a leader in the antifascist struggle and would later become a Christian Democrat minister, described in his *Idee sulla Democrazia Cristiana*, that the DC should have a "left wing" as did other parties and not embrace "the conservatives, even if the latter proclaim themselves and want themselves to be Catholics".[8] Similar ideas surfaced in several other manifestos and programs of the Catholic Resistance, supporting plans for the socialisation of large industries and banks, while others stressed the need to effectively include the workers' interests within the state.[9] Giuseppe Dossetti, future leader of the left wing in the DC, suggested in 1945 that the end of the war and the victory of the

---

5. Traniello, "Guerra e religione". The volume De Rosa, *Cattolici, Chiesa, Resistenza*, is of fundamental importance for the vast coverage it gives to this topic. It furnishes a synthesis of the reseach developed on a regional scale and published in the following volumes, all of which were published by Il Mulino in 1997: Gariglio, ed., *Cattolici e Resistenza nell'Italia settentrionale*; De Rosa, ed., *I cattolici e la Resistenza nelle Venezie*; Bocchini Camaiani and Giuntella, eds., *Cattolici,Chiesa, Resistenza nell'Italia centrale*; Mazzonis, ed., *Cattolici, Chiesa e Resistenza in Abruzzo*; Violi, ed., *La Chiesa nel Sud tra guerra e rinascita democratica*. For a broader view of events in Italy in these years see: Vecchio, Saresella and Trionfini, *Storia dell'Italia contemporanea*.
6. Olivelli was one of the main protagonists in the Italian Resistance. Influenced by Catholic university students supporting the *Federazione degli Universitari Cattolici* (FUCI), he was also persuaded to support the fascist regime, of which he began to distance himself after criticising the racial laws of 1938. An officer in the Alpine Artillery, he was captured by the Germans in September 1943. He escaped and joined the underground Resistance. He was recaptured and died in Hersbruck prison camp, after a severe beating for having tried to help a sick companion (Caracciolo, *Teresio Olivelli*).
7. Cited in Bianchi Iacono, *Aspetti dell'opposizione dei cattolici*, 33.
8. Taviani, "Idee sulla Democrazia Cristiana".
9. The main accounts are collected in Varnier, *Idee e programmi*. See also Campanini, "I programmi del partito democratico-cristiano".

Labour Party in England would open not simply a "new chapter" but rather a "new volume" in European history.[10] In 1945 a cultured rural priest, Father Primo Mazzolari (about whom below), wrote a piece entitled *La rivoluzione cristiana*.

The Catholic presence in the Resistance movement was therefore of great significance, especially if one enlarges the concept of the Resistance and one considers not only the episodes of actual armed struggle, but also all of the acts of hostility and "illegality" in the confrontation with the Germans and the fascists: offering hiding places to those in danger, passive resistance, sabotage, distribution of propaganda, graffiti on walls, failure to report for military service, etc. (*Resistenza disarmata*).[11] When regarding the actual armed struggle it is extremely difficult to establish how many of the combatants were actually from the parishes or from Catholic Action, in part because the numbers of partisans varied a great deal over the course of months, reaching the greatest number in the spring of 1945 with close to 200.000 men. Based on recent studies it is possible to assemble provisional numbers on the make up of the forces in the field. Approximately 46% belonged to the communist Garibaldi Brigades, 20% to the *Giustizia e Libertà* group (they consisted of the liberal-socialist and antifascist followers of Nello and Carlo Rosselli - brothers who had been assassinated in France under orders of the fascist regime in 1937); 7% to the Matteotti Brigades (socialists); over 4% to Catholic organisations, and 21% to independent units that rejected political or ideological labels.[12] These percentages are, however, open to interpretation, considering that in certain independent formations, such as the *Fiamme Verdi* or the *Osoppo*, the Catholic presence was very strong. It can be further observed that membership in such groups did not follow a clear ideological or political criterion; what counted more in the real world was the local situation, the influences of contemporaries or local friends, or the vicissitudes of chance. There were, therefore, Catholic militants in the Garibaldi Brigades (a typical case being the future Christian Democrat Secretary Zaccagnini, a member of the XXVIII Garibaldi Brigade) or, vice versa, non-Catholics that entered a military unit that made reference to the Catholic world. One can, however, confirm that the Catholic presence in the Resistance was far from insignificant.

Nevertheless, the memory of this victory did not inspire a political program nor did it become a fundamental component of the Italian Church. It is also worth observing that a large part of the population (that of the South) only endured the German presence for a few weeks and therefore did not have a direct experience with the Resistance. Moreover the bishops and priests were foremost preoccupied with the strong presence of the communists among the partisans and were therefore interested in avoiding giving the communists any further advantage. Indeed, in the spring of 1945, many prelates (or bishops) - beginning with Cardinal Schuster in Milan - had made attempts to find a way to prevent the final "revolution of the people" against

---

10. Cited in Formigoni, "La memoria della guerra e della Resistenza", citations on pp. 8-10.
11. On these and other important themes, see Parisella, *Sopravvivere liberi*.
12. Ilari, "Le formazioni partigiane alla Liberazione", 141ff.

the Germans, while the communists were instead attempting to speed up its arrival.

The historian Guido Formigoni has astutely observed that at the end of 1945 the memory of the Resistance was not sufficient to sustain proposed projects for a profound social and political reorganisation in Italy. Indeed, as he goes on to suggest, what resulted was an interpretation in which the Resistance had been led and appraised above all as a moral and religious act and therefore without any ideological and political profile. This tends, therefore, to reduce the partisans' struggle to simply a contingent act, however noble it may have been. Or, on the other extreme, there is the tendency to exaggerate the concept of the Resistance to encompass every type of struggle for liberty. De Gasperi himself has been credited with the idea that the Resistance continued with the struggle against communism (an idea reinforced by the killing of numerous priests by militant communists in the period following the war). Faced with the current conception in which the Resistance was Italy's "second Risorgimento", numerous Catholic authors have arrived at the opposite view, according to which the true "second Risorgimento" was on 18 April 1948, that is the date of the triumphant electoral victory of the Christian Democrats. With this approach they opened the way to appropriate any type of operation. For example, the Christian Democrats' *Martirologio* (Book of Martyrs), prepared by the President of Catholic Action, Luigi Gedda, placed those who had received a gold medal for their participation in the Resistance side by side with those who had received the same recognition of military valor for their participation in the Spanish Civil War in the ranks of the fascist army.[13]

The Resistance did not become a fundamental element of postwar Catholic political culture. The fact that these memories were avoided in a specific and punctual manner - in order to avoid having to remember, in the Cold War years, that the Catholics had previously collaborated with socialists and communists - can be explained as a psychologically understandable selective "memory loss". This did not happen to everyone, but it was certainly a factor for many Catholics. This facilitated the attempt on the part of the PCI to appropriate *completely* the tradition of the Resistance, in order to consolidate its own image as the party representing every authentic libertarian and populist. It is impossible to claim that all Italian Catholics voluntarily chose to forget about the Resistance particularly amongst left and reformist elements, for whom the memory was not lost, often due to direct personal experience. It is sufficient to remember that, among the principal DC leaders, other than the already mentioned Taviani, Giuseppe Dossetti had been a partisan leader, Giuseppe Lazzati had been imprisoned in a German jail, Giorgio La Pira was an antifascist fugitive, Enrico Mattei a member of the military command of the *Comitato di Liberazione Nazionale Alta Italia* (CLNAI), and so on. Likewise, the figures more likely to be open to reform were also most likely to have had direct and personal contact with fascists and the Germans; this was the case with Father Primo Mazzolari, Father Zeno Saltini, Father David Maria Turoldo and many others. It can also be said that many of the priests that were active during the

---

13. Formigoni, "La memoria della guerra", 39.

Resistance dedicated their lives after the war to improving the lives of the poor. For example, Father Giacomo Vender of Brescia campaigned on behalf of homeless families. This raises the issue of whether there was a link between personal experiences during the war and later engagement in social work "on the frontier".

3. The Social Question between World War and Cold War.

The possibilities of developing more advanced social service dimensions within Italian Catholicism were limited, although the intense charity works of the bishops and priests during and after the war tended to give an official character to such tasks, as there had been a great deal of energy invested in them. Very solid and established institutions and organisations supported the unquestionably great works of charity carried out by the Church during the war. Among these were the *Pontificia Commissione Assistenza Profughi*, aiding refugees, and the *Pontificia Commissione Assistenza ai Reduci*, aiding returning soldiers, both fusing into the *Pontificia Commissione di Assistenza* (PCA) in 1945, finally becoming transformed into the *Pontificia Opera di Assistenza* (POA) in 1953.[14] Active information bureaus existed in each diocese to aid individual citizens and families, and these were directly connected with the Vatican. The head of the PCA and the POA was Monsignor Ferdinando Baldelli (1886-1963), a priest from the Marches region who had, since 1914, been responsible for the charitable initiatives on behalf of miners, farmers and emigrants. In 1926, he was called to Rome under a contract with the Viscosa Company to provide religious welfare to the workers inside the factory. In 1930 Baldelli established *Opera Nazionale Assistenza Religiosa e Morale degli Operai* (ONARMO), an organisation aimed at coordinating the activities of "workers' chaplains" devoted to proselytising among the working class. During the 1930s, ONARMO developed thanks both to favorable support from industrialists and the fascist regime. It also became active in the FIAT factories in Turin, where it gradually acquired its own unique character, thanks mostly to the work of Father Giuseppe Pollarolo, who attempted to create greater continuity in pastoral work. Pollarolo was not willing to simply limit his work to extemporaneous initiatives such as the celebration of Easter mass in the factory. After 1943 the workers' chaplains in Turin had to face new problems: first and foremost was the presence of the Germans (Pollarolo was arrested and, once liberated, fled into the mountains), then came the hostility of communist workers. While chaplains in other Italian cities remained tied to a more traditional mentality, those in Turin were forced to adapt to the realities of working class life. For example, they refused to campaign actively for the Christian Democrats in the 1948 elections and, later on, they tried to become familiar with the Belgian and French experiences of the *Jeunesse Ouvrière Chrétienne* (JOC).[15]

---

14. Giovagnoli, "La Pontificia Commissione Assistenza e gli aiuti americani".
15. Bertini and Casadio, *Clero e industria a Torino*. With regards to the JOC, it should be recalled that the first tentative importation of its model actually occurred in Turin in 1943, under the impetus of the workers' chaplain, Father E. Bosco. From this arose the

After 1945 ONARMO enjoyed years of considerable support and during the Cold War Baldelli received considerable aid from the Americans, as they spent lavishly to finance their anticommunist campaigns. In fact, the presence of workers' chaplains came to be seen with favour among many of those who wanted to limit at all costs the strength of the communists inside the factories. Baldelli had tried to create the basis for a real labour movement, a cause that proved to be untenable, given the prior existence of the *Associazioni Cristiane dei Lavoratori Italiani* (ACLI), the latter, starting in 1944, having the task to assist Catholic workers enlisted within the unified trade union, the *Confederazione Generale Italiana del Lavoro* (CGIL), in educational and cultural matters. The ACLI was organised on capillary lines moving from the national level to territorial circles and then to cells for each industrial concern. Enrollment expanded very quickly and with remarkable success, from 250 circles in 1945 to 3690 in 1947, with 4110 cells. These contributed to the formation and reorganisation of a new union, following the trade union division of July 1948 and the breaking of ties with the communist and socialist workers' organisations.

Nevertheless, the number of workers' chaplains grew considerably, from approximately 160 in 1945 to over 600 ten years later. It is important to point out, however, that these chaplains were very different from working class priests: they maintained their sacerdotal clothing and carried out only religious and charitable activities. With ONARMO, these priests collaborated more than others with the sensitive requirements of the workers' world and therefore sought out new forms and approaches for their pastoral work. Such was the case of the Florentine Father Giulio Facibeni (1884-1958), who was active in the working class neighbourhood of Rifredi and founder of the *Opera della Divina Provvidenza Madonnina del Grappa*.

It is impossible to find a similar phenomenon in Italy compared to that of the French worker priests or initiatives similar to the *Mission de France*. This is because - unlike the French case - in Italy one firmly believed that there was no need yet for a concerted effort at rechristianisation. Certainly, the signs of the disconnectedness between faith and daily experience were evident to everyone, but the majority of bishops and priests believed that these were the outcomes of the contingencies of the war. Or, more particularly, that these were the products of communist propaganda, secularism or even Protestants, or a result of the spread of immorality and secularism in the Italian press. From this line of thought emanated continued pressures, first on the fascists and then on the DC government, to limit the spaces for free speech and freedom of the press. This belief also led to the conviction that Italians may have been strongly shaken by the war, but did not necessarily require the introduction of new forms of evangelisation. One can look, for example, at the concentration of political skirmishes and great manifestations connected with the Holy Year (1950), the Year of Mary

---

first organisation, the *Gioventù Italiana Operaia Cristiana* (GIOC), which must have had to compete with the strength of the *Gioventù Italiana Azione Cattolica* (GIAC), with the latter supported by the Vatican's Central Office. In 1950, representatives of the GIOC participated as observers at the International Congress of the JOC in Brussels, and in the same year Joseph Cardijn came to Rome to meet with the Italian leaders of the GIOC (see Panero, "GIOC").

(1954) or the so-called "missions". Although these religious activities and public mobilisations were concentrated in a short period of time, they were designed precisely to give a healthy jolt to "lazy souls" or, worse yet, to those attracted to communism.

After all, the first Italian worker priests did not emerge on the scene until the end of the 1950s, when Father Sirio Politi (1920-1988) assumed work as a manual labourer in the shipyards of Viareggio (1956). In 1959, the Church hierarchy issued him an ultimatum, and Father Politi decided to remain a priest while maintaining a close relationship with the dockworkers and occasionally working with them as a stevedore. In the years that followed, he lived in a community of laymen and priests and participated at the heart of the political struggles against hunger, nuclear war, and in solidarity with conscientious objectors.[16] His experience as a worker priest began to bear fruit only some years later. Following the Vatican II Council, between 1965 and 1968, there existed about ten worker priests in Italy. In 1969, the first national meeting of worker priests was held at Chiavari, which gave rise to national coordination efforts and the clear separation of the organisation from the paternalistic traditions of the ONARMO chaplains.[17]

At any rate, Catholics did not lack debates over how best to address the problems of the working class and the poor. The logic of these, shaped as they were by clashes with the communists and the pressures of the Church hierarchy, tended ultimately to lead to a position of accommodation. After the electoral victory of 18 April, 1948, the internal battles in the DC between the followers of De Gasperi and the left wing followers of Dossetti were carried out in part over the major issues in economic and social politics. Above all the writing of Giorgio La Pira aroused concern with his *L'attesa della povera gente*, published in the review *Cronache Sociali* in January 1950, and his follow-up piece, *Difesa della povera gente*.[18] This essay was an attempt to counter the absolute dominance of neoclassical economic laws and constituted an important chapter in the Dossetti camp's critique against the monetarist and quasi-liberal economic line of the Minister of the Budget, Pella, himself a Christian Democrat. La Pira (1904-1977) became Mayor of Florence in 1950 and tried to put into action his convictions concerning peace and social justice. During the 1950s and 1960s many of his initiatives provoked ferocious criticisms. For example, he organised the requisition of vacant houses to make them available for the homeless; demanded aid from the ENI of Mattei[19] in order to save the Pignone factory; he transferred private property to public uses; organised interfaith conventions in Florence with Muslims and Jews; and he undertook a series of dialogues with Soviet leaders, from the mayor of Moscow to even Nikita S. Krushchev himself.

---

16. Raffaelli, "Politi, Sirio".
17. Guasco, *Storia del clero in Italia dall'Ottocento a oggi*, 287-288.
18. See Balducci, *Giorgio La Pira*.
19. The *Ente Nazionale Idrocarburi* (National Corporation for Hydrocarbons) was founded by Enrico Mattei in 1953 for the research of, and trade in, oil and gasoline resources. This corporation engaged in a protracted struggle with American oil companies, such as Standard Oil and Texaco.

Attention to the poor and the working class was also a constant in the thought of Father Primo Mazzolari (1890-1959).[20] In 1932, as a parish priest in Bozzolo, a country town in Mantova province (but in the Cremona diocese), he had already made a name as a non-conformist priest: decidedly antifascist, he endured threats and repeated arrests, then joining the underground in 1944. As a brilliant and original writer, he quickly had to reckon with the censors of the Holy Office, to which his book *La più bella avventure* had been submitted for the imprimatur in 1935. Beyond the already cited *Rivoluzione cristiana* (written in 1945 but published posthumously in 1967), Father Mazzolari published numerous texts between the 1930s and 1950s, including *La via crucis del povero* (1939), *Il compagno Cristo* (1945), and *La pieve sull'argine* (1952). His activities as a preacher in a number of Italian cities were equally intense. In 1949 Mazzolari founded the fortnightly *Adesso*, that was meant to be a newspaper whose debates were outside the normal lines, so much so that Mazzolari became the target for numerous interventions by ecclesiastical censors and of prohibitions from Rome and the Bishop of Cremona. *Adesso* distinguished itself for its ability to describe the living conditions of diverse categories of the poor (unemployed people, labourers, immigrants, peasants, those living in shanties or homeless, prisoners, etc.), publishing numerous direct testimonies, and recalling the duties of Christians towards such groups. The review's polemics were directed equally against the paternalism of the Church, the inequalities of capitalism, and communist materialism. It was significant that the review made an attempt to speak to the poor and for the poor. Amongst the more important regular columns of *Adesso* must be counted those entitled, *La parola ai poveri* (Voice to the Poor), *L'oro e il tempio dei poveri* (Gold and the Temple of the Poor), *La città e i poveri* (Society and the Poor), *I diseredati* (The Disinherited). Near the end of the 1950s there appeared two new columns (*Cronaca dei paesi sottosviluppati* and *Angoli d'Europa*) that devoted space also to the poor of the world at large. It is important to note that Mazzolari was particularly attentive to the experiences of French Catholicism, whose works and journals he avidly read. *Adesso* also expressed many of the intellectual traditions of the following writers: the Auxiliary Bishop of Lyon, France, Alfred Ancel; the noted theologian Jean Danielou; the Archbishop of Paris Cardinal Maurice Feltin, and of his predecessor, Cardinal Emmanuel Suhard; as well as the editor of *Esprit*, Jean-Marie Domenach, Jacques Maritain and many others, while also following closely the experiences of the worker priests.

Notwithstanding the strong efforts on the part of the Church hierarchy and the DC leadership to maintain a compact Catholic word - always believing that every tiny crack could open the way to communism -, the dissenting voices such as *Adesso* could not be extinguished. (The journal folded only in 1962, three years after the death of Father Mazzolari.) The signs of uneasiness were clear even at the center of Catholic Action and became ever

---

20. Bellò, *Primo Mazzolari*; Bergamaschi, *Presenza di Mazzolari*; Bedeschi, *L'ultima battaglia di don Mazzolari*; Chiodi, *Primo Mazzolari*; Campanini and Truffelli, eds., *Mazzolari e Adesso*. In Bozzolo (Mantova) the *Fondazione Don Primo Mazzolari* is active as the custodian of his private archives and in promoting the further diffusion of his thought (Address: via Castello 15, Bozzolo).

more frequent throughout the 1950s.[21] The association was at the apex of its organisational potential and of its capacity to influence larger sections of society during this period, thanks mostly to the dynamism of its president, Luigi Gedda, one of the authors of the electoral fortunes of the DC. But Gedda's approach, other than being socially conservative and rigidly anti-communist, was also very autocratic and hostile to every autonomous tendency coming from the four principal "pillars" composing Catholic Action (young men, young women, men, and women). In 1952, he chose not to renew Carlo Carretto's position as president of *Gioventù Italiana di Azione Cattolica* (GIAC), giving the position instead to Mario V. Rossi. Two years later, however, both leaders were forced to resign by the Holy See, provoking a noisy struggle that had repercussions within all youth associations. Also in 1954, the national assistant of the GIAC, Father Arturo Paoli, was forced to leave his assignment and was transferred from Rome. The leadership of the GIAC, in fact, stood close to the left wing of the Christian Democrats and emphasised the secular nature of politics. In 1953 Rossi wrote: "Young people want politics to be made up of political choices and not religious choices: religion should be an inspiration to politics and not a substitute for it. Therefore laymen must create their politics at their own personal risk, without using the Church to support a political position".[22] Moreover, they agreed to search for new forms of association and to increase their presence in the workplace, taking their example from the Belgian and French model of the JOC. In contrast once again to Gedda's convictions, Rossi emphasised the importance of religious training and contemplation as a means to overcome the limits of activism. Influencing this new orientation were the readings of Rossi and his circle - once again French writers, above all Mounier, but also Maritain, Congar, and Chenu.

The diverse life experiences of these men deserve reflection: Carlo Carretto (1910-1988) entered the *Petits Frères de Jésus* of Father Charles de Foucauld and spent ten years in the Sahara, to finally become the guiding spirit of a monastic community in Spello (Perugia); Mario Vittorio Rossi (1925-1976) worked closely with the European Coal and Steel Community, studied industrial medicine and likewise dedicated himself to the study of psychoanalysis and psychopathology. While never ending his personal search for a more liberated faith, he collaborated closely with the previously mentioned newspaper *Adesso*, edited by Father Mazzolari; Arturo Paoli (born in 1913) also joined the *Petits Frères* and eventually settled down in Latin America where he dedicated his life's work to the causes of the poor and the destitute.

In this panorama of voices that shared a commitment to concrete action in social issues, perhaps the most original experience was that of the Emilian Father Zeno Saltini (1900-1981), a truly remarkable figure. Born in Carpi (in the province of Modena), he had been diocesan president of the

---

21. For an introduction to the history of Catholic Action in Italy, see Formigoni, *L'Azione Cattolica Italiana*; Casella, *L'Azione Cattolica nell'Italia contemporanea*, not to mention the numerous entries in Traniello and Campanini, eds., *Dizionario storico del movimento cattolico in Italia* and in Traniello and Campanini, *Dizionario storico. Aggiornamento 1980-1995*.
22. Cited in Giuntella, "Cristiani nella storia. Il 'caso Rossi'", citation on p. 356.

Giuventù Cattolica, went on to graduate in jurisprudence from the Catholic University and then became a priest, choosing soon after to adopt a young ex-convict as his son. From the 1930s onwards he gave life to numerous social initiatives, gathered collectively under the name *Opera Piccoli Apostoli*. Over a number of years many children and young people were taken in by Father Zeno, and in 1941 one young woman of his parish began to devote herself entirely to his calling. She became the first *mamma per vocazione*, and she was soon followed by many others. These women made the decision to forgo having their own families, but instead, while remaining part of the laity, to adopt a number of young children and give them the same affection as would a true mother. In the same period, Father Zeno also attempted to give life to an *Unione dei Padri di Famiglia*. In 1945, Father Zeno published a book with the meaningful title, *La rivoluzione sociale di Gesù Cristo*, and in 1947 he took over with his followers the Fossoli Prison (near Carpi) that had been, during 1943 and 1944, the principle German transit camp in Italy and the place were many Jews and antifascists were held before their deportation to Germany and Poland. The prison camp was renovated and became the center for work projects designed to render the community independent. In 1948 an internal constitution was approved for the *Opera Piccoli Apostoli*, entitled "Nomadelfia", a neologism that expressed "fraternity is law". These were the years of greatest success for Father Zeno, for which he gained support from both church and secular leaders. Nomadelfia's population grew to over 1000 inhabitants, with some 850 "children" received. On the occasion of performing the first marriages between Nomadelfia residents, the new couples were taught to receive with equal love their own children as well as those adopted from outside the community. Father Zeno had originally attempted to widen the definition of a priest's work until he had indeed given life to a real political movement, one capable of taking in all of the "poor". His charged polemics were always lively, and in those years he came to be seen as a communist sympathiser. In reality, Father Zeno had hoped to defeat the communists, but in the Cold War climate his language and non-conformist nature created a number of adversaries both within the Church and in the Christian Democratic Party. Their alarm would increase in 1950 when the Emilian priest launched a proposal for a political movement called the *Movimento della Fraternità Umana*; the Church hierarchy quickly moved to block its development. Between 1951 and 1952 the crisis of Nomadelfia finally matured, due in part to poor administrative management and to growing financial deficits, as the expenses incurred in maintaining hundreds of children and young people were in fact quite enormous. In 1952 the Holy Office ordered Father Zeno to abandon Nomadelfia, while the Minister of the Interior, Mario Scelba (DC), arranged for the evacuation of Fossoli and the forced removal of the minors, entrusting them to boarding schools. Father Zeno requested and obtained for himself the demotion to lay status so that he could more freely dedicate himself to the solution of social problems. The community was resurrected on a landed estate near Grosseto, and in time Father Zeno returned to celebrate mass (1962) and was named parish priest. Still today Nomadelfia constitutes a unique experiment of communitarian life, one that refuses to accept the concepts of private property and money within its borders.[23]

The example of Father Zeno Saltini is significant for understanding some of the particularities of "Left Catholicism" in Italy. His social and political positions constituted very strong polemical arguments and these were of course viewed as "dangerous" and labelled "communist" (which explains the fury of Mario Scelba against Nomadelfia). But the intention of Father Zeno was in reality to defeat communism with a more radical proposition. His concept of society was basically rural, tied to the image of the patriarchal family in which he had been raised; while his theological training and his mentality were purely traditional in nature. Along these lines, in the last years of his life Father Zeno argued vehemently against the introduction of divorce and the legalisation of abortion.[24]

4. The Problem of Peace and Catholic Pacifism

During the Cold War and the most intense political and ideological clashes with communism, the topic of peace ended up being neglected, or better, reduced to the existing split between the two great international blocks. Italian Catholics clearly privileged a pro-western position, and therefore they tended to judge every discussion of peace as a symptom of weakness or, worse yet, as a sign of complicity with the Soviet Union (unless, naturally, the discussion of peace was limited to the Christian definition of peace, a point made many times by Pius XII). The dissenting voices were very few in number. Among those worthy of discussing were the supporters of the *Movimento Cristiano per la Pace* (MCP), founded in January 1948 by Guido Miglioli (1879-1954), previously leader of the extreme left current in the Italian Popular Party during the first postwar period, and then exiled to Moscow during the fascist period. In addition to Miglioli, other significant figures were Ada Alessandrini and Pio Montesi. The MCP had its own unitary vision of politics and trade unionism, aligning themselves decisively on the Left. It took part, together with the communists and socialists, in the Popular Democratic Front that opposed the Christian Democrats in the 1948 elections. After the split in the trade union movement, the MCP made the decision that its members would stay within the CGIL. Nevertheless, it was a very limited experience from the numerical point of view, as a matter of fact the remnants of the MCP disappeared by the second half of 1948 and early 1949. Various exponents of the MCP, beginning with Ada Alessandrini, maintained an independent leftist politics and in successive years collaborated closely with the initiatives of the Partisans of Peace, an organisation directly supported from Moscow and active in numerous

---

23. Internet site: www.gol.grosseto.it/asso/nomadelfia. See also the volume *Nomadelfia. Un popolo nuovo*.
24. Ciceri and Gazzi, eds., *Zeno. Un'intervista, una vita*; Saltini, *Don Zeno*; Sgarbossa, *Don Zeno*. In October 1999 two national conferences were held (one in Carpi, the other in Grosseto) on the life of Father Zeno, with the proceedings, edited by Nomadelfia, currently in press.

European and non-European countries.25 Their choice, however great its significance, did not provoke any particular repercussions within the Church, as these were the opinions of only a few individuals, lone voices within a unified and decidedly anticommunist Catholic world, even if internally diverse. But it was clear that every attempt at a relationship or dialogue between these Catholic organisations and the Partisans of Peace was always harshly rejected.

A somewhat more polemical issue was raised when the Partisans of Peace engaged the services of the Genoan Father Andrea Gaggero, connected with the Philippine fathers. He brought with him a past of Resistance (as a chaplain amongst the partisans) that had led to his arrest, deportation, and torture by the Nazis at the Mauthausen prison camp. His outspoken positions, marked as they were by an evangelic love and a strong dose of enthusiasm, drew a great deal of attention from the Left as well as criticism from within the Catholic world and the ecclesiastical hierarchy. Gaggero participated in the World Peace Conference held in Warsaw in November 1950; and in that and other circumstances he appealed to the universal feelings of peace and brotherhood, without entering into specific political or ideological topics. Because of his relationship with the Partisans of Peace, however, he was deprived of his position as a religion teacher and was subsequently reduced to lay status (1953). Throughout the 1950s, he continued to be engaged inside communist pacifist organisations, so much so as to be awarded the Lenin Peace Prize.26

In contrast to Gaggero, Father Primo Mazzolari refused to collaborate directly with the Partisans of Peace, contesting their ambiguities and partialities. According to the parish priest from Bozzolo, "the conquest and defense of peace is of such great import that it cannot become monopolised". In fact, "war is already declared at the very moment when a people or a class considers with less horror the possibility that a war could bring them justice, freedom and peace".27 In 1950, when addressing the so-called "Stockholm Appeal", launched by the international peace movement to demand a ban against the atomic bomb, Mazzolari was said to be disposed to signing the appeal and suggested an impartial debate with Christians on this theme, representing his evangelical and radical pacifism.28 This position taken in *Adesso* did not go unnoticed and indeed provoked the direct intervention of the hierarchy, as Cardinal Marchetti Selvaggiani, Vicar of Rome and Secretary of the Holy Office, corresponded with the Bishop of Cremona, Cazzani, in order to get information and speed up sanctions against *Adesso*. At the end of the same year, 1950, Mazzolari participated in a "Dialogue on Peace", an exchange of letters with the communist journalist Davide Lajolo and the Christian Democrat deputy Igino Giordani.29

25. For a general study, refer to Vecchio, *Pacifisti e obiettori di coscienza nell'Italia di De Gasperi*.
26. On Gaggero, see his autobiography *Vestìo da omo*. In addition, see the biographical entry in *Enciclopedia dell'antifascismo e della Resistenza*, II, 464.
27. Maprim [P. Mazzolari], *La pace di Parigi*, in *Adesso*, 30 April 1949.
28. Mazzolari wrote this article, entitled "La bomba atomica e ogni arma sterminatrice fuori legge", under the pseudonym Father Stefano Bolli, in *Adesso*, 1 July 1950.
29. P. Mazzolari, "Un sacerdote si unisce al dialogo tra un democristiano e un comunista", *L'Unità*, 29 December 1950.

On the whole, one sees a growing consciousness of the need to follow the road of non-violence and passive resistance to oppression in the reflections of Mazzolari: "By placing myself onto the evangelical plane, I did not renounce the defense of justice, nor did I confuse good and evil by accepting to take a neutral or resigned behaviour. The sheep has no wish to turn himself into a wolf, nor to reason with the wolf: he only understands how to resist the wolf as a sheep, that is the only way he can defeat him. Perhaps that is something which we, as Christians, have missed and continue to miss, something that now requires a concrete demonstration, complete and heroic, that justice for the poor and the oppressed can be arrived at without war".[30]

With these ideas Mazzolari aligned himself in favour of conscientious objection, which, in the immediate postwar period and especially in 1948 and 1949, had become a "hot" topic in Italy and France as well. It is worth noting that in the summer of 1941 Mazzolari had written a long reply to a Catholic young man who had asked his opinions on the purpose of war.[31] Mazzolari's interventions on these themes during the Cold War years were numerous. His conceptions of war and peace were ultimately published in his famous pamphlet, *Tu non uccidere!* (Thou shalt not kill!) written at the end of 1952 but not published until 1955.[32] In this text a total and non-refutable refusal of war is welded together with realistic recollections of the material disasters and human suffering in the recent world war. He also denounces the hypocrisy of the self-styled "Christian civilisation" and combines his critique with a message overflowing with hope and inner coherence. His enumeration of dramatic questions lead to the conclusion of the impossibility of a "just war", and he then binds his argument together with precise instructions on alternatives such as non-violence and conscientious objection. His criticism of the contradiction within communist pacifism does not preclude his questioning of Christians' tardiness in addressing the issue of war and peace; the causes of peace are tied to those of social justice and the struggle against the causes of misery. Whatever one might make of such a diverse and distinguished scheme with regards to the contingent political worries and alignments, it is clear that Mazzolari was successful in providing directions that, despite their utopian appearances, turned out to be quite durable.

In *Tu non uccidere!* the point of departure once again was the conviction that the communist peace movement should not be confronted by "pointing out the irony of their rituals or making a mockery of their initiatives" but with a testimonial of Christian coherence, "out of inner conviction, rather than out of fear", without fear of possible instrumentalisation.[33] The parish priest of Bozzolo insisted as well on the complexity of actual war conditions, on the mixing of economic, diplomatic, propagandistic, and

30. P. Mazzolari, "Per avere ragione del lupo non è necessario che la pecora si faccia lupo", *Adesso*, 15 December 1950.
31. P. Mazzolari, "Risposta ad un aviatore (I problemi della ricostruzione cristiana)", dated 10 August 1941, subsequently published in Mazzolari, *La Chiesa, il fascismo e la guerra*, citation on p. 78.
32. P. Mazzolari, *Tu non uccidere!*. For a complex interpretation of the small volume, see also Campanini, *Don Primo Mazzolari*, 59-77 and Bedeschi, *L'ultima battaglia*, 60-63.
33. P. Mazzolari, *Tu non uccidere*, 12-13 (in the 1980 edition of this work).

political factors that made it extremely difficult to carry out a serious analysis; at the same time, there was clear evidence of the interlocking elements of social and national self-interests hiding themselves behind the affirmations of principles or ideals. By reviewing and citing numerous theological affirmations, all of them critically opposed to the ideas of a "just war", Mazzolari could bring up the difficult issues of "mind sets", of "tacit acquiescence" and of "criminal activities" that bring about war "from a distance but with certainty".[34] He goes on to reject the much abused appeal to the concept of the nation (*patria*) to justify war: "War murders the nation, which is not simply a name, but made up of real citizens and their homes".[35]

In addition to Father Mazzolari, one must also mention the already cited Igino Giordani (1894-1980), the then Christian Democratic deputy. He carried on his shoulders a rich and varied human experience, both in politics and religion, that made him a truly unique figure[36]: wounded and decorated with honours during World War I, representative of the Popular Party, journalist, he was an attentive observer of international questions. After the arrival of fascism, he found work at the Vatican library (as did De Gasperi), and traveled to the United States for specialised library studies. He devoted himself to the study of the Church Fathers and to social doctrine, having begun to update *Le encicliche sociali dei Papi* (The Social Encyclicals of the Popes). At the beginning of 1949 Giordani started his own periodical, *La Via*, with the goal of "reclaiming at all costs an open dialogue", avoiding any associations with "those manicheans who, compartmentalising humanity into honest and dishonest, poor and rich, exploited and exploiter, east and west, entrench themselves into a block, fatalistically awaiting a clash".[37] Giordani also engaged himself in a public relations campaign on the North Atlantic Treaty as well as subscribing to the realism of De Gasperi's politics; he therefore managed to maintain a very perplexing combination of ideals and meta-politics. His delusions drew their origins from his understanding of the impotence of Christian nations to find a more adequate way to live peacefully with each other than by means of military pacts. Thus, at the occasion of a parliamentary debate on Italian participation in the Atlantic Alliance, Giordani used harsh words against war while also bitterly criticising the conduct of the communists and the anti-atlanticist opposition: "Every war - I assert - is a failure of Christians [...] Every war is murder". Therefore, now that every war was above all "a crazy extermination of values and people", no war could be considered "just".[38] In this way, Giordani most notably anticipated the future instructions of the Church, recognising before others the epochal significance of the advent of the atomic bomb: after Hiroshima it was no longer possible for there to be a "just" war. On the basis of these considerations, Giordani started quite quickly to promote conscientious objection showcasing objectors as "a sign of the reconstituted Christian consciousness against the madness of a civilisation

---

34. Ibid., 85.
35. Ibid., 37.
36. For a background discussion of his life and work, see Casella, *Igino Giordani*; Sorgi, ed., *Igino Giordani*.
37. I. Giordani, "La via della ragione," in *La Via*, 29 January 1949.
38. Atti Parlamentari, Camera dei Deputati, *Discussioni*, 16 March 1949, 6956-6963.

that goes on under the nightmare of nuclear war".[39] Therefore, conscientious objection assumes for him "a heroic importance, nearly paradoxical" in the confrontation against the "monstrous sin" constituted by modern total war.[40] In 1949 Giordani presented, together with the Social Democratic Deputy Umberto Calosso, a bill for the recognition of conscientious objection, which was, however, quickly shelved and never discussed in Parliament. The unique contribution of Giordani was his ability to remain on a level of moral and cultural denunciation of war, without entering into specific political analyses.

Neither Mazzolari nor Giordani would have likely accepted the label "Left Catholicism". In the context of the Cold War, therefore, their message assumed an explosive meaning within a Catholic world that had accepted dogmatically an extremist anticommunism, coloured by strong nationalistic sentiments that were the bequest of fascism. It was not therefore by chance that Mazzolari experienced numerous prohibitions and disciplinary measures, while Giordani failed to be reelected in 1953, paying thus for his pacifist positions.

5. Anticipations of the Vatican II Council in the 1950s

During the course of the 1950s the most critical voices within Italian Catholicism were confronted as well by the difficult relationship between the Church and contemporary society. The struggles with the communists (officially excommunicated from the Church in 1949) and the intensive movements of people during and after the war had, in fact, created a crisis for the traditional parishes. Each solemn pronouncement made by the Church was followed with numerous episodes of reciprocal intolerance that often led to situations approaching tragicomedy, and there remained, therefore, obvious symptoms of a profound gulf dividing the population. There were frequent clashes related to the celebration of funerals, caused by the requests of leftist militants to carry their red flags into the church, which was often met with objections by the parish priest. At other times, in various places, the parish priests had a habit of suspending the traditional processions for the patron saints as a sign of their condemnation of the electoral victories given to the communists by the local population. The very popular characters of Father Camillo and Peppone, created by the writer Giovanni Guareschi, did not have to venture far from reality for inspiration. This was because - after all - each of the two personae in question came from the same rural and traditional world which was still recognisable for millions and millions of Italians. Perhaps this was the motive for the extraordinary success of the films directed by Julien Duvivier, which began with *Don Camillo* (1952).

---

39. I. Giordani, "Gli obiettori di coscienza," *La Via*, 17 December 1949.
40. I. Giordani, "Bomba a idrogeno e obiezione di coscienza," *La Via*, 11 March 1950;
    I. Giordani, "Teologia degli obiettori di coscienza," *La Via*, 27 May 1950;
    I. Giordani, "Gli obiettori di coscienza io li vedo così," *L'Avvenire d'Italia*,
    3 December 1949.

The problems faced by the parish priest received ample space in the work of Primo Mazzolari, strengthened by his many decades as a parish priest. During his entire adult life, he questioned the role of the priest in the Church and in contemporary society, raising the question of a possible "dialogue" with the "estranged" and the renewal of traditional pastoral methods. But the most radical critic of the pastoral method came from a Florentine priest, Father Lorenzo Milani (1923-1967).[41] He had come from a well-off bourgeois family, of great cultural depth; his mother, Alice Weiss, was Jewish. In 1947 Father Milani was made chaplain at S. Donato Calenzano, a church in the industrial zone near Florence, where he could experience directly the effects of secularisation and the passage from a rural to a working class society. Critical of traditional forms of Catholic association, the young priest dedicated himself above all to the organisation of a popular school, one which included communist youth among its students. It was in this context that he undertook to write a book, subsequently published in 1958 with the title *Esperienze pastorali* (Experiences of Pastoral Work). In it he developed a pitiful and realistic analysis of the Church's actions, demonstrating its separation from the reality of people's lives. The book was judged to be "inappropriate" by the Holy Office, which gave orders to ban its further sales.[42] Therefore, in 1954, Father Milani was placed as prior (parish priest) at S. Andrea di Barbiana, an extremely isolated rural parish with very few inhabitants, in the area of Mugello. Here he dedicated his life to an original form of education and instruction for peasant youth, providing them with an education based on a revolutionary methodology, on the reading and discussion of newspapers, on comparative study, and on direct connections between everyday life and culture, and with the will not to see a single student drop out. This work became renowned in Italy in the following years. During the student movement of 1968 and for a long period thereafter, Father Milani was revered as a "prophet", especially after the publication of *Lettera a una professoressa* (1967)[43], edited together with the young residents of Barbiana, which constituted a strong denunciation of the classical character of Italian schooling. Father Milani was also at the center of another well-known case during these years, in which he was charged with inciting civil disobedience, having publicly defended the right of conscientious objection to military service (1965).[44]

The atmosphere in Florence was, in the 1950s and 1960s, particularly lively and produced many individuals and experiences that could be catalogued under the "Left Catholic" label. One should not forget in this regard the groundbreaking role of the Mayor, Giorgio La Pira. Among the religious activists, one man who began to make a name for himself was Father Ernesto Balducci (1922-1992), a member of the congregation of the *Chierici regolari poveri della madre di Dio delle scuole pie*.[45] In his case too, the most

---

41. Scattigno, "Milani, Lorenzo"; Fallaci, *Dalla parte dell'ultimo* (with additional and various new editions).
42. *Don Lorenzo Milani tra Chiesa, cultura e scuola.*
43. Scuola di Barbiana, *Lettera a una professoressa.*
44. Milani, *L'obbedienza non è più una virtù* (containing his writings on this topic and the document sent by Father Milani to his judges).
45. Gaudio, "Balducci, Ernesto".

activist portion of his career and the greatest notoriety came in the 1970s and lies thus beyond the scope of this study. But already in the 1950s Balducci had begun to disseminate throughout Italy the thinking of Teilhard de Chardin, and in 1958 he started the review *Testimonianze*, which became a reference point for progressive Catholics and those on the political Left. In 1959, the Holy Office forced Father Balducci to leave Florence and to establish himself first in Frascati and then in Rome.

Balducci's *Testimonianze* and Mazzolari's *Adesso* were not the only critical Catholic reviews originating in that period. Apart from those journals openly political or linked to the Christian Democratic Left, one should at least recall *Il Gallo* (The Rooster). It began in Genoa in 1946 under the editorship of Nando Fabro. The title is in reference to the biblical episode in which the rooster crows after Peter's repeated betrayal of Jesus. The paper intended to put aside trepidation and to create a point of dialogue between Christians and marxists. Always very attentive to literature and culture, *Il Gallo* insisted on the necessity of transforming consciousness, stepping outside of rigid political oppositions and often making comparative references to the thought of Maritain. After 1950, such themes as the relationship between the lay population and the Church hierarchy, the autonomy of the laity, and collaboration between believers and non-believers, were at the center of the paper's editorial concerns. In 1956, an interesting *Memoria breve sui cattolici di sinistra* (Short Memorandum Concerning Left Catholics) was published, written by Fabro, relating the history of various initiatives, such as the efforts of Antoine-Frédéric Ozanam and Father Henri Maret who, in the context of 1848 France, through the intermediary of the paper *L'Ere nouvelle*, aimed to arrive at a reconciliation between Catholicism and democracy and, on this occasion, launched the slogan "Christian Democracy".[46]

A significant role was played in those years by Father David Maria Turoldo[47] (1916-1992), a member of the order of the *Servi di Maria*, who had already distinguished himself in Milan during the war years for his ties with the Resistance and his intense work attending to and protecting those whose lives were in danger. Attentive to the political proposals of the Christian Left of that time, Turoldo declared himself hostile to the hypothesis of a single unified Catholic Party and therefore avoided getting caught up in the Catholic mobilisation of 1948. In the more openly critical years of Italian and international political confrontation, Turoldo operated above all on a religious and cultural level. In 1951, still in Milan, together with Father Camillo De Piaz, he created the *Corsia dei Servi* cultural center, destined to quickly become one of the more active centers for the encounter between Catholic and lay cultures. Beyond that it was one of the more significant

---

46. Guala and Severini, "Dialogo, obbedienza, 'critica' e dissenso nel 'Gallo'".
47. Turoldo was recognised as well for his intense artistic and poetic activities. Some of his principal works in those years include *Io non ho mani* (Bompiani, Milano, 1948); *Udii una voce* (Mondadori, Milano, 1952); *Gli occhi miei lo vedranno* (Mondadori, Milano, 1955). Amongst those published more recently, see *O gente terra disperata* (Paoline, Roma, 1987); *Il grande male* (Mondadori, Milano, 1987); *Canti ultimi* (Carpena, Sarzana, 1989), subsequently republished by Garzanti, Milano, 1991. The most recent anthology is *O sensi miei... Poesie 1948-1988* (Rizzoli, 1989). On the author himself, see Vecchio, "Turoldo, David Maria".

spaces for the maturation of ideas destined to contribute to the great experience of the Vatican II Council. Important in this regard were the efforts to increase the participation in the liturgy through the readings of the Gospel and the main prayers in Italian. Influenced by many religious poets and preaching friars of the Middle Ages, Turoldo proclaimed himself a traditionalist, rejecting the contemporary definitions given him by others, such as a "modern" priest, "of the left", or "troublesome". The consternation and the open criticisms emanating from traditionalist circles and the religious hierarchy against this religious figure grew more acute in connection with the open clash surrounding the case of Father Zeno Saltini mentioned above. Turoldo had in fact known the priest from Carpi and was familiar with the experience at Nomadelfia in 1948. This had convinced him to get involved even to the point of forming a solidarity committee and initiating assistance for Nomadelfia. The harsh campaign directed against Father Zeno - concluding with the forced abandonment of Nomadelfia and the defrocking of Father Zeno - had a profound impact on Turoldo as well. In fact, by the end of 1952 the order came from Rome for Turoldo to leave Italy - Cardinal Ottaviani is said to have advised him to "go and see the world" - and thus, for Turoldo, began a long phase of travels and short journeys to foreign countries. He spent more or less extensive periods in Switzerland, Austria, Germany and subsequently in England, the United States, Mexico, Chile, Canada and South Africa.

6. Conclusion

As stated in the introduction, it is highly debatable whether one may apply the "Left Catholic" label to the majority of personalities described here. It is also true that many of them would have rejected a definition that would risk reducing them to a singular political dimension; beyond that, it would also have created further difficulties for them with the Church hierarchy. Moreover, the accomplishments of the individuals described in this chapter are better characterised as pastoral, charitable, and social, and - with some exceptions - did not emanate from a direct wish to take part in politics as such. An additional reason to question the label is that almost every single one of them lacked any direct influence from marxism, nor did they have any more or less explicit linkages with the Communist Party or even the Socialist Party. In short, only those who had some ties to the MCP or religious figures like Father Gaggero tried to construct direct collaborative ties with the political organisations of the Left, at least on the issue of the struggle for peace. For all the others, communism remained the enemy to attack; and they dealt with it, if at all, by confronting it with its own weapons, while at the same time not forgetting the urgent need to create in Italy a more meaningful system of social justice. In addition, the influence of marxism at the cultural and philosophical level was limited, if not to say totally absent, as the outlines of reasoning and the language used by most had their roots in neo-Thomist philosophy studied in their youth, or, in other cases, influenced by a radical evangelical tradition. It follows then that most preferred to speak of "the poor" rather than the "proletariat".

The mentality of these men also remained heavily permeated with the attitude of opposition to contemporary culture and society that had characterised the atmosphere when they had been young and in training. Their mindset therefore remained imbued by the pre-Vatican II Council climate. These men were, however, different than the majority of Italian Catholics in that they were pushed by their intelligence and humane sensibilities to seek out new sources of thought. Difficulties of language also played a role, as it precluded many of them from having any direct contact with German and Anglo-Saxon Catholicism. This meant that the majority of them looked to French pastoral currents for inspiration, whose avant-garde authors served as constant points of reference.

As has been hinted at above, there existed another major difference between these dissident religious figures and the Church hierarchy as well as the majority of the clergy concerning the realistic assessment of the pastoral conditions within the Italian Church. For these men "of the frontier", it was never taken for granted that Italy was a "naturally" Catholic country by virtue of its historical past and the presence of the Pope in Rome. The idea that it was sufficient to apply with greater courage and determination the traditional criteria and methods in order to relate to society became the topic of debates. Voices stressing the need for a radical modification of the old methods in order to adapt them to a situation in which it was necessary to start again, to re-evangelise those who had lost their faith in the Church, began to be heard. In sum, here again, the trend toward secularisation found in France was concluded to be closer to the Italian situation than many would have wanted to believe.

The implacable opposition against communism and the vigilant gaze of the Vatican blocked for many years the necessary innovations at the local level. At the same time, the secular press used criteria of political convenience to judge all of the Catholic innovators. In this way the moderate papers clamored against those who "played the communist's game", while the Left press tried to speculate on the internal conflicts of the Church, always hoping to insert themselves into any active controversies. For the majority of Italian Catholics, however, the ideas discussed in this chapter were heard only as faint echoes, a problem that was in part attributable to the dispersion of these "frontier" forces, and because their messages were disseminated through journals and editorial houses with often minuscule resources. Yet, still, publications such as *Adesso* had a respectable circulation above all amongst the provincial clergy and the clergy of the countryside of Northern Italy.[48]

The true value of so many men and ideas was only slowly recognised, not really until the period of Pope John XXIII and Pope Paul VI. Carretto, Mazzolari, Milani and Turoldo came to be respected and cited authors, revered as authentic precursors or faithful interpreters of the Vatican II Council. Nevertheless, the popularity of their thought remained conditioned by the changing of times (Father Milani was particularly popular in

---

48. See Trionfini, "Gli uomini e le fortune di Adesso". This study was based on a careful examination of Father Mazzolari's personal archives. For the other newspapers cited, there still exist no comparable studies.

the years of mass protest during the late 1960s) and, more practically, by the relative difficulty to obtain their works. Even today their works are published by small publishing houses and only rarely are they picked up in the larger distribution channels of the publishing industry. There still persist prejudices and simplistic appraisals that now and again feed the old suspicion of their "communism" (the polemical recourse to the pejorative definition of *cattocomunisti* is easily made) or their supposed weakness vis-à-vis marxism, an accusation that is usually misplaced. On the whole, there still remains the problem of recovering and conserving a Catholic historical memory that is not limited to a narrow intellectual elite and one that - even if from a critical perspective - could withstand comparison with the heritage of those who have been discussed here. The fact that everything becomes reduced to the single dimension of the hierarchy (or even the pontiff) does not make it any easier to understand the past. Proof positive of this obstacle can be seen *ad abudantiam* in the frequently occurring discussions concerning the relationship between Pius XII and the extermination of the Jews, a discussion that almost always precludes a serious examination of the Church's attitude in its entirety (bishops, priests, and laymen).

SOCIALISM OUT OF CHRISTIAN RESPONSIBILITY.
THE GERMAN EXPERIMENT OF LEFT CATHOLICISM (1945-1949)

Andreas Lienkamp

1. In the Beginning

In his article, "Vergessene Brückenschläge", the Catholic socialist Walter Dirks recalls that after the Second World War Christianity and socialism, the two "powers of the soul", initially felt a close bond. "Both had survived persecution at the hand of the inhumane dictatorship, strengthened in their cause and in the certainty of their future, and weakened through the death or emigration of significant individuals. However, as life in the Federal Republic normalised itself, the former fronts were restored".[1] Immediately following 1945, similar to the post-World War I period, an initial atmosphere of fundamental change emerged in which no antagonism between Christianity and socialism could be detected in the political arena. "On the contrary: it was precisely these two powers that were regarded as the decisive, forward-looking factors shaping the reform of economic and social relations".[2] Yet spring did not last for long. Under the sign of the Cold War the militant antisocialism of the Adeanuer Era hindered the growth of the fragile buds of Left Catholicism, which did not blossom until the 1960s.

Like Walter Dirks, the Left Catholic *Bensberger Kreis*, co-founded by Dirks himself, looks back at the "forgotten bridges" between socialism and Catholicism in its memorandum, "Antisozialismus aus Tradition?". Thereby, the verdict concerning the significance of precisely that movement, which moved the issue of rapprochement in the first half of the 20th century forward the furthest, proves to be rather sobering: "After 1945 religious socialism revived, but only briefly. It did not survive the emergence of the Federal Republic of Germany".[3] This lapidary assessment seems to render a further preoccupation with German Left Catholicism unnecessary, since at first glance this assertion does not give any doubt as to the historical ineffectiveness of this movement, at least as far as the German context after 1949 is concerned.

In his analysis of the "idea of a Christian socialism within the Catholic social movement and in the *Christlich Demokratische Union* (CDU)", Franz Focke affirms that neither in the Weimar Republic nor in the post-World War II period did the "Catholic socialists" possess a distinct social and political influence. "Inasmuch as they once again began to work towards the

---

1. Dirks, "Vergessene Brückenschläge", 239-240.
2. See Dirks, Schmidt and Stankowski, "Einleitung: Christen für den Sozialismus", 7.
3. *Antisozialismus aus Tradition?*, 25.

same goal after 1945, they remained confined to smaller groups, like Steinbüchel, Michel and Mertens. They were called upon to provide inspiration, but they were neither willing nor capable of politically organising themselves and fighting for the acquisition of power".[4] Therefore, there is no place for Left Catholics in a historiography of victory and success.[5] Is it still worth examining them closer?

Despite his verdict concerning Left Catholics, it is evident that Focke makes an exception for Walter Dirks, who was closely associated with Steinbüchel, Michel and Mertens. His stance is justifiable, since Dirks is one of the key figures of Left Catholicism in post-World War II Germany.[6] He plays a significant role in the various efforts within Catholicism, not only on the party-political (co-founder of the "Christian socialist" CDU in Frankfurt), the theoretical (advocate for "socialism out of Christian responsibility"), the journalistic (co-editor of the Left Catholic *Frankfurter Hefte*), but also on the practical level (co-initiator of the demand for co-determination at the Catholic Convention in Bochum). These levels shall construct the framework for the ensuing attempt to reconstruct the German experiment with Left Catholicism in the second half of the 1940s and in the early years of the 1950s.

The term "Left Catholicism" shall be used as an after-the-fact label for those Catholic movements, thinkers and organisations, who understood themselves to be devout and crucial members of the Catholic Church, yet who also opted to take a socialist route (however individually natured). According to Stankowski, the term was not accepted as common linguistic usage until the beginning of the 1950s, when the differences between a majority and minority Catholicism became much more pronounced. In the immediate postwar period, the expression is to have been used in connection with progressive Catholicism in France[7], although even in Germany at this time it occasionally functioned as a way to identify either oneself or others as being socially oriented Catholics[8], in the latter case often with the intention to bring the others into disrepute.[9] Unlike structurally and institutionally organised social Catholicism, the quantitatively smaller Left Catholic milieu is much more difficult to identify. Left Catholicism was pub-

---

4. Focke, *Sozialismus aus christlicher Verantwortung*, 292.
5. See Dirks, Schmidt and Stankowski, "Einleitung", 8-9: Since Christians for whom socialism was not just a temporary fashionable movement "were politically defeated, memory of them was suppressed or destroyed. That history books ordinarily recount historical events from the victors' point of view is a well-known fact".
6. See Stankowski, "Katholiken für den Sozialismus", 10.
7. See Stankowski, *Linkskatholizismus nach 1945*, 12. He refers to Kogon, "Georges Bidault. Frankreichs Ministerpräsident". In this profile, Kogon portrays Bidault "as the most prominent man of the new Left Catholic party, the MRP". Ibid., 665.
8. See Stankowski, *Linkskatholizismus nach 1945*, 12 and 304 footnote 27. As an example of such self-identification he refers to Dirks, "Rechts und links". In this passage Dirks opts for a "socialist rebuilding of the economy and society" as a "Left Catholic" and out of "political love of one's neighbour". Ibid., 26, 35 and 24. The *Rheinischer Merkur*, in its 15 July 1950 issue, characterises Dirks in an intentionally critical manner as the head of a trend "that tends to be called 'Left Catholic' or 'Christian socialist'". Citation in: Stankowski, *Linkskatholizismus nach 1945*, 319 footnote 120. Stankowski could not find an example for the application of the term in the Weimar Republic.
9. See Dirks, "Ein 'anderer' Katholizismus?", 250.

licly represented by individual people and publication projects[10], by "partisans without the support of the masses", as Dirks so appropriately writes.[11]

2. The Pre-History: Left Catholicism in the Weimar Republic

Just as the moment of liberation from the tyranny of National Socialism through the efforts of the Allies did not truly represent the "zero hour" in terms of social, economic, political or ideological developments, but rather a multi-layered conglomerate of historical continuity and discontinuity[12], so also does Left Catholicism in post-world war Germany not begin as *tabula rasa*. For the most part, it were the same individuals, those with a "known record", those who already in the Weimar Period acted in the interest of Left Catholicism, who then, particularly in the last phase of the Second World War, once more began working with ideas and concepts linked to their previous preoccupations.

Associating the Catholic socialists of this era, who were in many ways quite different from each other, with one particular movement is not quite so unproblematic. At first glance, there appears to be more which separates than unites them. Included in this group are: the pastor and scholar Wilhelm Hohoff (1848-1923), who had attempted to use Thomas Aquinas' ideas to support the theories of Karl Marx and was basically isolated from the Catholic camp, referred to himself as a socialist, and yet viewed social democracy with a critical eye; the priest, philosopher, moral theologian and social philosopher from Cologne, Theodor Steinbüchel (1888-1949), a student of Hohoff, who interpreted "socialism as an ethical idea" and who acted as a mentor to the Catholic socialists[13]; the social scientist, adult educator and committed "lay-theologian" Ernst Michel (1889-1964) who was active in the Frankfurt trade union-run *Akademie der Arbeit* and like Hohoff considered himself to be a socialist independent from the *Sozialdemokratische Partei Deutschlands* (SPD); the political commentator and theologian Walter Dirks (1901-1991), a student of Steinbüchel, who, educated by Romano Guardini and the Catholic youth association *Quickborn*, became an editor of the Left Catholic *Rhein-Mainische Volkszeitung* in the Weimar Republic and who published the *Frankfurter Hefte* together with Eugen Kogon after the Second World War - he, too, saw himself as a Catholic socialist dissociated from social democracy; and finally, there is Heinrich Mertens (1906-1968), the only representative of this group to join the SPD, who came from Anton Orel's romantic Viennese school of thought, founded the association of Catholic socialists along with their publication, the

---

10. Ludwig and Schroeder, "Einleitung", 9.
11. Dirks, "Ein 'anderer' Katholizismus?", 250. See also ibid., 253 and 256-257: "On the whole, an unorganised and only in part interdependent complex of readers, friends, informal and formal groups, impossible to organise".
12. See Focke, *Sozialismus aus christlicher Verantwortung*, 275: "The tabula rasa syndrome, meaning the belief that one could completely rebuild from the ground up, was...more likely the product of political wishful thinking than a reasonable assessment".
13. In my dissertation, I am attempting to paint a more complete picture of Steinbüchel in the context of, above all, Catholic discussions of socialism in the first half of the 20th century. See Lienkamp, *Theodor Steinbüchels Sozialismusrezeption*.

Rote Blatt, and who was associated with the Protestant religious socialists. These five individuals did not comprise an actual group, but were set apart from contemporary Catholic antisocialism by an "option for socialism", an affinity of ideas, which bound them together despite all their differences. Klaus Kreppel formulates the common goal of the Catholic socialists as follows: they wanted "to politically refute, in the same manner as Wilhelm Hohoff, on whose ideas they had based their theoretical arguments, Bebel's popular thesis that Christianity and socialism stood opposed to one another like fire and water".[14]

The congenial thinkers Steinbüchel, Michel and Dirks cultivated the most intense personal and scholarly exchange of ideas - at least during the Weimar period but also after 1945 - although, as far as the reception of Marx and socialism is concerned, one can assume that Steinbüchel probably possessed the greatest influence. If, according to Ulrich Bröckling, Walter Dirks "evidently (belongs) to the few authors who already prior to 1933 had familiarised themselves with the early writings of Marx"[15], then one must - according to the opinion of Jürgen Habermas[16] - also include Steinbüchel in this group. It is even possible that it was Steinbüchel who inspired Dirks to read and analyse Marx' early writings. Dirks himself confirms this assumption: "Theodor Steinbüchel, who had opened the discussion within Catholic circles after the [First] World War in a positive and thorough manner with his book, *Der Sozialismus als sittliche Idee* (1921), had as the altogether first Catholic thinker thereupon recognised the philosophical and historical potential of early marxist ideas".[17] Despite the strong philosophical emphasis in Marx' work, Steinbüchel does not belong to those individuals, who clearly distinguish between the early *philosophical* Marx and the later *economist*. On the contrary: in his publications of the 1920s, as in his literature of the 1940s, Steinbüchel underscores the *abiding* synthesis of Marx's philosophy and socialism, the *combining* of economics and philosophy, as constituting the *essence* of marxism as well.[18]

---

14. Kreppel, "Feuer und Wasser", 5.
15. Bröckling, *Katholische Intellektuelle in der Weimarer Republik*, 144. See also Dirks, *Der singende Stotterer*, 19: "At that time, the two-volume Kröner edition of the early writings of Karl Marx was published, read with passion and discussed among friends, just like the brand new work of Lukács, *Geschichte und Klassenbewußtsein*".
16. See Habermas, "Zur philosophischen Diskussion", 167.
17. Dirks, "Christen zum Marxismus", 176, emphasis added- A.L.
18. See the interpretation, which heads in the same direction, of Landshut and Mayer, "Einleitung. Die Bedeutung der Frühschriften von Marx", XIII: "We make it our duty to dispose of a certain prejudice, which has its own history and which underlies not only the anti-marxist interpretation of Marx, but also marxist interpretations of Marx. This misunderstanding is that Marx, in his younger years, was 'still' oriented towards philosophy only, that he eventually freed himself from philosophical 'captivity' - first from Hegel himself, then from the young Hegelians (Bauer, Ruge), and eventually also from Feuerbach - and that towards the end of the forties he struggled to establish his final, purely economical interpretation of the historical world and its 'necessary' development. This view of Marx, which is still generally accepted today [1932- A.L.], can be much less sustained, however, now that the manuscript [meaning the Paris manuscript, 'Nationalökonomie und Philosophie' from 1844- A.L.], which until now remained completely ignored, has been published for the first time, revealing its straightforwardly and fundamentally philosophical basis of his economic theory. In a certain sense, this study is Marx's most central work".

Yet, the efforts of Steinbüchel, Michel, Dirks and Mertens encountered tremendous opposition within the Church as well as without. There were specifically two events that brought the Left Catholic projects and the Christian-socialist dialogue to an abrupt end on the eve of the Weimar Republic: the appearance of the encyclical *Quadragesimo Anno* and then, above all, the National Socialists' takeover of government control. As the fortieth anniversary of the first social encyclical, *Rerum Novarum* (1891) written by Leo XIII, drew closer, the unsolved problem, "Christianity and socialism", once again forced itself onto the agenda. Apparently the previous efforts of the Church authorities had not achieved the desired successes in this respect. Yet (not only) German Catholics still sympathised with socialism and participated in its specific movements, not least of all encouraged by the cautious opening of a dialogue between German social democracy and parts of Catholicism. Both sides began to relax their boundaries. Because of this situation, Pius XI saw it necessary to state his fundamental opinion clarifying his earlier, rather specific comments. On May 15, 1931, his encyclical *Quadragesimo Anno* appeared, whose goal was, among other things, to (re-) establish "a unified course for social Catholicism"[19], which the Catholic socialists had consciously abandoned primarily because of their stand on capitalism and socialism.

Addressing the social Catholics, the Pope clearly explained: "Whether considered as a doctrine, or a historical fact, or a movement, socialism, if it remains truly socialism... cannot be reconciled with the teachings of the Catholic Church because its concept of society itself is utterly foreign to Christian truth" (QA 117). Franz Focke is right in his judgement, when he writes that the passage in the encyclical on socialism may have ended the discussion in the Catholic camp for the time being regarding the possibility of a "Christian socialism".[20] The Left Catholic activities that still remained after the publication of *Quadragesimo Anno* were swept away when the National Socialists came to power on 30 January 1933.

3. German Left Catholicism in the Second Half of the 1940s and in the Early Years of the 1950s

"The jointly suffered persecution of the Protestant and Catholic churches, the terror practiced against communists, socialists and Christians, as well as the fight of these so differently constituted groups against the same totalitarian regime, were among the unforgettable experiences many people had during the national socialist tyranny. These experiences became the chief motive for a new form of political cooperation between Protestant

---

19. Schasching, *Zeitgerecht - zeitbedingt*, 9. That the encyclical did indeed effect social Catholicism in this way is substantiated by, for example, the commentary by Brauer, *Der soziale Katholizismus in Deutschland*, 6: "Whatever questions or doubt or differences of opinion were still remaining shall be settled here". Mertens, "Bilanz. Unser Ursprung", 69.
20. See also the title of the corresponding chapter in his work: "The Preliminary End of Christian-Socialist Discussions". Focke, *Sozialismus*, 173.

and Catholic Christians and for the attempts at a common journey of socialists and Christians immediately after the war".[21]

These initial circumstances caused political Catholicism and the Catholic socialist movement in Germany to completely reorganise. Yet, even though the Centre Party (1945) and quite a bit later the Christian trade unions (1955) were re-established, they did not manage to regain their previous strength in membership numbers and socio-political significance. The Catholic workers' associations did not escape a similar fate, despite their revival (tolerated by several bishops only as a result of the pressure from the Vatican). Even they could not attain to the same influence they had possessed in the 1920s after years of socio-political abstinence which had been forced upon them by the Nazis.[22] Instead of restoring the organisational framework used in the Weimar Republic, a large part of political Catholicism merged with the interdenominational CDU / CSU[23], and large parts of the Catholic workers' movement joined the party-politically and ideologically neutral *Deutscher Gewerkschaftsbund* (DGB).[24]

That which the DGB accomplished, namely the unification of Christian and socialist powers under the same institutional roof, was *not* achieved in the party-political sphere, although there were attempts at unification, even if only very weak and intermittent. At this point it would be appropriate to recall the (futile) efforts of Walter Dirks to create a *Sozialistische Einheitspartei Deutschlands* as the recognised heir of the SPD and the *Kommunistische Partei Deutschlands* (KPD), that was to unite workers, left wing democrats and social Christians.[25] In the first of his twelve theses which he drew up in May 1945 and presented to a group of Frankfurt antifascists, Dirks recognised an effective escape from the German and European chaos "only in a German and European socialism".[26] To accomplish this, "an unambiguous socialist theory" would be needed that would supplement and revive "the fundamental elements of marxism from the experiences of the last thirty years" (6th thesis).[27] Dirks identified the goal of this democratic socialism as "the organisation of the highly diversified

---

21. Stegmann, "Geschichte der sozialen Ideen im deutschen Katholizismus", 484.
22. See Focke, *Sozialismus*, 18, as well as Klönne, "Arbeiterkatholizismus", 42.
23. Regarding the formation and the program of the *Christlich Demokratische Union* (CDU), see my next subchapter 3.1. In the German parliament, the CDU joined up in a parliamentary bloc with its closely allied Bavarian sister party, the *Christlich-Soziale Union* (CSU).
24. See Focke, *Sozialismus*, 17-18. At the founding congress of the DGB in Munich on 12-14 October 1949, sixteen previously independent trade unions united under one roof. Adherence to the self-imposed principle of party-political neutrality was disputed from the beginning. Eventually, the DGB's relatively close association with social democracy led to the formation of the *Christliche Gewerkschaftsbewegung Deutschlands* in 1955 (since 1959: the *Christlicher Gewerkschaftsbund Deutschlands*) and thereby to the division of the Catholic workforce into two organisations.
25. See Dirks, "Vorwort", 7. In this context, see also Dirks, *Der singende Stotterer*, 26. Besides the resemblance of the name, Dirk's conception had nothing in common with the *Sozialistische Einheitspartei Deutschlands* (SED), which emerged in April 1946 in the Soviet occupation zone as a result of the forced merger between the KPD and the SPD. After its second party conference (20-24 September 1947), the SED was converted into a "party of a new type", modelled after the Soviet Communist Party.
26. See Dirks, "Thesen zu einer 'Sozialistischen Einheitspartei'", 33.
27. Ibid., 34.

national economy along socially responsible lines", yet not a "total collectivism in which personal identity, freedom, morality and dignity of the individual would be lost" (9th thesis).[28]

However, this plan to establish a "radical socialist Labour Party that was also influenced by Christians" was hindered by representatives of both traditional workers' parties, whose primary objective was the reestablishment of the former organisational structures. Whether or not Christians would have indeed traversed this path towards a Christian socialist party is questionable and in retrospect seems more than doubtful".[29]

3.1. The Chance to Realise a "Christian Socialism" in the CDU (1945-1949)

The idea of a social, even socialist, but not marxist "party of labour", modelled after the English Labour Party, had arisen already during the war.[30] Among these advocates of such a party was Walter Dirks[31], along with the Christian trade unionist and former Centre Party politician Jakob Kaiser (1881-1961) in Berlin; the former president of the federation of Christian trade unions and Vice-President of the German Centre Party, Adam Stegerwald (1874-1945) in Würzburg; Wilhelm Elfes (1884-1969), former editor of the *Westdeutsche Arbeiterzeitung*, the voice of the Catholic workers' association, and at that time chief mayor of Mönchengladbach[32]; Carl Spiecker (1881-1953) in Westphalia, who returned after having emigrated to Canada, a former assistant to Reich Chancellor Heinrich Brüning, as well as the former Reich Chancellor Joseph Wirth (1879-1956) in Freiburg. According to Franz Josef Stegmann, groups in Mannheim, Paderborn and with particular vigor the *Frankfurter Kreis* were to have also pursued the same goal.[33]

In Focke's view, Frankfurt, Cologne and Berlin belonged not only to the strongholds of the most important CDU regional or zonal parties. "Efforts were also made – based on very different ideological points of departure and based on equally different political conditions in each region or zone – to establish a socialism out of Christian responsibility (as in Frankfurt, but partly also in Berlin), or rather a Christian socialism (as in Cologne and Berlin). In Cologne these efforts were exemplified by an appreciation of natural right embedded in Catholic social philosophy. In Frankfurt they unmasked the nefarious admixture of traditional Christianity and bourgeois ideology through the confrontation of a new religious understanding with marxism. In Berlin these efforts took root as an attempt to theoretically establish the integration of various versions of socialism, in the context of an already sig-

---

28. Ibid., 35.
29. Bröckling, "Einleitung", in: Dirks, *Sozialismus oder Restauration*, 14.
30. See Stegmann, "Geschichte der sozialen Ideen", 484.
31. See Schmidt, *Zentrum oder CDU*, 162. Yet, at the same time, Schmidt points out the special nature of Dirks' political interpretation: "Walter Dirks' initial attempt, which was to lead to socialism in a roundabout way, tended…much more radically towards a thorough renovation and reorganisation of society than the concept of the Labour Party".
32. Until 1950 it was called München-Gladbach.
33. See Stegmann, "Geschichte der sozialen Ideen", 485.

nificantly more identifiable political constellation, and to proclaim this new vision as the basis for economic, domestic and foreign policy strategies".[34]

3.1.1. The *Kölner Leitsätze*: the "Original Programme of the CDU" (1945)

Through contact with his Father Superior Laurentius Siemer (1881-1956), the Dominican Eberhard Welty (1902-1965) became a member of the *Köln-Walberberger Widerstandskreis* in 1941, which grew out of the Catholic workers' movement and for which he developed fundamental principles for a new organisation of the state and of society. Then, in June 1945, his concepts served as a basis for discussion at the talks regarding the *Kölner Leitsätze*, "in which, for the first time amidst the CDU of the Rhineland then beginning to emerge, there was talk of a 'Christian socialism'... From the time of the *Kölner Leitsätze* in 1945 until the *Ahlener Programm* in 1947, at whose deliberations Welty played a significant role, [his ideas] acquired decisive influence upon the foundation of the Christian Democratic Union's program".[35]

Rudolf Uertz identifies the following as central elements of this "Christian socialism", closely related to the Dominican teachings on the common good: an economy providing for the needs of its people based on a self-administration of employers and employees; socialisation of large scale industries; a broad distribution of non-productive private property; an equitable distribution of manufactured goods; as well as an all-encompassing system of social justice.[36] The right to private ownership was to remain guaranteed, while property relationships were to be reformed according to the "fundamental principle of social justice".[37]

Consciously opposing a marxist-oriented socialism, the *Kölner Leitsätze* upheld a "true Christian socialism that had nothing in common with false collective objectives that fundamentally contradict the nature of human beings".[38] Behind this new abstract interpretation stood a strategic experiment "to introduce an antimarxist concept of socialism and thereby to create a Catholic social doctrine that was more appealing and that would

---

34. Focke, *Sozialismus*, 297. It was not the term but the idea of a "Christian socialism" that was already present in the first programmatic document of the CDU, "Aufruf an das Deutsche Volk", issued in Berlin on 26 June 1945. See Heimann, "Christlicher Sozialismus in der CDU", 113.
35. Ockenfels, "Welty", 957. The *Kölner Leitsätze*, which are known as the "original programme of the CDU", are based primarily on Welty's work, *Was nun?*, that summarises the discussions of the *Widerstandskreis*. The expanded version of this book appeared in 1946, entitled *Entscheidung in die Zukunft*. See Uertz, *Christentum und Sozialismus*, 27-29 and 205, as well as Ockenfels, "Eberhard Welty", 244.
36. See Uertz, *Christentum und Sozialismus*, 205.
37. Citation in Heimann, "Christlicher Sozialismus", 114.
38. "Kölner Leitsätze", 10.

attract the working classes to the Catholic Church".³⁹ However, these attempts proved unsuccessful, suffering a fate similar to the tactically motivated Christian socialist endeavours of Heinrich Pesch, Max Scheler and Theodor Bauer immediately following the First World War. According to Ockenfels, these earlier efforts diminished with equal speed as did Welty's "Christian socialism"⁴⁰ which survived only briefly in the CDU of the British zone, i.e. until the *Ahlener Programm*.⁴¹

However, according to Focke's analysis, the failure of "Christian socialism" can be traced back to a time before the economic and foreign policy conflicts between Jakob Kaiser and Konrad Adenauer (1876-1967) in 1946. This process started "already with the offensive of the bourgeois forces and their immediate demand for leadership in the summer of 1945. The concept "warding off a left bloc" won precedence over the view expressed by the authors of the *Kölner Leitsätze* that fascism had been the result of "militarisation and capitalist armament tycoons" and that a system based on 'true Christian socialism' would need to be created. The founding generation eventually withdrew into the background and the antisocialist impulse became integrated into the new socially heterogeneous party".⁴² The term "Christian socialism" had already been deleted from the party program in September 1945, when the revised version of the *Kölner Leitsätze* was published.⁴³ It was rarely ever used in public after Adenauer was elected chairman of the CDU of the Rhineland on 5 February and chairman of the British zone on 1 March 1946.⁴⁴

---

39. Ockenfels, "Welty", 957. Even Lothar Roos regards the attempt of the *Walberberger Kreis* associated with Welty "to portray the ethical and economic guidelines of Catholic social doctrine (essentially built on the principle of solidarity) as 'Christian Socialism'", as a mere "terminological baptism" which eventually had to be given up as the term "socialism" had a distinct "connotation" deriving from prior use in the history of ideas and party politics. Roos, "Kapitalismus, Sozialreform, Sozialpolitik", 130. Similarly, Uertz, *Christentum und Sozialismus*, 20, who believes the choice of terminology to have been motivated by its stronger appeal to the public.
40. See, for instance, Ruhnau, *Der Katholizismus in der sozialen Bewährung*, 240-242. See also Ockenfels, "Eberhard Welty", 245: Welty's "Christian 'socialism' was strictly antimarxist and was supposed to serve the sole purpose of an engaging catch-phrase for the description of his thomist social doctrine".
41. See Ockenfels, ed., *Katholizismus und Sozialismus in Deutschland*, 145.
42. See Focke, *Sozialismus*, 299. See ibid., 265: A militant anticommunism, according to Adenauer, was "much more likely to [serve] as a factor of integration for the socially heterogeneous party, which largely consisted of the former Centre Party and conservative voters", than the "Christian socialism" of Jakob Kaiser.
43. *Guiding Principles of the Christian Democratic Party (CDU) in Rhineland and Westphalia*, Second Edition of the Kölner Leitsätze.
44. See Uertz, *Christentum und Sozialismus*, 206. Of prime importance were the interventions of the Protestant members of the Union favouring a laissez-faire economy, who rejected a theological and ethical legitimisation of socio-political models of the social order. See also Heimann, "Christlicher Sozialismus", 112.

3.1.2. The *Frankfurter Leisätze*: The Program of "Indirect Socialism" (1945)

Contrary to the *Kölner Leitsätze*, which despite all the socialist semantics essentially described a rebirth of a Christian solidarism[45], the programmatic development in Hessen initially took a radically different course. In 1945, Eugen Kogon, Karl Heinz Knappstein, Walter Dirks and others endeavoured, with the creation of the CDU, to establish a Left Christian party in Frankfurt and to give it a specific theoretical foundation. "We called it the party of 'indirect socialism', because already in May 1945 we considered direct socialism – via the SPD and the KPD – fairly narrow-minded ... These two parties could not reach Catholics, peasant farmers, the petty bourgeoisie, including white collar employees. We wanted to bridge these gaps, specifically with an appeal to the Christian conscience. At that time we were convinced – as I still am today – that only a socialist reform could destroy the root of misery and injustice".[46] As always, the biblical basis that Dirks used was the parable of the Good Samaritan, which he transferred into the realm of politics.

After the above-mentioned failure of his illusionary advance in the direction of a socialist unity party, this "detour" was substituted for the desired solution.[47] "We wanted to offer a third party that was to have a socialist program. We hoped that these three parties together could be more powerful than the bourgeois parties which we expected to emerge".[48] With these goals, Dirks and his comrades distinctly separated themselves from the Christian Democratic mainstream. Therefore, the *Bensberger Memorandum* notes that "of all the many initial local programs of the CDU ... the *Frankfurter Leitsätze* were the first to display socialist tendencies".[49]

The section entitled "Socialism and Property" affirms an economic socialism built on a democratic foundation. The purpose was to strive for the conversion of the large scale producers of raw materials, industries and banks into collective property as well as a central management of the national economy, through which a reconstruction based not only on free enterprise but on the consideration of overall societal goals would be made possible. The attainment of the highest possible prosperity rate for the general population was supposed to be the essence and purpose of all the "socialist measures", in the long run also the establishment of ownership for the non-property owning classes. "As in its goals, so also should the methods of socialism be democratic and not dictatorial". Socialism would therefore have to be sustained by the people and their institutions and enough opportunities would have to be provided for the development of personal initiatives and for the competition of top-level performances. "It is therefore our

---

45. In this context I understand the term "solidarism" to mean the social-philosophical and social reform-oriented conception of Catholic social doctrine, basing itself on Heinrich Pesch (1854-1926), which believed itself to be a counter-movement opposing individualistic liberalism as well as collective socialism. See also Ruhnau, *Der Katholizismus in der sozialen Bewährung*.
46. Dirks and Glotz, "Jenseits von Optimismus und Pessimismus", 21. In addition, see also Dirks, "'Umwegiger Sozialismus'", 12.
47. Bröckling, "Einleitung", in: Dirks, *Sozialismus oder Restauration*, 14.
48. Dirks and Glotz, "Jenseits von Optimismus und Pessimismus", 21.
49. *Antisozialismus aus Tradition?*, 25-26.

socialist goal to secure a life of freedom from misery, of human dignity and of personal responsibility, for as many people as possible".[50]

However, in German society at that time, the idea of a leftist CDU with a socialist program was everything but capable of gaining majority support. "Opposition against the socialist programme developed rapidly within the CDU. The group that gathered around Walter Dirks and Eugen Kogon could not gain acceptance".[51] According to Walter Dirks, Konrad Adenauer, along with the majority of Catholic as well as Protestant Christians, destroyed his plans.[52]

3.1.3. The *Ahlener Programm* of the British Zone CDU (1947): The Last Chance for a "Christian Socialism" within the CDU?

The CDU's first declaration of its principles, the *Ahlener Wirtschafts- und Sozialprogramm,* drafted 3 February 1947, strictly speaking was only of regional significance, since the CDU and CSU were originally created on a zonal level. It was "neither recognised nor accepted by the governing bodies of the combined CDU".[53] Nevertheless, it had achieved supra-zonal respect and significance. At the first British zone CDU party conference on 14-15 August 1947, even Konrad Adenauer publicly described the *Ahlener Wirtschafts- und Sozialprogramm* as a "milestone in the history of German economic and social life"[54], although this recognition was probably more or less tactically motivated.[55]

The evident points of conformity with the *Kölner Leitsätze* are grounded in the fact that the main theoretical features of the *Ahlener Programm* were also conceptualized by the *Walberberger Kreis* under the leadership of

---

50. "Frankfurter Leitsätze vom September 1945", 11-12. Also in: Dirks, Schmidt and Stankowski, eds., *Christen für den Sozialismus,* 45-49, citation on pp. 47-48.
51. Bröckling, "Einleitung", in: Dirks, *Sozialismus oder Restauration,* 16.
52. See Dirks and Glotz, "Jenseits von Optimismus und Pessimismus", 21. Uertz believes that the main reason for the insignificant and only temporary influence of "Christian socialism" in Frankfurt on the Hessian party can be found "in the American occupational authorities' refusal to accept Karl-Heinrich Knappstein, who was nominated by the Christian socialist founding members as chairperson of the party. Instead, the American authorities appointed the conservative Jakob Husch. Thus, from the very beginning, the CDU in Hessen followed a path that was not desired by its founders. For this reason Dirks and Kogon, dissociated themselves quite early from the CDU". Uertz, *Christentum und Sozialismus,* 63, footnote 153.
53. Mommsen, ed., *Deutsche Parteiprogramme,* 576.
54. Deuerlein, CDU/CSU 1945-1957, 78, citation in Mommsen, ed., *Parteiprogramme,* 576.
55. See Uertz, *Christentum und Sozialismus,* 191-193, 211, as well as Focke, *Sozialismus,* 265 and 286: "Among other things, but in particular with the help of his flexible utilisation of programmes (*the Neheim-Hüstener* and *the Ahlener Programm*) - while carrying out a politics of moderate reforms -, Adenauer managed to obstruct the fundamental economic and social reorientation towards which the Christian socialists strove. Yet at the same time Adenauer, with the help of the Christian socialists, managed to attract a large number of workers into the party."

Eberhard Welty.[56] Like its forerunner, the *Ahlener Programm* possessed distinct anticapitalist features, which above all are revealed in its well-known preamble: "The capitalist economic system does not do justice to the vital interests of the German people pertaining to matters of state and civil society". A fundamental reform would be needed, whose content and intent could no longer be the "capitalist striving for profit and power", but only the welfare of the population.[57] Thus, the goal of the *Ahlener Programm* is an economy that provides for the needs of the people, which even "in normal times ... to a certain extent" requires planning and management of the economy. This planning and management would be carried out through self-governed corporate bodies controlled by parliament.

As indicated in the anticapitalist preamble, the program proposes the breaking up of big companies and an anti-trust legislation; the distribution of economic power and the "workers' right of co-determination regarding fundamental issues of economic and social planning", the socialisation of the coal mining industry and the iron producing big industry; the enlargement of the cooperatively-run sectors of industry; as well as profit sharing among workers.[58] However, at the same time, the document cautions against substituting a private capitalism with capitalism governed by the state, "which would be even more dangerous to the political and economic freedom of the individual".[59]

According to Franz Focke, it seemed imminent that the *Ahlener Programm* would make "Christian socialism" "the official program of the CDU, which in turn prepared itself to develop into the most powerful political party in Germany".[60] Yet, already when looking at the terminology employed, it becomes obvious that the term "Christian socialism" does not even occur once in the programme, as opposed to the case of the *Kölner Leitsätze*. In fact, the terminology associated with "socialism" appears only in a negative connotation.[61] Altogether, the document consists of three heterogeneous parts. First, the preamble which, according to Focke, may be traced back to the workers' leader Johannes Albers (1890-1963). Second, a section of the fundamental principle, which stands opposed to the preamble and takes up the central economic points of Adenauer's *Neheim-Hüstener Programm* of February 1946.[62] And third, the actual *Ahlener Wirtschaftsprogramm*, "which must be explained as a reaction to the demand for socialisation by the English government as well as the German

---

56. See Uertz, *Christentum und Sozialismus*, 207, as well as ibid., 97-99. Focke calls Adenauer the author of the first draft. See Focke, *Sozialismus*, 255. According to Uertz, *Christentum und Sozialismus*, 101, Adenauer's proposal was created as an alternative to the Walberberg draft. The informal *Walberberger Kreis* - to which, among others and in addition to Welty, belonged former Christian trade unionists, such as Johannes Albers (1890-1963) and Karl Arnold (1901-1958) - was, according to Uertz, "the actual group of people which had prepared the intellectual and theoretical ground in regards to its programmatic intent". See Uertz, *Christentum und Sozialismus*, 98.
57. "Das Ahlener Wirtschaftsprogramm", 576-577.
58. Ibid., 579-581.
59. Ibid., 579.
60. Focke, *Sozialismus*, 18.
61. "Das Ahlener Wirtschaftsprogramm", 578, where the economic system of the years 1933 until 1945 is twice characterised as "state socialism in disguise."
62. See Focke, *Sozialismus*, 235-241.

working class and in which were included the demands of the small-industry-oriented CDU of the Wuppertal region for sponsorship of private entrepreneurial activity and the protection of legally acquired property".[63] The indecisiveness, ambiguity and even contradictions within the document can be explained by the fact that this document was a compromise, which also contributed to the controversy that arose later along with diverging interpretations within the CDU.

After the western powers paved the way for the creation of a West German Federal Republic in the summer of 1948, the Frankfurt economic administration of the *Vereinigte Wirtschaftsgebiet* (i.e. the three western zones) under the leadership of Ludwig Erhard (1897-1977), who later became the Federal Minister of Economic Affairs and then Chancellor of the Federal Republic, introduced economic liberalisation, which strongly influenced the monetary reform of 20 June 1948.[64] In light of the socio-economic upswing that took place after 1950, the assertions of the *Ahlener Programm* now seemed outdated. "It had been the intention of the *Ahlener Programm* to let the social Christian trend influence the CDU. In times of a seemingly perpetual prosperity, allowing reformed Christian social ideas to become tradition or cultivating Christian worker movement's traditions seemed more and more unnecessary".[65] In the time to come, under the leadership of Adenauer, the CDU/CSU increasingly developed into a modernised conservative bourgeois political party[66], primarily by surmounting the fragmentation of the bourgeois non-socialist camp and by means of the dissolution of the denominational division between Protestants and Catholics. Only the CDU social commissions kept the Christian social ideas of the *Ahlener Programm* alive, "yet without exercising any major influence upon the economic organisational policy of the Federal Republic".[67] Instead, the neo-liberal *Düsseldorfer Wirtschaftsprogramm* gained much more influence, becoming the CDU platform in the first federal election campaign in 1949. The CDU emerged from this campaign, along with the CSU, as the most powerful party. According to Uertz, this officially confirmed "the end of Christian socialism in the CDU".[68]

---

63. Ibid., 257.
64. See Hildebrand, "Erhard", 355, as well as Uertz, *Christentum und Sozialismus*, 211.
65. Klönne, "Arbeiterkatholizismus", 43.
66. See Schmidt, *Zentrum oder CDU*, 345. See Focke, *Sozialismus*, 273: "As a result of the absence of a party on the political Right and the enforced move towards a few large parties as a result of the experiences in the Weimar Republic, the conservative groups automatically gathered within the CDU, where they activated the traditional antisocialist potential of Catholic social doctrine in order to prevent cooperation between Christian socialists and social democrats".
67. See Uertz, *Christentum und Sozialismus*, 211. From 1945 onwards, social Christian workers consolidated into "social commissions" that perceived themselves to be "transmission belts" of the CDU within the proletariat and at the same time representatives of the workers' interests. See Schroeder, *Katholizismus und Einheitsgewerkschaft*, 285.
68. Uertz, *Christentum und Sozialismus*, 202.

3.1.4. "Christian Socialism" in the CDU of the Soviet Occupation Zone and the Role of Jakob Kaiser

Already during the Weimar Republic, Jakob Kaiser acted as a functionary of the Christian trade unions and member of the Reich Executive Committee of the Centre Party. Then, during the period of National Socialism, he became actively involved in the resistance movement. Later (as of 1949), he became chairman of the CDU social commissions as well as Federal Minister for All-German Affairs (1949-57). After the death of Stegerwald on 3 December 1945, Jakob Kaiser was not only promoted to become a leading Christian trade unionist, but also to become chairman of the CDU in Berlin and the Soviet occupation zone (SBZ), a position which he held from 20 December 1945 until his dismissal by the Soviet military administration on 20 December 1947.[69] Unanimously supported by the CDU of the eastern zone, he managed in February 1946 to make "Christian socialism" the foundation of the party's program.[70] Kaiser's originality, according to Focke, was notable in that Christian socialism "for the first time seemed to have been given a real political chance".[71]

Because of the key position that the CDU assumed within the German party system in the post-world war period, the dissension within the Union regarding "Christian socialism" – Focke refers to an actual "class struggle"[72] – carried more than simply an internal party significance. "As the most prominent Christian socialist, Jakob Kaiser was not just one among other opponents of Adenauer, but an advocate of what his fellow party members already at that time believed to be the sole recognised major alternative concept to the ideas of the later chancellor. Yet again, this would not have been possible, had Kaiser not been able to base his ideas on a Christian socialist tradition".[73]

At the CDU convention in Berlin from 15-17 June 1946, when the efforts to create a German Labour Party had already been made history, Jakob Kaiser spoke of "the conventional bourgeois social order belonging to a lost generation, an order that will be replaced with an age belonging to working people, by the era of socialist forms of existence". More important than the security of the individual and his property, a "fundamentally new construction of our social and economic structure" would be needed. Kaiser therefore summoned the German nation to take "the step toward socialism" out of a Christian and democratic responsibility. "Considering the overwhelming misery of the people, all attempts to re-establish the obsolete past appear inappropriate. Let us recognize what is needed: socialism has the floor".[74]

---

69. See Kosthorst, "Kaiser", as well as Schroeder, "Katholizismus und Einheitsgewerkschaft", 375.
70. See Focke, *Sozialismus*, 235, 295 and 297 as well as 283-284: "While Adenauer had to fight against strong opposition within his zonal party, the CDU of the Soviet occupation zone gave Kaiser 100% support."
71. Ibid., 297.
72. Ibid., 296.
73. Ibid., 18.
74. Kaiser, "Um Deutschlands Schicksal", 9 and 11. Citation in Stegmann, "Geschichte der sozialen Ideen", 485.

According to Focke's interpretation, Kaiser had always believed the economic and social reform of Germany to be part and parcel of the acquisition of German unity, established with the help of an agreement between the political parties based on a broad socialist consensus. As the attempted agreement as well as the restoration of German unity became increasingly hopeless, even the goal of a "Christian socialism" faded more and more into the background. Since July 1947 at the latest, when a convention of the enlarged CDU executive of the eastern zone and Berlin took place, Kaiser and his political comrades no longer referred to the term "Christian socialism".[75]

Since Kaiser was finding himself under increasingly strong pressure in the eastern zone from the SED and the Soviet military administration, which ultimately dismissed him from his position as the CDU chairman of the SBZ, he attempted to find support within the party in the western zones. Yet his attempts failed hopelessly, despite the strong encouragement from the organised Christian trade unionists within the party. In response to his petition not to ignore the "socialist trend of the times", he was told at the first zonal party convention of the British zone CDU in August 1947 that there was a "certain fear of a marxist socialist thought process intruding" into the party.[76] Sharing this fear, Adenauer responded to Kurt Schumacher's observation that the CDU had given up its socialism, contending that the SPD chairman's assertion was totally illogical, since the CDU had never advocated a socialism in the first place.[77] With Kaiser's dismissal from the office of CDU chairman of the SBZ, the CDU of the British zone under Adenauer's leadership lost their most powerful opponent and could therefore rise unhindered to become the dominant zonal branch of the CDU.[78]

"Christian socialism may have been conceptualized in 1945 by academic and religious circles (the Frankfurt group of intellectuals, the Dominicans in Walberberg), but only after these circles had been pushed aside was it adopted by the party's social commissions and by certain individuals within the party leadership structures - primarily by former Christian trade unionists and friends of Jakob Kaiser, such as Johannes Albers, Karl Arnold and Heinrich Strunk".[79] From the beginning, the position of these individuals within the Union had been too weak to give the CDU, which considered itself a people's party, distinct socialist features. Although Kaiser's concept found some support within the party in the western zones, he was still incapable of gaining majority support either inside or outside the party boundaries. According to Uertz, his influence remained largely restricted to Berlin as a result of the peculiar situation in the Soviet occupation zone and "Adenauer's clever resistance".[80]

---

75. See Focke, *Sozialismus*, 269.
76. Ibid.
77. As stated in the course of a rally in Eutin. See ibid., 270.
78. See Uertz, *Christentum und Sozialismus*, 200.
79. Focke, *Sozialismus*, 271-272.
80. See Uertz, *Christentum und Sozialismus*, 206-207.

3.2. The German Centre Party – A Left Catholic Alternative to the Union?

On 14 October 1945, former Centre Party parliamentarians founded a new *Deutsche Zentrumspartei* (DZ) in the Westphalian city of Soest, an organisation that defined itself as a Christian "party of the creative center and of social balance".[81] Initially, they wanted to find their place between the groups that were expected to develop within the conservative Christian and the left socialist factions. Yet, as the spectrum of political parties developed in an entirely different fashion than originally expected, strong forces under the influence of Carl Spiecker soon pressed to "establish the DZ to the left of the CDU as an ideologically neutral power (*Essener Richtung*), similar to the British Labour Party".[82]

According to the analysis of Ute Schmidt, even after 1945 Spiecker's vision reflected the goals of the left republican wing of the Weimar Centre Party. These objectives included political independence from the clergy, social reform, willingness to form a coalition with the SPD, a strengthened republican-democratic mentality and a foreign policy oriented towards *détente*. In September 1946, Spiecker published a summary of his plans for a post-capitalist federal Germany in a federal Europe. In this summary he stresses that property ownership should be established primarily to benefit the public, instead of promoting the ownership rights of individuals. The most recent war had made the inequality of property distribution intolerable. Therefore the misery resulting from the war "inevitably" demanded that the distribution of burdens be staggered according to individual ability to perform. Spiecker contended that socialisation was no longer a fear-inspiring word. But it by no means solely implied state control, but instead the transformation of private into common property, "either of the state, communities, cooperatives or of the workforce". Therefore the Centre Party supported the demand for the inclusion of employees in running their businesses and benefiting from these businesses' profits.[83]

Spiecker's efforts to commit the whole party to this programme, located somewhere between the CDU and the SPD, was nonetheless frustrated by the resistance of the traditionalist majority. Through disputes within the party during the years 1946-1947, it became apparent "that the ideas of Spiecker's group were not to be adopted", Ute Schmidt contends.[84] In view of the CDU/CSU's increasing influence, the *Zentrum* was collectively destined to rapid disintegration in the time to come and remained hardly more than a marginality in the German federal party system.[85]

---

81. Morsey, "Deutsche Zentrumspartei", 17-18.
82. Ibid., 18.
83. Carl Spiecker, "Das neue Zentrum", *Tagesspiegel*, 19 September 1946, citation in Schmidt, *Zentrum oder CDU*, 242.
84. Schmidt, *Zentrum oder CDU*, 242-243. Spiecker himself joined the CDU in 1949. See ibid., 353.
85. See Schmidt, *Zentrum oder CDU*, 344. At the first parliamentary elections the percentage of votes cast for the *Zentrum* sank from 3.1% in the year 1949 down to 0.8% in the year 1953. Even in North Rhine-Westphalia, which was the Centre Party's stronghold, the party continually lost ground in the state elections. Their voter return in this most populous state of Germany shrank from 9.8% (1947), 7.5% (1950), 4.0% (1954), 1.1% (1962) to finally under one percent. See ibid., 361.

3.3. The Catholic Socialists after 1945

Following the discussion of a variety of attempts to establish "Christian socialism" within the party political spectrum, now Ernst Michel, Walter Dirks and Theodor Steinbüchel, three of the Left Catholic theorists already active in the Weimar Republic, move to centre stage.

3.3.1. Ernst Michel: "The Christian in the Socialist Movement"

In his study on Ernst Michel, Peter Reifenberg objects to "all reductionist and narrow-minded interpretations which only focus on the political Michel of the Weimar Period", and he believes Michel's main focus to be much more theologically, anthropologically and ethically oriented.[86] Yet a distinction between the political Michel and the theological, anthropological and ethical Michel does not seem to carry much credibility - at least if one interprets this dichotomy to mean that the publications during the Weimar Period did not possess a theological, anthropological, and ethical foundation and the publications after 1945 did not have a political basis nor a political aim. Nonetheless, it is certainly correct that Ernst Michel "did not resume his political activities (with the exception of his late *Sozialgeschichte* [of 1947- A.L.]) after the interruption of the Nazi Period".[87] However, this does not mean that Michel had abandoned or even denied his former views. Here it is helpful to glance at Michel's 1947 work, *Renovatio – Zur Zwiesprache zwischen Kirche und Welt*.

With respect to the church authorities' determination to ward off the socialist movement, Michel contends in this study that the question had been posed time and again in past decades, whether a Christian could also be a socialist and join the socialist movement, even if it meant rejecting certain doctrines and a certain narrow-mindedness due to the political conjuncture. "Natural law" and a religious social doctrine based on this law were regarded as criteria by which to evaluate the answer to this question and by which to examine the socialist movement. The requirements and boundaries for a "church-approved or even 'Christian' socialism" developed out of these criteria. As a result of the abandonment or moderation of certain heretical doctrines that originated in the early days of the socialist movement and the neutralisation of socialist antireligious slogans, the church authorities seemed to have achieved a "certain tolerance for socialists among the congregation", even if "socialism" continued to be in practice rejected.

Yet, Michel's critical attitude towards a "'Christian' socialism" that can be gleaned from some of his passages should not be misunderstood as abandonment of his previous support for Catholics in the socialist movement.

---

86. Reifenberg, "Ernst Michel", 499.
87. Dirks, "Vorläufer Ernst Michel", 71. The object of discussion is Michel, *Sozialgeschichte der industriellen Arbeitswelt*, which, according to Dirks, is a belated fruit of his intensive educational work at the *Akademie der Arbeit*. This work is a compilation of his lectures, primarily from the years 1929 to 1933. See also Haunhorst, "Selbstbestellte Vermittler", 262-264, where Haunhorst views Michel's defence of socialism as "merely an episode" (263).

He very clearly shares the opinion "that the historical circumstances urged the realisation of socialism and that a Christian in his responsibility to the world owes his efforts to this movement". Therefore, no objections should be made against attempts to obtain a space for socialist activism on the basis of natural law, Catholic social doctrine and the teachings of the Church. Such attempts would only be suspect if they would develop into a "religious" or "Christian socialism". For this special form of socialism cannot exist legitimately, just as little as a "Christian state".[88] A Christian is simply called upon to place himself squarely in the middle of proletarian misery and to take responsibility for the mission towards socio-economic revolution and reform. Thereby the possibility "that he will become a socialist out of principle, for doctrinal reasons", is eliminated. Such a possibility would necessarily result "in a self-glorifying dictatorship of the spirit over life, a rape of living history and of the differently structured organs of public and private life".[89] Michel believes that a Christian can and should not become a "follower of 'socialism as an ideology'".[90] Operating as a Christian in the socialist movement has "purpose and justification", not as a fundamental response but as a conjunctural action with purposeful intent".[91] Even after the Second World War it is obvious that Michel holds firmly to the views of the "political Michel of the Weimar Period". Thus, Reifenberg's preoccupation with the alleged "theological, anthropological, and ethical Michel" stands in danger of prohibiting other aspects of Michel's arguments to be expressed and of misinterpreting Michel's ideas.

3.3.2. Walter Dirks: "Socialism out of Christian Responsibility"

With the benefit of hindsight Walter Dirks describes the social, political and economic situation in the year 1945 in an evocative manner: "The liberal economic powers ... appeared to have been compromised once and for all through their pact with National Socialism. Its representatives either sat in some allied prison cell or secluded in the countryside. Industry was set in motion much more by the influence of municipal and regional politicians and the trade unions than by mandates of property owners. Even banks were without power and influence during the near-total inflation. Capitalist society seemed to be ruined. We acted on that assumption. We expected and wanted not the reconstruction of the system that had been used in the Weimar period, but that a new societal structure would develop out of it".[92]

Walter Dirks believed it to be a matter of course that Catholics would have a crucial part in this discussion, although at that time the expectations within Catholicism of their objectives differed quite radically. According to Dirks, most people expected a reformed capitalism freed from the predominance of capital, as expressed in the social encyclicals *Rerum Novarum* and *Quadragesimo Anno*. "Only a minority hoped for what they called 'social-

---

88. Michel, *Renovatio*, 65.
89. Ibid., 65-66.
90. Ibid., 66.
91. Ibid., 116, footnote 9.
92. Dirks, "Das gesellschaftspolitische Engagement der deutschen Katholiken", 73-74.

ism out of Christian responsibility'".[93] Dirks makes no secret out of the fact that he also belonged to that minority. The Catholic socialists, with whom he identifies himself, recognised the approaching opportunity to manage key industries and banks as common property. In addition, they favoured the idea of cooperatives, although they did not fundamentally object to private ownership of the means of production.

Without confusing the model of society for which they were striving with the kingdom of God, they believed "that a people purified in times of affliction would want to and would have the ability to rebuild the social structure amidst the wilderness of ruins according to fundamental standards of social justice". However, Dirks' summarising remark bears an unmistakable tone of resignation: "Socialism out of Christian responsibility did not result in anything at all, and not much resulted from other versions, in any case not the restructuring of society".[94]

But what did Dirks' program consist of? Ulrich Bröckling, a friend and co-worker of Dirks, primarily stresses the concept of a socialist "Third Way" and the notion of Europe as a "Third Power" between the blocs. "Those were the two elementary central points of that 'productive utopia', which Dirks postulated in April 1945 as the goal and path of the German republic".[95] In October 1946 Dirks summarised his thesis in an article defending the word "socialism". "At the centre...lies the idea of the 'socialised planned economy'; we describe it as 'socialist', because its essential prerequisite contains something that all socialisms have in common: the socialisation of the principal means of production. We call it socialist in order to identify and proclaim the 'leap', that qualitative difference which exists between the old and the new order, between a socially reformed capitalism that is restricted at every turn, yet fundamentally free, and a social economy dedicated in principle to public welfare and administered by society but given as much freedom as possible".[96]

Bröckling asserts that with this statement Dirks sets himself apart from the social reform-oriented concepts of Oswald von Nell-Breuning as well as from the antisocialist "Christian socialism", which Eberhard Welty based on natural law. With a strong emphasis on economic democracy, the concept of cooperatives, federalism and the European idea, Dirks' point of view clearly distinguished itself from the Schumacher SPD's decidedly anticommunist and nationalist perception that aimed at nationalisation, central planning and state centralised power.[97] "Like many intellectuals after 1945, who based their interpretations on Marx, Walter Dirks aimed to expose the humanist truths of marxism and to separate it from the reality of stalinist terror".[98] However, his goal to establish a coalition between Christians and socialists as a foundation of the second German republic, a goal towards which he strove "with the antifascist pathos that was a hallmark of the ini-

---

93. Ibid., 75.
94. Ibid., 75-76.
95. Bröckling, "Der 'Dritte Weg' und die 'Dritte Kraft'", 71-72. Bröckling relies on Dirks, "Die Zweite Republik".
96. Dirks, "Das Wort Sozialismus", 642.
97. See Bröckling, "Einleitung", 18.
98. Ibid., 21.

tial postwar period", proved to be illusory. "Christians simply did not form a political group nor even a coalition comparable to the socialists".[99]

3.3.3. Theodor Steinbüchel: "Socialism as an Ethical Idea"

Theodor Steinbüchel died on 11 February 1949, leaving him barely four years after the disintegration of National Socialism and the close of the Second World War. Yet one must take into account that Steinbüchel was able to build on the preliminary research he had carried out prior to 1945. After the National Socialists shut down the Munich Catholic Theology Department at the end of the winter semester of 1938-1939, and until he assumed the position of visiting professor of moral theology in Tübingen in the summer of 1941, Steinbüchel was forced to take a leave of absence, though with pay. In addition he was released from "military duties" due to his status as a theology professor.[100] During this time he was able to devote himself wholly to scholarship, apart from his pastoral duties. His brother Anton writes: "One might observe that he published very little during the period between 1938 and 1941. Yet those were exactly the years of his politically forced retirement in Munich. These years are definitely among his most fruitful, since Theodor Steinbüchel used them all the more intensely to prepare for his literary projects in an anticipated near and better future".[101] However these preliminary studies would most likely not have touched upon the range of themes relating to Marx and socialism, since Theodor Steinbüchel after 1938 burned all those documents which he believed to be dangerous. He did this "because it was important to him to survive those times for the sake of scholarship, which was then very much under assault".[102]

This short final period of his life and of his career in Tübingen became increasingly stressful as a result of additional duties: dean of the Department of Catholic Theology; then, above all, president of the university and finally its vice-president. This demanding workload allowed Steinbüchel "only limited time to devote to his scholarly work".[103] Therefore both his planned and his completed projects deserve all the more respect. Among the first of these projects is Steinbüchel's intended new edition of his theological dissertation, *Der Sozialismus als sittliche Idee* . In 1929 he had refused to authorise a new print-run of his unrevised dissertation, "since he considered a thorough revision necessary", probably as a result of the publication of the complete works of Marx and Engels begun in 1927.[104] Apart from Alfons Auer[105], Marcel Reding confirms that Steinbüchel stuck to this plan for a

---

99. Focke, *Sozialismus*, 272-273.
100. Nachlaß Theodor Steinbüchel, at the chair of Prof. Dr. Gerfried W. Hunold, Department for Theological Ethics, Tübingen, folder 10, document 4.
101. Anton Steinbüchel, Theodor Steinbüchel. *'Sein eigenes Menschenbild'*, *Zur 75. Wiederkehr seines Geburtstages am 15.6.1963*, in Nachlaß Steinbüchel.
102. Ibid., 227.
103. Auer, "Vorwort".
104. Letter from Paul Böhringer (Druckerei und Verlag L. Schwann, Düsseldorf) to Anton Steinbüchel dated 13 April 1949. Nachlaß Steinbüchel, folder 13, document 6.
105. Interview with Prof. Dr. Alfons Auer, Biberach/Riss (Oberschwaben), 23 February 1995.

revised edition until his death. Reding was a student and co-worker of Steinbüchel in Tübingen, who even after Steinbüchel's death took part in the deliberations for a new edition.[106] According to Reding, this work would have "needed to be reworked using the new material as a foundation". However, the early death of Steinbüchel prevented these plans from coming to fruition.[107] Aside from his lectures, Steinbüchel offered "courses on moral theology" (*Moraltheologische Übungen*) at Tübingen in the winter semester of 1946-1947 and in the following semester, entitled "Socialism as an Ethical Idea".[108] The fact that Steinbüchel thus picked up the thread that had been severed by National Socialism suggests, in addition to the planned revision of his theological dissertation, that socialism and the ethical concepts related to it were ongoing themes with which Steinbüchel concerned himself all his life.

During the summer semester 1948, the university in Tübingen organised a lecture series with the title, "The Year 1848", honouring the one-hundredth anniversary of the revolution. As vice-president, Steinbüchel was called upon to hold two lectures, entitled "Catholicism and the Catholic Social Concept in 1848" and "The Idea of Socialism in 1848".[109] But likewise in discussions outside of the lecture halls, Steinbüchel promoted a more open relationship between Christians and Marx and between Christians and socialism. Two important talks dealing with Karl Marx constitute something like a framework for this final period of his career. A few months before his death, Steinbüchel gave a lecture on "The Nature of the Proletariat According to Karl Marx".[110] In this lecture Steinbüchel states that "it is *marxist* socialism which determines the views of the workers to a large degree. And if it is another kind of socialism, then it cannot survive unless it *originates* from *Marx*. For this reason, the thorough and intense study of marxism is important to Catholic thought, especially in France. We can learn much from the intensity and depth with which French Catholicism carries out this research even today!"[111] In Steinbüchel's words, in which he commends French Catholicism's reception of socialism, one can recognise simultaneously an implicit criticism of German Catholicism's reception of socialism, whose considerations on marxism, according to his interpretation, pale in comparison to efforts in neighbouring France.

---

106. However this plan was never carried out. In 1956-1957 Dirks still considered *Der Sozialismus als sittliche Idee* topical: This "significant book" is "still almost as important today … as it was 33 years ago". Dirks, "Der Sozialismus als sittliche Idee", 18. Reding, in 1970, thought similarly. See Reding, "Theodor Steinbüchel", 151.
107. Ibid.
108. Apparently these lectures were in high demand, for in the published schedule for the summer semester 1947 one finds the supplemental remark: "pre-registration required; numbers limited." See Eberhard-Karls-Universität Tübingen. Namens- und Vorlesungsverzeichnis. Sommer-Semester 1947, 20. Archive of the Eberhard-Karls University in Tübingen.
109. On 3 and 24 June 1948. The first lecture served also as a draft for a subsequent presentation, which Steinbüchel gave on 7 July 1948 in Stuttgart, entitled "Catholicism and the Catholic Social Concept in 1848". This version is published in the posthumous anthology: Steinbüchel, *Sozialismus*, 234-271.
110. Walberberg, 10 October 1948. Posthumously published in Steinbüchel, *Sozialismus*, 99-123.
111. Steinbüchel, "Das Wesen des Proletariats nach Karl Marx", 116. Similarly, see Dirks, "Ein 'anderer' Katholizismus?", 256.

Of even more significance is a lecture that Steinbüchel gave only one year after the conclusion of the war and that likewise concerned itself with Marx. "After the years in which research on Marx was banished, Steinbüchel derived a new view of Marx from the publication of the early philosophical manuscripts in the 1930s. He introduced this new idea in his presentation on 'Karl Marx, Person –Work –Ethos', which he gave at the occasion of the *Sozialethische Arbeitstagung christlicher Studenten* in July 1946".[112] Perhaps it was this international, ecumenical and interdisciplinary conference, which caused Franz Focke to observe that Steinbüchel continued the discussion of socialism after the war "among student circles".[113] In a conference report, probably written by Walter Dirks, the goal of the conference was said to be "the pursuit, from an ethical point of view, of the question whether and, if appropriate, how a dialogue between Christianity and socialism would be possible, i.e. a true synthesis and not just a cheap compromise".[114] Among other things, the detailed discussions focused on the possibility "to infuse Christian moral standards into the everyday life of society". This led "to a renewed emphasis on the obligation for responsible cooperation, even in the realm of politics. Only with this consideration does it become possible to come closer to a solution of the social problems of the present in a manner that the conscience dictates: the principle of a 'personalist socialism', in which the individual and the community are equally important".[115]

In her dissertation, *Die Katholischen Sozialisten*, Susanne Hedler refers to Steinbüchel's lecture, which portrayed "the revolutionary and philosophical Marx in a completely new light".[116] She uses this lecture to support her thesis that Steinbüchel "was the *only one* of the mentioned individuals, who resumed his efforts to foster *understanding* between the Church and socialism in a similar fashion after the war".[117] She even supports the interpreta-

112. Reding, "Theodor Steinbüchel", 151. Steinbüchel's essay was published in the following year in a collection, *Zur sozialen Entscheidung*, edited by Nikolaus Koch. In the Archiv der sozialen Demokratie of the Friedrich-Ebert-Stiftung in Bonn, one may consult a seven page type-written report of this conference that Dirks himself most likely wrote. "From 27-29 July [1946], an interzonal workshop of Christian students, sponsored and supported by the French military government, took place in Tübingen at which delegates from most of the universities in Germany as well as French and Swiss guests were present. Only representatives of the eastern zone were unfortunately unable to attend, although invitations had been sent to them as well. Also attending the conference was [Theophil] Wurm, a provincial bishop of the Protestant Church, and [Direktor Dr. Solter- A.L.], an authorised representative of the bishop of Rottenburg. The conference (was) organised by the *Sozial-Praktische Arbeitsgemeinschaft der Katholischen und Evangelischen Studentengemeinde Tübingen* under the direction of Dr. Nikolaus Koch". Dirks, *Sozial-ethische Arbeitstagung christlicher Studenten*, [1]. Nachlaß Dirks, shelf mark 358 (*Sozialismus aus christlicher Verantwortung 1945-1949*). Steinbüchel's talk is an expanded and revised version of his 1928 article. See Steinbüchel, "Karl Marx. Gestalt und Ethos", 27-46. The far-reaching convergence of his views on Marx as 'person' and Marx' 'ethos' in both versions is proof of the continuity present in Steinbüchel's position.
113. See Focke, *Sozialismus*, 265, footnote 1091.
114. Dirks, "Sozial-ethische Arbeitstagung", [1]. Next to and above the word "synthesis" there are alternative suggestions noted, which possibly originate from Dirks: "produkt. Auseinandersetzg". ("productive dialogue") and "posit. Ergebn." ("positive outcome").
115. Ibid., [6].
116. Ibid., [1].
117. Hedler, *Die katholischen Sozialisten*, 129.

tion that, except for Theodor Steinbüchel, *not one* of the representatives of the Catholic socialist movement during the Weimar period – this includes Ernst Michel, Vitus Heller, Heinrich Mertens and Otto Bauer – "acted politically as a Catholic socialist after 1945".[118]

But it would be hasty to conclude that Steinbüchel specifically expresses his views on Marx and socialism only in *those* speeches that explicitly name these themes in their title. Steinbüchel's presidential speech, *Europa als Verbundenheit im Geist*, delivered on 2 May 1946, is a notable counterexample. In this programmatic presentation[119] given almost precisely one year after the end of National Socialism and the conclusion of the Second World War, Steinbüchel strove to demonstrate intellectual and cultural European unity - including Russia and America! - and dedicated a notably lengthy section to socialism. As if wanting to justify this detailed preoccupation, he explains that it was necessary, "in view of the tremendous significance of marxism for Europe"[120], to emphasize the "*ethical* idea", the "*meaning*" of marxist socialism, in order to identify a spiritual side of this movement of European dimension that connected the various parts of Europe at that time. Once again the issue for Steinbüchel is the ethical idea of socialism, its humane ethos of liberation, which to him embodies one of the intellectual bonds uniting Europe.[121]

In this speech, Steinbüchel repeatedly referred to the Catholic French philosopher Jacques Maritain (1882-1973), who in his critique on culture exposed the insufficient utilization of "the social possibilities of Christianity".[122] Steinbüchel found it surprising, yet understandable considering the situation and given the issue, that Maritain granted marxism "considerable attention". In this way, Steinbüchel argued, the French thinker meets up with German theology, ethics and philosophy of history.[123] Yet, to support this argument Steinbüchel only refers to his own studies of socialism. Similar to Maritain's work, which criticises Marx's positivism and atheism as well as the lurking danger of the loss of individuality in marxism, his studies reveal the anthropological and ethical idea present in marxism. "By denouncing the inhumanity and loss of individuality that results from an economic and social order in which a person, as Kant would say, is regarded as a means to an end rather than the end in itself, Marx's critique of capitalism found favour with humanist socialism and Christian social ethics".[124]

It is particularly worth emphasizing that in this speech Steinbüchel still supports his early research of socialism dating from the 1920s.[125] The positive reference to these writings, without any restrictions, can be interpreted as a further proof of the continuity in Steinbüchel's view of socialism.

---

118. Ibid., 18.
119. See Hunold, "Theodor Steinbüchel", 232.
120. Steinbüchel, "Europa als Verbundenheit im Geist", Presidential inaugural speech delivered at the University in Tübingen (Universität Tübingen 36) (Tübingen, 1946) 15.
121. Ibid., 18.
122. See ibid., 14.
123. See ibid., 15. He felt a close affinity with Maritain on account of his similar "insight into the secularised-messianic, eschatological-chiliastic character of Marx' interpretation of history". Ibid., 19.
124. Ibid., 18-19.
125. Ibid., 18, footnote 2.

This continuity originated during the time when he worked as a chaplain in the Rhineland during and after the First World War and continued up through his later pronouncements as president of Tübingen University immediately after the Second World War.

On the whole, it becomes apparent that Steinbüchel developed a special interest for the "underground" representatives of socialism, the thinkers going against the grain and the "dissenters", including the democratic socialist Eduard Bernstein, whose revisionist views were officially condemned by his party; Georg Beyer, who was heavily reproached as a result of his connections with Catholicism;[126] the ethical socialists of the Marburg school, whose attempts to establish a synthesis of Kant and Marx were rejected by the orthodox socialists; or the nonconforming "moral philosopher" Georg Lukács, whose most important work was officially accused of leading a revisionist attack on marxism.

Steinbüchel also developed an especially pronounced interest in the early writings by Marx, viewed unfavourably by the official Soviet line.[127] The connection between the early Marx and Marx as the author of *Das Kapital* was clearly seen by Steinbüchel, but was disputed by the guardians of "orthodoxy". When reading Steinbüchel's writings one gets the impression that Steinbüchel wanted to liberate Marx from narrow interpretations and the various marxist attempts to use and abuse Marx for ulterior purposes. In 1948 he noted that "Marx himself was simply not a dogmatic marxist. Marx' disparaging comment addressed to the popularisers and systematizers, 'I am not a marxist', is well-known".[128] In Steinbüchel's view, Marx himself becomes a "dissident", whom Steinbüchel intends to defend from the machinations of his epigones, who want to appropriate Marx and distort him.

Not only during the Weimar Republic, but with equal vigour after 1945, Steinbüchel worked towards creating an atmosphere in which a discussion of modernity, including a dialogue with Marx and with socialism, could find voice and vote in the Church, even if with some delay and in a too hesitant form. He helped to create an atmosphere in which Oswald von Nell-Breuning was allowed to comment that "we all ... [are standing] on the shoulders of Karl Marx"[129] and in which political theologies and liberating theologies could develop that, unlike their opponents, seriously regarded "marxism as a challenge to theology".[130] Steinbüchel is one of the architects not only of the reorganisation within the Catholic Church and its the-

---

126. With his work, *Katholizismus und Sozialismus* (Berlin, 1927), Georg Beyer (1884-1943), the cultural editor of the *Rheinische Zeitung*, gave expression to the attempt at a rapprochement between social democracy and Catholicism that was widely noticed at that time. See Haunhorst, "Katholizismus und Sozialismus", as well as Lienkamp, *Theodor Steinbüchels Sozialismusrezeption*, Part B, Chapter 1.1.3., "Georg Beyers Vermittlungsversuch".
127. See Landshut, "Vorwort", VI: "It did not happen by chance that the official Soviet interpretation of Marx never took notice of these writings".
128. Steinbüchel, "Existenzialismus und christliches Ethos", 139. This quote from Marx is also referred to by Dirks, "Marxismus in christlicher Sicht", 126.
129. Von Nell-Breuning, "Wir alle stehen auf den Schultern von Karl Marx".
130. Metz, "Marxismus als Herausforderung an die Theologie?", as well as Lienkamp, "Die Herausforderung des Denkens".

ology, but also of the bridge built across the "abhorrently" wide gap between Christianity and socialism, between Christian and socialist ethics.

3.4. *The* Frankfurter Hefte: *The Most Significant Periodical of German Left Catholicism in the Postwar Period*

The *Frankfurter Hefte*, edited by Eugen Kogon starting in April 1946 together with Walter Dirks and (between 1948 and 1950) Clemens Münster, with its 50.000 to 75.000 subscribers must be regarded as one of the political and cultural periodicals with the highest print-run in the immediate postwar period.[131] In order to evaluate the influence of the *Frankfurter Hefte*, one must take into consideration that the number of people who read this periodical was significantly higher - a poll in 1947 revealed three to four readers per copy - and that at times up to 150.000 subscription requests could not be granted as a result of the fixed quota for paper.[132] Following the monetary reform, the circulation of the *Hefte* decreased, "although the *Frankfurter Hefte* remained the most widely-distributed cultural-political monthly into the 1950s".[133] According to the visions of the editors, the *Frankfurter Hefte* were not only to give running commentaries on political events, but above all also to contribute programmatic suggestions for the new construction of Germany.[134] Therefore, contrary to many other periodicals that emerged in postwar Germany, the *Hefte* were characterised by a more consistent position and a more precise conception of that which was to come.[135]

A clearly recognisable plea for "socialism out of Christian responsibility" was part and parcel of this plan. Already in their original prospectus, Kogon and Dirks ascribed a particular role in the creation of a new Europe under socialism to the working class and to Christians. According to Kogon and Dirks the periodical's task was to work "on the theoretical and practical rapprochement between workers and Christians, between Christianity and socialism".[136] In a similar manner Karl Heinz Knappstein, the cofounder of the "socialist" CDU in Hessen, emphasises in an article entitled "The Hour of Social Reform", published in the June issue of the first

---

131. Bröckling, "Der 'Dritte Weg' und die 'Dritte Kraft'", 71.
132. See Stankowski, *Linkskatholizismus nach 1945*, 81.
133. See Bröckling, "Einleitung", in Dirks, *Sozialismus oder Restauration*, 12.
134. See Bröckling, "Der 'Dritte Weg' und die 'Dritte Kraft'", 71.
135. Prümm, "Entwürfe einer zweiten Republik", 330. In addition to the *Frankfurter Hefte*, the journal *Ende und Anfang*, which was in circulation since April 1946 (appearing every two weeks), should also be mentioned. It was published by a group of young Left Catholics from the youth movement *Quickborn* which a number of "Christian socialists" from Munich joined, including Theo Pirker. "Of all the Left Catholic groups of the immediate postwar period, *Ende und Anfang* engaged in the most intensive dialogue with marxism". After the monetary reform and in the course of the increasingly pervasive climate favouring restoration, the journal found itself in economic difficulties and was forced to discontinue its publication in February 1949. Editor's note in Dirks, *Sozialismus oder Restauration*, 283. See also Stankowski, *Linkskatholizismus nach 1945*, 27-63, as well as Schmidt, "Linkskatholische Positionen nach 1945 zu Katholizismus und Kirche im NS-Staat", in particular pp. 134-140, who refers to the intensive contacts between this journal and French Left Catholics (ibid., 135).
136. Citation in Stankowski, *Linkskatholizismus nach 1945*, 72.

volume, that "political cooperation between Christians and the workers' movement would lead to concrete realisations of socialist demands" and that this was not only possible, but historically desirable. "Socialism out of Christian responsibility is no empty slogan, no unrealistic whim but neither is it deceiving bait. Rather, it is a system of practical economic policy measures"[137], the most important being the following three: first, the *socialisation* of privately owned big businesses and key industries for reasons of public welfare, i.e. the transformation of these properties into cooperative property (nationalisation only in a few unavoidable cases); second, *indicative planning* of the overall contours of the economy, serving the interests of the "little man", above all in the area of investment, with sufficient room for self-initiative and personal responsibility (not state bureaucracy, but sensible self-management of the economy by the people composing its workforce); third, co-determination of workers over the uses of capital funds on which their economic existence depends (genuine economic equality and co-determination also regarding the business decisions of workplaces, profit sharing and the sharing of economic risks) and in all institutions of the planned economy and in the directing of the overall economy.

This would, according to Knappstein's prognosis, "return millions of proletarians back home to society after many decades of division and ostracism. These masses would then no longer be objects or raw materials of the economy, but rather its responsible co-leaders". Only in this way could the social question be truly solved and class struggle overcome, not only in word but in deed. The author is convinced that "the path to such a goal is called socialism. If we proclaim ourselves adherents of this path, then we do so out of a Christian responsibility for the masses – our neighbours".[138] It becomes evident that the *Hefte* took a wholly different approach from that of the prominently antisocialist representatives of a "Christian socialism", such as Welty and Siemer.

In the commemorative volume written particularly for Walter Dirks' 80th birthday, Eugen Kogon gives a retrospective account of the *Frankfurter Hefte*'s programme. "Never again racism, tyranny and exploitation; no more cowardly conformity; freedom in responsibility". With these words Kogon described the editors' intentions.[139] The general purpose of the periodical was devotion to ethical pursuits, to fundamentally innovative reflections, education in the sense of the conveyance of values, and information. The lesson from Nazi barbarism was to be a radically consistent humanism as a standard for thought and deed. Therefore, according to Kogon, the editors had decided to pursue political journalism - in the sense of observation, analysis, criticism and advice - instead of engaging in party politics.[140] But the editors of the *Hefte* also wanted to influence politics and to utilise the opportunity, "reminiscent of the Old Testament", "to allow politics to develop out of ethical concerns, which rarely ever happens".[141]

---

137. Knappstein, "Die Stunde der Sozialreform", 1.
138. Ibid., 3.
139. Kogon, "Fragende Erinnerung", 255.
140. See ibid., 255-257.
141. Ibid., 255.

In numerous fundamental articles, Dirks in particular outlined the spiritual framework of the anticipated new German republic. According to Kogon, "we have co-drafted the concept of a 'socialism in liberty', a libertarian socialism".[142] Yet, in the end the efforts to create a different Germany west of the Elbe failed. The decisions opposing all that the editors of the *Hefte* deemed right, desirable and realistically possible were already made early on. "It began with the strictly capitalist currency reform in 1948, which permitted the former property relationships to persist unchanged, and which was carried out against all those of us who were expropriated except for forty marks". Rearmament marked the second major defeat, which was to be followed by many others.[143] Thus, according to Kogon's pessimistic conclusion, the potential of the unique historical opportunity for a genuine new beginning was not even close to being utilised, much less successfully realised.[144]

Despite these misfortunes, the *Frankfurter Hefte*, "as an independent Left Catholic periodical beyond social democracy and official communism", still performed "an important function within the intellectual environment of the Federal Republic of Germany", as Ute Schmidt summarised it in her analysis of Left Catholic activities after 1945. "The periodical created a space, or rather a niche, that could provide a solid base for a civil, peace-promoting and enlightened way of thinking".[145]

3.5. The Demand for Co-Determination at the 1949 Catholic Convention in Bochum – the Swan Song of Left Catholicism"?

Soon after its establishment, the socialist and Christian powers within the trade union movement that had united to form the DGB made economic co-determination their primary objective.[146] Yet their demand did not remain uncontested within the Catholic realm. The majority of Catholics, according to Bröckling, feared infringements upon the right to property, the influence of "non-business elements", or even steps towards socialism based on economic democracy.[147] It was not an unfounded concern, at least as far as Left Catholic intentions were concerned. That is why Walter Dirks, one of their advocates, concurred with those employers who recognised "the right to co-determination as a 'step towards socialism'".[148]

---

142. Ibid., 259.
143. See Ibid.
144. See ibid., 261.
145. Schmidt, "Linkskatholische Positionen nach 1945", 146-147.
146. "Co-determination" means the institutionalized participation of employees or their representatives (factory committees, trade unions) in the administration and organisation of businesses and enterprises, as well as in all social, economic and socio-political decisions in a broader sense. See Rüthers and Kleinhenz, "Mitbestimmung", 1176.
147. See Bröckling, "Einleitung", in: Dirks, *Sagen was ist*, 33.
148. Dirks, "Der Kampf um die Mitbestimmung", 688.

The parliamentary elections in 1949 resulted in the *Kleine Koalition* (namely the CDU/CSU, the FDP and DP), favoured by Adenauer, taking control of government duties.[149] Shortly thereafter, from 31 August to 4 September 1949, the 73rd German Catholic Convention took place in Bochum attended by five hundred thousand participants, which proved to be one of the largest mass meetings in the postwar period. At this second Catholic Convention following the end of the Second World War[150], the social and Left Catholic forces succeeded in standing their ground against their rivals within the Catholic Church[151] and established a counterpoint against the neo-liberal orientation of economic politics that was officially implemented by the government.[152] So it happened that the Catholic Convention at that time adopted a sensational resolution of the workshop on "Employers and Workers". This resolution called for the statutory establishment of the "right to co-determination of all workers regarding social, personnel and economic issues".[153] Up until this point, this summons had never been presented so clearly and with such impact upon the public by forces emanating from within Catholicism. According to Wolfgang Schroeder, however, the real "scandal" was the fact that the resolution declared the right to co-determination as a natural right ("a divinely ordained natural right"), thereby putting it on an equal level with the right to own property.[154]

Yet the Bochum resolution assumed the establishment of co-determination based on the principles of corporatism and the autonomy of each individual business, with "non-business elements", such as trade unions, not welcome. All the same, the resolution was gladly welcomed by the DGB and its chairperson Hans Böckler as an important starting-point for the democratization of the economy.[155] "At the same time, however, the representatives of the trade unions overestimated the significance 'of this swan song of Left Catholicism in Germany after 1945' (Theo Pirker) and failed to recognise the corporate idea, stressing the notion of the workplace as a performance-oriented community of employers and employees, which the demand for co-determination coming out of Catholic circles reflected. Walter Dirks saw things differently. He recognised co-determination as the field in which at least initial steps toward economic democracy had been achieve – even if on a much lesser scale than anticipated between 1945 to 1948".[156]

---

149. An influential group under the leadership of Jakob Kaiser had pleaded in vain for the Grand Coalition consisting of the CDU/CSU and the SPD. The *Freie Demokratische Partei* (FDP) emerged in December 1948 as a result of a merger of West German liberal parties. After 1947 the *Deutsche Partei* (DP), which emerged out of the *Niedersächsische Landespartei* (founded in 1945), supported a federal and national-conservative programme.
150. The first Catholic Convention after the war took place on 1-5 September 1948 in Mainz and had as its theme "The Christian in Times of Misery". It was also the first Catholic Convention after the National Socialists' accession to power.
151. See Bröckling, "Einleitung" in: Dirks, *Sagen was ist*, 33.
152. See Schroeder, *Katholizismus und Einheitsgewerkschaft*, 112-113.
153. *Gerechtigkeit schafft Frieden*, 114.
154. Schroeder, *Katholizismus und Einheitsgewerkschaft*, 113.
155. See ibid., 113-114.
156. Bröckling, "Einleitung", in: Dirks, *Sagen was ist*, 34.

Schroeder contradicts Pirker's thesis, which referred to the resolution as "the product of Left Catholic powers". Schroeder claimed that the different social and Left Catholic trends had goals regarding the politics of trade unions that were too diametrically opposed and that the intentions of the participants in drafting the resolution were too different. Participants included a whole spectrum of individuals ranging from the conservative head of the *Katholische Arbeiterbewegung* (KAB), Hermann-Josef Schmitt, to the Left Catholic Walter Dirks.[157] As a result, in the post-Convention period, marked by sharp internal attacks against the Bochum resolution, social Catholic groups increasingly withdrew their support of the resolution. This was illustrated in a letter from the Left Catholic entrepreneur Wilhelm Haurand to Hans Böckler, dated 9 November 1949, in which he states: "In the meantime, the struggle opposing the decision made in Bochum concerning the right to co-determination of the worker has developed into a true witch-hunt that takes on ever more grotesque forms everyday. One cannot help but wonder how those individuals expect to be taken seriously, who after long and tedious deliberations proclaimed to the whole world the clear, unmistakable decision in Bochum and today do everything possible to sabotage the realisation of this decision".[158] According to Haurand, the fate of the Bochum resolution now lay solely in the hands of the trade unions. The Catholic critics of the decision for co-determination not only received support from Archbishop Joseph cardinal Frings from Cologne[159], but also from Pope Pius XII, who, in his speech delivered 3 June 1950, emphasised the fundamental importance of the right to own property while declaring out of bounds the defense of the right to co-determination based on natural law. "Neither the nature of the employment contract as such nor the nature of an enterprise logically calls for such a right".[160] However, according to Lothar Roos, when examining the context of the Bochum resolution more

---

157. Schmitt was the former secretary-general of the *Reichsverband der Katholischen Arbeiter- und Arbeiterinnenvereine Deutschlands*, which was rather influential during the Weimar Republic. In 1946 he was instructed by Archbishop Joseph Frings of Cologne to take charge of the reconstitution of the *Westdeutscher Verband der Katholischen Arbeiter- und Arbeiterinnenvereine*, which included Welty and Nell-Breuning amongst their advisers. In 1947, the founding of the *Werkvolk - Süddeutscher Verband Katholischer Arbeitnehmer* came about, which stood in the tradition of the *Verband Süddeutscher Katholischer Arbeitervereine*. Not until 1971 was a *Bundesverband der Katholischen Arbeitnehmer-Bewegung Deutschlands* created.
158. Citation in Schroeder, *Katholizismus und Einheitsgewerkschaft*, 114. Haurand was a friend of Wilhelm Hohoff. See Haurand, "Wilhelm Hohoff". Along with Chaplain Joseph Rossaint of Düsseldorf and Theo Pirker, the latter belonging to the group around *Anfang und Ende*, Haurand belonged to the *Bund christlicher Sozialisten* that was established in Oberhausen, consisted mainly of Catholics and whose history remains largely unexplored to this day. See Dirks, Schmidt and Stankowski, eds., *Christen für den Sozialismus*, 11, 29-34.
159. See Schroeder, *Katholizismus und Einheitsgewerkschaft*, 114. For Frings, "the enemy [stood] on the Left", reversing Joseph Wirth's famous expression. Letter from Joseph Frings to Wilhelm Hamacher dated 29 March 1946. Citation in Schmidt, *Zentrum oder CDU*, 240.
160. See Pius XII, "Ansprache an die Teilnehmer", 3266. Highly suggestive is the title of this section called "The Threat to Private Property Through Economic Co-Determination by Wage-Earners". This danger was seen as similar to the socialist threat.

closely, it becomes evident that the Catholic Convention never actually made such a claim.161

Even if the co-determination of the coal, iron and steel industries, which was legally established in 1951 and which guaranteed co-determination in economic issues, was not achieved until the trade unions threatened to go on strike, it can perhaps still be considered as a consequence of the Catholic Convention in Bochum.162 Yet, as Eugen Kogon notes in a sobering remark, already one year later, the constitutional law governing the administration of private enterprises, called for more significant limitations of the rights of employees.163

4. The 1950s: An Epoch Marked by Restoration

In September 1950, Walter Dirks published a widely read article entitled "Der restaurative Charakter der Epoche", in which, according to Peter Glotz, he captured the spirit of the times.164 "The restoration of the old world", the article stated, "is so complete that one must, first of all, accept it as a fact".165 Dirks discovered symptoms of restoration not only in the CDU166, but "in all parties, in the economy and everyday life, in city planning, in literature, philosophy and theology ... Actual blame must be placed on those indistinct Christians and socialists, who had been called upon to actively participate in a renewal, but have failed to take up this responsibility due to complacency and lack of vision".167 According to Walter Dirks himself, this article marked the conclusion of the period in which the *Frankfurter Hefte* had attempted to oppose the movement towards restoration led by Adenauer and had hoped "to realise the concept of European socialism, of a socialist Europe".168 Now the only task remained "to recognise and to proclaim what has become reality today".169 For Bröckling, this

---

161. Roos, "Kapitalismus, Sozialreform, Sozialpolitik", 115, footnote 112.
162. Co-determination of the coal, iron and steel industries, established 21 May 1951, guarantees the fully proportional representation of workers' delegates on the board of directors. Moreover, it ensures that the interests of the workers in these industries are brought to the attention of the board of directors through a "director of labour", who cannot be appointed nor voted out without the support of a majority of the workers' representatives on the board of directors. See Rüthers and Kleinhenz, "Mitbestimmung", 1178.
163. See Kogon, "Fragende Erinnerung", 259-260. The constitutional law governing the administration of enterprises, enacted 11 October 1952, was passed after a sometimes bitter fight, in which the supporters of economic democracy lost out to the supporters of free enterprise. See Naendrup, "Betriebsverfassungsrecht", 739.
164. Dirks and Glotz, "Jenseits von Optimismus und Pessimismus", 21. According to Focke, *Sozialismus*, 275, Dirks "was amongst the first to recognise and identify the process of restoration in West Germany."
165. Dirks, "Der restaurative Charakter der Epoche", 942.
166. Ibid., 948: This union of Christians did not develop into "a force that [would] renew the face of the earth", a goal intended by those who founded it, among them Dirks himself. "Even today, reading the *Frankfurter Leitsätze* and *the Ahlener Programm* is a painful process".
167. Bröckling, "Einleitung", in: Dirks, *Sozialismus oder Restauration*, 29.
168. Dirks, "Vorwort", in: Dirks: *Sozialismus oder Restauration*, 8.
169. Dirks, "Der restaurative Charakter der Epoche", 943.

line of reasoning was equivalent to an acknowledgement of defeat. In addition, this line of reasoning reflected Dirks' continued refusal to reconcile himself with the status quo.[170]

A shift in the trend began to manifest itself, not only on the political level, but also within the Church. The Catholic Convention in Bochum had promoted the motto "Justice Creates Peace". Already in the selection process of a theme for the Catholic Convention in Passau and Altötting in 1950, a counter movement evolved and the Convention took place under the motto " First the Kingdom of God".[171] Out of the controversy over co-determination that erupted as a result of the meeting in Bochum, a monolithic Catholic view regarding society, economy and politics emerged in which "everyone who did not accept or even denied this course stood in danger of being rejected".[172]

By contrast, continues Schroeder, a relative openness regarding fundamental social and economic reforms was present in social Catholicism for the first few years following the war, despite all scepticism towards new political developments. Left Catholics were regarded as well-liked conversation partners within the CDU and within Catholicism. Socialism, communism and the Church's view of these ideologies were discussed in Catholic publications, and even the project of the Catholic worker priests in France was closely followed.[173] Stankowski maintains that the influence from France should not be underestimated, a country where German Left Catholics, "out of curiosity and maybe even with jealousy, observed a natural cooperation between Christians and communists and whose theological and political projects they became aware of through the Allied press and soon by means of personal contacts".[174] Primarily the groups associated with the most widely distributed Left Catholic publications, *Frankfurter Hefte* and *Ende und Anfang*, nurtured active contacts with Left Catholics in neighbouring France.[175]

"Even if the sceptics and the open-minded formed two different groups, a combination of them, both favouring economic and social renewal, constituted a force that was not to be underestimated. The exclusive orientation of the Catholic camp on the CDU/CSU, the latter becoming dominant in the 1950s, had not yet come about. Yet in the years 1949-1950, this relative openness turned into fixed positions and exclusivity".[176] All sociopolitical motives and measures which were not solidly anchored in "the middle" were attacked in the name of anticommunist doctrine. According to Schroeder, this phase initiated the "shift of German Catholicism towards the Right".[177]

---

170. See Bröckling, "Einleitung", in: Dirks, *Sozialismus oder Restauration*, 29.
171. See Schroeder, *Katholizismus und Einheitsgewerkschaft*, 115.
172. See ibid.
173. See ibid., 116.
174. Stankowski, "Katholiken für den Sozialismus", 11.
175. Ibid.
176. Schroeder, *Katholizismus und Einheitsgewerkschaft*, 116.
177. Ibid.

5. Last But Not Least

The "restoration", however, was not the final word and neither did it mark the end of Left Catholic activities in Germany. Running parallel to the international political and social developments of the 1960s and 1970s - decolonization, the Cuban revolution, the Prague Spring, as well as the student and women's movement, to name a few key events –, new openings began to emerge within the Church. Soon after the succession of Pope Pius XII by Pope John XXIII, who introduced the *aggiornamento* into the Church, Left Catholicism in Germany experienced a certain renewal, despite the repeated instances of resistance and losses incurred from various frictions. This opening was marked by many progressive steps including: the creation of the Second Vatican Council and the opening of the Church to the "world", especially encouraged by *Gaudium et Spes*; the Christian-marxist conversations (starting in 1965), inspired by the *Paulusgesellschaft*; the *Bensberger Kreis*, which was co-founded by Walter Dirks (in 1966), along with his ringing plea for anticapitalism out of socialist conviction; the journals established in 1968: *Internationale Dialog-Zeitschrift*, *Publik*, as well as *kritischer Katholizismus* - publications in which Dirks repeatedly published his articles[178]; the establishment of theologies of liberation, hope, revolution, and the new political and feminist theology; the creation of the German branch of *Christen für den Sozialismus* (1973); and the common synod of the dioceses of the Federal Republic of Germany in Würzburg and, above all, their resolution *Kirche und Arbeiterschaft* (1975).

Although the thesis purporting direct connections between Left Catholicism of the immediate postwar period and its corresponding movement in the 1960's and 1970's is controversial, nonetheless ideological and personal continuities, for which Walter Dirks is a prime example, can be found. In addition, scholars and political commentators began a historical and literary assessment of the history of Left Catholicism[179], in part also serving the purpose of confirming the authors' own concealed roots, and contributing to the Christian socialist rediscovery of its own identity.[180]

Last but not least, we should return to the question posed initially, whether it is still worthwhile to examine German Left Catholicism of the 1940s and 1950s, despite its relative failure. In a response to this question, we shall let Ulrich Bröckling have the final word: "Historiography tends to portray the past in such a way as if everything that happened, had to happen the way it did. The disregard of all defeated alternatives avoids the danger that arises from memories of past battles: There are alternatives, and future struggles have the potential to end differently".[181]

---

178. See Bröckling, ed., *Walter Dirks Bibliographie*.
179. See the comments made by Stankowski, *Linkskatholizismus nach 1945*, 3-4, as well as by Focke, *Sozialismus*, who sees his book as a contribution to the historiography of "German Left Catholicism". Ibid., 11.
180. See Walter Dirks, "Nachbemerkung", 160: "Whoever does not want to give up faced with the second period of impending restoration in the mid-1970s should remember the forefathers and history".
181. Bröckling, "Einleitung", in: Dirks, *Sozialismus oder Restauration*, 11.

MULTI-FACETED RELATIONS BETWEEN CHRISTIAN TRADE UNIONS AND LEFT CATHOLICISM IN EUROPE

Patrick Pasture

1. The Christian Labour Movement, or "the Catholic Left"?

In the literature on Left Catholicism the Christian labour movement[1] and the Christian trade unions in particular are usually omitted. However, at first sight one could consider them Left Catholic, as being to the "left" of the Catholic centre.

According to the definition adopted in the introduction, Left Catholicism is a conjunctural left wing movement within Catholicism, i.e. an expression of a "moment of opportunity and crisis" in the 1940s. Since the Christian trade unions exist since the late 19th century, they cannot be considered "Left Catholic" by definition. However, the features attributed to Left Catholicism also apply to a great extent to the Christian trade unions. Both focus on the defence of the working class and have very similar objectives. Obviously, the Christian trade union movement is an expression of the emancipation of the workers by themselves. Moreover, with the possible exception of the Dutch Catholic trade union movement that was integrated and de facto subject to a clerical officialdom until 1945/1963[2], the Christian trade unions and political worker leagues always were independent lay movements, certainly as regards their "core business", the actual trade union activities or political representation, even if they subscribed to a political perspective of defence of the Catholic interests as well, which the unions, moreover, only reluctantly did.[3]

---

1. In most countries (however not in France) the Christian trade unions were integrated within a broader Christian labour movement, which included not only trade unions but also co-operatives, cultural and apostolic associations, as well as political worker leagues. Therefore I sometimes refer to the Christian labour movement as an all-encompassing term which includes the Christian trade unions. Please take note that I do not make that difference just for purposes of alternating the terminology: the difference remains significant. In the following article I will nevertheless mainly emphasise the trade unions.
2. Pasture, "Diverging Paths".
3. It is impossible here to distinguish the nevertheless important differences in this respect between organisations and between countries. The oldest German and Belgian trade unions clearly considered themselves as non-confessional and neutral, and considered the British trade unions as their ideal in respect of their ideological stance. The integration of the trade unions into a political perspective always was a difficult process. In *Histoire du syndicalisme chrétien international*, chap. 1, I give a more detailed overview of the origins and features of the Christian trade unions in Europe up to 1920.

This perspective makes clear that the Christian trade unions also recognised the value of pluralism long before the appearance of Left Catholicism. The Christian unions originated mainly as a reaction against the mounting influence of socialism within the labour movement. Therefore they presented themselves as nonconfessional and even neutral. Although after 1900 the impact of the Catholic Church upon the Christian labour movement and the unions increased considerably and changed them deeply, this particular origin remained important and part of their heritage (most outspokenly so at an international level). Moreover, they owed their existence to pluralism, which they therefore welcomed in principle.[4] In the 1920s and 1930s the Christian trade unions - most clearly if not mainly so on the international level via the *Confédération Internationale des Syndicats Chrétiens* (CISC) - distinguished themselves by their fight for democratic liberties, in particular freedom of association, targeting fascism and marxism in equal terms.[5] After the Second World War, the Christian trade unions increasingly, and apparently without much discussion, opened their ranks to non-Christians. This was particularly the case for the *Confédération Française des Travailleurs Chrétiens* (CFTC) in the French overseas areas.[6] Incidentally, the ideas of Jacques Maritain as expressed in *Humanisme intégral* did find a particularly warm welcome in Christian trade union circles. They seemed to confirm the ideas the Christian unions defended since their origin.[7]

In his presentation of the innovations within the realm of theology, Gerd-Rainer Horn notes that the Left Catholic milieu left behind its "exclusionary anticommunism" and adopted a "competitive anticommunism". Certainly the Christian trade unions in 1945 had remained anticommunist and even antisocialist. However, essentially, their anticommunism and antisocialism followed the same logic as attributed to Left Catholicism: combating the enemy by combating social injustice. Fighting the causes that drove workers into the arms of socialism definitely was the perspective of the Christian labour movement from its very inception, and the international Christian trade union movement adopted the same line of conduct regarding communism.[8]

4. See esp. Strikwerda, *A House Divided*.
5. I cannot here develop the complex and, in the literature, disputed question of the attitude of the Christian trade unions towards fascism. See extensively my study *Histoire du syndicalisme chrétien international*, ch. 2 and 3.
6. I do not know if the Dutch Protestant union (Christelijk Nationaal Vakverbond, CNV) followed a similar policy in the Dutch colonies.
7. Maritain, "La personne humaine en général" (see also the resolution adopted by the CISC Congress in Paris on 6-8 September 1937, quoted in Pasture, *Histoire du syndicalisme chrétien international*, 196). On the influence of Maritain upon the Christian trade union movement, see also Vanistendael, "Jacques Maritain".
8. Incidentally, this attitude in the 1960s brought them to severely criticise US policy in this respect, particularly in Latin America. Pasture, *Histoire du syndicalisme chrétien international*, 315-323 and passim.

2. Oppositions: the Perception of Difference

Shall we conclude thus that the Christian trade unions were a "Left Catholic" movement avant la lettre? The parallels are indeed striking. Nevertheless, there are also differences. Left Catholics, for example, generally have a more "bourgeois", urban and intellectual background (see the other chapters in this book) compared to the working class character of the Christian labour movement - I assume, however, that Left Catholics would not appreciate this difference as being determining.

To a certain extent Left Catholic movements can be regarded as different in both size and organisation: Left Catholic movements were smaller, more fragmented, less organised and less bureaucratic but more militant than the Christian labour movement, apparently also more focused on formation and education rather than mass collective action. In a way they seem to anticipate the New Left of the late 1960s.[9] But I doubt if that difference is really to the point. Left Catholic political parties such as the early *Mouvement République Populaire* (MRP) and *Union Démocratique Belge* (UDB), but also the *Mouvement Populaire des Familles* (MPF), aimed at becoming mass movements, as was the Christian labour movement. Also, one should not overestimate the organisational strength of the latter: After all, the massive character of the Christian unions in Belgium, the Netherlands or France was a relatively recent phenomenon and only dated from the 1930s.

In my opinion subjective factors - perception and representation - carry more weight than the "objective" differences. Most certainly, the Left Catholic movements did *present* themselves as being new, and they also wanted to break out of the traditional "closed" Catholic community or "ghetto" and that certainly included the Christian labour movement. The surviving Christian trade unions after the war - limited to France, the Netherlands, Belgium, Luxembourg, and Switzerland - on the contrary explicitly aimed at restoring their prewar existence, and notwithstanding some hesitations they explicitly situated themselves in the Catholic or Christian Democratic camp. That was, as we shall see, to a certain extent even the case in France. This perspective explains the "institutional conservatism" or inertia that sometimes, rightly or wrongly, is associated with these unions. Incidentally, Christian trade unions would certainly reject the label "Left Catholic", not only because of their antisocialism (to which we will return) or because they still cultivated an ideal of aclericalism[10], non-confessionalism and independence, but also because they advocated "a third way", beyond the dichotomy between socialism and liberal capitalism.[11]

---

9. Compare Hamon and Rotman, *La deuxième gauche*. One could even think about the contrast between "new" and "old" social movements. However, as Kenneth H. Tucker emphasized (mainly regarding the work of Jürgen Habermas and Jean Cohen), the theoreticians of the New Social Movements show little understanding of the "old" social movements and are therefore useless for insight into the historical development of the latter. Tucker, "How New are the New Social Movements?".
10. Durand, *L'Europe de la démocratie chrétienne*.
11. See extensively Pasture, *Histoire du syndicalisme chrétien international*. Compare also Van Kersbergen, *Social Capitalism*.

The main difference in my opinion between Left Catholicism and the Christian labour movement, however, is to be found in its theoretical or theological underpinning. Left Catholicism referred to a very different conception of the role of the Christian in society, which was rooted in the "theology of Incarnation" and the separation of the spiritual and the temporal, as in the *Nouvelle théologie*. But this orientation had other antecedents too in Catholic Action.

Catholic Action was the vehicle of a particular view on the role of the Catholic layperson in society, which emphasised its individual responsibility in the apostolate of the church. This ideology - for an ideology it was - aimed at the rechristianisation of society; it was therefore essentially offensive, as expressed in the metaphor of the *miles Christi*. The Christian labour movement, on the contrary, in particular the trade unions, arose from a defensive reaction of the workers - laypersons - against socialism, sometimes supported by parts of the clergy but mostly against the wishes of the upper strata of the Church hierarchy, who tried to control or even to destroy them.[12] Under the influence of Catholic social doctrine the Christian labour movement finally stressed the collective responsibility of the Catholics in the defence of the faith against secularism and socialism. This marks an important difference with the views of Left Catholicism in the 1940s and 1950s.

Moreover, insofar as Left Catholic movements were rooted in Catholic Action and referred to its principles of the separation between the spiritual and the temporal, the Christian labour movement recognised in Left Catholicism an old enemy. Indeed, in the 1920s and 1930s the Christian labour movement had opposed Catholic Action, which it considered to be the expression of a clerical and antidemocratic reaction within the Catholic Church, which aimed at submitting the workers to the authority of the hierarchy and jeopardising freedom of association and democratic representation. The Christian labour movement saw itself as a movement directed by laypersons, who were responsible towards their own members (even if clerics, as "moral advisors" or *Directeurs d'œuvres sociales*, did play a considerable role as well)[13], while Catholic Action - contrary to how theologians and church historians usually represent it as an expression of the emancipation of the laypersons (following the recognition of the apostolic action of the laypersons in *Ubi Arcano Dei*, 1922) - aimed at restoring the authority of the hierarchy over the apostolate. Moreover, Catholic Action undermined the democratic representation of the workers, and in particular their defence against fascism. In Italy, for example, the *Azione cattolico* from 1924 onwards actively combated the "white" (=Christian) trade unions close to the *Partito Popolare*, already locked in a fight to the death with the fascists.[14] In Belgium Catholic Action associated itself in practice with reactionary con-

---

12. Kalyvas, *The Rise of Christian Democracy in Europe*; Conway, "Introduction".
13. The role of these clerics is difficult to explain. Certainly their actual influence went far beyond just "moral advising", and especially at the local level they sometimes carried the movement. However, they often acted in the first place as defenders of the labour movement towards the hierarchy, which is a quite different perspective from that of Catholic Action. See Pasture, *Histoire du syndicalisme chrétien international*, passim; Pasture, "Diverging Paths", and Gerard, *Église et mouvement ouvrier chrétien en Belgique*.
14. Pollard, *The Vatican and Italian Fascism*, 32-33.

servatives and seriously challenged the political activities of the Christian labour movement. As Emmanuel Gerard emphasised, at the very least Catholic Action therefore tended to alienate the Catholic community from democratic politics.[15] In the worst case, Catholic Action could turn into a fascist movement itself, as happened with the Belgian Catholic Action movement *Rex*.[16]

These events in the 1920s and 1930s left a lasting imprint in the memory of Christian trade unionists, and that would become an important factor in their relations with movements that referred to Catholic Action after the war, even if Catholic Action organisations after the destruction of the Christian trade unions had offered the Christian worker activists a safe haven against fascists.

The divergent orientations of the Christian labour movement and Left Catholicism resulted in a fundamental difference between the two, all the more so since, as Gerd-Rainer Horn describes in the introduction to this volume, Left Catholicism not only tended to alienate itself from its potential supporters, in this case the Christian labour movement, but even went as far as radically departing from its initial objectives, as becomes blatantly clear in the remarkable development of the French MPF - in earlier publications I have called this the "paradox of the lay apostolate", a phenomenon that we find again in many lay apostolic movements in the 1950s and 1960s.[17] This development brought these movements in direct conflict with the Christian labour movement.[18]

3. Intrusions and Parallels

Left Catholicism and the Christian labour movement thus appeared to be quite different after all. However, after the Second World War they adopted parallel positions; one may even argue that elements of Left Catholicism "infused" themselves into the Christian labour movement. These features especially come to the fore when we focus on the relations of the Christian labour movement with the non-Catholic Left.

---

15. Gerard, *De katholieke partij in crisis*; Gerard, "Adaptation en temps de crise", especially 187-194 and 233-236. See also several contributions in Buchanan and Conway, eds., *Political Catholicism in Europe*; Conway, *Catholic Politics in Western Europe*, 43-44, 52 ff. The conflict between the Christian trade unions and Catholic conservatives in France almost led to a condemnation of the former, but the CFTC eventually got off well (the Mathon case). See Launay, *La CFTC*, 227-287; *A propos du document romain sur la question syndicale*; Tessier, "L'Église catholique et le syndicalisme"; see also Mayeur, *Catholicisme social et Démocratie chrétienne*.
16. See Conway, "Building the Christian City"; Conway, *Collaboration in Belgium*; and, for the larger context, Conway, *Catholic Politics in Europe 1918-1945*.
17. Pasture, *Kerk, politiek en sociale actie*, chapter 4. See also the contribution by Bruno Duriez elsewhere in this volume.
18. However, as Kalyvas noted, because of its democratic lay character, Christian Democracy - and by extension also the Christian labour movement - had secularising effects as well (Kalyvas, *The Rise of Christian Democracy in Europe*, esp. 260-261) and thus also alienated itself from its origins.

3.1. Co-operation with the Non-Catholic Left

Left Catholics explicitly wanted to break out of the closed Catholic world and favoured some form of organisational unity with the socialists and even communists. In principle, this was difficult to adopt for the Christian trade unions, whose original identity was based upon antisocialism. This antisocialism had remained quite virulent in the 1920s and 1930s - in some countries socialists and Christians had been virtually on a war footing, the most tragic example being Austria. The appeal of popular fronts in the 1930s concerned communists and Social Democrats, but not directly Christians; in 1936 the CFTC made its breakthrough in France precisely because of its rejection of the popular front.[19]

But this antisocialist attitude was changing. To a certain extent a sense of common interests and of a common fate had developed. Incidentally, the Christian unions in principle always had been in favour of cooperation with non-Christian unions regarding concrete issues of the defence of the workers' interests.[20] Also the position of the CFTC towards the popular front in 1936 had not been just rejection as it had been the case for most Catholics. As Michel Launay emphasised, the leadership of this confederation, even if it did not accept the "main tendue" offered by the Communist Party leader Maurice Thorez as well as the socialist Léon Blum, remained cautious and in May 1936 even refused to condemn the workers' occupation of the factories.[21] In the fight against fascism the CISC had severely criticised the repression of the socialist labour movement (admittedly not always supported in this by the national rank and file), even when the local Christian unions were spared or went as far as supporting a fascist regime, as was the case in Austria where the opposition between the (small) Christian Social labour movement and the socialists was perhaps the most dramatic.[22] In his first postwar activity report CISC general secretary Serrarens had to recognise that socialism, at least in Europe, had "lost much of its anticlerical character" and that, even if most socialists still were materialists, "the number of those who recognise the existence of a moral law [was] increasing" - admittedly, an ambiguous statement.[23] In Italy, Germany and Austria - the former fascist countries, where the free Christian trade unions had been abolished for ten to twenty (Italy) years - the Christian labour leaders in 1944 supported the formation of unitary trade unions.

Also, within the Christian labour movement and the Christian trade unions Left Catholic factions or currents existed that openly favoured trade union unity and a fundamental renewal of "traditional" Christian trade union organisation and practice. These circles had often emerged from the *Jeunesse Ouvrière Chrétienne* (JOC) and were thus influenced by Catholic Action and receptive towards the new theology (Maritain, Mounier, Chenu etc.).[24] They explicitly invoked the experience of the Resistance (or, at least,

---

19. Launay, *La CFTC*, 301-380.
20. This has especially been underlined by Strikwerda, *A House Divided*.
21. Launay, *La CFTC*, 301-380; Pierrard, *L'Église et les ouvriers en France*, 533-539.
22. See extensively Pasture, *Histoire du syndicalisme chrétien international*, ch. 3 (on Austria, especially 171-182).
23. *L'Internationale Syndicale Chrétienne 1937-1945*, 229.
24. See Fouilloux, *Une Église en quête de liberté*.

the experience of fascism, dictatorship or occupation) and referred to the distinction between the spiritual and the temporal to underpin and justify their positions. During the liberation period, such currents actually exercised much influence over the bulk of the "traditional" Christian trade unions.

At the first postwar CISC Congress, held in Brussels on 8-10 October 1945 immediately after the creation of the World Federation of Trade Unions (WFTU), for example, Jean Brodier of the CFTC pleaded passionately not to burn the bridges with the new international federation and to strive at the very least for unity of action.[25] However, many obstacles existed against such unity, e.g. residual antisocialism within the Christian labour movement as well as - in the first place - anticlerical resentments among the European Social Democratic unions. The CISC rejected the affiliation to the WFTU if this came down to its own dissolution, while the remaining Christian movements did not fuse with their socialist competitors, let alone with communist organisations. Nevertheless, the Christian movements strongly advocated "joint action", and in 1949, after the split of the WFTU and the formation of the International Confederation of Free Trade Unions (ICFTU), they seriously considered an organisational collaboration with the new international.[26]

3.2. Left Catholic Currents Arising from the Christian Labour Movement itself: Belgium

Surprisingly, in Belgium the most salient Left Catholic initiatives - the MPF as well as the UDB - originated from the Christian labour movement itself. One of the breading grounds of Left Catholicism was the JOC, the young workers movement that was a constituent part of the Belgian organised Christian labour movement. The JOC combined the apostolic ambitions of Catholic Action, including its criticism of "traditional" Catholic social action, with an outspoken working class perspective. As Emmanuel Gerard convincingly argued, this particular situation and the recognition of "specialised" Catholic Action in Belgium was part of the "compromise" between Catholic Action and Christian Democracy in the 1920s, with long lasting and paradoxical implications, in particular regarding the political action of the Christian labour movement.[27] The "deconfessionalisation" of the Catholic Party, of which the UDB was an exponent, certainly was one of these lasting effects.[28] The MPF likewise came about as an extension of the JOC.[29]

---

25. *Het Internationaal Christelijk Vakverbond*, 1937-1945, 258; Brodier and Bouladoux, *Problèmes de syndicalisme international*, 4.
26. For a discussion of the different arguments, including strategic considerations, motivations and positions on this issue in the different countries and at an international level, see Pasture, *Histoire du syndicalisme chrétien international*, ch. 4, 209-252.
27. Gerard, *De katholieke partij in crisis*; Gerard, "Adaptation", especially 187-194 and 233-236.
28. Pasture, *Kerk, politiek en sociale actie*, ch. 1.
29. Zelis, "Les Équipes populaires", 545 ff.

Some trade union circles were initially receptive towards the question of trade union unity. An article in the francophone review of the Belgian Christian labour movement in December 1944 observed that *un véritable ouragan* (a veritable hurricane) in favour of trade union unity set ablaze the Walloon Christian trade unions.[30] Joseph Fafchamps, a leader of the Christian metalworkers' union in Liège, was one of the fiercest advocates of trade union unity.[31] Together with some other "Christian Democrats" he also joined the UDB National Committee and in 1945 stated that a majority of the activists in the Walloon Christian labour movement supported the new party.[32] However, the UDB, but also the MPF, utterly failed; one of the major reasons for their downfall was the reaction of the socialists, who preferred to rebuild their own movement, hoping they would grow strong enough to outnumber the Christians[33] - a considerable misjudgement, because it were the latter who registered the biggest progress. While they repudiated any rapprochement to the *Comités de lutte syndicale* (trade union fighting committees) of the Belgian Communist Party or the "syndicalist" *Mouvement Syndical Unifié* (unified trade union movement) of the Liège trade union leader André Renard, which had emerged during the war, the Belgian Christian labour movement, in particular the trade union confederation CSC (*Confédération des Syndicats Chrétiens*), strongly advocated "joint action" and even "structural cooperation" with the Social Democrats. They did, however, reject organic unity.[34]

3.3. "Reconstruction": A Trojan Horse in France?

In France, the movement called *Reconstruction* and the *minorité* that strove for the confessionalisation of the confederation in my view may be considered expressions of Left Catholicism (though I will nuance this observation further in the text). Paul Vignaux, who undoubtedly was the prime

---

30. "Le syndicalisme chrétien", 341. On the Left Catholic initiatives within the realm of the Christian labour mouvement, see Pasture, *Kerk, politiek en sociale actie*, 48-83.
31. Vansweevelt, "Pogingen tot progressieve frontvorming in de vakbeweging", 205-207. See also Vansweevelt, "Pogingen tot progressieve frontvorming in de vakbeweging tijdens de bevrijdingsperiode".
32. Jules Fafchamps to the editorial board of *Les Dossiers de l'Action sociale catholique*, 14 August 1945 (Leuven, KADOC, ACW Archives, 169). The term Christian Democrat in Wallonia is used for the political representatives of the Christian labour movement.
33. Incidentally, in the Netherlands the opposite happened: as Annemieke Klijn showed in her comparative analysis of Dutch and Belgian socialist party politics (*Arbeiders- of volkspartij: een vergelijkende studie van het Belgisch en Nederlands socialisme 1933-1946*), in the Netherlands the socialists reached out to the Christians, but it were the latter who rejected this rapprochement.
34. Pasture, *Kerk, politiek en sociale actie*, 48-51. See also the Belgian attitude at the CISC Congress, Brussels, 8-10 October 1945 (report in *L'Internationale Syndicale Chrétienne 1937-1945*).

figure of the *minorité* and the driving force behind *Reconstruction*, certainly offers a clear example of a Left Catholic activist.35

Vignaux in the 1930s was a *directeur d'études* and lecturer in medieval theology and a specialist in Thomism at the famous *École des Hautes Études* in Paris. In 1937 he founded the French trade union for teachers in public education, the *Syndicat Général de l'Éducation Nationale* (SGEN), which affiliated to the CFTC. By doing so, he introduced within the Christian confederation the idea of *laïcité*, which accepted the values of the Republic and the importance of the civil service. After the war, the groups *Reconstruction* stressed the working class character of the French confederation, which was by then still dominated by white collar workers. In 1944-1949, "enriched" by the experience of the war and the Resistance, these groups de facto formed a political faction within the CFTC that started to strive (1) for a rapprochement towards the socialists and communists at national and international levels (however, not necessarily by means of a unified trade union federation), (2) for a new internal organisation in which white collar and blue collar workers would be represented by joint industrial unions instead of separate unions, (3) for less explicit confessional references, in particular to the Catholic encyclicals (which illustrates the far more moderate character of this current compared to the MPF), and (4) against a political alliance with the MRP. The latter may surprise, but indeed, while many protagonists as well as scholars considered the MRP as a Left Catholic, nonconfessional party, the entrance of French Catholics into one single party can be viewed very differently, because no strong Catholic party had existed in France prior to 1945. Notwithstanding its relatively radical character at its origins, the MRP, in the eyes of its opponents - and from a critical comparative perspective as well - represented a greater confessionalisation of party politics and thus was dubbed *Mouvement des Révérends Pères* (Movement of the reverend fathers).36 Significant in this respect is that Jacques Tessier, the indisputable leader of the CFTC after the war - one of the founding fathers of the French confederation and one of the first trade union activists to join the Resistance - also stood at the cradle of the MRP.

This opposition faction, called the *minorité*, increasingly distanced itself from traditional Catholic doctrine as this was interpreted, in a fairly strict manner, by the leadership of the CFTC. In the 1940s and 1950s the minorité radicalised and simulatenously became more influential, eventually, as is widely known, in 1964, transforming the CFTC into the non-con-

---

35. On Vignaux, see *Paul Vignaux: un intellectuel syndicaliste*. On Reconstruction, see Vignaux' autobiographical book, *De la CFTC à la CFDT*. See also the literature on the CFTC/CFDT, esp. Adam, *La CFTC 1940-1958*; Branciard, *Histoire de la CFDT*, esp. 98-99 (Branciard strongly emphasises that the *minorité* in fact was composed of several circles and groupings); Groux and Mouriaux, *La CFDT*, 26-27.

36. Cholvy and Hilaire, eds., *Histoire religieuse de la France contemporaine*, III, 129. See the observations of Groux and Mouriaux, *La CFDT*, 28, on the new situation posed by the MRP and the relevance of the German/Alsatian model. Strangely enough this perspective has escaped the attention of most historians of the MRP and Christian Democracy in France: e.g. Mayeur, "La démocratie d'inspiration chrétienne en France" (but see also Fouilloux, *Les chrétiens français entre crise et libération*, 251, and - quite ambiguous, however - Letamendia, *Le Mouvement Républicain Populaire*).

fessional *Confédération Française Démocratique du Travail* (CFDT), which, in the 1960s, would advocate economic planning and later self-management.[37]

3.4. Unified Trade Union Experiences in the Former Fascist Countries

In the former fascist countries the Christian labour leaders opted for a unified non-confessional trade union movement, including communists. At first sight this can be interpreted as the trade union equivalent of political Left Catholicism such as in the UDB and the MRP, but its impact upon the working class was much greater. Paradoxically, however, in these countries the ideal of working class unity was not continued at the political level; in each of them a new Christian Democratic Party was created. Moreover, the advocates of trade union unity also wanted to establish a link with Christian Democracy; it was even considered a prerequisite for their participation within the unified trade union formula.

The motives of the Catholic labour leaders to favour a united, non-confessional trade union federation were diverse, complex and sometimes even contradictory: the simultaneous experience of the war and the weakness of the divided labour movement faced with the fascist tide, new views on the role of Christians in society, ideological radicalisation and even communist sympathies played a part alongside anticommunism as well as an interest in maximising their power. This was most clearly the case in Italy where the Christian Democratic leaders, in particular Alcide de Gasperi and Achille Grandi, forced through trade union unity, according to some sources even against the will of the Vatican.[38] From 1922 until its disappearance in 1925-1926 general secretary of the Italian Christian trade union confederation CIL (*Confederazione Italiana dei Lavoratori*), Grandi certainly was a declared partisan of labour unity; in 1923 he had supported the formation of a trade union defence front against the fascists.[39] Now, in 1945, he became one of three general secretaries of the unified CGIL (*Confederazione Generale Italiana del Lavoro*). For his generation of leaders, the reminiscence of the *Partito Popolare Italiano* (PPI) and the resistance against fascism were of utmost importance, but for the younger followers of Dossetti the influence of Catholic Action, the mysticism of incarnation and the separation of the spiritual and the temporal prevailed in their quest for trade union unity.[40]

---

37. On this development see (apart from the works quoted in note 35) Georgi, *L'invention de la CFDT*; Hamon and Rotman, *La deuxième gauche*.
38. That was at least what Pius XII affirmed to the Belgian Christian trade union leader August Cool in March 1947 (detailed notes of the secret audience in the appendix to the minutes of the CISC Board meeting, Paris, 4 June 1947; Leuven, KADOC, CISC Archives). Compare Fonzi, "Mondo cattolico, Democrazia Cristiana e sindacato", 748; Turone, *Storia del sindacato in Italia*, 107; Bedani, *Politics and Ideology in the Italian Workers' Movement*, 10 ff.; Romero, *The United States and the European Trade Union Movement*, 50 ff.; Durand, *L'Église catholique dans la crise de l'Italie*, 484.
39. Tramontin, "Sindacalismo e cooperativismo cristiano dall' giolittiana al fascismo", especially 263-286; Ciampani, *La buona bataglia*, especially 61 ff.
40. Fonzi, "Mondo cattolico".

The situation in Austria and Germany was not fundamentally different. Both in Germany and Austria former Christian trade union leaders from the 1930s supported the creation of a unified trade union movement, which was also favoured by the allied forces - for the Western Allies, on the one hand, this meant promoting British and American models of collective action, on the other it was designed as a deliberate strategy to counter communist dominance in the labour movement.[41] One of the few surviving prewar Christian trade union leaders in Germany, Jacob Kaiser, a man of irreproachable reputation and involved in active resistance, in 1947 even explicitly spoke out in favour of a socialist society.[42] But most of his former colleagues - such as Karl Arnold, a secretary of the prewar Christian trade union confederation and in 1947 minister-president of Rhineland-Westphalia, and Johannes Albers, one of the founders of the *Christlich-Demokratische Arbeitnehmerschaft* (CDA), the organised workers' faction in the *Christlich Demokratische Union Deutschlands* (CDU) - emphasised the political reconstruction of Germany and the development of a strong Christian Democratic party. They considered trade union unity a prerequisite for social stability and the reconstruction of a stable democracy.[43]

Incidentally, alongside the Christian trade unions in each of these countries apostolic workers movements tried to permeate Catholic workers with the Catholic social doctrine and to preserve them from communist influence. In Germany the *Katholische Arbeiterbewegung* (KAB) existed already since 1884 and had survived Nazism up to 1944.[44] In Italy, as a corollary to trade union unity, the *Assoziazione Cristiani dei Lavoratori Italiani* (ACLI) was set up for the education of the Catholic workers and the propagation of Catholic social doctrine.[45] While in France and (francophone) Belgium such apostolic organisations easily radicalised into Left Catholic movements (the "paradox of the lay apostolate"), this was not the case in those countries where unitary trade unions existed, at least not until the late 1950s.

The Cold War put strong pressures upon the unified trade unions, since communists and Western-oriented labour leaders reacted in diametrically opposed ways towards the Marshall Plan; tensions arose on other issues as well.[46] In Italy, trade union unity within the CGIL did not last. The

---

41. On the American and British influence in Germany see Fichter, *Besatzungsmacht und Gewerkschaften*, and Lademacher and Mühlhausen, "Die deutschen Westzonen". The attitudes of the Catholics are extensively covered by Schroeder, *Katholizismus und Einheitsgewerkschaft*. For Austria, see Reichhold, *Geschichte der christlichen Gewerkschaften Österreichs*.
42. Document regarding the situation in Germany for the CISC Board Meeting, Paris, 4 June 1947 (Leuven, KADOC, CISC Archives); Schroeder, *Katholizismus und Einheitsgewerkschaft*, 373-381. See also the contribution of Andreas Lienkamp elsewhere in this volume.
43. See Schroeder, *Katholizismus und Einheitsgewerkschaft*, with extensive biographical data on Kaiser as well as Arnold and Albers.
44. Schroeder, *Katholizismus und Einheitsgewerkschaft*.
45. Pasini, *Le Acli delle origini*; Pasini, "Associazione Cristiani dei Lavoratori Italiani (ACLI)"; Durand, *L'Église catholique*, 485-493.
46. The literature on the influence of the Cold War on European labour is abundant. Carew, *Labour under the Marshall Plan* still is the basic reference. Romero, "Guerra fredda e scissione sindacali: stato e prospettive della storiografia" offers the most recent state of the art on the historiography regarding this subject.

Catholics under the leadership of Giulio Pastore in 1948 quit the CGIL. However, the Libera CGIL and from May 1950 the *Confederazione Italiana Sindacati Lavoratori* (CISL), its successor, explicitly claimed to be a democratic, non-confessional trade union movement - though constituted almost exclusively of Catholics and de facto allied with the *Democrazia Cristiana* (DC).[47] In Austria tensions between communists, socialists and Christians provoked the formation of political factions within the unified *Österreichische Gewerkschaftsbund* (ÖGB), but the Christian Democratic leaders did not see the point of splitting up the confederation and putting the social and political stability at risk; also their anticommunism incited them to stay within the federation which allowed the democratic labour forces - as opposed to the experience within the CGIL where the communists dominated - to effectively control the communists.[48] In Germany the tensions between the different currents did not lead to similar organised political factions, but in 1955 a number of Christian trade unionists split from the *Deutscher Gewerkschaftsbund* (DGB) to create separate Christian trade unions. However, neither the churches, the CDU nor the apostolic organisations offered their support to the initiative, and most Catholic and Protestant workers remained within the unified confederation, notwithstanding their political minority status.[49]

In sum, when we discuss the relations between Christian trade unions and Left Catholicism it is necessary to make some distinctions: (1) We can consider the main Christian trade unions in Europe as different from Left Catholicism in perception and ideological underpinning, keeping in mind however that, objectively, the parallels are striking. (2) Nevertheless, within these Christian trade unions, since 1944 Left Catholic factions or currents existed, such as *Reconstruction* within the CFTC. (3) Trade union unity was achieved in Italy, Austria and also Germany. In a way we may consider this as the trade union version of Left Catholicism, equivalent to the political project of the UDB or MRP - but, it should be underlined, of far greater significance. However, the motives for trade union unity were often complex, and probably much less "idealistic" than in Left Catholicism. Moreover, the role of Catholic Action and the principal choice for a separation of the spiritual and the temporal played a minor role, especially in Germany and Austria. Paradoxically, anticommunism favoured the creation of nonconfessional and even of unified trade unions whenever communists constituted a significant minority. Incidentally, when communists were not regarded as

---

47. See, apart from general overviews of Italian trade union history, especially Pede, "La scissione in Italia"; Zaninelli, ed., *Il sindacato nuovo*; Bedani, *Politics and Ideology*; Saba, *Giulio Pastore sindacalista*; Saba and Bianchi, *La nascita della Cisl*; Romero, *The United States*.
48. Pelinka, *Gewerkschaften im Parteienstaat*; Reichhold, *Geschichte der christlichen Gewerkschaften Österreichs*.
49. See Schroeder, *Katholizismus und Einheitsgewerkschaft*; Pelinka, *Gewerkschaften im Parteienstaat*, for an interesting comparison with the ÖGB, and Ciampani, "Attori sociali e dinamiche internazionali durante la ricostruzione democratica", for an interesting Italian perspective.

being a considerable threat, as was in my view the case in Belgium[50], there was no pressure towards trade union unity either.

4. Christian Trade Unions and Left Catholics: Between Living Apart and Common Struggle

How did the Christian trade unions react to the different Left Catholic initiatives? Their reaction varied from no interference to outright opposition. Especially immediately after the war there were widespread sympathies towards some Left Catholic initiatives within Christian labour circles. A number of militants of prewar Catholic Action organisations, particularly of the JOC, were now involved in Christian trade unions.[51] However, with its antidemocratic and anti-union policies of the 1920s and 1930s still fresh in their memory, a strong "Catholic Action" character or background certainly was not of a sort to elicit much sympathy among Christian trade union leaders.

If Catholic Action was not put forward or if Left Catholics did not directly constitute a threat to their activities, the Christian unions tended to ignore the Left Catholics: they had other fish to fry. Apart from France where Vignaux and his companions stimulated an intensive ideological and political debate, they did not feel the need to write extensive philosophical tracts either, after 1945 even less so than in the 1920s and 1930s when their existence was much more disputed yet. With both feet firmly planted in the daily fight for the defence of the workers' interests, they seemed less interested in the theoretical underpinning of their programs, and references to theology or philosophy were virtually non-existent.

Perhaps the Left Catholic movements sometimes were too radical for them as well, as Left Catholic activists themselves liked to believe. I am not inclined, however, to give much credit to their explanation. For their part the Christian unions had their own programme, aimed at the transformation of the social economy according to a corporatist-personalist perspective (and which, by the way, was more radical than traditional Catholic social doctrine). However, their priorities were different and they fundamentally followed another logic than Left Catholics.

4.1. Demise and Recuperation of Left Catholicism by the Belgian Christian Labour Movement

In Belgium, the Christian trade unions at first ignored the (very moderate) Left Catholic initiatives, but soon reacted against them. However, in any case the political context did not favour a fundamental renewal.[52] The

---

50. In many publications Lode Wils has argued that communists did constitute a threat to the social and political order in Belgium (e.g. Wils, *Honderd jaar Vlaamse Beweging*, III, 243 ff.). This thesis, however, is widely rejected by contemporary scholars on Belgian political history.
51. See e.g. Béthouart, *Des syndicalistes chrétiens en politique*.
52. The following observations refer to Pasture, *Kerk, politiek en sociale actie*, 38-83.

"hurricane" in favour of trade union unity in reality proved to be little more than a storm in a teacup. The leadership of the CSC without much difficulty refuted an alliance with the communist *Comités de lutte syndicale*; the latter did fuse with the socialist unions, forming the *Fédération Générale des Travailleurs de Belgique* (FGTB), but this sealed the fate for any further attempt to unify with the new confederation. After the war, most attention of the CSC was devoted to economic reconstruction and the creation of a new social scheme, which, far from uniting both confederations, in practice pitted them against each other and reinforced competition between them.[53]

The CSC was reluctant to take action against the UDB mainly because of internal political divisions; also for reasons of principle the union claimed political independence. However, the Archbishop Cardinal Van Roey did not share such hesitations and underlined the necessity of political unity of all Catholics. Unlike its French model, the MRP, the UDB collapsed like a jelly in the first postwar elections in February 1946. More than a consequence of the archepiscopal interdiction, the UDB failed because of its astoundingly weak organisation as well as the growing polarisation between Catholics and the anticlerical forces after Liberation: the UDB only recruited in certain Walloon and Brussels intellectual circles but did not appeal to the masses, especially in Flanders, and certainly not among socialists. The major trade union leaders, who during the war had looked at the attempts for political renewal with a favourable eye, as was the case with the popular (French-speaking) president of the Belgian Christian trade union federation, Henri Pauwels, had withdrawn from the UDB already at the end of 1944.[54]

Things were different, however, with the MPF, which did prosper in Wallonia and Brussels. From the moment that the MPF started to radicalise along the lines of its French predecessor and seemed to get out of control, roughly from February 1946 onwards, the Christian trade union confederation and the leadership of the workers' leagues, supported by the bishop of Namur, Mgr Charue, actively combated the MPF. They had the means to do so, since the MPF was still part of the organised Christian labour movement, to which it was tied by personal and financial ties. The MPF's activities in the field of the apostolate within the Christian labour movement were soon taken over by the *Équipes populaires* and the women workers' leagues.[55]

The Christian labour movement in Belgium effectively neutralised Left Catholicism. But some of the Left Catholic values and interests were recuperated and re-integrated, mainly through the efforts of its educational organisations. Former UDB and MPF activists found a safe haven in the cultural and press services of the different branches, although measures were taken to prevent that they would, like in France, once again use these services to propagate Left Catholic ideals throughout the Christian labour movement. Left Catholic ideals nevertheless survived in the 1950s in the margins of the Walloon Christian labour movement, in particular in the intellectual circles that Jean-Louis Jadoulle describes elsewhere in this volume.

---

53. Pasture, "Belgium: pragmatism in pluralism".
54. Beerten, *Le rêve travailliste en Belgique*, 37.
55. Pasture, *Kerk, politiek en sociale actie*, 62-83; Zelis, "Les Équipes populaires".

4.2. The Transforming Power of Left Catholicism in France

The situation in France is more complicated. The *minorité* CFTC and the groups *Reconstruction* were given a hearing; even more, they managed to gain dominance within the training department, which proved to be a most effective instrument for propagating their ideas, even if, of course, they experienced opposition from the majority as well. But they succeeded in transforming the Christian confederation into a new kind of union, the CFDT, which in many ways can be considered the heir of Left Catholicism.[56] However, as Guy Groux and René Mouriaux make us observe, that was not yet the perspective just after Liberation. Fernand Hennebicq, one of the founding fathers of *Reconstruction* and one of the protagonists of the *minorité*, in December 1944 declared being profoundly deceived "to find comrades who, under the pretext of the (in [his] view utopian) myth of the conquest of the masses, aim at transforming the milieus of Catholic Action into members of the CGT". "I believe it is a good thing to do something against a tendency that is spreading a bit too much for the moment, and that consists of removing any Christian label. Finally one will end up by eliminating any Christian reference, and, bit by bit, all the Christian character will go away".[57]

Regarding the French MPF, the CFTC did not really combat it, though there were frictions between militants of both movements. But the JOC and the *Secrétariats sociaux* of Lille did react against it, and in 1946 the French bishops "observed" that the MPF could no longer be labelled Catholic Action; three years later the episcopacy concluded that the attempts to reanimate a Catholic workers' apostolate within the framework of the MPF had failed. The MPF fell apart and a new organisation was created (1950-51) which was to be obedient to the hierarchy, the *Action Catholique Ouvrière* (ACO).[58] However, the ACO once again stressed the separation of the spiritual and the temporal and developed its own version of the "paradox of the lay apostolate". In the first place, it turned into an important centre of support for the *minorité* CFTC.[59] In some places, the ACO and the CFTC came to blows.[60] More generally, the ACO developed a model for the Catholic working class different from the large integrated Christian labour movement as it existed in Belgium and the Netherlands; in the later 1950s the ACO laid the foundations of a new international organisation of Christian workers, which provoked a conflict with both the International Federation of Catholic Labour Movements (best known as *Fédération Internationale des Mouvements Ouvriers Catholiques*, FIMOC) and, especially, the International Federation of Christian Trade Unions, CISC.[61]

---

56. See, in particular, Hamon and Rotman, *La deuxième gauche*.
57. Quoted in Groux and Mouriaux, *La CFDT*, 31-32 (translation P.P.).
58. Pierrard, *L'Église et les ouvriers en France*, 220-222; Debès, *Naissance de l'Action Catholique Ouvrière*, 135 ff.
59. Debès, *Naissance de l'Action Catholique Ouvrière*, 198. See also Adam, *La CFTC*, 189-205.
60. Cholvy and Hilaire, *Histoire religieuse*, III, 229.
61. Gerard, "Le MOC-ACW", especially 612-619; Pasture, *Histoire du syndicalisme chrétien international*; Pasture, "Les différents modèles d'organisation ouvrière catholique".

The worker priests equally embarrassed the CFTC, since they almost all affiliated to the CGT and supported communist initiatives such as the *Mouvement de la Paix* in 1950. Sometimes they clashed. Accused of being "the accomplice of the government, the employers and the big privileges", CFTC President Gaston Tessier in 1953 even summoned eighteen worker priests to appear before the ecclesiastical court (the *officialité*) of Paris because of defamation. The incident is significant for the tense relations between the CFTC, especially the *majorité*, and the worker priests.[62]

But in fact the main threat to the CFTC did not come from these Left Catholic movements, but from the MRP, which soon departed from its Left Catholic origins - if it ever could be labelled as such - and adopted centre right positions. The association of trade union action with politics, of course, always is a difficult issue for any trade union[63], but in this case the increasingly conservative orientation of the MRP offered numerous opportunities for the *minorité* to develop and to challenge the leadership of the confederation that continued to support that party against all odds.[64] The attitude towards the MRP certainly was a major factor in the process that led to the deconfessionalisation of the CFTC in 1964, which in turn was quite a symbol of the change of climate within the Catholic community that undermined and finally provoked the ruin of the Christian Democratic project in France and the dissolution of the MRP in 1967.[65]

4.3. The Cases of Unified Trade Unions

In the cases of Germany, Austria and Italy it is hardly possible to speak about a Christian trade union reaction against Left Catholicism, since there were no longer Christian trade unions and the Christian labour leaders supported the unitary trade union movement. Perhaps in a unitary trade union context one should rather look at the organisation and positions of the Catholics within the unified confederation. Significant is the tension in Italy between the supporters of Grandi and De Gasperi on the one hand and the *dossettiani* on the other, who were accused by the former of integrism or of being "integralists".[66] More important is the 1947 secession when the Catholics, under the leadership of Giulio Pastore, a dedicated follower of

---

62. Cholvy and Hilaire, *Histoire religieuse*, III, 229. Incidentally, Tessier won this case.
63. See Crouch, *Trade Unions: the Logic of Collective Action*.
64. Adam, *La CFTC*; Branciard, *Histoire de la CFDT*; Guy and Mouriaux, *La CFDT*; Georgi, *Eugène Descamps, chrétien et syndicaliste*.
65. Letamendia, *Le Mouvement Républicain Populaire*, 288-290, 367 and passim.
66. Incidentally, the accusation of integrism or integralism (the distinction is mere rhetoric) was also expressed by the *dossettiani* against the followers of De Gasperi and the former *popolare*. The term referred to a general attitude of Christian integralism (*cristanesimo integrale*) and explicitly targeted the views of Jacques Maritain (see his major work *Humanisme intégral* from 1936). Obviously, however, it also referred to the virulent antimodernism of the *Sodalitium Pianum*, the secret antimodernist association of Mgr Benigni, dissolved by Benedict XV in 1921 (see Poulat, *Intégrisme et catholicisme intégral*). See the short discussion in Fonzi, "Mondo cattolico", 791, note 150. On the phenomenon of the *dossettiani*, see also the contribution by Antonio Parisella elsewhere in this volume.

Dossetti[67], followed by Republicans and socialists, left the CGIL. The *Libera CGIL* as well as, in 1950, the CISL presented themselves as being nonconfessional, but since virtually all Social Democrats and Republicans joined the *Unione Italiana del Lavoro* (UIL), the CISL was left with an exclusively Catholic membership. Moreover, the CISL became allied to the DC.[68] In the long run, it was perhaps rather the ACLI that somehow would take up the Left Catholic legacy of the unified confederation rather than the CISL, since from 1957 onwards the ACLI adopted more critical positions, particularly with regard to the DC.

In Germany the Catholic choice for a unified trade union was disputed and led to numerous conflicts within the DGB as well as between the DGB, the CDU, the bishops, and the KAB. But in the end the majority of the Catholic trade unionists decided to stay within the DGB, even after the creation of the *Christliche Gewerkschaften Deutschlands* in 1955 - with some 100-200.000 affiliates the latter remained marginal compared to the millions of the DGB. However, it proved difficult to maintain a Catholic opposition within the DGB, which allied itself with the German Social Democratic Party (SPD); by 1960 it became virtually impossible to distinguish a particular Catholic faction: unification was complete.[69] In Austria the Catholics united in a Christian Democratic faction, which functioned as the labour faction within the Austrian Christian Democratic Party (*Österreichische Volkspartei*, ÖVP); apparently they felt quite satisfied with the formula.[70]

5. Conclusion

To conclude this article I want to return to the meaning of the 1940s as a "moment of opportunity and crisis" for the Christian trade unions and the role of Left Catholicism and vice versa. First of all we have to observe that in the former fascist countries a completely new trade union landscape was created, in which there was no more room for explicitly Christian trade unions. Even if labour unity, mainly under the impact of the Cold War, was broken, a return to the Christian trade union model, for different reasons, had become impossible. In this fundamentally new orientation Left Catholic ideas had played a certain role alongside other factors. This new situation had implications for the development of Left Catholicism in the political and apostolic field: the realisation of trade union unity fundamentally altered the conditions for the apostolate and prevented the "paradox of the lay apostolate" to materialise, perhaps because an important objective of Left Catholicism was realised. The apostolic organisations in a context of

---

67. Baget-Bozzo, *Il partito cristiano al potere*; 175, 241 ff.; Pombeni, *Le "Cronache sociali" di Dossetti*, 163.
68. The relationship of the CISL with the DC is essential to any study about the CISL. See, in particular, Bedani, *Politics and Ideology*.
69. Schroeder, *Katholizismus und Einheitsgewerkschaft*.
70. See Reichhold, *Geschichte der christlichen Gewerkschaften Österreichs*. See also Kriechbaumer, *Parteiprogramme im Widerstreit der Interessen* and Pelinka, *Gewerkschaften im Parteienstaat*, for an insightful comparison of the German and the Austrian situation.

unified trade unionism concentrated on pastoral work and on assuring a link with Christian Democracy. It remains paradoxical, however, that Christian labour leaders in these countries could promote political pluralism and the formation of Christian Democratic parties, but reject trade union pluralism and promote unified or neutral trade unions, something which was unthinkable for their colleagues in countries where the political structures were not destroyed for such a long time by fascism. This paradox is, however, of a fundamental importance.

In these other countries at first sight the Left Catholic initiatives appear to be short-lived and of little significance for the Christian trade unions. Certainly the latter did not engage in support of Left Catholic movements; on the contrary, as long as Left Catholics did not interfere with Catholic trade unions, the latter simply ignored the former. The Christian trade unions seemed especially concerned with their own "restoration" and, it should not be forgotten, with the socio-economic issues at stake after Liberation, which did not leave much space for theoretical speculations which were so dear to the Left Catholics, who were true intellectuals, even if they became involved in party political action. Often, Christian labour activists considered Left Catholics as utopians. Incidentally, if the "Resistance" and the experience of war and occupation is often invoked as an explanation for growing rapprochement between Catholics and socialists and as a point of origin of Left Catholicism, these experiences also worked the other way round. Christian trade unionists, particularly in France, had won their spurs as well; their actions and behaviour raised their self-consciousness and gave them credit after the war. Moreover, the fascist initiatives to create unified trade union structures - sometimes supported by socialist and Christian trade unionists[71] - had reinforced the traditional Christian convictions regarding both the role of the State and unified trade union structures. Also, some particular experiences during the occupation in some cases, as in the Netherlands, deeply spoiled the relations between Christian and Social-Democratic unions.[72]

In fact, even when Christian trade unionists in 1944-45 did favour unified unions, they distanced themselves from people we would identify as Left Catholics. Politically the Christian trade unions searched for an alliance with Christian Democratic parties as they were formed after the war - they constituted the exact mix of renewal and tradition that suited them. As recent studies emphasise, these Christian Democratic parties indeed constituted something considerably new, especially in France and Italy, but also in

---

71. In Belgium, e.g., the unified trade union organisation was promoted by the former socialist party leader Hendrik De Man. For several months unions, incidentally mainly Christian, let themselves be drawn into this experiment, which led, among other things, to a split within the CSC. Most unions, however, refused to submit themselves to the authority of the Nazis and broke away from this unified union. See, in particular Steenhaut, *De Unie van Hand- en Geestesarbeiders*.
72. See Harmsen and Reinalda, *Voor de bevrijding van de arbeid*, 220, for the Netherlands and Mampuys, "Le syndicalisme chrétien", esp. 216-225, for Belgium.

Germany and Austria, as well as in Belgium and the Netherlands.[73] With their stress on their democratic, lay and non-confessional character (at least on paper and during the Liberation period) they conformed to the orientations that the Christian trade unions had nourished since their origins; moreover, the Christian trade union leaders were given a hearing in these parties, be it on a personal basis or via organisational representation as often had been the case in the interwar period, especially in Belgium and the Netherlands. But this trade union presence did not weaken the influence of Christian Democracy in general, neither in 1944-1946 nor in the long run. In fact, this conclusion also applies to the Christian Democratic parties in those countries where unified trade unions were formed; paradoxically, the anticommunist drive towards trade union unity in these cases benefited the Christian Democratic parties.[74]

Nevertheless, some Left Catholic ideas and concerns were adopted by the Christian trade unions, such as the importance attached to training and education. In the CFTC an internal opposition movement was created that in my view may be considered Left Catholic. It gradually gained influence and managed to transform the confederation into the CFDT, which became known as "la deuxième gauche" (the second Left). To a certain extent we can observe similar developments, though much less spectacularly so, in Switzerland, the Netherlands and even Belgium. It shows that Left Catholicism did not come to an end in 1949 but retained its significance, particularly in the 1960s, notwithstanding the spectacular downfall of some of its protagonists.

---

73. E.g. Durand, *L'Europe de la démocratie chrétienne*, 217-220 and ff.; Conway, "Introduction", 30-31. Lamberts, "General Conclusions: Christian Democracy in the European Union", rather emphasises the continuity of Christian Democracy with traditional conservatism.
74. Compare Conway, "Introduction", 30, and Durand, *L'Europe de la démocratie chrétienne*, 229 ff.

FROM PERMISSION TO PROHIBITION. THE IMPACT OF THE CHANGING INTERNATIONAL CONTEXT ON LEFT CATHOLICISM IN EUROPE

Peter Van Kemseke

The Left Catholic experiments that had emerged at the end of the Second World War and that had disappeared by 1950 were, at first sight, mainly national phenomena. They had their roots in the specific circumstances of the war, developed in a particular, national political configuration, and were embedded in a national jumble that by the end of the decade had gradually become less and less experimental. Transnational relations between Left Catholic movements were limited or non-existent. A Left Catholic International, for example, was never aimed for nor would have been within the realms of possibility. Consequently, the international context is either completely left out in the (few) studies on Left Catholicism that have been written, or it functions as a commonplace mentioned once or twice in the margins to "explain" the failure of Left Catholics. A more profound study of the complex interaction between party level, national and international elements has not yet been undertaken and can by no means be the ambition of this brief contribution. This article at most serves to outline a possible framework that introduces an international perspective onto the study of Left Catholicism. More specifically, it examines the relevance of the international context to the emergence and retreat of Left Catholic party political experiments between 1945 and 1950.

1. **The Left Catholic Eureka in a Permissive International Context (1944-1945). The Case of Left Catholic *Travaillisme***

With the outbreak of the Second World War in 1939, the principles that until then had characterised the organisation of the international system had become discredited. The dramatic events of the late 1930s and early 1940s had harshly laid bare the shortcomings of an international system that had been organised, however loosely, according to the often unpredictable logic of power balances. In this atmosphere of discontent, even revulsion, concepts of an alternative postwar international order found fertile soil. Blueprints aspiring to make an end to the traditional system of alliances, spheres of influence and unilateral initiatives flourished widely in political circles. Wilsonian ideals apparently got a second chance: another world war could only be prevented by a world order based on principles such as self-determination and collective security, preferably under the aegis of a world government.[1]

It is often forgotten that in 1944 and for at least part of 1945 these - with hindsight rather idealistic - prospects were not necessarily in contradiction with realities on the field. While the final chapters of World War II were being written, it was not yet clear which form the international system would take after the war, let alone that it would take the form of a "Cold War".[2] Relations between the United States, Great Britain and the USSR were exploratory and unsure but not by definition hostile. Of course, the political systems and ideologies of the Western powers and the USSR were very different, which aroused suspicion; the USSR had not forgotten the Allied intervention after World War I, while Stalin's pact with Germany was undoubtedly still fresh in the memory of the Allies. But as long as Germany and Japan had not been defeated, potential conflicts of interests were played down to safeguard the antifascist coalition, as was the case at the Tehran Conference at the end of 1943 and the Yalta conference in February 1945. In 1945, all three powers were convinced that it would be possible, desirable and even necessary to continue the wartime coalition.[3] Even Stalin's ambitions in Eastern Europe were, at first, no insuperable problem. They were at most one of many interfering elements, which also existed between the United States and the United Kingdom.[4] In general, however, the illusion prevailed that all uncertainties could be straightened out through regular consultation. The *Council of Foreign Ministers*, an instrument that was created during the Potsdam Conference in August 1945, was to serve that purpose.

This cooperative international climate, as well as the immense prestige of the USSR, both victor and martyr of World War II[5], the subsequent attraction of its revolutionary societal model, and the bankruptcy of rightist political formations in the whole of Europe, created a promising window of opportunity for ideological experiments at the national level.[6] Left Catholicism was one of these ideological experiments. As defined by G.- R. Horn in his contribution to this volume, Left Catholicism includes the whole "range of new departures and party-political projects" in the 1940s

---

1. Divine, *Second Chance*, 168-175.
2. Whether the origins of the Cold War can best be explained as the result of historical and/or geographical "laws" or primarily as the result of a series of "accidents" and misunderstandings between the main actors is still a controversial issue in Cold War historiography. See e.g. Gaddis, *We Now Know*, 1-26.
3. Recent documents from Russian archives underline this point for the USSR. See e.g. Pechatnov, *The Big Three After World War II*. See also Reynolds, *The Origins of the Cold War in Europe*.
4. Woods, *A Changing of the Guard*; Louis and Bull, *The Special Relationship*.
5. Recent figures indicate that the USSR lost 27 million citizens in World War II. Volkogonov, *Stalin: Triumph and Tragedy*, 505.
6. Jean-Pierre Rioux describes the atmosphere in France as follows: "When reading the press and the proclamations of that time, one could get the impression that the revolution was just around the corner. Many Frenchmen have experienced those months as a rupture with the old order (...) That period was, obviously, rather exceptional in our political history: the Right had disappeared with Vichy, while the Left, invested with the virtues of the Resistance, assumed the advantageous role of spokesperson of the deep interests of the nation". Rioux, *La France de la Quatrième République*, 77. The same goes without doubt for many other European countries at Liberation.

and early 1950s, "pushing the boundaries of Catholic politics further to the Left than in any previous historical conjuncture". It could safely be argued that the "permissive", left-leaning 1944-1945 international context left substantial room for and probably even facilitated such new political designs.

The international context was perhaps more than just a "facilitator". To some extent, it was also a source of inspiration. Although their concrete patterns of incarnation were primarily circumscribed by national contours, Left Catholic movements did not develop in complete isolation from their international surroundings. On the contrary, certain factors from abroad were an important and sometimes direct source of inspiration for Left Catholic initiatives. This complex interplay between national and international factors can be illustrated by focusing on one very important - though not intrinsic - characteristic shared by several if not all of these Left Catholic party political projects: their ambition to break through the shackles of the Catholic world and to create a mould of organisational unity with, amongst others, socialists.[7]

On the national level, the aspiration to combine forces was facilitated by wartime experience. The common struggle of Catholics, socialists and communists in their resistance against fascism and Nazism undoubtedly had favoured the rapprochement of former political rivals.[8] The climate of philosophical and ideological tolerance during the war convinced many Catholics that an agreement could be reached with non-Catholic parties safeguarding the rights of the Church and protecting denominational education.[9] In such circumstances, there would no longer be a need for a Catholic party, thus opening the door to postwar political cooperation with non-Catholics on other and in their opinion more important cleavages such as socio-economics. In the end, the *modus operandi* of Left Catholics was also strongly influenced by a second national factor: the strength and nature of their rival communist and socialist parties in general, the budding political landscape, the power configuration in which political Catholicism had to resume its activities.

On the international level, which is the focus of this article, the inspiring example of the British Labour Party quite often served as a point of reference in these *travaillist* endeavours. Especially to those Left Catholics who had spent the war in exile in the United Kingdom, *travaillisme* had a wide appeal. This was even more so after the overwhelming victory of the Labour Party in the July 1945 elections. In several Left Catholic experiments, British *travaillisme* was a recurring theme. In reality however, these *travaillist* schemes soon ended in failure.

---

7. In some cases, Catholics made an opening to communists too, as illustrated by e.g. the Italian *Partito Comunista Cristiano*, which had close ties with the *Partito Comunista Italiano* (PCI). Others, however, have always kept some distance towards communism while at the same time flirting with democratic socialism.
8. This rapprochement, however, is by no means self-evident. As Patrick Pasture points out in his contribution, certainly in the case of trade unions, relations between Catholics/Christian Democrats and socialists could also be spoiled during the Occupation, as was the case in the Netherlands.
9. The *Avant-projet de pacte de l'union travailliste* of 1941, to which later on the Belgian Left Catholic UDB would refer as its Charter, included a paragraph dealing specifically with education. Beerten, *Le rêve travailliste en Belgique*, 14.

In Germany, the idea of an interdenominational, reformist, left wing "labour party", inspired by the British example and including (at least part of) the *Sozialdemokratische Partei Deutschlands* (SPD) was very much cherished by a group of Catholic politicians who before Hitler's *Machtübernahme* had belonged to the left wing of the *Zentrumspartei* or to the Christian labour movement.[10] In June 1945, these *christliche Sozialisten* presented their *Kölner Leitsätze*, a provisional party programme with a rather radical leftist undertone, critical of capitalism, in particular of the role of big business, and very much in favour of socialisation and state intervention.[11] Three months later, negotiations started with leading figures from the SPD - especially SPD-leader Kurt Schumacher showed a great interest in these talks - but quite soon they broke down, partly on the instinctive anticlericalism of several socialists. By the end of the year, pioneers such as Johannes Albers had given up their *travaillist* dream. An alliance with more liberal-individualist Protestant groups on a denominational basis then seemed the logical outcome.[12] This resulted in the creation of the Christian Democrat CDU (*Christlich Demokratische Union*), in December 1945, of which the *christliche Sozialisten* would constitute the leftist, or Left Catholic wing.

In Italy too, the idea of going beyond a strictly Catholic party found ardent supporters among Left Catholics. During the war, Giuseppe Dossetti - who had played a leading role in the Resistance - had become convinced of the futility of a Catholic party. "Catholic parties have become an outdated reality", Dossetti argued in 1943, obviously to the dissatisfaction of several ex-*popolari*.[13] Instead, Catholics had to adhere to and influence other political formations that were close enough to their socio-economic ideas. These and other blueprints of a similar nature were, however, short-lived. In 1944, the ideal of a unitary Catholic party in Italy began to materialise at a time when alternative concepts were aggressively condemned by the Vatican.[14] In that climate, Dossetti preferred to situate his political activities primarily within the framework of the *Democrazia Cristiana*.[15] Like its

---

10. Uertz, *Christentum und Sozialismus*, 9 and 34. An interesting overview is given in Gurland, *Die CDU/CSU*, 31-35. Interesting, though rather superseded: Wieck, *Die Entstehung der CDU und die Wiedergründung des Zentrums*.
11. Gurland, *Die CDU/CSU*, 106-112.
12. Uertz, *Christentum und Sozialismus*, 38 and 345.
13. A similar idea would later be defended by Fanfani, who belonged to Dossetti's group, in his important article "Partiti di ispirazione cristiana e Chiesa Cattolica" in *Humanitas*, I (1946), 381-385. The term ex-*popolari* refers to the members of the *Partito Popolare Italiano* of the interbellum period, the forerunner of the DC. Pombeni, *Il Gruppo Dossettiano*, 172-173.
14. In June 1945 the *Osservatore Romano* condemned Catholic-communist experiments. See the article "Non conciliare l'inconciliabile", *Osservatore Romano*, 23 June 1945. In the same year, the *Partito della sinistra cristiana* was dissolved shortly after having been condemned by the Vatican. Malgeri, *La Sinistra cristiana*.
15. Pombeni is quite clear on this: "It is a fact that in the fall of 1944, Dossetti's activities became ever more intensive and got ever more the character of a political activity situated within the framework of the Christian Democratic party". Pombeni, *Il Gruppo Dossettiano*, 175. In general, several Left Catholics considered it politically wiser to operate within a strong party that enclosed all Catholics. Ravajoli's advice to Gerardo Bruni, founder of the unsuccessful *Partito cristiano-sociale* was telling: "There was no room for small parties. Democracy could only take the large parties into consideration".

German counterpart, Dossetti's Left Catholicism too tried to find its place within a broader Christian Democrat formation. Within the centrist DC of Alcide De Gasperi, the left wing Dossetti group defended its own programme and its own vision on the nature of the DC, and, like the German *christliche Sozialisten,* it often referred to the British Labour party's programme.16 It held on to the concept of a "deeply spiritual and socially just party" and associated this with "the sweeping welfare reforms, which the British Labour government had recently carried through".17

To some extent, the Belgian case was not that different. In Belgium, *travaillist* initiatives were taken as early as 1941, when a small group of prominent Christian Democrats and socialists concluded the so-called *"travaillist* agreement".18 The initiative won the support of some Catholic politicians in exile in London, who argued that the main political cleavage in postwar Belgium would be socio-economic rather than confessional. This opinion was directly and manifestly influenced by their position as eyewitnesses of the functioning of the British political system, which they wanted to imitate. Just as in Germany and Italy, however, these schemes came to nothing. The first postwar congress of the Belgian Socialist Party, in June 1945, where the *Belgische Socialistische Partij* (BSP) confirmed the *Charter of Quaregnon* as its guiding principle, closed any further discussions. After all, the radical discourse of *Quaregnon,* referring to the class struggle, was incompatible with the ideals of class harmony of *Rerum Novarum* and *Quadragesimo Anno* that would guide Belgian Left Catholics.19 However, what makes Belgian Left Catholics rather unique, is that after the failure of their *travaillist* blueprints, they did not choose to play a role within a more centrist, but in their eyes overwhelmingly conservative Christian Democrat PSC-CVP.20 Instead they decided to establish a new party, the *Union Démocratique Belge* (UDB), which was thought - mistakenly, as would soon appear - to be capable of vying with the *Parti Social Chrétien - Christelijke Volkspartij* (PSC-CVP).21

See Baget-Bozzo, *Il Partito Cristiano al Potere,* 102. If Dossetti personally followed the same reasoning is not entirely clear, though not impossible.

16. In August 1945, Dossetti launched in his home base Reggio Emilia the weekly *Tempo Nostro,* which showed a very strong sympathy for the British Labour Party. According to Pombeni, "that sympathy for the British Labour movement was also illustrated by the term *laburista cristiani* which was sometimes used to define the new tendency within Italian Catholicism". Pombeni, *Il Gruppo Dossettiano,* 197. The impact of the British experience on Italian Left Catholicism, and more specifically on the Dossetti group, remained important till the group's final collapse in 1951.
17. Ginsborg, *A History of Contemporary Italy,* 121.
18. Beerten, *Le rêve travailliste en Belgique,* 12.
19. On the motivation of Belgian socialists to keep off *travaillist* overtures, see Gotovitch, *C. Huysmans,* 30 ff.
20. It should be added, however, that a large number of prominent Catholics subscribed to the theses of the UDB, but preferred to modernize Christian Democracy from within the PSC-CVP. They found each other in the periodicals *La Relève* and *'t Westen.*
21. The Walloon trade unionists and politicians, who dominated the UDB and most of whom had played a significant role in the Resistance, did not want to be part of a party in which notorious francophone conservatives would continue to play an important role, a party that furthermore would be dominated by a Flemish wing that did not want to separate itself from some of its leaders, accused of a collaborationist attitude during the Occupation. Therefore, the community question in Belgium should be taken into account when trying to explain the unique character of Belgian Left Catholicism.

Ideologically, the political group in France that probably fits best within the *travaillist* experiments described above was *Jeune République* (JR).[22] Even though many of JR's leaders joined the newly founded *Mouvement Républicain Populaire* (MRP) in 1944, a majority of its members preferred to keep their distance. Instead, they chose to back the more radical Socialist Party *(Section Française de l'Internationale Ouvrière*, SFIO) and the *Union Démocratique et Socialiste de la Résistance* (UDSR), a small centre left political formation that had developed out of - the name is meaningful - the *Union Travailliste*. By August 1945, however, *travaillist* blueprints impinged on the fervent anticlericalism of the, at least rhetorically, marxist SFIO, even though they continued to inspire part of French Christian Democracy. Not all Christian Democrats, however, were enthusiastic about closely cooperating, let alone reaching some level of organisational unity, with the SFIO. MRP leader Georges Bidault's firm stance against collaboration with the socialist SFIO *(trop laïque)* and his reluctance towards any *travaillist* undertaking set the party somewhat apart from other contemporary Left Catholic initiatives.[23] The MRP is at best a controversial example of a Left Catholic movement or party. Some French scholars, and often for good reasons, have questioned the "leftist" orientation of the MRP. In the rest of this article, we will nevertheless focus on the MRP as an exponent of French Left Catholicism, rather than, say, on the "left-of-Left Catholic" *Jeune République*, and that for two reasons. Firstly, the MRP was a party in office for most of the Fourth Republic. Perhaps even more relevant: between 1944 and 1954 the MRP has, except for a very brief interval, continuously occupied the *Quai d'Orsay* (the French Foreign Office), which made the party particularly susceptible to evolutions on an international level.[24] Secondly, from an international perspective, i.e. compared to other Christian Democratic parties, the MRP was definitely situated left of the Catholic centre. It is significant that at least initially the MRP felt ideologically more congenial towards the Left Catholic - and, compared to the MRP, distinctly more moderate! - UDB than towards the Christian Democrat PSC-CVP.[25] On 17 February 1946, on the occasion of the Belgian elections, the MRP paper *L'Aube* unambiguously expressed its sympathy for the UDB. At the

---

Moreover, they denounced the "C" (of "Christian") in the name of the new party, for this went against their ideal of a completely deconfessional party. See *Rapprochements*, no 5-6, August 1945, 9.

22. *Travaillist* sentiments were also vivid among certain local groups of the former *Parti Démocrate Populaire*, such as the section in Marseille. See Delbreil, *Centrisme et démocratie-chrétienne en France*, 436. On *Jeune République*, see Guerrier, *La Jeune République de 1912 à 1945*.
23. Jean-Pierre Rioux is explicit in that respect: "Georges Bidault (...) thought he could easily win the bet: ignore the sirens of the SFIO - which was too laicist - or of a vague *travaillisme* and build the only political force capable of competing with the communists". Rioux, *La France de la Quatrième République*, 81.
24. Callot, *L'Action et l'Oeuvre Politique du Mouvement Républicain Populaire*, 107.
25. Unfortunately, at this moment too little is known on any transnational relations that might have existed between Left Catholic politicians, movements or parties.

same time, it was rather critical of the PSC-CVP of August De Schryver.[26] Also, there can be little doubt that the MRP's self-image as a progressive and even revolutionary party led to the party's reluctance to engage in the *Nouvelles Equipes Internationales*, the international network of Western European Christian Democratic parties, in which less reformist parties set the tone.[27]

This brief and by no means comprehensive overview suffices to indicate that within the same "international window of opportunity", and often with the same foreign source of inspiration, quite divergent expressions of Left Catholicism could manifest themselves, depending on and even largely determined by just as divergent factors on the national level.[28] In 1944 and 1945, the dynamics and development of Left Catholicism were primarily rooted in the national context. It is mainly a national angle that helps to understand the various shapes and forms Left Catholicism took on, especially since transnational cooperation between those movements seems rare.[29] The British Labour Party, which around that time started to unite the European socialist parties in the Socialist International Conference, could obviously not function as a rallying point, despite the attraction of its political programme. The international context surely left all possibilities open and offered some inspiration - perhaps it facilitated or even stimulated Left Catholic attempts at political renewal - but in general, its impact seems rather limited. This is illustrated by taking a closer look at the Belgian case.

26. "The recent emergence of the *Union Démocratique Belge* in political life is - finally - an original, new and important fact. In a country where the political classifications were essentially based on the distinction between 'believers' and 'non-believers', the young UDB fortunately passes the current boundaries between political groups". *L'Aube*, 17 February 1946.
27. Bichet, *La démocratie chrétienne en France: le MRP*, 243-244. *L'Aube*; Paris, 4 December 1950. According to Nicole Bacharan-Gressel, "the MRP distrusted the influence of the Belgian PSC. It denounced the reactionary, even aggressively confessional character of the party". Bacharan-Gressel, "Les Organisations et les Associations Pro-européennes", 47. Also worth noticing, but from a later date, is Léo Hamon's fear, expressed rather explicitly during the *Commission Exécutive* of 20 May 1948: "There is no way we could join forces with the Right. We have to act alone or with the socialists. Otherwise, we will go down". Archives MRP, Archives nationales, 350 AP/46. One of the parties that was particularly aimed at, was the PSC-CVP of Paul Van Zeeland, the former Prime Minister of Belgium. Jean Gilibert referred to Van Zeeland when arguing during the *Commission Exécutive* of 17 February 1949: "At this moment, there are many Christians in Europe that are no democrats". Archives MRP, Archives nationales, 350 AP/71. For Van Zeeland, see Dujardin and Dumoulin, *Paul van Zeeland*.
28. Still another shape was taken on in the Netherlands. There, several progressive/"Leftist" Catholics joined the *Nederlandse Volksbeweging* (NVB), a *travaillist* project, that, unlike those already mentioned, was from the very beginning dominated and initiated by the Dutch socialist party, the SDAP. See Bank, *Opkomst en ondergang van de Nederlandse Volksbeweging*. Considering the rather marginal role of "Leftist Catholics" within the NVB, this movement will not be developed here.
29. Further research should clear up if contacts indeed were limited to sending delegations to each others' congresses. In December 1945 for example, the UDB sent a small delegation to the MRP Congress in Paris. A week later, three MRP representatives attended the UDB Congress.

2. 1946: The (Ir)Relevance of the International Context in the Pre-Cold War Era: The Cases of Belgium and Germany

By the end of 1945, *travaillisme* had proved unfruitful on the continent. The French MRP, and more specifically its leader Georges Bidault, had had little interest in a rapprochement with socialism. Through their own choice, or after having been rejected by the Left, Left Catholics in Italy and Germany had started to operate within more centrist, Christian Democratic formations. Within these parties, they tried to strengthen their position and to influence the party line. Belgium was unique in that some Left Catholics had chosen to develop their own party.

Soon, however, the UDB turned out to be a still-born project after all. The February 1946 elections, with the UDB gaining hardly more than 2% of the votes, were a major disappointment and rang in the beginning of the end of the party. An international perspective adds little to our understanding of the fading away of the party. For Belgium in 1946, Gerd-Rainer Horn's hypothesis that "ultimately the failure of Left Catholicism to survive as a current with a measurable influence must be located in the international political conjuncture characterising post-liberation Europe" is problematic.[30] The international context did not have that impact yet. The failure of the UDB seems in the first place related to specific national conditions - foremost the Royal Question which revived the traditional confessional cleavage that the UDB had wanted to downplay - as well as to the nature and the functioning of the UDB itself.[31] From 1947 onwards, however, it could be argued that the international context did have a more considerable impact on what by then was still left of the UDB - mainly some small and isolated local groups in Brussels. When former *udebists* in Brussels tried to revive the movement and created the group *Renaissance*, the focus had shifted from *travaillist* aspirations to a liberal and rabidly anticommunist programme. But by then the international configuration had lost its permissive character and had become "prohibitive": it no longer facilitated ideological experiments, but on the contrary had started to congeal them.

Still, it would be premature to jump to conclusions based on just one case. Pre-Cold War Germany indeed gives a different picture. After Germany's unconditional surrender, its destiny lay in the hands of the occupying Allied forces and in the relations between these forces.[32] Therefore, an international perspective is relevant to the study of Left Catholicism in Germany. The British Labour government, which controlled an occupation zone in which Left Catholic ideological experiments flourished, followed the quarrels between the different fractions within the Christian Democratic CDU with great interest. As indicated above, the Left Catholic current, with its nerve-centre in Cologne, had in the first years of the party's existence a

---

30. See G.-R. Horn's introduction to this volume.
31. Beerten, *Le Rêve travailliste en Belgique*, 153-156.
32. Smyser, *From Yalta to Berlin*, offers a good and recent introduction to this complex topic.

rather solid position within the party.33 It had stood at the cradle of the party and it had developed its earliest (provisional) programme. Its opponents - mainly liberal Catholics with a bourgeois outlook who gathered around the figure of Konrad Adenauer, as well as Protestant groups like the *Wuppertal group* - initially existed alongside the Christian socialists. In the radical *Zeitgeist* just after the war, they were, however, unable to impose their project of a "Christian-motivated bourgeois movement as a counterpart to the 'leftist' parties".34 This became clear at the Bad Godesberg Conference, in December 1945, where the CDU was officially launched. On that occasion, the more liberal elements could not prevent the term *christlicher Sozialismus* from being included in the party programme.35 With the famous (or notorious) "Ahlen Programme", which was adopted by the CDU in early February of 1947, the Left Catholic wing undoubtedly reached the pinnacle of its influence. Even though it was a compromise, the document - which stressed the need for government intervention and nationalisations in a *gemeinwirtschaftlichen Ordnung* - clearly bore the mark of the Christian socialists.36

The British government welcomed the Ahlen Programme as a clear victory of the left wing against the conservative wing. From the beginning, the British Foreign Office had actively supported the left wing fraction of Karl Arnold as an antidote against the right wing of the CDU which it considered to be "extremely reactionary".37 This explains why in August 1946, for example, Britain proposed Arnold for the post of Minister of the Interior in Nordrhein-Westfalen.38 The British had high hopes that a strong position of the Christian socialists would allow them to put into practice their socialisation programme in their zone of occupation. London was very much aware that its programme depended to a large extent on the support of the leftist fraction of the CDU, which is illustrated by the following remark by Patrick Dean in October 1946. "Britain", he argued, "had every interest in the long term in reconciling the differences between at any rate the left wing of CDU and the SPD".39 In order not to alienate the former, the Labour government even kept its distance towards the SPD, even if this meant gag-

33. The dominance of the Christian socialists in the first years of the existence of the CDU is explicitly stressed by one of its representatives, Leo Schwering. Schwering, *Vorgeschichte und Entstehung der CDU*. Later publications tend to relativise or, like Adenauer himself, even ignore this "prelude" of the party. They stress that the CDU was from the very beginning a liberal-conservative party. On this historiographical debate, see Uertz, *Christentum und Sozialismus*, 11-13. See likewise the contribution by Andreas Lienkamp elsewhere in this volume.
34. Uertz, *Christentum und Sozialismus*, 41.
35. Ibid., 60-65.
36. "In general, it cannot be denied that the Ahlen Programme is primarily a document of Christian Socialism". Uertz, *Christentum und Sozialismus*, 185. See also Gurland, *Die CDU/CSU. Ursprünge und Entwicklung bis 1953*, 138.
37. Patrick Dean, Legal Advisor in the British occupation zone in Germany. Note of 9 October 1946, in Archives Foreign Office (London), 371/55372/C11985/2/18. PRO.
38. Hüttenberger, *Nordrhein-Westfalen und die Entstehung seiner parlamentarischen Demokratie*, 229. The CDU itself described Arnold as the "representative of the CDU explicitly wanted by the military government". Quoted in *Westfalenpost* (Soest), 1, (23 August 1946) 35, 2.
39. Patrick Dean, quoted in Steininger, "British Labour, Deutschland und die SPD", 212.

ging those leaders and militants of its own party who were in favour of closer relations between the British Labour Party (BLP) and its German counterpart, the SPD.[40] At the end of the year, the Foreign Office stated quite explicitly: "there is no question of backing the Social Democrat Party against other German Parties by giving them material or moral advantages on the spot".[41] In other words, the British left wing government, through its occupation policies, actively stimulated a political climate which favoured and strengthened the position of the German Left Catholics. This situation would change from 1947 onward, when the international situation began to change and the United States started to take the initiative in Germany.

3. The Economic Cold War, Cold War Economics and Left Catholicism, 1947: The Emergence of a "Dissuasive" International Context

The spring of 1947 was, at least symbolically, an important pivotal point in early postwar international relations. In collective memory, "1947" is associated with the beginning of the Cold War. During the course of 1946, tensions between the USSR and the United Kingdom had increased dramatically, with the German question as the main bone of contention. The *Council of Foreign Ministers* in Paris, which had ended its sessions in July 1946, had not done anything to mitigate these tensions. On the contrary, recent research suggests that precisely around this time, the British *Foreign Office* gave up the idea that a workable agreement with the USSR could still be reached.[42] More and more, the British fostered the idea to first build up the Western occupation zones, independently from the USSR, even if this would imply a "temporary" political division of Germany. By late 1946, the United States went with this analysis, toned down their claim for German unification and in the end agreed to join their occupation zone with the British one into what became known as *Bizonia*.[43] This coincided with the more active role the United States began to play in international politics. Until then, Truman had primarily sat on the fence. Unlike Bevin he had immediately distanced himself from Churchill's speech at Fulton. By the end of 1946 however - partly because of considerable pressure from the United Kingdom, partly because of growing dissatisfaction with Soviet policy - the

---

40. In the second half of 1946, BLP prominents repeatedly attempted to invite SPD representatives to London, but each time the British Minister of Foreign Affairs Ernest Bevin prevented such a visit. The official reason was that such a visit would seriously jeopardise relations with the USSR. In reality, however, the political situation in the British occupation zone was of more importance. Close relations with the SPD on the eve of an extensive socialisation programme could give the other parties the impression that the SPD enjoyed a privileged position, which would complicate relations with the (left of the) CDU. Steininger, *Deutschland und die Sozialistische Internationale*, 65. See also Steininger, "Die Rhein-Ruhr-Frage", 111-166, and Steininger, "British Labour", 188-225.
41. Telegram Foreign Office #1275 to British Embassy in Paris, 13 December 1946, in Archives Foreign Office, 371/55377/C15383/2/18.
42. Deighton, *The Impossible Peace*, 55-78 and 81-102. See also the excellent article of Farquharson, "From Unity to Division".
43. A good overview of the role of Great Britain in the early Cold War can be found in Reynolds, "Great Britain", 80-83. The "leading" role of Great Britain, however, is considerably toned down by the American historian Gaddis, *We Now Know*, 43.

United States took over the leading role.[44] The Truman Doctrine and the Marshall Plan - "two halves of the same nutshell"[45] - were a clear and unambiguous expression of Truman's commitment to the "free world". The Marshall Plan put an end to the uncertainties of the first postwar years: from then on, everyone had to follow suit.

The "changing of the guard" on the international level and the outbreak of the Cold War no doubt influenced the context in which Left Catholics had to operate. The Marshall Plan, and its foreseeable rejection by the USSR, established two economic blocks, centred around economic principles that began to play an increasingly important role as elements in the identification process and concomitant rhetoric of both parties. This was, obviously, particularly clear in the case of Western Germany, where the Americans, first in their own occupation zone but soon, in cooperation with the British, on the bizonal level as well, controlled and influenced daily life.[46] The German historian Rudolf Uertz argues, rather easily perhaps, that a crucial mistake made by the Christian socialists was that they had not taken into account the tremendous impact the United States was securing on the German occupation zones.[47] By contrast, Uertz contends, their "opponent" Adenauer had indeed anticipated all along that it would not take too much time before "Liberal America" and no longer "Labour Britain" would set the tone.[48] Therefore, in Adenauer's words, he had always tempered his opposition against socialist influences within the party and waited until the general climate was more favourable for his liberal economic programme.

Whether or not Adenauer's explanation is a classic example of *Hineininterpretierung*, the climate did change under the influence of the Americans. Since the second half of 1947 and particularly in the course of 1948, reforms aimed at a steady liberalisation of the economy of the future West German state were gradually implemented. The *Foreign Assistance Act* of 1948, i.e. the legislation for the European Recovery Programme, defined US policy as "to sustain and strengthen principles of individual liberty, free institutions, and genuine independence in Europe through assistance to those countries of Europe which participate in a joint recovery program based upon self-help and mutual cooperation".[49] Even though, in strictly juridical terms, this held no obligation to establish a free market economy in Western Germany, the concrete regulations of the programme were in fact powerful "means to control and influence the use of the Marshall aid and the general economic policy of the recipient countries", as Manfred Knapp has rightly argued.[50] The orders given to US occupation commander General Lucius Clay were unequivocal: "to give the German people an

---

44. US involvement in Greece and Turkey since February 1947, on the request of Great Britain, illustrates this "changing of the guard" very well.
45. Truman quoted in LaFeber, *America, Russia and the Cold War*, 62.
46. Gradually, the Americans began to dominate the British in Western Germany. It is illustrative for example that in early 1947 the State Department pressed the British to suspend their plans for the socialisation of German coal mines in the Ruhr.
47. Uertz, *Christentum und Sozialismus*, 70.
48. Konrad Adenauer, quoted in Uertz, *Christentum und Sozialismus*, 186n1.
49. US Department of State, *A Decade of American Foreign Policy, Basic Documents 1941-49*, 1299-1300.
50. Knapp, "US Economic Aid and the Reconstruction of West-Germany", 48.

opportunity to learn of the principles and advantages of free enterprise", a directive which actually corresponded with Clay's personal preferences.[51] In such a climate of material as well as psychological-ideological support, the neoliberal theories of the German economist Ludwig Erhard, the then director of the *Verwaltung für Wirtschaft des Vereinigten Wirtschaftsgebietes*, flourished. They evoked, however, fierce criticism of some Christian socialists within the CDU while others, quite significantly, started to barter their socialist outlook for a more neoliberal one.[52] When Erhard joined the CDU around June 1948 and became the catalyst of an ideological revision of the party programme, the glorious days of the German Left Catholics within the CDU were numbered.[53] Between the summer of 1947, when the Ahlen Programme was accepted, and the summer of 1948, when a new socio-economic orthodoxy was introduced in the party, the CDU underwent a remarkable development. A development which in the end resulted in the *Düsseldorfer Leitsätze* of July 1949, a new party programme which definitively superseded the Ahlen Programme.

The presence of the United States in Western Germany made the impact of the unfolding Cold War on the domestic political context, and consequently on (the disappearance of) Left Catholicism, relatively direct. In France, where there was no such far-reaching American dominance as in Germany, the impact of the Cold War on the MRP was primarily indirect. Specific national factors, and in particular the political landscape in France which had been firmly rebuilt soon after the end of World War II, "filtered" the developments on the international level.

In the first two years after Liberation, French politics were dominated by the main exponents of the ideals of the Resistance. Coalition governments composed of the SFIO, the PCF and the MRP gave shape to the period of *tripartisme*. Despite some fundamental differences of opinion, mainly between the PCF and the "Left Catholic" but fiercely anticommunist MRP[54], *tripartisme* managed to survive until the beginning of 1947. In February, however, serious dissensions between the MRP and the communists came to the fore on defence policy. Tensions increased again in April when the PCF threw its weight behind the wave of strikes that paralysed the country. Hardly a month later, on 5 May, the SFIO and the MRP decided to exclude the communists from the government. In doing so, France was not unique: also in other countries where communists were in office, such as Belgium and Italy, communist participation in public affairs was terminat-

---

51. Second Basic Directive to the Commander in Chief of the U.S. Forces of Occupation regarding the Military Government in Germany, JCS 1179, 11 July 1947, in Departmnet of State, *Germany 1947-1949*, 40.
52. Uertz, *Christentum und Sozialismus*, 196 and 200n43.
53. Ibid., 197. At the second rally of the CDU of the British zone, in August 1948 in Recklinghausen, Erhard gave the keynote address on "Marktwirtschaft moderner Prägung", which illustrates the important ideological role he by then played within the party. See Konrad Adenauer Stiftung, *Konrad Adenauer und die CDU der Britischen Besatzungszone*, 657.
54. Precisely because of its anticommunism, the MRP managed to attract a large part of the rightist electorate, which saw in the MRP, at least until the creation of the RPF, "the only stronghold against the marxist bloc". Rioux, *La France de la Quatrième République*, 94. On the early years of the MRP, see also the contribution by Jean-Claude Delbreil elsewhere in this volume.

ed.55 The expulsion of communists was closely related to some dramatic events on the international level. First of all, the speculations surrounding the Marshall Plan undoubtedly played a considerable role. Non-communist parties like the MRP feared that American aid would not flow as generously to countries where communists were in office as to those in which they were not. Secondly, the radical break with the communists came less than two weeks after the spectacular breakdown of negotiations between the Foreign Ministers of the Big Four in Moscow, in April 1947. Upon his return from Moscow, the French MRP Minister of Foreign Affairs, Georges Bidault, drew his conclusions: "It's over! Any agreement with Russia is impossible. There is no more alliance or union of the Big Three, no more possibility of reaching an understanding with the communists. A new era has begun. We have to draw the conclusions".56 The era of the French-Russian pact of friendship, signed in December 1944 by Georges Bidault for France, had obviously come to an end. Both a Russian "stick" - Stalin's intransigence - and an American "carrot" - France welcomed the much-needed American aid only too eagerly - determined France's "decision" to ensconce itself in the Western block. From then on, Bidault stowed away the idea of a large European block, led by France and capable of a mediating role between East and West, and he decisively chose the Atlantic option.

This "voluntary subjection" to the US - for it was tantamount to that - had its consequences. The MRP's German policy for example made a remarkable about-turn and almost became an extract of US foreign policy in Germany.57 Slightly more interesting from our point of view is that the "accommodation" of the French political system to the changing national and international reality, *in casu* through the collapse of *tripartisme*, had considerable consequences for the MRP's domestic position too. After the expulsion of the communists, socialists and popular republicans no longer enjoyed a parliamentary majority. To form a government, they had no choice but to collaborate with the more centre-rightist *radicaux*, partisans of a liberal economic policy and opponents of state intervention, nationalisations and comprehensive social security programmes. The centre Left and centre Right were literally drawn towards each other, squeezed as they were between two political extremes which continuously attacked them: the communists to the Left and the Gaullist *Rassemblement du Peuple Français* (RPF), which had been created as a new political party in April 1947, to the Right.58 Moreover, this very appearance of the RPF - not completely unre-

---

55. Communists were excluded from office on 20 March 1947 in Belgium and on 13 May 1947 in Italy.
56. Elgey, *La République des illusions*, 282.
57. This change in policy aroused a lot of criticism within the MRP. Prominent figures like Robert Schuman argued: "France has no German policy; it simply follows the United States". Quoted in Callot, *L'Action et l'Oeuvre Politique du Mouvement Républicain Populaire*, 140.
58. In French political history, this period is therefore called the period of the "Troisième Force", the "Third Force" between leftist and rightist extremes.

lated to the Cold War climate either[59] - gradually began to push the MRP toward the Right.[60] At the same time, in order to keep its left wing aboard, the MRP tried to maintain a radical social and economic programme, with a clear focus on some form of economic planning and social reforms. Nevertheless, declarations that sounded too leftist were soon tuned down; they were simply incompatible with the continuance of a coalition in which moderates and radicals gradually managed to strengthen their position.[61] The economic plan of the French Minister of Finance René Mayer, approved by the government of Robert Schuman in January 1948, is a case in point.[62] Its plea in favour of the free play of market economics and its pronounced denunciation of state intervention swept away all illusions of a collectivist economy cherished at the time of Liberation.

The slipping away of the party from its initial, quite radical programme led in the summer of 1948 to the emergence of a left wing fraction within the MRP. That fraction continuously reminded the party's leadership of the roots and ambitions of the MRP. Particularly in trade union milieus, there were serious concerns about the development of the MRP.[63] The criticism that part of the MRP voiced at the inauguration of the government of André Marie in July 1948 - eighteen MRP representatives abstained, especially those with close ties to the CFTC - underlines this.[64] The French historian Jean-Pierre Rioux later described the evolution of the party quite accurately: "The ideologists succumb. The cure of centrism destroys the novelty that the popular republicans cherished in the Resistance and at Liberation (...) That young party slips further and further into the waters of a pale Christian Democracy and is alienating the laity by its position regarding denominational education (...) it still seduces many women, executives, the self-employed and civil servants, but the party loses ground amongst youngsters, workers and small agricultural labourers. It is reduced to the middle classes, where it meets the radicals, the Right and the RPF".[65] This reproach of having betrayed the hopes of "1945", however, is not shared by all historians. For Jean-Marie Mayeur, such criticism is meaningless for it could be applied to every new party that is confronted with the realities of power.[66] Indeed,

---

59. On the creation of the RPF, see d'Abzac-Epezy and Agostino, *De Gaulle et le Rassemblement du peuple français*. In 1946, relations between the MRP and De Gaulle had become tense. In the referendum on the French Constitution on 13 October 1946, for example, the MRP and De Gaulle were direct opponents. This led De Gaulle to form his own party in 1947, the RPF.
60. With a programme which stressed nationalism, liberalism, anticommunism and the defence of the rights of Catholics, the RPF strongly appealed to centrist and rightist elements within the MRP. In order not to alienate its conservative electorate, the MRP was therefore forced to put, to give but one example, the school question on the political agenda, thereby burdening its relationship with the SFIO.
61. On 5 September, 1948, e.g., R. Schuman formed a government in which the SFIO received the Ministry of Finance, while the MRP defended a leftist socio-economic programme. This government did not receive the support of the moderates and collapsed after two days.
62. See Rioux, *La France de la Quatrième République*, 255.
63. Groux and Mouriaux, *La CFDT*, 28.
64. See Callot, *L'Action et l'Oeuvre Politique du Mouvement Républicain Populaire*, 336.
65. Rioux, *La France de la Quatrième République*, 222.
66. Mayeur, "La démocratie d'inspiration chrétienne en France", 82.

since the collapse of *tripartisme* and the expulsion of the communists, the political centre of gravity had moved to the centre, even the centre right. If the MRP wanted to continue to be the pivot of French politics, it thought it had but little choice than to follow, even if this meant being part of coalitions that revered the principles of economic liberalism and state authority. Being the most "leftist" party in such coalitions was hardly a consolation for those who wanted to hold in esteem, or reinstate, the initial - call it - Left Catholic programme of *la révolution par la loi*.[67]

The party context in which Italian Left Catholics had to operate was slightly different from that in Germany or France. In Germany, Left Catholics *initially* had played a dominant role within the CDU. In France, the MRP as a whole had adopted a "leftist" pose. In Italy, however, Left Catholics, though initially quite popular, had to compete with more influential currents within their party.[68] Despite De Gasperi's slogan of 1945 - "el partito di centro che si muove verso sinistra"[69] - the DC was a party in which from the very foundation the idea of economic liberalisation had become firmly rooted.[70] The Christian Democratic party aroused expectations among farmers and industrial workers but also among sections of big business, which - compared to France - had been less compromised by its wartime behaviour. Quite soon after the end of hostilities, leading entrepreneurs left the elitist Liberal PLI and considered the DC a more promising instrument for the realisation of their neoliberal demands. The financial support of these supporters undoubtedly was a serious check on any collec-

67. Mayeur, *Des partis catholiques à la démocratie chrétienne*, 159. The developments that had started in 1947 would reach a climax in the 1951 elections. The SFIO - which had left the government in early 1950 because of the latter's increasingly liberal economic policy - and the MRP suffered great losses, thus making an end to the period of "third force" governments. The RPF, which scored a huge victory, could no longer be ignored: in March 1952, a government could only be formed with the support of twenty-seven RPF votes, thereby further anchoring the government in the rightist camp. Immediately after the elections, the RPF launched a new round in the struggle on education, thereby alienating the MRP even more from the Left.
68. Dossetti himself wrote several times to party leader De Gasperi that he had a strong feeling that his viewpoints were hardly accepted within the DC. Pombeni, *Il Gruppo Dossettiano*, 207. It is important to take into account that the fortunes of the Dossettists repeatedly rose and fell in the course of a few years. After the December 1946 congress of the DC, Dossettism was the victim of the shift to the Right within the party. From the middle of 1949 onwards, and particularly in early 1950 however, in a period of widespread revulsion in the country, Dossetti's influence again increased considerably. In March 1950, he was reappointed vice-secretary of the party. Ginsborg, *A History of Contemporary Italy*, 130.
69. "The centrist party that moves towards the Left". De Gasperi used this expression during the first national convention of the DC, in Rome, 31 July to 3 August 1945. He was quoted in *Il Popolo*, 2 August 1945. Pietro Scoppola noticed the stress on a more progressive, egalitarian society, based on land reform, social services, and parliamentary democracy in the DC wartime program. Scoppola, *La proposta politica di De Gasperi*. Baget-Bozzo, however, remarked in his study: "De Gasperi's declarations varied fast and radically according to the circumstances". Baget-Bozzo, *Il Partito Cristiano al Potere*, 82n9.
70. Harper describes the economic policy of the DC as a "confusing and incoherent mixture of liberal and interventionist elements". Harper, *America and the Reconstruction of Italy*, 20.

tivist illusions the party might have had. De Gasperi's choice of the orthodox liberal Epicarmo Corbino as Minister of the Treasury in December 1945 is a case in point.[71]

Not only the party context in which Italian Left Catholics operated was different. The complex interaction between the national context and international developments - the environment in which Left Catholics had to find their position - was also quite particular. Consequently, the relevance of international factors is not the same as in the French or German cases. The image of Germany, where to a considerable extent a neoliberal order was imposed by the US, can definitely not be applied to Italy.[72] Especially in the first postwar years, US influence on the Italian economic and political recovery, and the impact of the international system in general, should not be overestimated. American aid funds for Italy were initially very limited. Also, the US departments that had to deal with Italy were hopelessly divided, which often resulted in contradictory directives. Neither "Hullian" neoliberals nor "New Dealers" were in such a position as to influence American foreign policy in Italy. In general, there was a painful lack of understanding of local conditions.[73] Finally, the imposition of neoliberal policies would almost certainly have been resisted by a large part of Italian industry.[74]

In 1945 and 1946, it was rather De Gasperi who, for domestic reasons, enthusiastically sought the support of the US. The Italian leader wanted to avoid a peace treaty which would be too detrimental to Italian interests. Close relations with Washington would also increase his personal prestige. And besides, he counted on American financial support to stimulate the recovery of the Italian economy. At least as important a consideration was that US support, both financial and political, would allow De Gasperi to confront the Left. This was an urgent request of conservative landed estate owners, part of the private sector and the Vatican, which threatened to transfer its support to the right wing *Uomo Qualunque* movement.[75] Since the Left - and mainly the communist Left - became ever less an appropriate partner, especially if Italy wanted American aid[76], De Gasperi seemed "condemned" to the Right.

In other words, the exclusion of the PCI from the government in May 1947 was at least as much the initiative of the Italian Right, which in Pinzani's opinion found "a suitable exponent" in De Gasperi, as it was the

---

71. Corbino's liberal policy, supported by Einaudi, then Governor of the Bank of Italy, increased tensions within the coalition, which included the socialist PSIUP and the communist PCI.
72. The influence of the United States on Italian policy has been put in perspective by, amongst others, Scoppola, *La proposta politica di De Gasperi*.
73. Harper, *America and the Reconstruction of Italy*, 19 and 101. "Hullian" refers to then Secretary of State Cordell Hull.
74. In those years, only a few sectors or companies, such as the textile industry and FIAT, would have welcomed the end of protectionism and the institution of open markets.
75. Pinzani, "May 1947", 324.
76. The conditions attached to the Marshall Plan, such as tough stabilisation measures, could hardly be fulfilled with the PCI in the government. Moreover, the American Congress, dominated by a Republican majority, would never have allowed aid to governments which included communists.

consequence of the changing international environment. In that respect, the Italian case does not differ that much from the situation in France.[77]

By the second half of 1947, bipartisan consensus on massive aid programmes and on the necessity of an anticommunist crusade, made American foreign policy remarkably more efficient. Italy's "accommodation" to the conditions set forth by the Marshall Plan (or the European Recovery Programme) led, very much as in the rest of Western Europe, to a growing impact of neoliberal schemes.[78] The Italian scholar Pier Paolo D'Attorre remarked that by the time "the first ships carrying the ERP goods arrived, the debate between the 'planners' and the 'free traders' had almost been settled in favour of the latter".[79] The fact that De Gasperi included the neoliberal technocrat Einaudi, who was closely linked to the leading classes of Italian society, in his new government in May 1947 is quite significant in that respect.[80]

Whether primarily caused by the ever more dominant influence of the US or by pressure from the Right in Italy itself, which De Gasperi needed to stay in power, the result was the same: a political environment that did not favour Left Catholicism. Not surprisingly then, it coincided with a reduction of Dossetti's influence within the DC. At the DC congress of December 1946 - where Dossetti tabled his vote of no-confidence against De Gasperi - the election of the party executive clearly did not work out to the Dossetti group's advantage.[81] At the same time, leading leftists began to move to the De Gasperi camp.[82]

Unlike Germany, however, the considerable loss of influence did not lead to a complete marginalisation of Left Catholics. On the contrary, in Italy it even led to a greater *visibility* of the dissidents. For Dossetti, the series of events that had started with De Gasperi's visit to the US in January 1947 and that had reached a climax in May 1947 with the formation of the new government, were a clear warning that the party was "turning itself into a conservative party".[83] It is hardly a coincidence that, precisely in May 1947, the Dossetti group launched its periodical *Cronache Sociali*, a vehicle for sharp criticism of the liberal market economy, of Einaudi and of the United States, while at the same time paying tribute to the British Labour

---

77. Pinzani, "May 1947", 328.
78. To what extent this was really due to American pressure is a controversial issue. Antonio Gambino argued that Washington's intervention did not play any determinant role in the adoption of the Einaudi measures. This was mainly the responsibility of the business-financial sector. See Gambino, *Storia del dopoguerra dalla liberazione al potere DC*, 362-374.
79. D'Attorre, "The European Recovery Program in Italy", 83.
80. Malgeri described Einaudi as "an influential person in the economic field and supporter of the market economy, a term then excluded from the vocabulary of the Left". Malgeri, "La Democrazia Cristiana in Italia", 95. See also Harper, *America and the Reconstruction of Italy*, 170.
81. Baget-Bozzo called it "a break with both the *dossettiani* and the trade unionists" and "a shift to the right within the party". Baget-Bozzo, *Il Partito Cristiano al Potere*, 143.
82. An illustration of this evolution is Emilio Taviani. His experiences during the Resistance had strengthened his leftist convictions. At the end of 1946, however, he sided with De Gasperi.
83. "Il Consiglio Nazionale della DC" in *Cronache Sociali*, 30 May 1947. Dossetti was very pessimistic about the new government, directed by "the liberal upper class". See e.g. his article "La fiducia e la prova" in *Cronache Sociali*, 30 June 1947.

government.[84] But this increased visibility could not disguise that in 1947 Dossettism was completely isolated within the DC, as became clear once again at the Naples Conference of November 1947. As in the rest of Western Europe, the bipolarisation on the international level had led to a similar polarisation of the Italian political landscape, thereby stifling all discussions within the party.[85] More specifically for the Italian context, the impact of the Vatican and the Catholic hierarchy was detrimental for "leftist rebels" within the DC.[86] And finally, for the DC, the isolation of the Dossettists was partly due to the fact that De Gasperi was more than ever in charge of the party, while the Dossetti group was divided.[87] Others would argue that to some extent, Dossetti's Left Catholics isolated themselves by staying at a distance from the dominant "ideology of the West" around which some kind of consensus could be built within the heterogeneous DC.[88] It is this mixture of elements, on the international, national and party level that explains the isolation of the Left Catholic Dossetti group within the DC. Nevertheless, domestic social problems as well as international tensions on the politico-military field, and especially the creation of NATO, gave it another opportunity to raise its voice.

4. The Politico-Military Cold War and Left Catholicism ... or What was Left of it. The "Prohibitive" International Context (1948-1950).

The Marshall Plan of June 1947 had laid the foundations of the bipolar international system that would dominate the 1950s. After Soviet Foreign Minister Molotov had left the Marshall Plan negotiations in Paris in early July 1947, the American aid scheme served as the demarcation line between Eastern and Western Europe. Upon this economic cleavage, the formation of politico-military blocks was gradually grafted. During the *Council of Foreign Ministers* which took place in London in December 1947, tensions rose so high that Marshall, Bevin and Bidault left the summit meeting, leaving behind a flabbergasted Molotov. Before the American and French Foreign Ministers left London, they agreed on new measures to arrive at closer Western European and transatlantic cooperation. After the *coup* in

---

84. This was even more explicit after Frederico Caffè joined *Cronache Sociali*. Caffè stayed in Britain since the autumn of 1947 and reported on the accomplishments of the Labour government. He had an important influence on Dossetti's thinking.
85. Pombeni, *Il Gruppo Dossettiano*, 374. In the middle of 1949, however, Dossettism again would win ground, garnering 35% of the vote at the June 1949 Venice Congress.
86. The pontificate of Pius XII displayed ever more authoritarian characteristics, on the theological (see *Humani generis*, 1950) as well as on the political field. See Cornwell, *Hitler's Pope*, chapter 19. Even though the DC constantly attempted to safeguard its autonomy, the Catholic hierarchy was a political factor to be reckoned with.
87. The appointment of Fanfani by De Gasperi as Minister of Labour in the government that was so much attacked by Dossetti, divided the Dossetti group. By this manoeuvre, De Gasperi integrated the left wing of the DC into the government. See Pombeni, *Il Gruppo Dossettiano*, 356.
88. This argument is elaborated by D'Attorre, "The European Recovery Program in Italy", 79-80. D'Attorre argues that the Italian Left failed to perceive "the potential of the 'reformism' intrinsic to the ERP ideology". Ibid., 81.

Prague, in February 1948, this ambition gained momentum.[89] In March, the *Brussels Pact* was signed and in June the Vandenberg Resolution gave the US government the authority to conclude alliances in peacetime with partners outside the American continent. The creation of NATO, in April 1949, was the logical outcome.

Taking into consideration the evolution of MRP foreign policy during the course of 1947-48, it is no surprise that the French MRP Minister of Foreign Affairs, Georges Bidault, welcomed the transatlantic system of collective security. In March 1948, just after the Prague events, he wrote to his American colleague: "The moment has arrived to resume as rapidly as possible, in the political field as well as in the military field, the collaboration between the old and the new world, both sharing a deep respect for the only precious [Western] civilisation". In April of the same year, he formally asked Marshall to jointly develop a collective security regime.[90] In the ratification debate on the NATO Treaty, the Atlantic alliance was firmly defended by Robert Schuman and, in the name of the MRP, by Teitgen. By then, and at least on this issue, the MRP seemed to have more in common with the DC than with the Left Catholic group of Dossetti within the DC.

Like its sister parties in the rest of Western Europe, the Italian *Democrazia Cristiana* of De Gasperi too was a loyal supporter of the Atlantic construction. All his life, De Gasperi had been an ardent anticommunist who considered the principal political battle of his life to be that between Christianity and communism.[91] Therefore, when growing tensions between the Soviet Union and the United States came to the fore, the principled choice of integrating Italy firmly into the Western camp was made relatively early. It was undoubtedly strengthened by American aid to the Italian Christian Democrats during the election campaign of 1948. The modalities of transatlantic cooperation, however, and more specifically the entry of Italy into NATO, led to a sharp debate within the party at the end of 1948. Unlike De Gasperi, who showed himself a supporter of NATO, the Left Catholic fraction led by Dossetti as well as the trade union wing of the DC, were very critical. Dossetti, supported by Gronchi, argued that NATO was unnecessary since there was no immediate threat against Italy. Moreover, he repeatedly warned against US imperialism.[92] Instead, he preferred close economic and political collaboration with other European countries, outside the context of military alliances.[93] At this point, in 1949, leftist opinion

---

89. After the Czechoslovakian president Eduard Beneš and the non-communist ministers in the government had given clear indications that they wished to participate in the Marshall Plan, the USSR increased pressure on Czechoslovakia. A power struggle within the government in the end led to the resignation of eleven non-communist ministers. In the tumult that accompanied this power struggle, two ministers, one of them named Jan Masaryk, died in mysterious circumstances. Shortly after these events, all Czech parties were rolled up or integrated within the Czech Communist Party.
90. Callot, *L'Action et l'Oeuvre Politique du Mouvement Républicain Populaire*, 121.
91. Ginsborg, *A History of Contemporary Italy*, 49.
92. The Dossetti group had always been very critical of the intentions of the US. In June 1947 S. Majerotto wrote on the Marshall Plan: "this is a new and more decisive offensive of the dollar diplomacy through the construction of an Atlantic federation". S. Majerotto, "Riflessioni sull'offerta Marshall", *Cronache Sociali*, 30 June 1947.
93. Ginsborg, *A History of Contemporary Italy*, 158.

within the DC was - again - not insignificant. In 1949, the Dossetti group controlled a third of the party.[94] The untenable situation in the countryside[95] made the demand for land reform louder, which strengthened the position of the reformist Dossetti group within the party. In March 1950, when public indignation about the repression used against workers and farmers reached a peak, De Gasperi even reappointed Dossetti vice-secretary of the party. At the same time, other reformists were included in the new government that was formed by De Gasperi after he had excluded the antireformist Liberal Party from office. It had become clear that the "Einaudi line" provoked so much tension that it would not lead to social stability. The United States too insisted on a change of policy, preferably by including Saragat's social democratic PSLI into the government.[96]

It was, however, one of the last convulsions positively affecting the left wing within the DC. The strength of the Dossetti group was relative and was not translated into any concrete measures. In the discussion on NATO, the pro-Atlantic majority of the DC, openly supported by the "chaplain of the Atlantic Alliance", Pius XII, outnumbered its opponents.[97] In the House of Representatives, the DC approved Italy's entry into NATO almost unanimously, with only three opposing votes. As far as land reform was concerned, the picture was very much the same. The reformist rhetoric of the DC contrasted sharply with the very poor record on the field. It was clear that in a party which was influenced *to some extent* by big business and the Vatican, devoted to a centrist position and to being in office, and led by someone who was more of a Cold War warrior than a reformer[98], Left Catholicism could hardly leave its mark. The more so as both the national and international context did not favour collectivist experiments. In the early 1950s, with the outbreak of the Korean War and the economic achievements of capitalist recipes, the climate would not improve. In the summer of 1951, Dossetti drew his conclusions. With all illusions of a strong Catholic, reformist party gone, he left politics at the age of thirty-eight, and found a new destination in monastic life. In the same year, *Cronache Sociali* came to an end. And so did Left Catholicism ... for the time being.

5. Conclusion

To what extent did international developments, and more specifically the dramatic changes between 1945 and 1950, influence the emergence, development and retreat of Left Catholic movements in Europe? A careful-

---

94. Ibid., 130. As mentioned above, the chief motion of the Dossetti group at the June 1949 Venice Congress got the support of 35% of the participants.
95. On 29 October 1949 repression of farmers occupying land resulted in three casualties in Melissa, on this see Ginsborg, *A History of Contemporary Italy*, 122. On 9 January 1950 six people were killed during a workers' demonstration in Modena.
96. The PSLI was strongly supported by the US. In the opinion of the US, it could function as a left wing signboard of De Gasperi's policies.
97. See the radio message of Pius XII, on Christmas Eve 1948, quoted in Di Capua, *Come l'Italia aderì al patto Atlantico*, 148-150. Also: Hebblethwaite, "Pope Pius XII", 74.
98. This description is Ginsborg's, *A History of Contemporary Italy*, 142.

ly balanced answer to this question should take into account a twofold distinction.

First distinction: the remarkable difference between the "permissive" international context of 1945-1946 and the "prohibitive" international context of later years. Early 1947, when the United States made the transition from a search for global multilateralism to a policy of reconstructing and integrating Western Europe, serves as a turning-point. In the first postwar years the international context facilitated, even stimulated, ideological experiments, of which Left Catholicism's urge to political renewal was one manifestation. The climate of international cooperation between the victors of World War II, the euphoria of Liberation, the immense prestige of the USSR and of its societal model, and the bankruptcy of the political Right opened a window of opportunity. The success of the British Labour Party was a direct source of inspiration for those Left Catholics who - often after having spent the war as exiles in Britain - embarked on a *travaillist* adventure. In general, however, the impact of the international context in 1945 and 1946 was mainly indirect; the explanatory value of an international perspective is rather limited. It cannot explain why *travaillist* experiments in Germany, France, Italy and Belgium failed, nor why Left Catholics in Belgium managed to form their own party while in other countries they decided to play a role within broader Christian Democratic parties. It cannot explain the particular form and content of Left Catholic movements, some being rather radical, others rather moderate. The specific circumstances of the Occupation, the postwar national political configuration and even the role of individuals are far more revealing factors.

The impact of the "prohibitive" international context after 1947 - with the dramatic bipolarisation between East and West, and the leading and infiltrating role of the United States - turns out to be more important. The retreat of Left Catholicism cannot be adequately explained without including US foreign policy and the Cold War climate. The impact, however, was quite different from one country to another. This is the second basic distinction which has to be made.

In the German case, an international perspective is highly relevant. Initially, German Left Catholics were actively supported by the British Labour government, which needed the support of part of the CDU to realise its socialisation programme. When the United States started to take the lead and introduced a free market economy in Bizonia, their days were numbered. The presence of the United States in Western Germany thus made the impact of the unfolding Cold War on Left Catholicism relatively direct.

In France, the impact was more indirect. Developments at the international level were "filtered" by the national political configuration. After the communists were removed from office - a decision directly related to the outbreak of the Cold War, and more specifically to the Marshall Plan - the political centre of gravity first moved to the centre, then to the centre Right, especially after the appearance of the RPF. The initially Left Catholic MRP - hoping to remain in office - followed a similar course.

The same complex interaction characterised the fate of Left Catholics in Italy as well. Pressure from conservative forces - the Vatican, owners of large landed estates, and part of the private sector - drove the DC of De Gasperi relatively early into the hands of the United States. The US for its part strongly supported the neoliberal line which Dossetti attempted to counter. Initially, Left Catholics in Italy were - unlike their German counterparts - able to form a relatively influential fraction within the DC, but in the end they found themselves in complete isolation. Dossetti, quite appropriately, ended up in monastic life. By that time, the tremendous pressure from the international situation, aggravated by the outbreak of the Korean War, could no longer be counteracted.

LEFT CATHOLICISM IN EUROPE IN THE 1940S. ELEMENTS OF AN INTERPRETATION

Martin Conway

The currents of Left Catholicism present in Europe during the 1940s pose an awkward challenge to historians of Catholic politics. The reality is undeniable; much less easy to explain are its origins, nature and, more especially, its significance. It is upon this final element that this contribution will attempt to focus. As the essays in this collection well demonstrate, diverse movements of Left Catholicism emerged in a number of West European states during the final years of the Second World War, rallying significant numbers of Catholics behind their urgent message of spiritual and social transformation.[1] But what importance should we attach to this phenomenon? In some respects, this question seems more difficult to answer now than it would have done two decades ago. The dominant interpretation of modern Catholicism which held sway during the 1960s and 1970s tended to focus not surprisingly on the Second Vatican Council as a historic caesura when the Catholic Church and its social and political affiliates decisively embraced the reality of the modern, pluralist society.[2] Seen from this perspective, Left Catholicism appeared to be almost a dress rehearsal for the events of the 1960s: though the forces of change and progress within Catholicism were on that occasion defeated, their eventual success could not be long delayed.[3]

Nowadays, this essentially teleological framework no longer seems entirely adequate. As the Second Vatican Council has receded into history, so its consequences no longer seem so emphatic and unidimensional. At the same time, historical perceptions of the evolution of Catholicism from the militancy of the interwar years to the transformations of the 1960s have become considerably more complex. The 1940s and 1950s were a much more interesting and diverse era in the development of European Catholicism than is suggested by regarding them as a mere prelude to the changes introduced by John XXIII. Though forces of theological, political and social innovation were indeed emphatically present, they were not the only story. The papal triumphalism of Pius XII was much more than an absurd anachronism and the defensive *Lagerkultur* espoused by Catholicism since the end of the 19th century retained a powerful hold over Catholic

---

1. See especially the contribution of Gerd-Rainer Horn to this volume.
2. Jedin, "The Second Vatican Council", 146-147.
3. See the classic "progressive" interpretation of Catholic politics presented in Fogarty, *Christian Democracy in Europe*. For a more recent and considerably more sophisticated version of this thesis, see McMillan, "France", 34 and 59-68.

mentalities.[4] Placed in this context, the significance of the Left Catholicism of the 1940s has come to seem to lie less in what it heralded for the future of Catholicism than in what it revealed about the Catholic past. Many of the movements conventionally defined as having formed part of Left Catholicism, such as the worker priests and the *Mouvement Populaire des Familles* (MPF), belonged to a tradition which owed more to the social Catholic traditions of the 1890s and even the Catholic Action movements of the interwar years than it did to the post-Vatican II Catholicism of the 1960s.[5] Put crudely, it is easier to see where Left Catholicism came from than where it led.

In the light of these complexities, it would be tempting to dissolve (or at least substantially dilute) "Left Catholicism" by questioning its very existence. Like any such conceptual label, it is of course no more than a convenient abbreviation for a reality which was considerably more diverse. To bring together under a single heading, for example, the worker priest movement in France and Dossetti's left Christian Democrats in Italy must inevitably raise the question as to how much these phenomena really had in common. The differences between them were most obviously ones of national circumstance and tradition but also of ambition and temperament. The Dossettian movement was predominantly political in ambition and reformist in temperament, reflecting its origins in the fluid political alliances forged during the long hiatus in Italian politics between the initial collapse of the Mussolini regime and the final liberation of northern Italy.[6] In contrast, the French worker priests were emphatically spiritual rather than political in ambition, revolutionary rather than reformist in temperament, and arose primarily from the determination of radicalised sections of the clergy to bring Catholicism to a "dechristianised" working class.

And yet to take refuge in these very real differences would seem in many respects to be too easy a means of evading the interpretative challenge presented by the various Left Catholic movements. They may have differed in significant ways but, as the essays in this collection rightly remind us, they nevertheless occupied the same space. Rather than a unified or self-contained movement, Left Catholicism is perhaps best regarded as part of a common *champ d'action* inhabited by various radical Catholic groups during the 1940s. Seen in this way, questions of definition would seem to be less important than ones of proportion: How important were the Left Catholic movements? How did they arise and what legacy did they leave? In sum, what was their significance?

The starting-point of such an analysis must be the recognition that they always remained relatively small movements. None of the Left Catholic groups, with the partial exception of the MRP in France during its post-liberation efflorescence, ever became mass movements to rival their more mainstream Catholic rivals, such as the *Jeunesse Ouvrière Chrétienne* (JOC)

---

4. Logan, "Pius XII: *romanità*, prophecy and charisma", 237-247; Müller, Plasser and Ulram, "Wähler und Mitglieder der ÖVP", 163; Altermatt, *Katholizismus und Moderne*, 161-164; Imhof, "Wiedergeburt der geistigen Landesverteidigung", 184-204.
5. E.g. Misner, *Social Catholicism in Europe*; Winock, *Histoire politique de la revue "Esprit"*, 353-361.
6. Durand, *L'église catholique dans la crise de l'Italie*.

in France and Belgium. Numbers are, of course, not everything. The ideas advanced by radical Catholic groups during the 1940s undoubtedly enjoyed an influence which stretched beyond their declared supporters and seem to have exercised a formative influence on the new generation of prelates who came to the fore within European Catholicism in the 1960s and 1970s.[7] Nevertheless, it is undeniable that in terms of simple numbers the Left Catholic groups always remained no more than marginal components of the broader Catholic community.

This note of caution is perhaps all the more essential because of the tendency to approach the history of all such Catholic movements in terms of their origins. By tracing back the intellectual and political heritage of the Left Catholic groups to the social Catholic and "Christian Democrat" groups of the 1890s, as well as interwar dissident movements such as Marc Sangnier's *Jeune République* (JR), it is difficult to avoid appearing to invest them with a rather inflated significance.[8] As the latest manifestation of this half-submerged, half-visible Catholic progressive tradition, there is an inevitable temptation to suggest that, regardless of their modest size, the Left Catholic movements must have been important.

One corollary of such an approach is that it tends to displace responsibility for their failure onto factors external to the Left Catholic movements themselves. Especially among historians broadly sympathetic to Left Catholic ideals there has long been a tendency to explain the demise of the Left Catholic movements in the late 1940s in terms of an unpropitious combination of external circumstance and ill-will.[9] If only secular left forces had been more responsive to their ideas, the Cold War had not polarised European politics or the papacy had not been so implacable in its opposition, perhaps Left Catholicism would have enjoyed its rightful success. These are tempting "might have beens", but, by stressing external factors, they tend to distract attention from the more fundamental reasons why Left Catholic groups never became a major force within postwar European Catholicism.

Perhaps the most obvious such reason was the failure of the Left Catholic groups to build a durable alliance with the formidable and powerful network of Catholic working class organisations: the trade unions, political lobby-groups and youth leagues. The expansion of these groups over the previous half century had been remarkable and, if the Left Catholics had been able to win significant support among the JOC of Cardijn, the *Confederazione Italiana Sindacati Lavoratori* (CISL) or the *Algemeen Christelijk Werkersverbond-Mouvement Ouvrier Chrétien* (ACW-MOC) in Belgium, they would have been powerfully placed to influence postwar Catholic politics and indeed Catholicism in general. The reality of course proved to be entirely otherwise: whatever the appeal of radical alternatives at the initial moment of Liberation, Catholic working class movements opted predomi-

---

7. E.g. Suenens, *Memories and Hopes*, 38-40.
8. E.g. Durand, "La mémoire de la démocratie chrétienne en 1945".
9. A characteristic example of this broadly sympathetic approach is Arnal, *Priests in Working-Class Blue*. Two excellent monographs demonstrate the virtue of a more hard-headed but certainly not hostile approach: Letamendia, *Le Mouvement Républicain Populaire* and Beerten, *Le rêve travailliste en Belgique*.

nantly to re-enter the Catholic "pillar" and to remain loyal both to clerical leadership and the cross-class politics represented by the nascent Christian Democratic parties. The extent of this "repillarisation" did of course vary according to national circumstance: if it was most emphatic along the Rhine-Alps axes of European Catholicism, Catholic political and institutional pluralism remained (as it had long been) more strongly present within France. Nevertheless, almost everywhere in Europe, Catholic working class movements ultimately chose to privilege confessional loyalty over the ideological and political experiments represented by the Left Catholic movements.

The reasons why this should have been so owed much to the immediate political circumstances prevailing in Europe during the mid and late 1940s. The fears evident among Catholics throughout Europe of local or national communist seizures of power as well as the more immediate threat of a secular Popular Front of anticlerical forces acted as a powerful conservative counterweight to the new opportunities for alliances with non-Catholic groups created by wartime resistance to German rule. These fears were especially deeply-rooted among Catholic trade union activists, for whom socialist and latterly communist militants were not a distant spectre but immediate and formidable rivals in the struggle for the hearts and minds of the unstructured, disoriented and radicalised European working class which emerged from the war years.

This intense and often bitter rivalry was particularly evident in Belgium. As Carl Strikwerda's recent stimulating account has rightly stressed, a powerful logic of antisocialism had been inherent in Catholic trade unionism from its origins[10]; but at no time since perhaps the 1890s was the rivalry of the Catholic working class organisations with their secular opponents as strongly felt as during the years immediately following the Second World War. The years of German occupation had destroyed much of the former pillarised structure of working class life and had enabled a plethora of local organisations to emerge. In this new and much less certain world, the tasks of organisational reconstruction and the retention of the loyalty of their members were the principal priorities of most Catholic trade unionists who tended, not without some justification, to regard the proposals of fusion advanced by their secular rivals as devious attempts to undermine the distinctive character of Catholic trade unionism.[11] Both during the occupation and again after the Liberation, the Catholic trade union confederation, the *Confédération des Syndicats Chrétiens* (CSC), repulsed socialist calls for union, declaring emphatically that "Christian trade unionism is more indispensable than it ever was".[12]

---

10. Strikwerda, *A House Divided*.
11. A. Gillet to Mgr. Creusen, 17 Dec. 1944, Centre d'études et de documentation Guerre et Sociétés contemporaines, Brussels (CEGES-SOMA), PF2. See the excellent analysis in Hemmerijckx, "La CMB dans la clandestinité". For a characteristic example of the intense rivalry between the different union federations, see Syndicat Unique de la Région de Charleroi to Van Acker, 2 Nov. 1944, Rijksarchief Brugge (RAB), Van Acker Papers, 498. I am grateful to Michel Nuyttens for permission to consult the Van Acker archive.
12. *Les Dossiers de l'Action Sociale Catholique*, July-Aug. 1945, 362; Hemmerijckx, "La CMB dans la clandestinité", 376-378 and 389; Pasture, "Redressement", 258-259.

This defensive mentality also governed the suspicious attitude which Catholic working class militants adopted towards the various political initiatives launched after the Liberation to bring about a "deconfessionalisation" of Belgian politics. The *rapprochement* brought about by the war, especially within francophone Belgium, between certain progressive Catholic and socialist intellectuals bore fruit after the Liberation in the foundation of a new *travailliste* political movement, the Union Démocratique Belge (UDB), as well as in numerous discussion groups and periodicals, all of which proclaimed the virtues of a broadly-based alliance of progressive forces.[13] Yet, it is striking that Catholic working class figures were almost entirely absent from these initiatives. With the exception of a few prominent Catholic trade unionists initially active within the UDB, they remained predominantly middle-class and intellectual groups which operated outside of Catholic working class organisational structures. In the months following the Liberation, the umbrella organisation of the Catholic working class movement, the ACW-MOC, sought to maintain a political neutrality which reflected the reluctance of many of its affiliates, especially within francophone Belgium, to endorse the re-emerging "official" Catholic party, the *Christelijke Volkspartij-Parti Social Chrétien* (CVP-PSC). Gradually, however, the logic of "repillarisation" drew the ACW-MOC back into the mainstream of the Catholic organisational world, thereby hastening the demise of dreams of a deconfessional realignment of Belgian politics.[14]

Suspicions of new political forces were reinforced by the weight of institutional conservatism. Catholic working class movements across most of Europe were by the 1940s mature bureaucratic organisations controlled by firmly-entrenched leaderships who regarded new rivals with distrust and turned a deaf ear to pressures for innovation. The confessional ghetto mentality of Paul Segers as President of the ACW in Belgium clearly expressed such attitudes[15] but so too did an organisation such as the JOC in France and Belgium, within which the initial *élan* had been largely supplanted by formal hierarchies and a quasi-permanent cadre.[16] These leaders tended, not surprisingly, to measure success in institutional terms: increases in membership and in the scale of their activities seemed more important than a revolutionary rechristianisation of the working class. So too, in the uncertain political circumstances of the post-liberation years, did the recovery of their influence within the committees and corridors of Catholic politics. The new (or restructured) Christian Democratic parties which emerged throughout Western Europe in the later 1940s predominantly adopted structures of individual membership and centralised leadership which offered few oppor-

---

13. Beerten, *Le rêve travailliste*, 12-25; *Forces Nouvelles*, 24 Nov. 1945, 1, 4 and 5, "Socialistes et Chrétiens".
14. O. Grégoire to G. Hoyois, 23 Apr. 1945, CEGES-SOMA, PH 25; *Les Dossiers de l'Action Sociale Catholique*, Mar. 1945, 25-35, "Oeuvres sociales et politique" and Feb. 1946, 149-151, "Notre chronique politique"; Pasture, "Redressement et expansion", 251-254 and 264-267.
15. E.g. Verslag van P.W. Segers over de Kath. Partij [Oct.1944] and Vergadering der secretarissen 6 June 1945, Archives Générales du Royaume, Brussels (AGR), Papers of Gaston Eyskens, Docs. 495 and 4128. I am grateful to Mark Eyskens for permission to consult the papers of his father.
16. Arnal, "Toward a Lay Apostolate of the Workers", 211-227.

tunities for the collective and informal influence over party policy which had been formerly enjoyed by many Catholic working class organisations. Catholic politics had become less permeable to their influence, forcing the Catholic working class movement to adopt new strategies to regain the necessary access to the key forums of political and economic decision-making.[17]

The consequence of the cautious if not downright hostile attitude of working class Catholic organisations to Left Catholic movements and ideas was to render them more vulnerable to the efforts of the Church authorities to clamp down on actions and ideas that were perceived as unorthodox or even heretical. The key role played by ecclesiastical hierarchies and in particular the papacy in the marginalisation of Left Catholic movements has long been recognised. The history of the worker priest movement or the MPF, for example, became dominated in France at the end of the 1940s by the various initiatives by the papacy and the French bishops to suppress these movements or, more subtly, to integrate them within larger "authorised" organisations. This reassertion of clerical control was of course not limited to Left Catholic groups; it formed part of the much wider project of the Vatican under Pius XII to impose a neo-monarchical and authoritarian culture on European Catholicism after the greater national independence which had existed during the war years.[18] It was, however, perhaps especially striking because many of those spiritual initiatives which after the war became associated with Left Catholicism had their origins in officially-approved actions by the ecclesiastical authorities. Tempting though it is to present movements such as the worker priests as having always been inherently oppositional in nature, this is in many respects a retrospective illusion. During the pontificate of Pius XI, the Vatican had encouraged the clergy to implement innovative "scientific" pastoral practices through the use of modern propaganda techniques as well as the establishment of mass lay organisations on the model of Catholic Action.[19] These efforts to reach out to a more educated and diverse laity did much to inject a tone of dynamic optimism into Catholic life during the interwar years and provided the stimulus for the wartime decision to send priests to "accompany" deported workers to Germany as well as the postwar expansion and increased specialisation of the Catholic Action organisations. Initiatives such as the MPF and the worker priests were not therefore radical new departures but were the consequence of the new pastoral techniques developed by the papacy and by national hierarchies over the preceding decades. This was especially so in France, where the publication during the war years of the famous report *France, pays de mission?* by Godin and Daniel stimulated Cardinal Suhard and his fellow bishops to recognise both the reality of working class dechristianisation and the need to respond to it in innovative and radical ways.[20]

---

17. See, for example, Smits, "De afbouw van de autonome politieke actie van het ACW en de oprichting van de CVP".
18. Walsh, "Pius XII", 20-26.
19. Agostino, *Le pape Pie XI*; Holmes, *The Papacy in the Modern World*, 80-81; Fouilloux, "Le catholicisme"; Adoumié, "Le réveil religieux landais".
20. Godin and Daniel, *La France, pays de mission?*; Arnal, *Priests in Working-Class Blue*, 53-60.

Thus, in moving to suppress initiatives such as the worker priests and the MPF, the Vatican and its national allies were not so much clamping down on dissident groups as seeking to reassert their control over phenomena which they had done much to encourage. The initial cadre of French worker priests had been trained at the seminary of Lisieux and enjoyed influential episcopal support. Subsequently, however, the tendency of many of the worker priests to abandon traditional notions of their sacerdotal office caused apprehensions among the French bishops and, more especially, in Rome, where the subsequent condemnation of the worker priest experiment served as a means of holding the line against dangerous pastoral innovations as well as a convenient means of asserting the Vatican's ascendancy over the French Church at a time when the disruptions of the war years and their aftermath had fostered a perceived revival in Gallican tendencies.[21]

That this expression of papal disapproval contributed substantially to the marginalisation of the spiritual currents of Left Catholicism would seem to be beyond question. Just as the papal condemnation of *Action Française* in 1926 had restricted the extreme right newspaper's audience among French Catholics to limited circles of committed supporters, so Pius XII's disapproval of the worker priests served to ensure that they remained throughout the 1950s a small and isolated minority within the French Church. But it would be inaccurate to portray the actions of the papacy both in France and elsewhere as fundamentally at variance with the mood of European Catholics as a whole. Especially after the Second Vatican Council, it became tempting to regard the pontificate of Pius XII as a time when European Catholicism had been held artificially within an outmoded mould by the bonds of papal power. This would, however, seem at best to be only a partial truth. While it is certainly true that Pius' determination to strengthen Vatican control over the national ecclesiastical hierarchies as well as his doctrinal emphasis on the cult of the Virgin Mary created substantial and durable tensions, there was much within the papal message of intransigence and defence of the "Catholic fortress" with which many European Catholics, be they clerical or lay, instinctively identified.[22] In contrast, the spiritual and political ideas advanced by the Left Catholic groups, with their quasi-millennial rhetoric and calls for radical change, went against the grain of Catholic opinion. In a time of overwhelming uncertainty, most Catholics understandably preferred to hold close to the comforts of established truths, and it was this wider reality which would seem to explain why, once papal and national ecclesiastical approval for these groups was withdrawn, they should have dwindled so rapidly into institutional insignificance and personal obscurity.

---

21. Arnal, *Priests in Working-Class Blue*, 137-154. The prolonged conflict after Liberation between the French state and the Vatican over the demands of the French authorities for the dismissal of perceived "collaborationist" bishops provides the essential backdrop for understanding the motivations which underlay the subsequent papal *revanche*: see Latreille, *De Gaulle, la libération et l'église catholique*.
22. Pius XII, "Mediator Dei"; Hastings, "Catholic History from Vatican I to John Paul II", 3; Hebblethwaite, *John XXIII*, 225-230.

This divergence between the Left Catholics and the wider Catholic community reflected the origins of Left Catholicism in a particular social constituency which itself was marginal within Catholic ranks. Left Catholicism was predominantly a movement of young, urban, and male intellectuals which through its intellectual periodicals and elite organisations reached a restricted audience composed overwhelmingly of like-minded young male intellectuals.[23] Confined within this milieu, the Left Catholic groups of the 1940s tended to lack the ability to address the spiritual and material preoccupations of most European Catholics. This was perhaps most obviously so in the case of the significant majority of practising European Catholics who were women. All Catholic movements of the time were of course dominated by men but, even by the standards of the age, the almost complete absence of women from Left Catholic groups would appear to have been distinctive. Movements such as the MPF certainly could rally female support when they campaigned on issues of pressing concern such as food rationing. But, in more general terms, the "christianisme de choc" advocated by many Catholic radicals[24] seemed to offer little which responded in concrete terms to a female agenda dominated, understandably enough, by concerns for family and social welfare. While the MPF called insistently for a revaluing by society of *la vie familiale*[25], it was in fact the conventional charitable organisations closely tied to the Church, such as the *Caritasverband* in Germany, which in 1945 provided the essential support for families and communities uprooted by the population movements of the latter war years and the collapse in the welfare systems of the public authorities.[26] Similarly, in the longer term, it was not the Left Catholic groups but the new Christian Democratic parties which captured most successfully the demand for enhanced welfare provision by their use of the financial resources of the state to deliver welfare programmes targeted not merely at employed adults but also at women, children, the self-employed and the elderly.[27]

Just as Left Catholic groups were overwhelmingly male, so they were also predominantly urban. In marked contrast to the success with which certain radical right movements had succeeded in reaching out to rural Catholic populations during the interwar years[28], the Left Catholics seemed to remain confined within metaphorical city walls. The reasons were partly practical: Left Catholic groups did not possess the financial resources, personnel or mass-circulation press which would have enabled them to address the rural Catholic populations. But these weaknesses were reinforced by the disjuncture which existed between the preoccupation of Left Catholics with the sufferings of the alienated factory worker (and of urban employees more generally) and the concern of rural communities for effective protection of their material interests against the perceived demands of urban populations for cheap food. Urban-rural tension formed a prominent theme of European

---

23. E.g. Molitor, *Souvenirs. Un témoin engagé dans la Belgique du XXe siècle*, 196.
24. E.g. Beinaert, *Pour un christianisme de choc*.
25. Vermeulen, "Positions du MPF", 38-40.
26. Frei, "Brot und Sinn"; Blessing, "'Deutschland in Not, wir im Glauben'".
27. Béthouart, "L'apport socio-économique de la démocratie chrétienne en France"; Wilensky, "Leftism, Catholicism and Democratic Corporatism".
28. E.g. Heilbronner, *Catholicism, Political Culture and the Countryside*; Etienne, *Le mouvement rexiste jusqu'en 1940*.

politics after the Second World War, and one which Left Catholic groups, in common with many others, failed to transcend. While many of the Christian Democratic parties established after 1945 rapidly emerged as the defenders of the rural world (including its more mundane concerns such as price-support measures for agricultural produce)[29], the Left Catholics remained in effect defenders of a working class which already had more vocal and effective Catholic and non-Catholic spokesmen.

This failure of Left Catholic groups to reach out to influential elements of the Catholic community contributes to a more sophisticated understanding of why they did not develop into a substantial and durable presence in post-1945 European politics. Their success was undermined not merely by the harsh winds of the Cold War or by the rumblings of papal discontent. It also reflected the significant divergence which existed between the rhetoric and preoccupations of the Left Catholic groups and majority Catholic opinion. While the former spoke an utopian and radical language of spiritual rechristianisation and social revolution, most Catholics emerged from the war with a heightened sense of the dangers posed by radical forces of Left and the Right as well as by the need for Catholics to unite in defence of their distinctive interests. As Mgr. Saliège, the highly popular and far from reactionary archbishop of Toulouse, commented frankly in a pastoral letter to the faithful in February 1944: "You are afraid of communism, and I am not saying that you are wrong".[30] Anticommunism was, however, merely one of the more visible elements of a much wider range of Catholic anxieties during the 1940s. The sufferings of the war years and the manifold uncertainties which surrounded the future contributed to a recentring of the Catholic faith around its core institutions and beliefs. Lay elites were often demobilised or discredited by the disruptions of the war years and, in their absence, it was the clerical hierarchy and, more particularly, diocesan bishops who assumed an enhanced prominence as the leaders of the Catholic community. This "reclericalisation" of Catholicism was both cause and symptom of the conservative and defensive mood in which many European Catholics entered the postwar world. They remained aware of the need to engage in public life at both a local and national level, but they were also newly conscious of how much they had to lose.[31]

In these circumstances it was far from surprising that the dominant tenor of Catholic politics from the later 1940s onwards was not revolutionary but conservative in tone. Horn, citing the important interpretative essay of Rudi Van Doorslaer, rightly cautions against defining the consequences of the Second World War in terms of either continuity or change.[32] This should, however, be accompanied by a second warning, against assuming that change broadly equated with radicalism while continuity was predominantly conservative. Indeed, perhaps the most durable change in European political life brought about by the war was in fact conservative in nature.

29. Van Molle, *Chacun pour tous*, 344-345 and 348; Parisella, "La base sociale della Democrazia Cristiana Italiana", 197; Müller, Plasser and Ulram, "Wähler und Mitglieder der ÖVP", 171-172.
30. Clément, *Monseigneur Saliège*, 260.
31. Conway, *Catholic Politics in Europe*, 92-95; Durand, "L'épiscopat italien", 95-108.
32. Van Doorslaer, "De oorlog tussen continuïteit en verandering", 17-26.

This was the establishment of a broad centre-right alliance which, under the title of Christian Democracy, dominated political life in much of Western and Central Europe until the 1960s.

The ingredients which contributed to the remarkable success of Christian Democracy as a political force were clearly several, and varied considerably according to national circumstance. At the heart of it, however, was the dynamic energy provided by a new generation of Catholic elites who succeeded in combining a centrist praxis of government with material policies which succeeded in rallying a broad middle-class and rural coalition of support. The electoral basis of Christian Democracy extended well beyond the ranks of the Catholic faithful, and most notably in Germany also acquired an inter-confessional dimension. Nevertheless, the predominantly Catholic character of the Christian Democratic parties during the 1940s and 1950s was never in question. Their social policies, their firm defence of the interests of the Catholic Church and their close ties to the imposing network of Catholic social organisations were all manifestations of the rootedness of Christian Democracy within the Catholic subculture. Indeed, in many respects, the 1950s can be regarded as having marked the historic highpoint of Catholic influence in European politics. During that decade, Germany, Italy, Austria, Switzerland, Belgium, the Netherlands, Luxembourg, Ireland and to a lesser extent France (as well as the rather distinctive cases of Spain and Portugal) were all governed by coalition regimes within which Catholic parties and politicians played an often preponderant role.[33]

In comparison with the rapid growth of Christian Democracy, the Left Catholic groups must inevitably appear as something of a historical footnote. Operating either outside or within the Christian Democrat parties, they were powerless to prevent the evolution of Catholic politics into a centre-right mould which in terms of its acceptance of the bipolar logic of the Cold War and of a largely capitalist economic system was to a large extent the antithesis of their ideological goals. This emphatic failure does, however, risk obscuring the real significance of Left Catholicism which lay not in its very modest impact on the politics of the age but in what it revealed about the diverse and to some extent contradictory currents which co-existed within European Catholicism during the era stretching from approximately 1943 to 1949 when the horizon of "open-ended possibilities"[34] created by the Second World War had not yet been replaced by the rigid frontiers of Cold War politics.

Perhaps the most important such dimension revealed by Left Catholicism was the renewed energy which the events of the war years gave to dreams of a Catholic restructuring of Europe's social and political order. The war, in much of Europe, was anything but a dechristianising experience and, alongside the largely circumstantial rises in religious practice, the events of the war years caused many Catholics to approach their faith with

---

33. The historical literature on Christian Democracy remains remarkably weak. See the attempt at an analysis of its initial development in Conway, "The Age of Christian Democracy". See also the survey volume: Lamberts, ed., *Christian Democracy*. On the conservative reorientation of postwar politics, see the suggestive comments of Richard Vinen in *"The Parti Républicain de la Liberté"*, 183 and 203.
34. Judt, "Introduction", 25.

a new sense of emotional commitment.[35] The large-scale Catholic pilgrimages and parades which occurred in many areas of Europe during and after the war were one dimension of this heightened intensity[36]; but so, less visibly, was the way in which the horrors and sufferings of the war caused many Catholics to question the secular values which had governed Europe's modern development. Responsibility for the war was presented in Catholic sermons and writings in terms much broader than the clash of rival nationalisms or the evil actions of certain leaders. Instead, the war was seen as reflecting a deeper crisis of civilisation, to which the only salvation lay in an integral return to the truths of primitive Christianity stripped of the accretions of institutional and political power.[37] This was especially so in Germany, where the final collapse of the Nazi regime and of effective structures of national and local government gave the Catholic Church an unprecedented centrality in public life in southern and Western Germany as well as prompting widespread calls by both the clergy and laity for a "rechristianization" of Germany.[38]

None of this was of course entirely new. The impulses of intense radicalism generated by the events of the war and its turbulent aftermath were in many respects the continuation of the new mood of religious militancy which had been evident in many areas of Catholic Europe during the 1930s. But, while the campaigns of Catholic Action movements and the cult of Christ the King had been largely confined in the interwar years to a younger generation of educated and predominantly middle-class Catholics[39], during the 1940s this radicalism was more widely diffused. Among the clergy and organisations of the Catholic laity as well as simply in the fabric of parish life, there was a new determination to place a distinctively Catholic agenda of values at the centre of public and private life.

There seems no doubt, however, that the war had its most profound radicalising impact on a particular milieu of Catholic intellectuals (both clerical and lay) for whom the real revelation of the war was not so much the horrors of Nazism as the sufferings of working people which the war served both to heighten and to reveal with a new starkness. Some of these militants had been active before the war in Christian Democrat groups but others were simply Catholics whom the accidents of war threw into contact with the life of the working class. Especially in small industrial communities, such as the mining areas of northern France and Belgium, the material and spiritual hardships of the war were intense. The shortages of food and clothing, the impact of harsh manual labour and the suppression of the prewar trade unions as well as the deportation during the latter war years of large num-

---

35. See the interesting study of the parishes of Paris during the war years: Drapac, *War and Religion*.
36. See, for characteristic examples, Avon, "Le pèlerinage du Puy 12-15 août 1942"; Laury, "Le culte marial dans le Pas-de-Calais"; Mindszenty, *Memoirs*, 31.
37. Hebblethwaite, *John XXIII*, 191; Sauvage, *La Cité Chrétienne*, 220-221. Even the very worldly and conservative Cardinal Van Roey of Belgium began to adopt such language, declaring in his 1942 Lent message that Christianity was, first and primarily, a religion: Van Roey, *La vocation terrestre du christianisme*.
38. Löhr, "Rechristianierungsvorstellungen im deutschen Katholizismus", 25-41; Mitchell, "Materialism and Secularism".
39. Conway, "Building the Christian City".

bers of young men to the Reich caused destitution on a scale unprecedented in these communities since at least the First World War.[40] It was therefore not surprising that for those Catholic priests and laity who witnessed and to some extent shared in this suffering the overriding legacy of the war was an intense, occasionally almost millennial desire to build a new social order in which working people and their families would be freed from the brutal bleakness of lives of labour and isolation.

Left Catholicism was one of the manifestations of this new social commitment. As Yvon Tranvouez has rightly observed, the political and the missionary impulses were always inextricably intertwined within the various Left Catholic groups which emerged during the 1940s.[41] Both were facets of the same essentially social goal of liberation. In part, this ambition remained couched in the language of rechristianisation which had become such a familiar feature of militant Catholic rhetoric during the interwar years. As the Belgian leaders of the newly-founded MPF declared at their inaugural study week in the spring of 1945, their purpose was to "reconquer the working class to Christ".[42] But there was now also a recognition that reconversion was not the sole or even the primary need, which lay instead in a broader liberation of the workers from what one Belgian Catholic trade unionist and putative UDB politician termed "the triple oppression of machines, of money and of material appetites".[43] It was this novel emphasis upon what the President of the Belgian MPF called in 1945 "a real liberation" of the working class[44] which made the Left Catholicism of the 1940s much more than a fusion of themes inherited from the social Catholicism of the 1890s and the Catholic militancy of the interwar years. The activists of the 1940s owed much to both of these traditions but they also brought to it a new and more material focus which reflected the particular atmosphere of social and spiritual urgency fostered by the war. Liberation had ceased to be an abstract metaphor but had become a package of social and more especially economic changes which would render possible the achievement of a regime of material well-being and human dignity for all working people.[45]

The possible political trajectories which emerged out of this wartime radicalisation varied considerably. A very few, as is well known, were tempted by the *main tendue* offered by communism[46]; while many more, often strongly influenced by their experiences in Resistance groups, aspired to cre-

---

40. The wartime social history of the working class remains a remarkably understudied field. For a vivid first-hand description, see Rapport du Capitaine Drapier, 10 Jan. 1945, RAB, Van Acker Papers, 498. See also Behan, *The Long Awaited Moment*; Kirk, "Nazi Austria: the limits of dissent".
41. Tranvouez, "Un cryptocommunisme catholique?", 236-237.
42. "Introduction", *Mouvement Populaire des Familles. Première Semaine d'Etudes*, 3.
43. Fafchamps, *L'UDB et les travailleurs*, 8.
44. Michel, "Ascension des travailleurs et mission du MPF", 21.
45. The example of the largely industrial diocese of Tournai in Western Belgium well demonstrates the new radical momentum given to existing structures of social Catholicism by the German Occupation: Maerten, "Le clergé du diocèse de Tournai", 127-165.
46. See the contribution of Yvon Tranvouez to this volume as well as Tranvouez, "Un cryptocommunisme catholique?", 227-239 and Kelly, "Catholics and Communism in Liberation France", 187-202.

ate a new progressive politics which would transcend the confessional frontier between Catholics and non-Catholics.[47] More profoundly, however, the Left Catholic movements formed an important element of the intellectual and political trends which contributed to the emergence of the Christian Democratic parties in postwar Europe. This was particularly so in certain of the newly-liberated territories of Western Europe, such as northern Italy, northeastern France, Belgium and the southern Netherlands, where the combination of political radicalisation, economic suffering and spiritual engagement created a radical nexus of forces which provided the initial momentum behind the foundation of parties such as the MRP, the *Democrazia cristiana* (DC) and the PSC-CVP. In these areas, ideas of a Catholic-inspired transformation of the political and more especially social order, as expressed most dramatically in the revolutionary language of the founding programme of the MRP[48], possessed a plausibility and an urgency which motivated a largely new generation of Catholic militants to devote their energies to the doctrinal and organisational construction of the new parties.[49]

Any attempt to construct a dichotomy between Left Catholicism and the Christian Democracy of the immediate postwar era would therefore be misleading. Indeed, it was the subsequent development of Christian Democracy into a predominantly centre-right political force which caused Left Catholicism to become defined as a dissident and ultimately heretical force within the postwar Catholic world. In this respect, it was not so much Left Catholicism which changed as Christian Democracy itself. The evolution of Christian Democracy from its radical origins in the latter war years to the conservative movement of the 1950s could not have been prevented. As this article has sought to demonstrate, the forces which lay behind a conservative and defensive "reconfessionalisation" of Catholicism were simply more powerful than the actions of isolated intellectual and political elites. Both, however, contributed to the distinctive character of Catholicism in the later 1940s and 1950s which, while presiding politically over the postwar reconstruction of Western Europe, retained within it the intellectual components of a profound critique of the liberal and individualist values which underpinned that same process of reconstruction.

---

47. Durand, *L'Europe de la Démocratie Chrétienne*, 220-226; Winock, *Histoire politique de la revue "Esprit"*, 256-266.
48. Letamendia, *Le Mouvement Républicain Populaire*, 77.
49. Codaccioni, "Le M.R.P. à travers le journal *Nord-Eclair*", 543-561; Van den Wijngaert, *Onstaan en stichting van de CVP-PSC*. See also Ricquier, "Auguste De Schryver", 27.

ABBREVIATIONS

ACA	Assemblée des Cardinaux et Archevêques
ACJF	Association Catholique de la Jeunesse Française
ACLI	Assoziazione Cristiane dei Lavoratori Italiani
ACMO	Association Chrétienne du Mouvement Ouvrier
ACO	Action Catholique Ouvrière
ACW	Algemeen Christelijk Werkersverbond
AFO	Associations Familiales Ouvrières
APF	Associations Populaires Familiales
APFS	Associations Populaires Familiales Syndicales
BIR	Bulletin d'Information et de Recherche
BLP	British Labour Party
BSP	Belgische Socialistische Partij
CCI	Confederazione delle Cooperative Italiane
CCO	Centre de Culture Ouvrière
CDA	Christlich Demokratische Arbeitnehmerschaft
CDU	Christlich Demokratische Union
CFDT	Confédération Française Démocratique du Travail
CFTC	Confédération Française des Travailleurs Chrétiens
CGIL	Confederazione Generale Italiana del Lavoro
CGT	Confédération Générale du Travail
CGT-FO	Confédération Générale du Travail-Force Ouvrière
CIL	Confederazione Italiana dei Lavoratori
CISC	Confédération Internationale des Syndicats Chrétiens
CISL	Confederazione Italiana Sindacati Lavoratori
CLCV	Consommation, Logement et Cadre de Vie
CLN	Comitato di Liberazione Nazionale
CLNAI	Comitato di Liberazione Alta Italia
CNR	Conseil National de la Résistance
CNV	Christelijk Nationaal Vakverbond
CSC	Confédération des Syndicats Chrétiens
CSCU	Corrente Sindacale Cristiana Unitaria
CSCV	Confédération Syndicale du Cadre de Vie
CSF	Confédération Syndicale des Familles
CSU	Christlich-Soziale Union
CVP	Christelijke Volkspartij
DC	Democrazia Cristiana
DGB	Deutscher Gewerkschaftsbund
DP	Deutsche Partei
DZ	Deutsche Zentrumspartei
FDP	Freie Demokratische Partei
FGTB	Fédération Générale des Travailleurs de Belgique

FIMOC	Fédération Internationale des Mouvements Ouvriers Catholiques
FR	Fédération Républicaine
FUCI	Federazione degli Universitari Cattolici
GIAC	Gioventù Italiana Azione Cattolica
GIOC	Gioventù Italiana Operaia Cristiana
GRMF	Groupement pour la Recherche sur les Mouvements Familiaux
ICAS	Instituto Cattolico di Attività Sociali
ICFTU	International Confederation of Free Trade Unions
JAC(F)	Jeunesse Agricole Catholique (Féminine)
JEC	Jeunesse Etudiante Chrétienne
JOC(F)	Jeunesse Ouvrière Chrétienne (Féminine)
JR	Jeune République
KAB	Katholische Arbeiterbewegung
KPD	Kommunistische Partei Deutschlands
LAC	Ligue Agricole Catholique
LOC(F)	Ligue Ouvrière Chrétienne (Féminine)
MCC	Movimento dei Cattolici Comunisti
MCI	Movimento dei Cristiani Indipendenti
MCL	Movimento Cristiano del Lavoro
MCP	Movimento Cristiano per la Pace
MCS	Movimento Cristiano Sociale
MFR	Mouvement Familial Rural
MLC	Movimento dei Lavoratori Cristiani
MLO	Mouvement de Libération Ouvrière
MLP	Mouvement de Libération du Peuple
MOC	Mouvement Ouvrier Chrétien
MPF	Mouvement Populaire des Familles
MPL	Movimento Politico dei Lavoratori
MRP	Mouvement Républicain Populaire
MSC	Movimento di Sinistra Cristiana
MSC	Movimento Socialista Cristiano
MUCP	Movimento Unitario dei Cristiani Progressisti
NVB	Nederlandse Volksbeweging
OCM	Organisation Civile et Militaire
ÖGB	Österreichische Gewerkschaftsbund
ONARMO	Opera Nazionale Assistenza Religiosa e Morale degli Operai
ÖVP	Österreichische Volkspartei
OVP	Ouvriers de la Vierge des Pauvres
PCA	Pontificia Commissione di Assistenza
PCC	Partito Comunista Cristiano
PCF	Parti Communiste Français
PCI	Partito Comunista Italiano
PDA	Partito d'Azione

PDP	Parti Démocrate Populaire
POA	Pontificia Opera di Assistenza
PPI	Partito Popolare Italiano
PSA	Parti Socialiste Autonome
PSC	Parti Social Chrétien
PSC	Partito della Sinistra Cristiana
PSDI	Partito Socialista Democratico Italiano
PSI	Partito Socialista Italiano
PSIUP	Partita Socialista Italiano di Unità Proletaria
PSLI	Partito Socialista dei Lavoratori Italiani
PSU	Parti Socialiste Unifié
RDR	Rassemblement Démocratique Révolutionnaire
RPF	Rassemblement du Peuple Français
RSI	Repubblica Sociale Italiana
SBZ	Sowjetische Besatzungszone
SDS	Sozialistischen Deutschen Studentenbund
SED	Sozialistische Einheitspartei Deutschlands
SFIO	Section Française de l'Internationale Ouvrière
SGEN	Syndicat Général de l'Éducation Nationale
SPD	Sozialdemokratische Partei Deutschlands
STO	Service du Travail Obligatoire
UCP	Union des Chrétiens Progressistes
UDAF	Union Départementale des Associations Familiales
UDB	Union Démocratique Belge
UDSR	Union Démocratique et Socialiste de la Résistance
UGS	Union de la Gauche Socialiste
UIL	Unione Italiana del Lavoro
UNAF	Union Nationale des Associations Familiales
USI	Unione dei Socialisti Indipendenti
WFTU	World Federation of Trade Unions

BIBLIOGRAPHY

A propos du document romain sur la question syndicale. Discours de Jules Zirnheld. Brochure n° 1, Lille: Éditions du "Nord social", s.a. [speech delivered on 6 October 1929].

Adam, G. La CFTC 1940-1958: histoire politique et ideologique. Paris: Colin, 1964.

Adoumié, V. "Le réveil religieux landais au XXe siècle". Annales du Midi, 108 (1996) 377-394.

Agostino, M. Le pape Pie XI et l'opinion publique (1922-1939). Rome: Ecole Française de Rome, 1991.

"Das Ahlener Wirtschaftsprogramm, February 1947" in: W. Mommsen, ed. Deutsche Parteiprogramme. Munich: Isar, 1960, 576-582.

Alessandrini, A. "Guido Miglioli e il Movimento cristiano per la pace" in F. Leonori, ed. La figura e l'opera di Guido Miglioli 1879-1979. Rome: Quaderni del Centro di documentazione dei cattolici democratici, 1981, 209-239.

Allen, L. "Resistance and the Catholic Church in France" in S. Hawes and R. White, eds. Resistance in Europe: 1939-1945. Middlesex, England: Penguin Books, 1976 [1975], 77-93.

Alessandrini, A. " Incontri e scontri con Gerardo Bruni. Dalla Biblioteca Vaticana alle lotte del dopoguerra per la democrazia e per la pace" in A. Parisella, ed. Gerardo Bruni e i cristiano-sociali. Rome: Edizioni Lavoro, 1984, 247-274.

Altermatt, U. Katholizismus und Moderne. Zur Sozial- und Mentalitätsgeschichte der Schweizer Katholiken im 19. und 20. Jahrhundert. Zürich: Benziger, 1989.

Andolfatto, D. "Attitudes religieuses et implications syndicales" in P. Bréchon, B. Duriez and J. Ion, eds. Religion et action dans l'espace public. Paris, 2000.

Antisozialismus aus Tradition? Memorandum des Bensberger Kreises zum Verhältnis von Christentum und Sozialismus heute. Reinbek near Hamburg: Rowohlt, 1976.

Antonetti, N. L'ideologia della Sinistra cristiana. I cattolici tra Chiesa e comunismo (1937-1945). Milan: Angeli, 1976.

Antonetti, N., De Siervo, U. and Malgeri, F., eds. (introduction by G. De Rosa). I cattolici democratici e la Costituzione. 3 vols. Bologna: Il Mulino, 1998.

Ardigò, A. "Jacques Maritain e 'Cronache Sociali' (ovvero Maritain e il dossettismo)" in G. Galeazzi, ed. Il pensiero politico di Jacques Maritain. Milan: Massimo, 1974, 195-202.

Arnal, O.L. "Beyond the Walls of Christendom: The Engagement of the Mission de France and its Seminary (1941-1954)". Contemporary French Civilisation, 7 (Fall 1982) 1, 41-62.

Arnal, O.L. "A Missionary Main Tendue Toward French Communists: The Témoignages of the Worker-Priests". French Historical Studies, 13 (Fall 1984) 4, 529-556.

Arnal, O.L. Ambivalent Alliance: The Catholic Church and the Action Française. Pittsburgh: University of Pittsburgh Press, 1985.

Arnal, O.L. Priests in Working-Class Blue: The History of the Worker-Priests (1943-1954). New York: Paulist Press, 1986.

Arnal, O.L. "Toward a Lay Apostolate of the Workers: Three Decades of Conflict for the French Jeunesse Ouvrière Chrétienne (1927-1956)". The Catholic Historical Review, 73 (1987) 211-227.

Arnal, O.L. "Theology and Commitment: Marie-Dominique Chenu". Cross Currents, 28, 1, 71-75.

Atti dell'VIII Congresso Tomistico Internazionale sull'enciclica Aeterni Patris 8-13 sett. 1980. 2 vols. Vatican City: Ed. Vaticana, 1981.

Aubert, P. "Léon XIII" in *I Cattolici italiani dall'800 ad oggi*. Brescia,1963, 205-206.

Aubert, R. "Aspects divers du néo-thomisme sous le pontificat de Léon XIII" in G. Rossini, ed. *Aspetti della cultura cattolica nell'età di Leone XIII. Atti del convegno tenuto a Bologna il 27-28-29 dicembre 1960*. Rome: Lune, 1961, 133-227.

Aubert, R. "Le contexte historique et les motivations doctrinales de l'encyclique 'Aeterni Patris'" in B. d'Amore, ed. *Tommaso d'Aquino nel I centenario dell'enciclica "Aeterni Patris"*. Rome, 1981, 15-48.

Auer, A. "Vorwort" in: T. Steinbüchel. *Sozialismus*. Gesammelte Aufsätze zur Geistesgeschichte 1 (A. Auer, ed.). Tübingen, 1950.

Augros, L. *De l'église d'hier à l'Église de demain: L'aventure de la Mission de France*. Paris: Cerf, 1980.

Avon, D. "Le pèlerinage du Puy 12-15 août 1942". *Revue d'histoire de l'Eglise de France*, 83 (1997) 395-434.

Bacharan-Gressel, N. "Les Organisations et les Associations Pro-européennes" in S. Berstein, ed. *Le MRP et la Construction européenne*. Brussels: Complexe, 1993.

Baget Bozzo, G. "Il fascismo e l'evoluzione del pensiero politico cattolico". *Storia contemporanea*, 4 (1974) 671-697.

Baget-Bozzo, G. *Il partito cristiano al potere. La DC di De Gasperi e di Dossetti 1945-1954*. Florence: Vallecchi, 1974.

Balbo, F. "La sfida storica del comunismo al cristianesimo e le sue conseguenze filosofico sociali". *Il Mulino*, 77 (1958). (reprinted in F. Balbo, *Opere*, introduction by M. Ranchetti. Torino: Boringhieri, 1966, 333-334).

Balducci, E. *Giorgio La Pira*. S. Domenico di Fiesole: Edizioni Cultura della Pace, 1986.

Bank, J. *Opkomst en ondergang van de Nederlandse Volksbeweging (NVB)*. Deventer: Kluwer, 1978.

Barrau, G. *Le Mai 68 des catholiques*. Paris, 1998.

Barré, J.-L. *Jacques et Raïssa Maritain: les mendiants du ciel*. Paris, [1995].

Bartolozzi Batignani, S. *Dai progetti cristiano-sociali alla Costituente. Il pensiero economico di Paolo Emilio Taviani*. Florence: Le Monnier, 1985.

Bedani, G. *Politics and Ideology in the Italian Workers' Movement. Union Development and the Changing Role of the Catholic and Communist Subcultures in Postwar Italy*. Oxford-Providence: Berg, 1995.

Bédarida, R. *Les Armes de l'Esprit, Témoignage Chrétien (1941-1944)*. Paris: Éditions Ouvrières, 1977.

Bedeschi, L. *La Sinistra cristiana e il dialogo con i comunisti*. Parma: Guanda, 1963.

Bedeschi, L. *Cattolici e comunisti. Dal socialismo cristiano ai cristiani marxisti*. Milan: Feltrinelli, 1974.

Bedeschi, L. et al. *I cristiani nella sinistra dalla Resistenza a oggi*. Rome: Coines, 1976.

Bedeschi, L. *L'ultima battaglia di don Mazzolari: "Adesso" 1949-1959*. Brescia: Morcelliana, 1990.

Beerten, W. *Le rêve travailliste en Belgique. Histoire de l'UDB 1944-1947*. Histoire du mouvement ouvrier en Belgique 11. Brussels: Vie Ouvrière, 1990.

Behan, T. *The Long Awaited Moment. The Working Class and the Italian Communist Party in Milan 1943-1948*. New York, 1997.

Beinaert, L. *Pour un christianisme de choc*. Brussels, 1943.

Bellò, C. *Primo Mazzolari. Biografia e documenti*. Brescia: Queriniana, 1978.

Belouet, E. "La JOC et les organisations syndicales (1927-1997)". *Cahiers de l'Atelier*, 484 (April-June 1999).

Belouet, E. and Viet-Depaule, N. "Albert Bouche ou l'itinéraire d'un frontalier". *Cahiers de l'Atelier*, (2000).

Benoît, G. et al. *Le Ciel était Rouge*. Nancy: Éditions Serpenoise, 1994.

Bergamaschi. *Presenza di Mazzolari. Un contestatore per tutte le stagioni*. Bologna: Edizioni Dehoniane, 1986.

Berstein, S. et al., eds. *Le MRP et la construction européenne*. Brussels: Complexe, 1993.

Berti, E. and Campanini, G., eds. *Dizionario delle idee politiche*. Rome: Ave, 1993.

Bertini, B. and Casadio, S. *Clero e industria a Torino. Ricerca sui rapporti tra clero e masse operaie nella capitale dell'auto dal 1943 al 1948*. Milan: Franco Angeli, 1979.

Béthouart, B. "L'apport socio-économique de la démocratie chrétienne en France'"in E. Lamberts, ed. *Christian Democracy in the European Union. Proceedings of the Leuven Colloquium, 15-18 November 1995*. KADOC-Studies 21. Leuven: Leuven University Press, 1997, 336-362.

Béthouart, B. *Des syndicalistes chrétiens en politique. De la Libération à la Ve République (1944-1962)*. Lille: Presses universitaires du Septentrion, 1999.

Beyer, G. "Erinnerungen an einen 'vergessenen Brückenschlag'". *Neue Gesellschaft/ Frankfurter Hefte*, 32 (1985) 80-86.

Bianchi Iacono, C. *Aspetti dell'opposizione dei cattolici di Milano alla Repubblica Sociale Italiana*. Brescia: Morcelliana, 1998.

Bichet, R. *La démocratie chrétienne en France: Le Mouvement Républicain Populaire*. Besançon: Jacques et Demontrond, 1980.

Blessing, W. "'Deutschland in Not, wir im Glauben...'. Kirche und Kirchenvolk in einer katholischen Region, 1933-1949" in M. Broszat, K.-D. Henke and H. Woller, eds. *Von Stalingrad zur Währungsreform. Zur Sozialgeschichte des Umbruchs in Deutschland*. Munich, 1988, 3-111.

Bocchini Camaiani, B. and Giuntella, M.C., eds. *Cattolici, Chiesa, Resistenza nell'Italia centrale*. Bologna: Il Mulino, 1997.

Boffi, G. "Domenico Ravaioli e 'Politica d'oggi'. Alle origini della DC romana" in F. Malgeri, ed. *Storia della DC*. Rome: Cinque Lune, 1987, IV, 347-396.

Boland, C. *Dure perçée: récit d'un premier prêtre-ouvrier (1924-1964)*. Brussels: Foyer Notre Dame, 1968.

Botti, A. *Religione, questione cattolica e DC nella politica comunista 1944-45*. Rimini: Maggioli, 1981.

Boucault, P. "La représentation des usagers dans les élections sociales" in GRMF. *La solidarité en actes. Services collectifs et expression des usagers dans le Mouvement Populaire des Familles 1940-1955*. Les Cahiers du GRMF 11. Villeneuve d'Ascq, 2000.

Bouckaert, G. "Mounier en de beweging rond Esprit" in L. Bouckaert and G. Bouckaert, eds. *Metafysiek en engagement: Een personalistische visie op gemeenschap en economie*. Leuven: Acco, 1992, 123-142.

Boulard, F. *Problèmes missionaires de la France rurale*. Paris: Cerf, 1945.

Bourdais, H. *La JOC sous l'occupation allemande*. Paris: Les Editions de l'Atelier - Editions Ouvrières, 1995.

Bousquet, H. *Hors des barbelés*. Paris: Spes, 1946^2.

Branciard, M. *Histoire de la CFDT. Soixante-dix ans d'action syndicale*. Paris: La Découverte, 1990.

Brauer, T. *Der soziale Katholizismus in Deutschland im Lichte von Quadragesimo Anno*. Religiöse Quellenschriften 96. Düsseldorf, 1935.

Bréchon, P. and Denni, B. *Attitudes religieuses et politiques des catholiques pratiquants. Enquête par questionnaire dans huit assemblées dominicals grenobloises*. Grenoble: BDSP-IEP, 1982.

Brena, G.L. and Pirola, G. *Movimenti cristiani di sinistra e marxismo in Italia*. Assisi: Cittadella, 1978.

Bressolette, M. "Jacques Maritain et la guerre civile en Espagne". *Cahiers Jacques Maritain*, 9 (April 1984) 33-42.

Brezzi, C. *Il cattolicesimo politico in Italia nel '900*. Milan: Teti, 1979.

Brizzolari, B. *Un archivio della Resistenza genovese. [L'archivio cospirativo di Paolo Emilio Taviani]*. Genova: Di Stefano, 1974.

Bröckling, U. "Einleitung" in: W. Dirks. *Sozialismus oder Restauration. Politische Publizistik 1945-1950*. Gesammelte Schriften 4. Zürich, 1987, 11-32.

Bröckling, U. "Einleitung" in: W. Dirks. *Sagen was ist. Politische Publizistik 1950-1968*. Gesammelte Schriften 5. Zürich, 1988, 15-40.

Bröckling, U. *Katholische Intellektuelle in der Weimarer Republik. Zeitkritik und Gesellschaftstheorie bei Walter Dirks, Romano Guardini, Carl Schmitt, Ernst Michel und Heinrich Mertens*. Munich, 1993.

Bröckling, U. "Der 'Dritte Weg' und die 'Dritte Kraft'. Zur Konzeption eines sozialistischen Europas in der Nachkriegspublizistik von Walter Dirks" in: J. Köhler and D. van Melis, eds. *Siegerin in Trümmern. Die Rolle der katholischen Kirche in der deutschen Nachkriegs-gesellschaft*. Konfession und Gesellschaft 15. Stuttgart, 1998, 70-84.

Brodier, J. and Bouladoux, M. *Problèmes de syndicalisme international*. Paris: CFTC, [1945].

Buchanan, T. and Conway, M., eds. *Political Catholicism in Europe 1918-1965*. Oxford: Clarendon Press, 1996.

Callot, E.-F. *L'Action et l'oeuvre politique du Mouvement Républicain Populaire*. Paris: Champion-Slatkine, 1986.

Campanini, G. *Fede e politica 1943-1951. La vicenda ideologica della sinistra d c*. Brescia: Morcelliana, 1976.

Campanini, G. *Cristianesimo e democrazia. Studi sul pensiero politico cattolico del '900*. Brescia: Morcelliana, 1980.

Campanini, G. "I programmi del partito democratico-cristiano (1942-1947)" in B. Gariglio, ed. *Cristiani in politica. I programmi politici dei movimenti cattolici democratici*. Milan: Angeli, 1987, 183-211.

Campanini, G. *Don Primo Mazzolari fra religione e politica*. Bologna, 1989.

Campanini, G. and Traniello, F., eds. *Dizionario storico del movimento cattolico in Italia*. 5 vols. Casale Monferrato: Marietti, 1981 (revised edition 1997).

Campanini, G. and Trufelli, M., eds. *Mazzolari e "Adesso". Cinquant'anni dopo*. Brescia: Morcelliana, 2000.

Caracciolo, A. *Teresio Olivelli*. Brescia: La Scuola, 1975.

Carew, A. *Labour under the Marshall Plan. The Politics of Productivity and the Marketing of Management Science*. Manchester: Machester University Press, 1987.

Caron, J. *Le Sillon et la démocratie chrétienne 1894-1910*. Paris: Plon, 1967.

Casella, M. *Igino Giordani. "La pace comincia da noi"*. Rome, 1990.

Casella, M. *L'Azione Cattolica nell'Italia contemporanea (1919-1969)*. Rome: AVE, 1992.

Casula, C.F. *Cattolici-comunisti e sinistra cristiana (1938-1945)*. Bologna: Il Mulino, 1976.

Casula, F. *Guido Miglioli. Fronte democratico popolare e Costituente della terra*. Rome: Edizioni Lavoro, 1981.

Cesbron, G. *Les Saints vont en enfer*. Paris: R. Laffont, 1952.

Chauvière, M. "Le baptême républicain de l'Union nationale des associations familiales". *Les Cahiers de l'Animation*, INEP, 57/58 (December 1986).

Chauvière, M. "Mobilisation familiale et intérêts familiaux" in M. Chauvière et al. *Les implicites de la politique familiale*. Paris: Dunod, 2000.

BIBLIOGRAPHY

Chauvière, M. "Une entrée en politique: les catholiques sociaux du Mouvement Populaire des Familles dans le compromis familialiste de 1945" in *Chrétiens et ouvriers de la fin des années 1930 au début des années 1970*. Paris: Archives de France-Editions de l'Atelier, forthcoming.

Chenaux, P. *Une Europe Vaticane? Entre le Plan Marshall et les Traités de Rome*. Brussels: Ciaco, 1990.

Chenu, M.-D. *Pour une théologie du travail*. Paris: Seuil, 1955.

Chiodi, *Primo Mazzolari. Un testimone in Cristo con l'anima del profeta*. Milan: Centro Ambrosiano, 1998.

Cholvy, G. and Hilaire, Y.M., eds. *Histoire religieuse de la France contemporaine*. Toulouse: Privat, 1985.

Christophe, P. *1936, les catholiques et le front populaire*. Paris: Éditions Ouvrières, 1986.

Christophe, P. *1939-1940: les catholiques devant la guerre*. Paris: Éditions Ouvrières, 1989.

Ciampani, A. *La buona bataglia. Giulio Pastore e i cattolici sociali nella crisi dell' Italia liberale*. Milan: Franco Agnelli, 1990.

Ciampani, A. "Attori sociali e dinamiche internazionali durante la riconstruzione democratica: I processi per l'unità sindacale nel sindacalismo tedesco" in M. Antonioli et al., eds. *Le scissioni sindacali. Italia e Europa*. Milan-Pisa: BFS Edizioni, 1999, 89-113.

Ciceri, G. and Gazzi, E., eds. *Zeno. Un'intervista, una vita*. Florence: Libreria Editrice Fiorentina, 1986.

Clément, J.-L. *Monseigneur Saliège, archevêque de Toulouse 1929-1956*. Paris, 1994.

Cocchi, M. and Montesi, P., eds. *Per una storia della Sinistra cristiana. Documenti 1937-1945*. Rome: Coines, 1976.

Coco, J.-P. and Debès, J. *1937, L'élan jociste. Le dixième anniversaire de la JOC-Paris-juillet 1937*. Paris: Editions Ouvrières, 1989.

Codaccioni, F.-P. "Le M.R.P. à travers le journal *Nord-Eclair* de septembre 1944 à mai 1947". *Revue du Nord*, 57 (1975) 543-561.

Cole-Arnal, O. "Shaping Young Proletarians into Militant Christians: The Pioneer Phase of the JOC in France and Quebec". *Journal of Contemporary History*, 32 (1997) 4, 509-526.

Cole-Arnal, O.-L. "Roman Catholic Church in France" in B.M. Gordon, ed. *Historical Dictionary of World War II France*. Westport, Connecticut: Greenwood Press, 1998, 318-320.

Comte, B. *L'honneur et la conscience: Catholiques français en Résistance 1940-1944*. Paris: Atelier, 1998.

Conway, M. "Building the Christian City. Catholics and Politics in Inter-war Francophone Belgium". *Past and Present*, 128 (August 1990) 117-151.

Conway, M. *Collaboration in Belgium. Leon Degrelle and the Rexist Movement 1940-1944*. New Haven: Yale University Press, 1993.

Conway, M. "Introduction" in T. Buchanan and M. Conway, eds. *Political Catholicism in Europe 1918-1965*. Oxford: Clarendon Press, 1996.

Conway, M. *Catholic Politics in Western Europe 1918-1945*. London-New York: Routledge, 1997.

Conway, M. "The Age of Christian Democracy. The Frontiers of Success and Failure" in T. Kselman, ed. *Christian Democracy: Comparative Perspectives and Future Prospects*. Notre Dame Ind., forthcoming.

Cornwell, J. *Hitler's Pope: The Secret History of Pius XII*. London: Viking, 1999.

Coutrot, A. *Élites et militants dans la société française contemporaine*. Rapport pour le doctorat de science politique, Institut d'études politiques de Paris, 1983.

Crouch, C. *Trade Unions: The Logic of Collective Action*. Glasgow: Fontana/Collins, 1982.

Cuminetti, M. *Il dissenso cattolico in Italia 1965-1980*. Milan: Rizzoli, 1983.

Curtis, D.E. *The French Popular Front and the Catholic Discovery of Marx*. Hull: University of Hull Press, 1997.

d'Abzac-Epezy, C. and Agostino, M. *De Gaulle et le Rassemblement du Peuple Français (1947-1955)*. Paris: Colin, 1998.

D'Attorre, P.P. "The European Recovery Program in Italy: Research Problems" in *The Role of the United States in the Reconstruction of Italy and West Germany, 1943-1949*. Papers presented at a German-Italian Colloquium held at the John F. Kennedy-Institut für Nordamerikastudien. Berlin, June 1980.

Dall'Asta, G. "Maritain e il movimento dossettiano" in R. Papini, ed. *Jacques Maritain e la società contemporanea*. Milan: Massimo, 1978, 275-289.

De Berranger, O. *Alfred Ancel: Un homme pour l'évangile, 1898-1984*. Paris: Centurion, 1988.

De Greef, D. *Les prêtres-ouvriers en Belgique*. Mém. de license, Université Catholique de Louvain, 1985.

De Jonghe, E. "Het integraal humanisme van Maritain" in L. Bouckaert and G. Bouckaert, eds. *Metafysiek en engagement: Een personalistische visie op gemeenschap en economie*. Leuven: Acco, 1992, 89-122.

De Rosa, G., ed. *Cattolici, Chiesa, Resistenza*. Bologna: Il Mulino, 1997.

De Rosa, G., ed. *I cattolici e la Resistenza nelle Venezie*. Bologna: Il Mulino, 1997.

De Soignie, P. *Culture et milieux populaires*. Tournai: Casterman, s.a.

De Soignie, P. *Leçons familières d'économie politique*. Paris: Casterman, 1945.

De Soignie, P. *Mystique chrétienne et ascension ouvrière*. Tournai: Casterman, 1946.

Debès, J. and Poulat, E. *L'Appel de la JOC, 1926-1928*. Paris: Cerf, 1986.

Debès, J. *Naissance de l'Action catholique ouvrière*. Paris: Editions Ouvrières, 1982.

Declich, A., ed. *Cristiani non democristiani*. Rome: Editori Riuniti, 1981.

Deighton, A. *The Impossible Peace: Britain, the Division of Germany, and the Origins of the Cold War*. New York: Oxford University Press, 1990.

Del Noce, A. *Il cattolico comunista*. Milan: Rusconi, 1981.

Delbreil, J.-C. *Centrisme et démocratie-chrétienne en France: Le Parti Démocrate Populaire des origines au MRP (1919-1949)*. Paris: Publications de la Sorbonne, 1990.

Delbreil, J.-C. *Marc Sangnier. Témoignages*. Paris: Beauchesne, 1997.

Deliat, R. *Vingt Ans chez Renault*. Paris: Éditions Ouvrières, 1973.

Department of State. *Germany 1947-1949. The Story in Documents*. Washington, 1950.

Deuerlein, E. *CDU/CSU 1945-1957*. Cologne, 1957.

Di Capua, G. *Come l'Italia aderì al patto Atlantico*. Rome, 1969

Dillard, V. *Suprême Témoignage*. Paris: Spes, 1946.

Dirks, W. "Das Wort Sozialismus". *Frankfurter Hefte*, 1 (1946) 628-643.

Dirks, W. "Die Zweite Republik. Zum Ziel und zum Weg der deutschen Demokratie". *Frankfurter Hefte*, 1 (1946) 12-24.

Dirks, W. "Rechts und links". *Frankfurter Hefte*, 1 (1946) 6, 24-37.

Dirks, W. "Marxismus in christlicher Sicht". *Frankfurter Hefte*, 2 (1947) 125-143.

Dirks, W. "Christen zum Marxismus. Bücher aus Frankreich, England und Deutschland". *Frankfurter Hefte*, 4 (1949) 175-177.

Dirks, W. "Der Kampf um die Mitbestimmung". *Frankfurter Hefte*, 5 (1950) 685-692.

Dirks, W. "Der restaurative Charakter der Epoche". *Frankfurter Hefte*, 5 (1950) 942-954.

Dirks, W. "Der Sozialismus als sittliche Idee (Theodor Steinbüchel)". *Die Mitarbeit*, 5 (1956/57) 3, 17-20.

Dirks, W. "Vergessene Brückenschläge. Das Gespräch mit dem Sozialismus 1918-1933" in W. Dirks. *Das schmutzige Geschäft? Die Politik und die Verantwortung der Christen.* Freiburg: Olten, 1964, 233-240.

Dirks, W. "Ein 'anderer' Katholizismus? Minderheiten im deutschen Corpus catholicorum". *Frankfurter Hefte*, 21 (1966) 247-260.

Dirks, W. "'Umwegiger Sozialismus'. Bemerkungen zur Gründung der CDU in Frankfurt vor 25 Jahren". *Kritischer Katholizismus*, 4 (1971) 6, 10-12.

Dirks, W. "Nachbemerkung" in W. Dirks, K. Schmidt and M. Stankowski, eds. *Christen für den Sozialismus.* Stuttgart, 1975, 159-160.

Dirks, W. *Der singende Stotterer.* Autobiographische Texte. Munich, 1983.

Dirks, W. "Vorläufer Ernst Michel". *Orientierung*, 50 (1986) 6, 69-71.

Dirks, W. "Thesen zu einer 'Sozialistischen Einheitspartei'" in W. Dirks. *Sozialismus oder Restauration. Politische Publizistik 1945-1950. Gesammelte Schriften 4.* Zürich, 1987, 33-36.

Dirks, W. "Vorwort" in W. Dirks. *Sozialismus oder Restauration. Politische Publizistik 1945-1950. Gesammelte Schriften 4.* Zürich, 1987, 5-10.

Dirks, W. *Sozialismus oder Restauration. Politische Publizistik 1945-1950. Gesammelte Schriften 4.* Zürich, 1987.

Dirks, W. "Das gesellschaftspolitische Engagement der deutschen Katholiken" [1964] in: W. Dirks. *Politik aus dem Glauben. Gesammelte Schriften 6.* Zürich, 1989, 73-99.

Dirks, W. *Bibliographie* (edited and introduced by U. Bröckling). Bonn: Archiv der sozialen Demokratie, Friedrich-Ebert Stiftung, 1991.

Dirks, W. and Glotz, P. "Jenseits von Optimismus und Pessimismus. Ein Gespräch". *Die Neue Gesellschaft / Frankfurter Hefte*, 36 (1989) 16-26.

Dirks, W., Schmidt, K. and Stankowski, M. "Einleitung: Christen für den Sozialismus" in W. Dirks, K. Schmidt and M. Stankowski, eds. *Christen für den Sozialismus. II. Dokumente (1945-1959).* Stuttgart, 1975, 7-10.

Divine, R.A. *Second Chance: The Triumph of Internationalism in America during World War II.* New York: Atheneum, 1967.

Don Lorenzo Milani tra Chiesa, cultura e scuola. Atti del Convegno su "Chiesa, cultura e scuola in don Milani" a venticinque anni dalla pubblicazione di Esperienze Pastorali. Milan: 1983.

Donegani, J.-M. *La liberté de choisir. Pluralisme religieux et pluralisme politique dans le catholicisme contemporain.* Paris: Presses de la Fondation nationale de sciences politiques, 1993.

Donegani, J.-M. "Identités religieuses et pluralité des rapports au monde" in P. Bréchon, B. Duriez and J. Ion, eds. *Religion et action dans l'espace public.* Paris: L'Harmattan, 2000.

Drapac, V. *War and Religion. Catholics in the Churches of Occupied Paris.* Washington DC, 1998.

Duhamel, E. *L'union démocratique et socialiste de la résistance. D'une résistance à l'autre.* Thèse d'histoire Université Paris-Sorbonne (Paris IV), 1993.

Dujardin, V. and Dumoulin, M. *Paul van Zeeland 1893-1973.* Brussels: Racine, 1997.

Duquesne, J. *Les catholiques français sous l'occupation.* Paris: Grasset, 1966.

Durand, J.-D. *L'église catholique dans la crise de l'Italie (1943-1948).* Rome: Ecole Française de Rome, 1991.

Durand, J.-D. "L'épiscopat italien" in J. Sainclivier and C. Bougeard, eds. *La Résistance et les Français.* Rennes, 1995, 95-108.

Durand, J.-D. *L'Europe de la démocratie chrétienne.* Brussels: Editions Complexe, 1995.

Durand, J.-D. "La mémoire de la démocratie chrétienne en 1945. Antécédents, expériences et combats" in E. Lamberts, ed. *Christian Democracy in the European Union 1945-1995. Proceedings of the Leuven Colloquium, 15-18 November 1995*. KADOC-Studies 21. Leuven: Leuven University Press, 1997, 13-26.

Duriez, B. and Chauvière, M. "Un dispositif de co-histoire dans l'étude des mouvements sociaux contemporains. Le Groupement pour la recherche sur les mouvements familiaux". *Politix*, 26 (second trimester 1994).

Elgey, G. *La République des illusions 1945-1951 ou la vie secrète de la IVe République*. Paris: Fayard, 1965.

Elia, L. "La Commissione dei 75, il dibattito costituzionale e l'elaborazione dello schema di Costituzione" in *Il Parlamento italiano*. XIV. Milan: Nuova Cei Informatica, s.a., 123-142.

Enciclopedia dell'antifascismo e della Resistenza. Milan-Rome, 1971.

Etienne, J.-M. *Le mouvement rexiste jusqu'en 1940*. Paris: Colin, 1968.

Fafchamps, J. *L'UDB et les travailleurs*. Brussels, [1945].

Falciatore, M., ed. *Il Codice di Camaldoli*. Special issue of *Civitas*, 2 (1988).

Fallaci, N. *Dalla parte dell'ultimo. Vita del prete Lorenzo Milani*. Milan: Milano Libri, 1974 (with additional and various new editions).

Farquharson, J. "From Unity to Division". *European History Quarterly*, 26 (1996) 1.

Faupin, J. *La Mission de France*. Paris: Casterman, 1960.

Fichter, M. *Besatzungsmacht und Gewerkschaften. Zur Entwicklung und Anwendung der US-Gewerkschaftspolitik in Deutschland 1944-1948*. Opladen: Westdeutscher Verlag, 1982.

Fievez, M. and Meert, J. *Cardijn*. Brussels: EVO, 1969.

Focke, F. *Sozialismus aus christlicher Verantwortung. Die Idee eines christlichen Sozialismus in der katholisch-sozialen Bewegung und in der CDU*. Wuppertal: Hammer, 1981.

Fogarty, M. *Christian Democracy in Western Europe 1820-1953*. London: Routledge and Kegan Paul, 1957.

Fonzi, F. "Mondo cattolico, democrazia cristiana e sindacato (1943-1955)" in S. Zaninelli, ed. *Il sindacato nuovo. Politica e organizzazione del movimento sindacale in Italia negli anni 1943-55*. Milan: Franco Agnelli, 1981, 717-820.

Formigoni, G. *L'Azione Cattolica Italiana*. Milan: Editrice Ancora, 1988.

Formigoni, G. "La memoria della guerra e della Resistenza nelle culture politiche del 'mondo cattolico' (1945-1955)". *Ricerche di storia politica*, (1996) 11, 7-42.

Formigoni, G. *La democrazia cristiana e l'alleanza occidentale (1943-1953)*. Bologna: Il Mulino, 1996.

Fouilloux, E. "Le catholicisme" in J.-M. Mayeur, ed. *Histoire du Christianisme*. XII. *Guerres mondiales et totalitarismes (1914-1958)*. Paris, 1990, 215-239.

Fouilloux, E. *Les chrétiens français entre crise et libération 1937-1947*. Paris: Seuil, 1997.

Fouilloux, E. *Une église en quête de liberté: La pensée catholique française entre modernisme et Vatican II 1914-1962*. Paris: Desclée de Brouwer, 1998.

Fourcade, M. "Jacques Maritain inspirateur de la Résistance". *Cahiers Jacques Maritain*, 32 (June 1996) 14-57.

Franceschini, C., Guerrieri, S. and Monina, G. *Le idee costituzionali della Resistenza*. Rome: Presidenza del Consiglio dei Ministri, 1996.

Frei, E. "Brot und Sinn. Katholizismus und Caritasarbeit in der Zusammenbruchgesellschaft 1945". *Historisches Jahrbuch*, 117 (1997) 129-146.

"Frankfurter Leitsätze vom September 1945". *Kritischer Katholizismus*, 4 (1971) 11-12.

Fumasi, E., ed. *Mezzo secolo di ricerca storiografica sul movimento cattolico in Italia dal 1861 al 1945: contributo a una bibliografia*. Brescia: La Scuola, 1995.

Gaddis, J.L. *We Now Know. Rethinking Cold War History*. New York: Oxford University Press, 1997.

Gaggero, A. *Vestìo da omo*. Florence: Giunti, 1991.

Galli, G. and Facchi, P. *La sinistra democristiana: Storia e ideologia*. Milan: Feltrinelli, 1962.

Gambino, A. *Storia del dopoguerra dalla liberazione al potere DC*. Bari: Laterza, 1975.

Gariglio, B., ed. *Cattolici e Resistenza nell'Italia settentrionale*. Bologna: Il Mulino, 1997.

Gaudio, A. "Balducci, Ernesto" in F. Traniello and G. Campanini, eds. *Dizionario storico del movimento cattolico. Aggiornamento 1980-1995*. Genova: Marietti, 1997, 234-236.

Gault, J.-P. *Histoire d'une fidélité: Témoignage Chrétien 1944-1956*. [Paris]: Témoignage Chrétien, [1962].

Georgi, F. *L'invention de la CFDT 1957-1970. Syndicalisme, catholicisme et politique dans la France d'expansion*. Paris: Les Éditions de l'Atelier/ Éditions Ouvrières/ CNRS, 1995.

Georgi, F. *Eugène Descamps, chrétien et syndicaliste*. Paris: Les Éditions de l'Atelier, 1997.

Gerard, E. *De katholieke partij in crisis. Partijpolitiek leven in België (1918-1940)*. Leuven: Kritak, 1985.

Gerard, E. *Église et mouvement ouvrier chrétien en Belgique. Sources inédites relatives à la direction générale des œuvres sociales 1916-1936*. Cahiers du Centre Interuniversitaire d'Histoire Contemporaine 102. Brussels-Leuven: Nauwelaerts, 1990.

Gerard, E. "Adaptation en temps de crise (1921-1924)" in E. Gerard and P. Wynants, eds. *Histoire du Mouvement Ouvrier Chrétien en Belgique*. KADOC-Studies 16. Leuven: Leuven University Press, 1994, I, 175-245.

Gerard, E. "Le MOC-ACW" in E. Gerard and P. Wynants, eds. *Histoire du mouvement ouvrier chrétien en Belgique*. KADOC-Studies 16. Leuven: Leuven University Press, 1994, II, 564-631.

Gerard, E. "Du parti catholique au P.S.C.-C.V.P." in W. Dewachter et al., eds. *Un parti dans l'histoire, 1945-1995. 50 ans d'action du Parti Social Chrétien*. Louvain-la-Neuve: Duculot, 1995, 11-32.

Gerard, E. "Van Katholieke Partij naar CVP" in W. Dewachter et al., eds. *Tussen staat en maatschappij: 1945/1995 Christen-Democratie in België*. Tielt: Lannoo, 1995, 13-27.

Gerard, E. "De Christelijke Volkspartij en het Sociaal Pact na de Bevrijding (1944-1948)" in D. Luyten and G. Vanthemsche, eds. *Het Sociaal Pact van 1944. Oorsprong, betekenis en gevolgen*. Brussels: VUB-Press, 1995, 325-344.

Gerard, E. "Christian Democracy in Belgium" in E. Lamberts, ed. *Christian Democracy in the European Union (1945-1995). Proceedings of the Leuven Collo-quium, 15-18 November 1995*. Leuven: Leuven University Press, 1997, 65-78.

Gérard-Libois, J. and Gotovitch, J. *Léopold III : de l'an 40 à l'éffacement*. Brussels, 1991.

Gerechtigkeit schafft Frieden. Der 73. Deutsche Katholikentag vom 31. August bis 4. September 1949 in Bochum. Paderborn, 1949.

Ginsborg, P. *A History of Contemporary Italy. Society and Politics 1943-1988*. London: Penguin Group, 1990.

Giovagnoli, A. "La Pontificia Commissione Assistenza e gli aiuti americani (1945-1948)". *Storia contemporanea*, 5-6 (1978) 1081-1111.

Giovanni, C. "Sull'integralismo cattolico". *Rivista di storia contemporanea*. VI. 1977.

Girardi, G. *Cristiani per il socialismo: perché?* Assisi: Cittadella, 1975.

Giuntella, M.C. "Cristiani nella storia. Il «caso Rossi» e i suoi riflessi nelle organizzazioni cattoliche di massa" in A. Riccardi, ed. *Pio XII*. Roma-Bari: Laterza, 1984, 347-377.

Giura Longo, R. *La sinistra cattolica in Italia. Dal dopoguerra al referendum*. Bari: De Donato, 1975.

Glisenti, M. and Elia, L., eds. *"Cronache sociali". Antologia.* San Giovanni Valdarno (Fi): Landi, 1965.

Godin, H. and Daniel, Y. *La France, pays de mission?* Paris: Abeille, 1943.

Gotovitch, J. C. Huysmans. *Geschriften en Documenten. De Belgische socialisten in Londen.* Antwerp: Standaard Antwerpen, 1981.

Gozzini, M. *Oltre gli steccati. Cattolici, laici e comunisti in Italia 1963-1993.* Milan: Sperling & Kupfer, 1994.

GRMF. *Les Mouvements familiaux populaires et ruraux.* Les Cahiers du GRMF 1. 1983.

GRMF. *De l'Action catholique au mouvement ouvrier. La déconfessionalisation du Mouvement populaire des familles. 1941-1950.* Les Cahiers du GRMF 2. 1984

GRMF. *L'action familiale ouvrière et la politique de Vichy.* Les Cahiers du GRMF 3. Villeneuve d'Asq, 1985.

GRMF. *Monde ouvrier, 1937-1957, une presse libre our des temps difficiles.* Les Cahiers du GRMF 4. 1986.

GRMF. *Femmes, famille et action ouvrière. Pratiques et responsabilités féminines dans les mouvements familiaux populaires (1935-1958).* Les Cahiers du GRMF 6. 1991.

GRMF. *La bataille des squatters et l'invention du droit au logement. 1945-1955.* Les Cahiers du GRMF 7. Villeneuve d'Ascq, 1992.

GRMF. *Une communauté brisée. Regards croisés sur la scission MLP-MLO de 1951.* Les Cahiers du GRMF 9. 1995.

GRMF. *La solidarité des actes. Services collectifs et expression des usagers dans le Mouvement populaire des familles. 1940-1955.* Les Cahiers du GRMF 11. Villeneuve d'Ascq, forthcoming.

Groux, G. and Mouriaux, R. *La CFDT.* Paris: Economica, 1989.

Guala, C. and Severini, R. "Dialogo, obbedienza, 'critica' e dissenso nel 'Gallo': momenti di una lunga presenza" in S. Ristuccia, ed. *Intellettuali cattolici tra riformismo e dissenso.* Milan: Edizioni di Comunità, 1975, 101-164.

Guasco, M. *Storia del clero in Italia dall'Ottocento a oggi.* Rome-Bari: Laterza, 1997.

Guellny, R. "Les antécédents de l'encyclique 'Humani Generis' dans les sanctions romains de 1942: Chenu, Charlier, Draguet". *Revue d'histoire ecclésiastique,* 81 (1986) 421-497.

Guerrier, C. *La Jeune République de 1912 à 1945.* Thèse d'état en droit. Université de Paris II, 1979.

Guizzardi, G. *L'unità dei cattolici in Italia. Origini e decadenza di un mito collettivo.* Milan: Guerini e associati, 1995.

Gurland, A.R.L. *Die CDU/CSU. Ursprünge und Entwicklung bis 1953.* Frankfurt am Main: Europäische Verlagsanstalt, 1980.

Haagdorens, L. "De mobilisatie van de katholieke zuil in de schoolstrijd tijdens het eerste jaar van de regering Van Acker (mei 1954-juli 1955)". *Revue belge d'histoire contemporaine,* 15 (1984) 3-70.

Habermas, J. "Zur philosophischen Diskussion um Marx und den Marxismus". *Philosophische Rundschau,* 5 (1957) 165-235.

Halls, W.D. *Politics, Society and Christianity in Vichy France.* Oxford: Berg, 1995.

Hamon, H. and Rotman, P. *La deuxième gauche. Histoire intellectuelle de la CFDT.* Paris: Ramsay, 1982.

Harmsen, G. and Reinalda, B. *Voor de bevrijding van de arbeid. Beknopte geschiedenis van de vakbeweging in Nederland.* Nijmegen: SUN, 1975.

Harper, J.L. *America and the Reconstruction of Italy, 1945-1948.* Cambridge: Cambridge University Press, 1986.

Hastings, A. "Catholic History from Vatican I to John Paul II" in A. Hastings, ed. *Modern Catholicism. Vatican II and After.* London-New York: SPCK, 1991.

Haunhorst, B. "Selbstbestellte Vermittler. Über katholische Intellektuelle in der Weimarer Republik". *Orientierung,* 57 (1993) 262-264.

Haurand, P.W. "Wilhelm Hohoff".
Frankfurter Hefte, 3 (1948) 161-165.

Hebblethwaite, P. *John XXIII. Pope of the Council*. London: Chapman, 1984.

Hebblethwaite, P. "Pope Pius XII: Chaplain of the Atlantic Alliance?" in C. Duggan and C. Wagstaff, eds. *Italy in the Cold war: Politics, Culture and Society 1948-1958*. Oxford: Berg, 1996.

Hedler, S. *Die katholischen Sozialisten. Darstellung und Kritik ihres Wirkens*. Hamburg, 1952.

Heilbronner, O. *Catholicism, Political Culture and the Countryside*. Ann Arbor, 1998.

Heimann, S. "Christlicher Sozialismus in der CDU" in T. Meyer et al., eds. *Lexikon des Sozialismus*. Cologne: Bund Verlag, 1986, 112-114.

Hellman, J. *Emmanuel Mounier and the New Catholic Left, 1930- 1950*. Toronto: University of Toronto Press, 1981.

Hellman, J. *The Knight-Monks of Vichy France, Uriage, 1940- 1945*. Kingston and Montreal: McGill-Queen's University Press, 1993.

Hemmerijckx, R. "La CMB dans la clandestinité: un syndicat entre la contestation et l'intégration" in *Chauffés au Rouge. Histoire de la Centrale des Metallurgistes de Belgique*. Ghent: Amsab, 1990, 363-420.

Het Internationaal Christelijk Vakverbond, 1937-1945. Van Parijs tot Brussel. Brussels: CISC, 1945.

Hildebrand, K. "Erhard" in *Staatslexikon*. II. Freiburg, 1986[7], 354-357.

Holmes, J.D. *The Papacy in the Modern World 1914-1978*. London, 1981.

Horn, G.-R. *European Socialists Respond to Fascism: Ideology, Activism and Contingency in the 1930s*. New York: Oxford University Press, 1996.

Houée, P. *Louis-Joseph Lebret: Un éveilleur d'humanité*. Paris: Atelier, 1997.

Hunold, G.W. "Theodor Steinbüchel - Leidenschaft für den Menschen. Zum 100. Geburtstag". *Theologische Quartalschrift*, 168 (1988) 230-234.

Huret, J.-M. and Combe, M. *Fidèle insoumission*. Paris: Cerf, 1999.

Hüttenberger, P. *Nordrhein-Westfalen und die Entstehung seiner parlamentarischen Demokratie*. Siegburg, 1973.

Ilari, V. "Le formazioni partigiani alla Liberazione" in *Commissione italiana di storia militare. L'Italia in guerra. Il sesto anno – 1945*. Rome, 1996.

Imhof, K. "Wiedergeburt der geistigen Landesverteidigung: Kalter Krieg in der Schweiz" in K. Imhof, H. Kleger and G. Romano, eds. *Konkordanz und Kalter Krieg*. Zürich, 1996, 184-204.

Isambert, F.-A. *Christianisme et classe ouvrière. Jalons pour une sociologie historique*. Tournai: Casterman, 1961.

Istituto nazionale di sociologia rurale, ed. *La riforma fondiaria: trent'anni dopo*. Milan: Angeli, 1979.

Jacquet, J. and Ancel, A. *Un militant ouvrier dialogue avec un évêque*. Paris: Éditions Ouvrières, 1982.

Jadoulle, J.-L. *La pensée de l'abbé Pottier (1849-1923). Contribution à l'histoire de la démocratie chrétienne en Belgique*. Louvain-la-Neuve: UCL-Collège Erasme, 1991.

Jadoulle, J.-L. "L'évolution du programme du Parti Social Chrétien / Christelijke Volkspartij (Noël 1945-1968): Éléments pour une histoire des idées sociales-chrétiennes" in W. Dewachter et al., eds. *Un parti dans l'histoire 1945/1995: 50 ans d'action du Parti Social Chrétien*. Louvain-la-Neuve: Duculot, 1996, 343-364.

Jadoulle, J.-L. *Chrétiens modernes? Regard sur quelques milieux intellectuels catholiques "progressistes" en Belgique francophone (1945-1958)*. Thèse de doctorat Histoire. Université Catholique de Louvain. Louvain-La-Neuve, 1999.

Jedin, H. "The Second Vatican Council" in H. Jedin and K. Repgen, eds. *History of the Church. X. The Church in the Modern Age*. London, 1981, 146-147.

Jervolino, D. *Questione cattolica e politica di classe*. Torino: Rosenberg & Sellier, 1979.

Judt, T. "Introduction" in T. Judt, ed. *Resistance and Revolution in Mediterranean Europe 1939-1948*. London-New York, 1989.

Julliard, J. and Winock, M., eds. *Dictionnaire des intellectuels français. Les personnes. Les lieux. Les moments.* Paris: Seuil, 1996.

Kaiser, J. "Um Deutschlands Schicksal" in *Deutschland und die Union. Die Berliner Tagung 1946. Reden und Aussprache.* Berlin, [1946], 5-21.

Kalyvas, S.N. *The Rise of Christian Democracy in Europe.* Ithaca-London: Cornell University Press, 1996.

Kaufmann, L. "Ansätze einer Theologie der Befreiung in Europa?" in H. Ludwig and W. Schroeder, eds. *Sozial- und Linkskatholizismus. Erinnerung - Orientierung - Befreiung.* Frankfurt am Main: Knecht, 1990, 261-284.

Keck, T. "Le père Montuclard, l'Action catholique et la mission (1936-1940)". *Revue d'histoire de l'Eglise de France*, 209 (July-December 1996) 301-310.

Kelly, M. "Catholics and Communism in Liberation France, 1944-47" in F. Tallett and N. Atkin, eds. *Religion, Society and Politics in France since 1789*. London-Rio Grande, 1991, 187-202.

Kesler, J.-F. "La Jeune République. 1912-1947". *Revue d'histoire moderne et contemporaine.* (January-March 1978) 61-85.

Kesler, J.-F. *De la Gauche dissidente au nouveau Parti Socialiste. Les minorités qui ont rénové le PS.* Toulouse: Bibliothèque historique Privat, 1990.

Kirk, T. "Nazi Austria: the limits of dissent" in T. Kirk and A. McElligott, eds. *Opposing Fascism. Community, Authority and Resistance in Europe.* Cambridge, 1999, 133-149.

Klijn, A. *Arbeiders- of volkspartij: een vergelijkende studie van het Belgisch en Nederlands socialisme 1933-1946.* Maastricht: Universitaire Pers Maastricht, 1990.

Klönne, A. "Arbeiterkatholizismus. Zur Geschichte des Sozialkatholizismus in Deutschland" in H. Ludwig and W. Schroeder, eds. *Sozial- und Linkskatholizismus. Erinnerung-Orientierung-Befreiung.* Frankfurt am Main: Knecht 1990, 32-45.

Knapp, M. "US Economic Aid and the Reconstruction of West-Germany: Political and Economic Implications of the European Recovery Program" in *The Role of the United States in the Reconstruction of Italy and West Germany, 1943-1949. Papers presented at a German-Italian Colloquium held at the John F. Kennedy-Institut für Nordamerikastudien.* Berlin, June 1980.

Knappstein, K.H. "Die Stunde der Sozialreform". *Frankfurter Hefte*, 1 (1946) 3, 1-3.

Kogon, E. "Georges Bidault. Frankreichs Ministerpräsident". *Frankfurter Hefte*, 1 (1946) 664-666.

Kogon, E. "Fragende Erinnerung" in F. Boll, M. Linz and T. Seiterich, eds. *Wird es denn überhaupt gehen? Beiträge für Walter Dirks.* Munich, 1980, 255-262.

"Kölner Leitsätze (1945)" in *Die Geschichte der CDU. Programm und Politik der Christlich Demokratischen Union Deutschlands seit 1945.* Bonn: CDU-Bundesgeschäftsstelle, 1980, 10-13.

-Konrad Adenauer Stiftung. *Konrad Adenauer und die CDU der Britischen Besatzungszone. Dokumente zur Gründungsgeschichte der CDU Deutschlands.* Bonn, 1975.

Kosthorst, E. "Kaiser" in *Staatslexikon*. III. Freiburg, 1987⁷, 274-276.

Kreppel, K. "Feuer und Wasser. Katholische Sozialisten in der Weimarer Republik". *Kritischer Katholizismus*, 4 (1971) 6, 4-5.

Kriechbaumer, R. *Parteiprogramme im Widerstreit der Interessen: die Programmdiskussion und die Programme von ÖVP und SPÖ 1945-1986.* Österreichisches Jahrbuch für Politik. Vienna, 1990.

L'Internationale Syndicale Chrétienne 1937-1945. Utrecht: CISC, 1945.

La Jeunesse Ouvrière Chrétienne: Wallonie Bruxelles, 1912- 1957. I- II. Brussels: Vie Ouvrière, 1990.

La Pira o gli anni di "Principi". La riflessione su Tommaso d'Aquino e la lotta alla dittatura. Florence: Cultura nuova, 1993.

Lademacher, H. and Mühlhausen, W. "Die deutschen Westzonen - Wiederaufbau und Intervention. Bemerkungen zur Gewerkschafts- und Strukturpolitik der Besatzungs-mächte" in H.J. Langeveld, ed. *Zwischen Wunsch und Wirklichkeit. Die belgischen, niederländischen und westzonalen deutschen Gewerkschaften in der Phase des Wiederaufbaus 1945-1951*. Münster: Zentrum für Niederlande-Studien, Universität Münster, 1994, 431-550.

LaFeber, W. *America, Russia and the Cold War 1945-1992*. New York: McGraw-Hill, 1993.

Lamberts, E. "Du personnalisme au social-personnalisme (1968-1995)" in W. Dewachter et al., eds. *Un parti dans l'histoire, 1945-1995. 50 ans d'action du Parti Social Chrétien*. Louvain-la-Neuve: Duculot, 1995, 365-376.

Lamberts, E. "L'influence de la Démocratie chrétienne en Belgique sur l'ordre politique" in E. Lamberts, ed. *Christian Democracy in the European Union (1945-1995). Proceedings of the Leuven Colloquium, 15-18 November 1995*. Leuven: Leuven University Press, 1997, 254-269.

Lamberts, E. "General Conclusions: Christian Democracy in the European Union (1945-1995)" in E. Lamberts, ed. *Christian Democracy in the European Union (1945-1995). Proceedings of the Leuven Colloquium 15-18 November 1995*. KADOC-Studies 21. Leuven: Leuven University Press, 1997, 473-481.

Lamberts, E., ed. *Christian Democracy in the European Union. Proceedings of the Leuven Colloquium, 15-18 November 1995*. KADOC-Studies 21. Leuven: Leuven University Press, 1997.

Landshut, S. "Vorwort" in K. Marx. *Die Frühschriften* (edited by S. Landshut). Stuttgart, 1953.

Landshut, S. and Mayer, J.P. "Einleitung. Die Bedeutung der Frühschriften von Marx für ein neues Verständnis" in K. Marx. *Der historische Materialismus. Die Frühschriften* (edited by Landshut and Mayer with the assistance of Friedrich Salomon), I, Leipzig, 1932, XI-XLI.

Latreille, A. "La pensée catholique sur l'État depuis les dernières années du XIXe siècle" in *L'ecclésiologie au XIXe siècle*. Paris, 1960, 281-295.

Latreille, A. *De Gaulle, la libération et l'église catholique*. Paris: Cerf, 1978.

Laudouze, A. *Dominicains Français et Action Française*. Paris: Éditions Ouvrières, 1989.

Launay, M. *Syndicalisme chrétien en France. Origine et développement*. Paris: Desclée, 1984.

Launay, M. *La CFTC. Origines et développement 1919-1940*. Paris: Publications de la Sorbonne, 1986.

Laury, S. "Le culte marial dans le Pas-de-Calais (1938-1948)". *Revue d'histoire de la deuxième guerre mondiale*, 128 (1982) 23-47.

LeBras, G. *Introduction à l'histoire de la pratique religieuse en France*. 2 vols. Paris: Presses Universitaires de France, 1942-1945.

Lebret, L.-J. *Les professions maritimes à la recherche du bien commun*. Paris: Dunod, 1939.

Leonori, F., ed. *La figura e l'opera di Guido Miglioli 1879-1979*. Rome: Quaderni del Centro di documentazione dei cattolici democratici, 1981.

Leprieur, F. *Quand Rome condamne. Dominicains et prêtres-ouvriers*. Paris: Cerf/Plon, 1989.

Letamendia, P. *Le Mouvement Républicain Populaire. Histoire d'un grand parti français*. Paris: Beauchesne, 1995.

Lienkamp, A. "Die Herausforderung des Denkens durch den Schrei der Armen. Enrique Dussels Entwurf einer Ethik der Befreiung" in F. Hengsbach, B. Emunds and M. Möhring-Hesse, eds. *Jenseits Katholischer Soziallehre. Neue Entwürfe christlicher Gesellschaftsethik*. Düsseldorf: Patmos, 1993, 191-212.

Lienkamp, A. *Theodor Steinbüchels Sozialismusrezeption. Eine christlich-sozialethische Relecture*. Paderborn, 2000.

Loew, J. *Les Dockers de Marseille*. L'Arbresle: Économie et Humanisme, 1945.

Loew, J. *Mission to the Poorest* (translated by P. Carswell). London: Sheed and Ward, 1950.

Loew, J. *Journal d'une mission ouvrière*. Paris: Cerf, 1959.

Logan, O. "Pius XII: romanità, prophecy and charisma". *Modern Italy*, 3 (1998) 237-247.

Löhr, W. "Rechristianierungsvorstellungen im deutschen Katholizismus 1945-1948" in J.-C. Kaiser and A. Doering-Manteuffel, eds. *Christentum und politische Verantwortung. Kirchen im Nachkriegsdeutschland*. Stuttgart: Kohlhammer, 1990, 25-41.

Louis, R. and Bull, H. *The Special Relationship: Anglo-American Relations since 1945*. Oxford: Clarendon Press, 1989.

Ludwig, H. and Schroeder, W. "Einleitung" in: H. Ludwig and W. Schroeder, eds. *Sozial- und Linkskatholizismus. Erinnerung-Orientierung-Befreiung*. Frankfurt am Main: Knecht, 1990, 7-9.

Ludwig, H. and Schroeder, W., eds. *Sozial- und Linkskatholizismus. Erinnerung-Orientierung-Befreiung*. Frankfurt am Main: Knecht, 1990

Lusi, A. "Un esempio di non conformismo negli anni cinquanta: don Primo Mazzolari e 'Adesso'" in S. Ristuccia, ed. *Intellettuali cattolici tra riformismo e dissenso*. Milan: Comunità, 1975, 59-97.

Maerten, F. "Le clergé du diocèse de Tournai face à l'occupation: la voie étroite" in F. Maerten, F. Selleslagh and M. Van den Wijngaert, eds. *Entre la peste et le choléra. Vie et attitudes des catholiques sous l'occupation*. Gerpinnes: Quorum, 1999, 127-165.

Maggi, G. "L'Istituto cattolico di attività sociale" in G. Campanini and F. Traniello, eds. *Dizionario storico del movimento cattolico in Italia*. Casale Monferrato: Marietti, 1981, I/2, 303-304.

Malgeri, F., ed. *Storia del movimento cattolico in Italia*. 6 vols. Rome: Il Poligono, 1981.

Malgeri, F. *La Sinistra cristiana (1937-1945)*. Brescia: Morcelliana, 1982.

Malgeri, F. "I programmi dei cattolici comunisti e della sinistra cristiana" in: B. Gariglio, ed. *Cristiani in politica. I programmi politici dei movimenti cattolici democratici*. Milan: Angeli, 1987, 135-154.

Malgeri, F.. *Voce Operaia. Dei cattolicico-munisti alla Sinistra cristiana (1943-1945)*. Rome: Studium, 1992.

Malgeri, F. "La Democrazia Cristiana in Italia" in E. Lamberts, ed. *Christian Democ-racy in the European Union 1945-1995. Proceedings of the Leuven Colloquium 15-18 November 1995*. KADOC- studies 21. Leuven: Leuven University Press, 1997, 93-108.

Mampuys, J. "Le syndicalisme chrétien" in E. Gerard and P. Wynants, eds. *Histoire du mouvement ouvrier chrétien en Belgique*. KADOC-Studies 16. Leuven: Leuven University Press, 1994, II, 150-277.

Maritain, J. *True Humanism*. London: Geoffrey Bless, 1938.

Maritain, J. "La personne humaine en général" in *L'Oeuvre de l'Internationale Syndicale Chrétienne 1934-1937*. Utrecht: CISC, 1939, 101-116.

Maritain, J. and Maritain, R. *Oeuvres Complètes* (edited by J.-M. Allion). 16 vols. Fribourg: Editions Universitaires, 1982-1999.

Maugenest, D., ed. *Le mouvement social catholique en France au XXe siecle*. Paris: Cerf, 1990.

Mayeur, J.-M. *Un prêtre démocrate chrétien. L'abbé Lemire, 1853-1928*. Tournai: Casterman, 1968.

Mayeur, J.-M. "Catholicisme intransigeant, catholicisme social, démocratie chrétienne". *Annales* ESC, 57 (1972) 2, 483-499.

Mayeur, J.-M. *Des partis catholiques à la démocratie chrétienne*. Paris: Colin, 1980.

Mayeur, J.-M. *Catholicisme social et démocratie chrétienne. Principes romains, expériences françaises*. Paris: Cerf, 1986.

Mayeur, J.-M. "La démocratie d'inspiration chrétienne en France" in E. Lamberts, ed.

Christian Democracy in the European Union (1945-1995). Proceedings of the Leuven Colloquium 15-18 November 1995. KADOC-Studies 21. Leuven: Leuven University Press, 1997, 79-92.

Mazzolari, P. *Tu non uccidere!* Vicenza: La Locusta, 1955.

Mazzolari, P. *La Chiesa, il fascismo e la guerra.* Florence, 1966.

Mazzonis, F., ed. *Cattolici, Chiesa e Resistenza in Abruzzo.* Bologna: Il Mulino, 1997.

McMillan, J. "France" in T. Buchanan and M. Conway, eds. *Political Catholicism in Europe 1918-1965.* Oxford: Clarendon Press, 1996.

Merli, G. *Le lezioni in Santa Giulia di don Roberto Angeli. Appunti di dottrina sociale cristiana.* Pisa: Giardini, 1989.

Mertens, H. "Bilanz. Unser Ursprung - Die katholische Kritik - Was wird?" *Das Rote Blatt der katholischen Sozialisten*, 1 (1929) 11, 12, 69 (reprinted, Glashütten, 1972).

Metz, J.B. "Marxismus als Herausforderung an die Theologie?" in J.B. Metz, ed. *Anfragen an den Marxismus und an das Christentum.* Munich, 1985, 53-66.

Michel, A.-R. *La JEC face au nazisme et à Vichy.* Lille, 1988.

Michel, E. *Renovatio. Zur Zwiesprache zwischen Kirche und Welt.* Aulendorf, 1947.

Michel, E. *Sozialgeschichte der industriellen Arbeitswelt - ihrer Krisenformen und Gestaltungsversuche.* Frankfurt am Main, 1947.

Michel, V. "Ascension des travailleurs et mission du MPF". *Mouvement Populaire des Familles Première Semaine d'Études 1945*, 21.

Michelat, G. and Simon, M. "Niveau d'intégration au catholicisme et vote" in: INSEE. *Données sociales.* 1990.

Milanesi, G. "Identità religiosa e impegno politico nei Cristiani per il socialismo" in *Religione e politica. Il caso italiano.* Rome: Coines, 1976, 206-233.

Milani, L. *L'obbedienza non è più una virtù.* Florence: Libreria Editrice Fiorentina, 1971.

Mindszenty, J. *Memoirs.* London, 1974.

Misner, P. *Social Catholicism in Europe: From the Onset of Industrialization to the First World War.* London: Darton, 1991.

Mitchell, M. "Materialism and Secularism: CDU Politicians and National Socialism, 1945-1949". *Journal of Modern History*, 67 (1995) 278-308.

Moine, J.-M. *René Boudot: Le Feu Sacré.* Nancy: Éditions Serpenoise, 1997.

Molette, C. *L'ACJF (1886-1908).* Paris: Colin, 1968.

Molitor, A. *Souvenirs. Un témoin engagé dans la Belgique du XXe siècle.* Paris-Gembloux: Duculot, 1984.

Mommsen, W., ed. *Deutsche Parteiprogramme.* Deutsches Handbuch der Politik 1. Munich: Isar, 1960.

Montesi, M. "Di qua, di là dal Tevere". *Il pensiero nazionale*, from 23-24 (1969) to 6-7 (1971).

Morsey, R. "Deutsche Zentrumspartei" in *Staatslexikon*, II, Freiburg, 1986[7], 17-18.

Moulier-Boutang, Y. *Louis Althusser. Une biographie. I. La formation du mythe (1918-1956).* Paris: Grasset, 1992.

Mounier, E. *Communisme, anarchie et personnalisme.* Paris: Seuil, 1966.

Mounier, E. *Le personnalisme.* Paris: PUF, 1949.

Müller, W., Plasser, F. and Ulram, P. "Wähler und Mitgleider der ÖVP 1945-1994" in R. Kreichbaumer and F. Schausberger, eds. *Volkspartei - Anspruch und Realität.* Vienna, 1995.

Murphy, F.J. *Communists and Catholics in France, 1936- 1939.* Gainesville: University of Florida Press, 1989.

Mustè, M. *Franco Rodano. Critica delle ideologie e ricerca della laicità.* Bologna: Il Mulino, 1993.

Naendrup, P.-H. "Betriebsverfassungsrecht" in *Staatslexikon*. I. Freiburg, 1985⁷, 739-743.

Nesti, A. "I gruppi minoritari cattolici come fenomeno di controcultura". *Problemi del socialismo*, 7-8 (1972) 61-93.

Nizey, J. "Naissance et développement du Mouvement Populaire des Familles (MPF) à Saint-Etienne" in D. Peschanski and J.-L. Robert, eds. *Les ouvriers en France pendant la seconde guerre mondiale*. CRHMSS-IHTP, CNRS Symposium, 22-24 November 1992. Supplement to the *Cahiers de l'IHTP*, 20 (1992).

Nomadelfia. Un popolo nuovo. Nomadelfia, 1999.

Ockenfels, W. "Eberhard Welty (1902-1965)" in J. Aretz, R. Morsey and A. Rauscher, eds. *Zeitgeschichte in Lebensbildern. Aus dem deutschen Katholizismus des 19. und 20. Jahrhunderts*. IV. Mainz: Mathias Grunewald, 1980, 240-249.

Ockenfels, W. "Welty" in *Staatslexikon*. V. Freiburg, 1989, 957-958.

Ockenfels, W., ed. *Katholizismus und Sozialismus in Deutschland im 19. und 20. Jahrhundert*. Beiträge zur Katholizismusforschung. Reihe A: Quellentexte zur Geschichte des Katholizismus 11. Paderborn: Schöningh, 1992.

Olhagaray, J. *Ce mur il faut l'abattre: Prêtre-ouvrier de la Mission de Paris*. Biarritz: Atlantica, 1999.

Ory, P. and Sirinelli, J.-F. *Les intellectuels en France de l'affaire Dreyfus à nos jours*. Paris: Collin, 1992².

Ossicini, A. *Il cristiano e la politica. Documenti e testi di una lunga stagione (1937-1985)*. Rome: Studium, 1989.

Ossicini, A. *L'isola in mezzo al fiume. Un isola nel Tevere*. Rome: Studium, Editori riuniti, 1999.

Pacetti, M., Papini, M. and Saracinelli, M., eds. *La cultura della pace dalla Resistenza al Patto atlantico*. Bologna-Ancona: Il lavoro editoriale, 1988.

Paci, R. "I Cristiani per il socialismo" in L. Bedeschi et al. *I cristiani nella sinistra dalla Resistenza a oggi*. Rome: Coines, 1976, 225-240.

Panero, T. "GIOC" in F. Traniello and G. Campanini, eds. *Dizionario storico del movimento cattolico. Aggiornamento 1980-1995*. Genova: Marietti, 1997, 214-217.

Papini, M. *Tra storia e profezia. La lezione dei Cattolici comunisti*. Rome: Euroma-La Goliardica, 1987.

Papini, M. "La formazione di un giovane cattolico nella seconda metà degli anni trenta. Franco Rodano tra la Congregazione mariana 'La Scaletta' e il Liceo Visconti (1935-1940)". *Cristianesimo nella storia*, 16 (1995) 553-586.

Parisella, A. "I cattolici-comunisti e la sinistra cristiana. Note sulla storiografia". *Idoc-internazionale*, 1-2 (1978) 30-36.

Parisella, A. "Memoria di parte sull'esperienza italiana dei Cristiani per il socialismo". *Il tetto*, 100-102 (1980) 429-444 (sources and bibliography in no. 103).

Parisella, A. "Unità proletaria o Democrazia cristiana? Guido Miglioli e i cristiano-sociali 1945-46" in F. Leonori, ed. *Guido Miglioli. La figura e l'opera 1879-1979*. Rome: Centro di documentazione dei cattolici democratici, 1981, 195-208.

Parisella, A. "Bruni Gerardo" in *Dizionario biografico degli italiani*. XXXIV. Roma: Istituto dell'Enciclopedia italiana, 1984, 535-538.

Parisella, A. "Cristiani per il socialismo, cultura cattolica, compromesso storico". *Il tetto*, 123-124 (1984) 306-318.

Parisella, A. "Il Partito cristiano-sociale" in F. Malgeri, ed. *Storia del movimento cattolico in Italia*. Rome: Il Poligono, 1981, 53-139 (offprint, Biblioteca di studi cristiano-sociali, Rome 1984).

Parisella, A. *Il Partito Cristiano-Sociale 1939-1948*. Rome: Biblioteca di Studi Cristiano-Sociali, 1984.

Parisella, A., ed. *Gerardo Bruni e i cristiano-sociali*. Rome: Edizioni Lavoro, 1984.

Parisella, A. "I programmi dei cristiano-sociali italiani dal fascismo all'Italia repubblicana" in B. Gariglio, ed. *Cristiani in politica. I programmi politici dei movimenti cattolici democratici*. Milan: Angeli, 1987, 155-181.

Parisella, A. "Il laicato cattolico" in
B. Bocchini Camaiani and M.C. Giuntella,
eds. *Cattolici, Chiesa, Resistenza in Italia
centrale*. Bologna: Il Mulino, 1997,
61-97.

Parisella, A. "La base sociale della
Democrazia cristiana. Elettorato, iscritti e
organizzazione" in E. Lamberts, ed.,
*Christian Democracy in the European
Union. Proceedings of the Leuven
Colloquium, 15-18 November 1995.*
KADOC-Studies 21. Leuven: Leuven
University Press, 1997, 189-209.

Parisella, A. "Guido Miglioli" in
Il Parlamento italiano. XI. Milan:
Nuova Cei informatica, s.a., 252-255.

Parisella, A. *Sopravvivere liberi. Riflessioni
sulla storia della Resistenza a cinquant'anni dalla Liberazione.* Rome: Gangemi,
1997.

Pasini, G. *Le Acli delle origini*. Rome:
Coines, 1974.

Pasini, G. "Associazione Cristiane dei
Lavoratori Italiani (ACLI)" in F. Traniello
and G. Campanini, eds. *Dizionario storico
del movimento cattolica in Italia
1860-1980*. Turin: Marietti, 1981, I/2,
170-176.

Pasture, P. *Kerk, politiek en sociale actie.
De unieke positie van de christelijke arbeidersbeweging in België 1944-1973.*
HIVA-reeks 13. Leuven/ Apeldoorn:
Garant, 1992.

Pasture, P. "Redressement et expansion
(1945-1960)" in E. Gerard and
P. Wynants, eds. *Histoire du Mouvement
Ouvrier Chrétien en Belgique.*
KADOC-Studies 16. Leuven: Leuven
University Press, 1994, II, 246-301.

Pasture, P. "Diverging Paths:
The Development of Catholic Labour
Organisations in France, the Netherlands
and Belgium since 1945".
Revue d'histoire ecclésiastique, 88 (1994)
1, 54-90.

Pasture, P. "Belgium: pragmatism in pluralism" in P. Pasture, J. Verberckmoes and
H. De Witte, eds. *The Lost Perspective?
Trade Unions between Ideology and Social
Action in the New Europe.* Avebury:
Aldershot, 1996, I, 91-135.

Pasture, P. "Les différents modèles d'organisation ouvrière catholique au niveau
international 1945-1968". Paper presented at the conference on *Chrétiens et
ouvriers 1930-1950*. Roubaix, 13-15
October 1999. Forthcoming.

Pasture, P. *Histoire du syndicalisme chrétien international. La difficile recherche
d'une troisième voie.* Paris: L'Harmattan,
1999.

Paul Vignaux: un intellectuel syndicaliste.
Paris: Syros, 1988.

Paul, H.W. *The Second Ralliement:
The Rapprochement Between Church and
State in France in the Twentieth Century.*
Washington DC: Catholic University of
America Press, 1967.

Pechatnov, V.O. *The Big Three After World
War II: New Documents on Soviet
Thinking about Post-War relations with the
United States and Great Britain*. S.l., 1995.

Pede, A. "La scissione in Italia" in
M. Antonioli et al., eds. *Le scissioni
sindacali. Italia e Europa.* Milan-Pisa:
BFS Edizioni, 1999, 115-126.

Pelinka, A. *Gewerkschaften im
Parteienstaat. Ein Vergleich zwischen
dem Deutschen und dem Österreichischen
Gewerkschaftsbund.* Berlin: Duncker und
Humblot, 1980.

Pelletier, D. *Économie et humanisme:
De l'utopie communautaire au combat
pour le tiers-monde (1941-1966).* Paris:
Cerf, 1996.

Perrin, H. *Journal*. Paris: Seuil, 1945.

Perrin, H. *Itinéraire d'Henri Perrin*. Paris:
Seuil, 1950, 1958.

Perrin, H. *Priest and Worker* (translated
by B. Wall). New York: Holt, Rinehart
& Winston, 1964 [1958].

Petrie, J., ed. *The Worker Priests*. London:
Routledge & Kegan Paul, 1956.

Pierrard, P. *L'Église et les ouvriers en
France, 1940-1990*. Paris: Hachette, 1991.

Pierrard, P., Launay, M. and Trempé, R.
La JOC. Regards d'historiens. Paris:
Les Éditions Ouvrieres, 1984.

Pinzani, C. "May 1947: The End of the Left's Participation in the Government" in *The Role of the United States in the Reconstruction of Italy and West Germany, 1943-1949. Papers presented at a German-Italian Colloquium held at the John F. Kennedy-Institut für Nordamerikastudien.* Berlin, June 1980.

Pirard, T. "Un météore dans la vie politique et intellectuelle de la Wallonie: Forces Nouvelles (1945-1946)". *La Vie Wallonne*, 65 new series (1991) no 414-415, 129-154.

Pirker, T. "Kleine Arbeitstheologie" reprinted in H. Ludwig and W. Schroeder, eds. *Sozial- und Linkskatholizismus. Erinnerung - Orientierung - Befreiung.* Frankfurt am Main: Knecht, 1990, 149-166.

Pius XII. "Mediator Dei" in Catholic Truth Society, ed. *Selected Letters and Addresses of Pius XII.* London, 1949, 169-249.

Pius XII. "Ansprache an die Teilnehmer des internationalen Kongresses für Sozialwissenschaft: 3. Juni 1950" in A.-F. Utz and J.-F. Groner, eds. *Aufbau und Entfaltung des gesellschaftlichen Lebens. Soziale Summe Pius XII.* Fribourg, 1954, 3258-3272.

Pollard, J.F. *The Vatican and Italian Fascism, 1929-32. A Study in Conflict.* Cambridge: Cambridge University Press, 1985.

Pombeni, P. *Le "Cronache Sociali" di Dossetti 1947-1951: Geografia di un movimento di opinione.* Florence: Vallecchi, 1976.

Pombeni, P. *Socialismo e cristianesimo (1815-1975).* Brescia: Queriana, 1977.

Pombeni, P. *Il gruppo dossettiano e la fondazione della democrazia italiana (1938-1948).* Bologna: Il Mulino, 1979.

Portelli, H. *Gramsci e la questione religiosa.* (Introduction by E. Fattorini). Milan: Mazzotta, 1976.

Possenti, V. *Cattolicesimo modernità: Balbo, Del Noce, Rodano.* Milan: Ares, 1996.

Poulat, E. *Naissance des prêtres-ouvriers.* Paris: Casterman, 1965.

Poulat, E. "Modernisme et intégrisme. Du concept polémique à l'irénisme critique". *Archives de Sociologie des religions,* 27 (1969) 3-28.

Poulat, E. *Intégrisme et catholicisme intégral. Un réseau secret international antimoderniste "La Sapinière" (1909-1921).* Paris-Tournai: Casterman, 1969.

Poulat, E. "Pour une nouvelle compréhension de la démocratie chrétienne". *Revue d'histoire ecclésiastique,* 70 (1975) 5-38.

Poulat, E. *Catholicisme, démocratie et socialisme. Le mouvement catholique et Mgr Benigni de la naissance du socialisme à la victoire du fascisme.* Tournai: Casterman, 1977.

Poulat, E. *Eglise contre bourgeoisie. Introduction au devenir du catholicisme actuel.* Tournai-Paris: Casterman, 1977.

Poulat, E. *Une Eglise ébranlée.* Tournai: Casterman, 1980.

Poulat, E. "L'intégrisme. Phénomène catholique ou catégorie universelle?" *Cultures et foi,* 110-111 (1986) 32-36.

Poulat, E. *Liberté, laïcité. La guerre des deux France et le principe de la modernité.* Paris: Cerf/Cujas, 1988.

Poulat, E. *Les Prêtres-ouvriers: Naissance et fin.* Paris: Cerf, 1999.

Prost, A. "Changer le siecle". *Vingtième siècle,* special issue on "Les engagements du 20e siècle", 60 (October-December 1998).

Prümm, K. "Entwürfe einer zweiten Republik. Zukunftsprogramme in den 'Frankfurter Heften' 1946-1949" in T. Koebner, G. Sautermeister and S. Schneider, eds. *Deutschland nach Hitler. Zukunftspläne im Exil und aus der Besatzungszeit 1939-1949.* Wiesbaden: Westdeutscher Verlag, 1987, 330-343.

Raffaelli, F. "Politi, Sirio" in F. Traniello and G. Campanini, eds. *Dizionario storico del movimento cattolico. Aggiornamento 1980-1995.* Genova: Marietti, 1997, 411-412.

Ramos Regidor, J. and Gecchelin, A. *Cristiani per il socialismo. Storia, problematica, prospettive.* Milan: Idoc-Mondadori, 1977.

Ravitch, N. *The Catholic Church and the French Nation, 1589-1989.* London-New York: Routledge, 1990.

Reding, M. "Theodor Steinbüchel 1888 - 1949". *Theologische Quartalschrift,* 150 (1970) 148-151.

Régnier, J. "Les choix de Mgr Guerry" in D. Maugenest, ed. *Le mouvement social catholique en France au XXe siècle.* Paris: Cerf, 1990.

Reichhold, L. *Geschichte der christlichen Gewerkschaften Österreichs.* Vienna: Verlag des ÖGB, 1987.

Reifenberg, P. "Ernst Michel - der 'erste ernstzunehmende Laientheologe'". *Stimmen der Zeit,* 212 (1994) 119, 498-500.

Rémond, R. *Les catholiques, le communisme et les crises, 1929-1939.* Paris: Colin, 1960.

Reynolds, D. "Great Britain" in D. Reynolds, ed. *The Origins of the Cold War in Europe: International Perspectives.* New Haven: Yale University Press, 1994, 80-83.

Reynolds, D., ed. *The Origins of the Cold War in Europe: International Perspectives.* New Haven: Yale University Press, 1994.

Richou, F. *La Jeunesse ouvrière chrétienne. Genèse d'une jeunesse militante.* Paris: L'Harmattan, 1997.

Ricquier, J.C. "Auguste De Schryver: Souvenirs politiques et autres". *Revue générale,* (June-July 1982).

Rigobello, A. "Persona" in E. Berti and G. Campanini, eds. *Dizionario delle idee politiche.* Rome: Ave, 1993, 619-625.

Rioux, J.-P. *La France de la Quatrième République. L'ardeur et la nécessité 1944-1952.* Paris: Seuil, 1980.

Rochefort-Turquin, A. *Front populaire. Socialistes parce que chrétiens.* Paris: Cerf, 1986.

Rodhain, J. *Une charité inventive: le père Guichardan interroge Monseigneur Rodhain.* Paris: Centurion, 1975.

Roggi, P. "Il mondo cattolico e i 'grandi temi' della politica economica" in G. Mori, ed. *La cultura economica nel periodo della ricostruzione.* Bologna: Il Mulino, 1980, 547-590.

Roggi, P. *Riviste cattoliche e politica economica in Italia negli anni della "ricostruzione". Un contributo allo studio di Keynes in Italia.* Florence: Università degli Studi di Firenze-Istituto di Scienze economiche, 1979.

Romero, F. *The United States and the European Trade Union Movement.* Chapel Hill-London: University of North Carolina, 1992.

Romero, F. "Guerra fredda e scissione sindacali: stato e prospettive della storiografia" in M. Antonioli et al., eds. *Le scissioni sindacali. Italia e Europa.* Milan-Pisa: BFS Edizioni, 1999, 1-15.

Roos, L. "Kapitalimus, Sozialreform, Sozialpolitik" in A. Rauscher, ed. *Der soziale und politische Katholizismus – Entwicklungslinien in Deutschland 1803-1963. Gesellschaft und Staat* 247-249 and 250-252. II. Munich-Vienna: Olzog, 1981, 52-158.

Rositi, F., ed. *La politica dei gruppi. Aspetti dell'associazionismo di base in Italia dal 1967 al 1969.* Milan: Comunità, 1970.

Rotelli, E., ed. *I gruppi spontanei e il ruolo politico della contestazione.* Milan: Feltrinelli, 1969.

Rotelli, E. "I gruppi spontanei del '68" in L. Bedeschi et al. *I cristiani nella sinistra dalla Resistenza a oggi.* Rome: Coines, 1976, 184-198.

Rousso, H. *Le Syndrome de Vichy de 1944 à nos jours.* Paris: Seuil, 1990.

Rouxel, J.-P. *Les Chrétiens Progressistes, de la Résistance au Mouvement de la Paix.* Thèse Université de Rennes, 1976.

Ruffilli, R., ed. *Cultura politica e partiti nell'età della Costituente. I. L'area liberaldemocratica. Il mondo cattolico e la Democrazia cristiana.* Bologna: Il Mulino, 1979.

Ruggieri, G. and Albani, R. *Cattolici comunisti? Originalità e contraddizioni di un'esperienza lontana.* Brescia: Queriniana, 1978.

Ruhnau, C. *Der Katholizismus in der sozialen Bewährung. Die Einheit theologischen und sozialethischen Denkens im Werk Heinrich Peschs.* Abhandlungen zur Sozialethik 18. Munich, 1980.

Rüthers, B. and Kleinhenz, G. "Mitbestimmung" in *Staatslexikon.* III. Freiburg, 1987, 1176-1185.

Saba, V. and Bianchi, G. *La nascita della Cisl (1948-1951).* Rome: Edizioni Lavoro, 1990.

Saba, V. *Giulio Pastore sindacalista. Dalle Leghe bianche alla fondazione della Cisl (1918-1958).* Rome: Edizioni Lavoro, 1983.

Saltini, *Don Zeno, il sovversivo di Dio.* Bologna: Edizioni Calderini, 1990.

Sauvage, P. *La Cité Chrétienne (1926-1940). Une revue autour de Jacques Leclercq.* Brussels: Académie Royale de Belgique, 1987.

Scattigno, "Milani, Lorenzo" in F. Traniello and G. Campanini, eds. *Dizionario storico del movimento cattolico in Italia, 1860-1980.* II. *I protagonisti.* Casale Monferrato: Marietti, 1982, 384-386.

Schasching, J. *Zeitgerecht - zeitbedingt. Nell-Breuning und die Sozialenzyklika Quadragesimo Anno nach dem Vatikanischen Geheimarchiv.* Bornheim, 1994.

Schmidt, U. *Zentrum oder CDU. Politischer Katholizismus zwischen Tradition und Anpassung.* Schriften des Zentralinstituts für sozialwissenschaftliche Forschung der Freien Universität Berlin 51. Opladen: Westdeutscher Verlag, 1987.

Schmidt, U. "Linkskatholische Positionen nach 1945 zu Katholizismus und Kirche im NS-Staat" in H. Ludwig and W. Schroeder, eds. *Sozial- und Linkskatholizismus. Erinnerung-Orientierung-Befreiung.* Frankfurt am Main: Knecht, 1990, 130-147.

Schroeder, W. *Katholizismus und Einheitsgewerkschaft. Der Streit um den DGB und der Niedergang des [traditionellen] Sozialkatholizismus in der Bundesrepublik bis 1960.* Bonn: Dietz, 1992.

Schwering, L. *Vorgeschichte und Entstehung der CDU.* Köln: Deutsche Glocke, 1952.

Scoppola, P. "La democrazia nel pensiero politico cattolico del '900" in L. Firpo, ed. *Storia delle idee politiche, economiche e sociali.* VI. Turin: Utet, 1973, 110-190.

Scoppola, P. *La proposta politica di De Gasperi.* Bologna: Il Mulino, 1977.

Scuola di Barbiana, ed. *Lettera a una professoressa.* Florence: Libreria Editrice Fiorentina, 1967.

Sgarbossa, M. *Don Zeno... e poi vinse il sogno.* Rome: Città Nuova, 1999.

Sidoti, F. "'Questitalia' e la polemica sui temi dell'organizzazione politica dei cattolici" in S. Ristuccia, ed. *Intellettuali cattolici tra riformismo e dissenso.* Milan: Comunità, 1975, 167-227.

Siefer, G. *The Church and Industrial Society.* London: Darton, Longman and Todd, 1964.

Singer, M. *Histoire du SGEN 1937-1970: le Syndicat général de l'Éducation nationale.* Lille: Presses universitaires de Lille, 1987.

Sircana, G. "L'origine della Sinistra indipendente" in *Il Parlamento italiano.* XXI. Milan: Nuova Cei informatica, s.a., 453.

Sirinelli, J.-F., ed. *Dictionnaire historique de la vie politique en France au XXe siècle.* Paris: PUF, 1995.

Six, J.-F. *Cheminements de la Mission de France, 1941- 1966.* Paris: Seuil, 1967.

Smits, J. "De afbouw van de autonome politieke actie van het ACW en de oprichting van de CVP" in E. Gerard and J. Mampuys, eds. *Voor kerk en werk. Opstellen over de geschiedenis van de christelijke arbeidersbeweging 1886-1986.* KADOC-Jaarboek 1985. Leuven: Universitaire Pers Leuven, 1986, 313-353.

Smyser, W.R. *From Yalta to Berlin. The Cold War Struggle over Germany.* New York: St. Martin's Press, 1999.

Sorgi, T., ed. *Igino Giordani. Politica e morale.* Rome: Città nuova, 1995.

Stankowski, M. "Katholiken für den Sozialismus" in: W. Dirks, K. Schmidt and M. Stankowski, eds. *Christen für den Sozialismus*. Stuttgart, 1975, 10-19.

Stankowski, M. *Linkskatholizismus nach 1945. Die Presse oppositioneller Katholiken in der Auseinandersetzung für eine demokratische und sozialistische Gesellschaft*. Cologne, 1976.

Steenhaut, W. "De Unie van Hand- en Geestesarbeiders. Een onderzoek naar het optreden van de vakbonden tijdens de bezettingsjaren 1940-1944". Doct. verh. Universieit Gent. Ghent, 1983.

Stegmann, F.J. "Geschichte der sozialen Ideen im deutschen Katholizismus" in: H. Grebing, ed. *Geschichte der sozialen Ideen in Deutschland*. Deutsches Handbuch der Politik 3. Munich: Olzog, 1969, 325-560.

Steinbüchel, T. *Der Sozialismus als sittliche Idee. Ein Beitrag zur christlichen Sozialethik*. Abhandlungen aus Ethik und Moral 1. Düsseldorf, 1921.

Steinbüchel, T. "Karl Marx. Gestalt und Ethos". *Der Morgen*, 4 (1928) 27-46.

Steinbüchel, T. "Existenzialismus und christliches Ethos". *Theologische Quartalschrift*, 128 (1948) 1-27, 129-160.

Steinbüchel, T. "Das Wesen des Proletariats nach Karl Marx" in W. Dirks. *Sozialismus oder Restauration. Politische Publizistik 1945-1950*. Zürich, 1987, 99-123.

Steininger, R. "British Labour, Deutschland und die SPD 1945/46". *Internationale wissenschaftliche Korrespondenz zur Geschichte der deutschen Arbeiterbewegung*, 15 (1979) 188-225.

Steininger, R. "Die Rhein-Ruhr-Frage im Kontext britischer Deutschlandpolitik 1945/46". *Geschichte und Gesellschaft*, Sonderheft 5 (1979) 111-166.

Steininger, R. *Deutschland und die Sozialistische Internationale nach dem Zweiten Weltkrieg: die deutsche Frage, die Internationale und das Problem der Wiederaufnahme der SPD auf den internationalen sozialistischen Konferenzen bis 1951*. Bonn-Bad Godesberg: Neue Gesellschaft, 1979.

Stengers, J. *Léopold III et le gouvernement: les deux politiques belges de 1940*. Paris, 1980.

Sternhell, Z. *Ni droite, ni gauche. L'idéologie fasciste en France*. Paris: Seuil, 1983.

Strikwerda, C. *A House Divided. Mass Politics and the Origins of Pluralism: Catholicism, Socialism and Flemish Nationalism in Nineteenth Century Belgium*. Lanham: Rowman & Littlefield, 1997.

Suenens, L.J. *Memories and Hopes*. Dublin, 1992.

"Le syndicalisme chrétien". *Les Dossiers de l'Action sociale catholique*, 21 (1944) 5-6, 341.

Talmy, R. *Histoire du mouvement familial en France (1896-1939)*. 2 vols. Paris: UNCAF, 1962.

Tamburini, G. *Une politique de l'agir. Stratégie et pédagogie du Mouvement populaire des familles*. Les Cahiers du GRMF 10. 1997.

Tassani, G. "Le 'Avanguardie cristiane' a convegno" in *Il Parlamento italiano*. XVI. Milan: Nuova Cei informatica, s.a., 18.

Tassani, G. *Alle origine del compromesso storico. I cattolici comunisti negli anni '50*. Bologna: Ed. Dehoniane, 1978.

Tassani, G. *La Terza Generazione. Da Dossetti a De Gasperi, tra Stato e rivoluzione*. Rome: Edizioni Lavoro, 1988.

Taviani, P.E. "Idee sulla Democrazia Cristiana" in G. B. Varnier, ed. *Idee e programmi della democrazia cristiana nella Resistenza*. Special issue of *Civitas*, 2 (1984) 57-67.

Tessier, G. "L'Église catholique et le syndicalisme". *L'Internationale Syndicale Chrétienne*, 7 (Dec. 1929) 12, 182-189.

Tétard, F. and Lefeuvre, C. *Culture et Liberté. Une naissance turbulente*. Paris: Collection Culture et Liberté, 1998.

Theunissen, P. *1950, le dénouement de la question royale. Cinq mois qui ébranlèrent la Belgique*. Brussels: Complexe, 1986.

Thibault, P. *Savoir et pouvoir. Philosophie thomiste et politique cléricale au XIXe siècle*. Québec: Presses de l'Université Laval, 1972.

Tramontin, S. *Sinistre cattoliche di ieri e di oggi*. Torino: Marietti, 1974.

Tramontin, S. "Sindacalismo e cooperativismo cristiano dall' giolittiana al fascismo" in F. Malgeri, ed. *Storia del movimento cattolico in Italia*. Rome: Il Poligno, 1980, III, 205-318.

Tramontin, S. "Partito cristiano-sociale" in G. Campanini and F. Traniello, eds. *Dizionario storico del movimento cattolico in Italia*. Casale Monferrato: Marietti, 1981, I/2, 349-352.

Traniello, F. "Cattolicesimo e società moderna" in L. Firpo, ed. *Storia delle idee politiche, economiche e sociali*. V. Turin: Utet, 1973, 551-652.

Traniello, F. "Guerra e religione," in G. De Rosa, ed. *Cattolici, Chiesa, Resistenza*. Bologna: Il Mulino, 1997, 31-60.

Tranvouez, Y. "Guerre froide et progressisme chrétien. *La Quinzaine* (1950-1953)". *Vingtième siècle*, 13 (1987) 83-93.

Tranvouez, Y. *Catholiques d'abord: Approches du mouvement catholique en France (XIXe – XXe siècle)*. Paris: Editions Ouvrières, 1988.

Tranvouez, Y. "Mission et communisme: la question du progressisme chrétien (1943-1957)". *Le Mouvement Social*, 177 (Oct.-Dec. 1996) 49-69.

Tranvouez, Y. "Un cryptocommunisme catholique? Les chrétiens progressistes en France, du début de la guerre froide à la mort de Staline (1947-1953)" in J. Delmas and J. Kessler, eds. *Renseignement et propagande pendant la guerre froide 1947-1953*. Brussels, 1999.

Tranvouez, Y. *Catholiques et communistes: La crise du progressisme chrétien, 1950-1955*. Paris: Cerf, 2000.

Trionfini, P. "Gli uomini e le fortune di 'Adesso': la diffusione, i collaboratori, la risonanza" in: G. Campanini and M. Truffelli, eds. *Mazzolari e 'Adesso'. Cinquant'anni dopo*. Brescia: Morcelliana, 2000, 155-192.

Tucker, K.H. "How New are the New Social Movements?". *Theory, Culture and Society*, 8 (1991) 75-98.

Turone, S. *Storia del sindacato in Italia, 1943-1980*. Rome-Bari: Laterza, 1981.

Tyssens, J. *Guerre et paix scolaires, 1950-1958*. Brussels: De Boeck, 1997.

Uertz, R. *Christentum und Sozialismus in der frühen CDU. Grundlagen und Wirkungen der christlich-sozialen Ideen in der Union 1945-1949*. Schriften der Vierteljahreshefte für Zeitgeschichte 43. Stuttgart: Deutsche Verlags-Anstalt, 1981.

Urettini, L. "I cristiano-sociali di Treviso. Note e documenti sulla figura di Silvio Zorzi" in A. Parisella, ed. *Gerardo Bruni e i cristiano-sociali*. Rome: Edizioni Lavoro, 1984, 211-221.

US Department of State. *A Decade of American Foreign Policy, Basic Documents 1941-49. Prepared at the Request of the Senate Committee on Foreign Relations*. 81st Cong., 1st sess., Doc. No.123. Washington, 1950.

Van den Wijngaert, M. *Ontstaan en stichting van de CVP-PSC: De lange weg naar het Kerstprogramma*. Antwerp: De Nederlandsche Boekhandel, 1976.

Van den Wijngaert, M. "De lange weg naar het Kerstprogramma (1936-1951)" in W. Dewachter et al., *Tussen staat en maatschappij: 1945/1995 Christen-Democratie in België*. Tielt: Lannoo, 1995, 28-42.

Van Doorslaer, R. "De oorlog tussen continuiteit en verandering: vragen en problemen" in L. Huyse and Kris Hoflack, eds. *De democratie heruitgevonden: Oud en nieuw in politiek België 1944-1950*. Leuven: Van Halewyck, 1995.

Van Kersbergen, K. *Social Capitalism. A Study of Christian Democracy and the Welfare State*. London-New York: Routledge, 1995.

Van Molle, L. *Chacun pour tous. Le Boerenbond belge 1890-1990*. KADOC-Studies 9. Leuven: Universitaire Pers Leuven, 1990.

Van Roey, J.E. *La vocation terrestre du christianisme*. S.l., 1942.

Vandenbussche, R. "Le mouvement familial : la Ligue ouvrière chrétienne sous l'occupation". *Revue du Nord*, special issue on "Églises et chrétiens pendant la seconde guerre mondiale dans le Nord-Pas-de-Calais", 237-238 (1978).

Vandenbussche, R. "L'évolution de la Ligue ouvrière chrétienne dans la région du Nord" in GRMF. *Les mouvements familiaux populaires et ruraux. Naissance, développement, mutations. 1939-1955.* Les Cahiers du GRMF 1, 1983.

Vanistendael, A. "Jacques Maritain e il movimento sindacale d'ispirazione cristiana" in R. Papini, ed. *Jacques Maritain e la societa contemporanea. Atti del Convegno internazionale organizzato dall' Istituto Internazionale "Jacques Maritain" e dalla Fondazione Giorgio Cini.* Venezia, 18-20 ottobre 1976. Milan: Massimo, 1976, 145-153.

Vansweevelt, I. *Pogingen tot progressieve frontvorming in de vakbeweging tijdens en na de Tweede Wereldoorlog.* Lic.verh. VUB, Brussels, 1987.

Vansweevelt, I. "Pogingen tot progressieve frontvorming in de vakbeweging tijdens de bevrijdingsperiode (1944-1947)" in E. Witte, J.-C. Burgelman and P. Stouthuysen, eds. *Tussen restauratie en vernieuwing. Aspecten van de naoorlogse Belgische politiek (1944-1950).* Brussels: VUB-Press, 1989, 149-166.

Varnier, G.B. *Idee e programmi della Dc nella Resistenza.* Special issue of *Civitas*, 2 (1984).

Vecchio, G. *Pacifisti e obiettori di coscienza negli anni di De Gasperi (1948-1953).* Rome: Studium, 1993.

Vecchio, G. "Il laicato cattolico di fronte alla guerra e alla Resistenza: scelte personali e appartenenze ecclesiali" in G. De Rosa, ed. *Cattolici, Chiesa, Resistenza.* Bologna: Il Mulino, 1997, 251-294.

Vecchio, G. "Turoldo, David Maria" in F. Traniello and G. Campanini, eds. *Dizionario storico del movimento cattolico. Aggiornamento 1980-1995.* Genova: Marietti, 1997, 467-470.

Vecchio, G., Saresella, D. and Trionfini, P. *Storia dell'Italia contemporanea. Dalla crisi del fascismo alla crisi della Repubblica (1939-1998).* Bologna: Monduzzi, 1999.

Verlhac, J. "La jeune génération catholique en 1944 et le Parti communiste" in X. de Montclos et al., eds. *Églises et chrétiens dans la IIe guerre mondiale.* Lyon: Presses Universitaires de Lyon, 1982, 501-505.

Vermeulen, R. "Positions du MPF". *Mouvement Populaire des Familles. Première Semaine d'Etudes 1945.* S.l., s.a., 38-40.

Verstraeten, J. "De sociale leer van de Katholieke Kerk en de 'Derde Weg'" in L. Bouckaert and G. Bouckaert, eds. *Metafysiek en engagement: een personalistische visie op gemeenschap en economie.* Leuven: Acco, 1992, 51-61.

Vignaux, P. *De la CFTC à la CFDT. Syndicalisme et socialisme. "Reconstruction" (1946-1972).* Paris: Éditions Ouvrières, 1980.

Vinatier, J. *Le cardinal Liénart et la Mission de France.* Paris: Centurion, 1978.

Vinatier, J. *Le cardinal Suhard.* Paris: Centurion, 1983.

Vinatier, J. *Les Prêtres Ouvriers, Le Cardinal Liénart & Rome.* Paris: Éditions Ouvrières, 1985.

Vinatier, J. *Le Père Augros.* Paris: Cerf, 1991.

Vinen, R. "The *Parti Républicain de la Liberté* and the Reconstruction of French Conservatism 1944-1951". *French History*, 7 (1993).

Violi, R.P., ed. *La Chiesa nel Sud tra guerra e rinascita democratica.* Bologna: Il Mulino, 1997.

Voillaume, R. *Charles de Foucauld et ses premiers disciples: du désert arabe au monde des cités.* Paris: Bayard, 1998.

Volkogonov, D. *Stalin: Triumph and Tragedy.* New York: Grove Weidenfeld, 1991.

von Nell-Breuning, O. "Wir alle stehen auf den Schultern von Karl Marx". *Stimmen der Zeit*, 194 (1976) 616-622.

Walsh, M. "Pius XII" in A. Hastings, ed. *Modern Catholicism: Vatican II and After.* London-New York: SPCK, 1991, 20-26.

Wattebled, R. *Stratégies catholiques en monde ouvrier dans la France d'après-guerre*. Paris: Editions Ouvrières, 1990.

Wieck, H.G. *Die Entstehung der CDU und die Wiedergründung des Zentrums im Jahre 1945*. Düsseldorf: Droste-Verlag, 1953.

Wieviorka, O. *Une certaine idée de la résistance: Défense de la France 1940-1949*. Paris: Seuil, 1995.

Wilensky, H. "Leftism, Catholicism and Democratic Corporatism: The Role of Political Parties in Recent Welfare State Development" in P. Flora and A.J. Heidenheimer, eds. *The Development of Welfare States in Europe and America*. New Brunswick-London: Transaction, 1981, 345-382.

Willame, J.-C. "L'Union Démocratique Belge (UDB): Essai de création 'travailliste'". *Courrier Hebdomadaire du CRISP*, 743-744 (26 November 1976).

Wils, L. *Honderd jaar Vlaamse Beweging. III. Geschiedenis van het Davidsfonds in en rond Wereldoorlog II*. Leuven: Davidsfonds, 1989.

Winock, M. *Histoire politique de la revue "Esprit"*. Paris: Seuil, 1975.

Winock, M. *"Esprit". Des intellectuels dans la Cité, 1930-1950*. New edition. Paris: Seuil, 1996.

Woods, R.B. *A Changing of the Guard: Anglo-American Relations, 1941-1946*. Chapel Hill: University of North Carolina Press, 1990.

Zaninelli, S., ed. *Il sindacato nuovo. Politica e organizzazione del movimento sindacale in Italia negli anni 1943-55*. Milan: Franco Agnelli, 1981.

Zanuttini, A. "Gli archivi dei gruppi parlamentari della Sinistra indipendente. Una recente acquisizione dell'Archivio centrale dello Stato" in *Gli archivi dei partiti politici*. Rome: Ministero per i beni culturali e ambientali, 1996, 176-184.

Zelis, G. "Les Équipes Populaires" in E. Gerard and P. Wynants, eds. *Histoire du mouvement ouvrier chrétien en Belgique*. KADOC-Studies 16. Leuven: Leuven University Press, 1994, II, 544-563.

Zunino, P.G. *La questione cattolica nella sinistra italiana. I. 1919-1939. II. 1940-1945*. Bologna: Il Mulino, 1975 and 1977.

INDEX

Adam, Roger 96
Adenauer, Konrad 98, 196, 204, 206-210, 223, 225, 255, 257-258
Albers, Johannes 207, 210, 238, 250
Alessandrini, Ada 153, 164, 168, 186
Amaury, Emilien 51
Ancel, Alfred 36, 130, 137, 183
Angeli, Roberto 145, 155
Aquinas, Thomas 24, 198
Archambault, Paul 61
Ardigò, Achille 163
Arnold, Karl 207, 210, 238, 255
Aubert, Roger 104, 106, 113
Augros, Father 135
Avinin, Antoine 53, 59

Bacon, Paul 55, 74-76
Badoglio, Pietro 148
Balbo, Felice 148-149, 169
Baldelli, Ferdinando 180-181
Balducci, Ernesto 191-192
Barreau, Henri 130-134
Bartesaghi, Ugo 168
Basso, Lelio 42
Baudry, Georges 129
Bauer, Otto 218
Bauer, Theodor 204
Baussart, Elie 106
Benedict XV 243
Beneš, Eduard 265
Benigni, mgr 243
Berdiaev, Nicolaj 152
Bernstein, Eduard 219
Beugniez, Louis 55
Bevin, Ernest 256, 264
Beyer, Georg 219
Bianchi, Carlo 177
Bidault, Georges 50, 76, 120, 251, 254, 259, 264-265
Blocq-Mascart, Maxime 74
Blum, Léon 233
Böckler, Hans 223, 224
Boisselot, R.P. 96
Boland, Charles 34, 123-124, 131, 138
Bordet, Michel 128, 133-134
Bosco, E. 180
Bouche, Albert 81
Boulier, Jean 69, 135
Bourdais, Henri 71
Bourdan, Pierre 58
Bourgy, Paul 105-106
Bousquet, Hadrien 125
Bouxom, Fernand 76
Bouyer, Louis 135, 137

Briefs, Goetz 31
Bröckling, Ulrich 214, 225, 227
Brodier, Jean 234
Bruni, Gerardo 145, 150, 152-155, 157, 161, 172, 250
Brüning, Heinrich 202
Buron, Robert 51

Caffè, Frederico 264
Cagne, Bernard 122, 135, 137
Calamandrei, Piero 167
Calosso, Umberto 190
Cardijn, Joseph 16, 38, 67, 69, 119, 123, 180, 271
Carretto, Carlo 184, 194
Catoire, Jules 55
Cazzani, mgr. 187
Cesbron, Gilbert 118
Champetier de Ribes, Henri 52
Chappoulie, mgr. 80
Charue, mgr. 241
Chatagner, Jacques 96
Chenu, Marie-Dominique 25, 27-32, 36, 41, 93, 95-96, 100, 184, 233
Churchill, Winston 256
Claudius-Petit, Eugène 51, 58-59, 80
Clay, Lucius 257-258
Cohen, Jean 230
Collard, Léo 111
Congar, Yves 32, 41, 184
Cool, August 237
Cools, Hector 124
Corbino, Epicarmo 167, 262
Costa, Angelo 157, 161
Courtoy, Albert 124, 132
Cru, Jacques 96
Cucchi, Valdo 167

D'Amico, Fedele 148-149
Daniel, Yvan 34, 35, 121, 274
Danielou, Jean 183
Day, Dorothy 99
De Bernis, Gérard 96-97
De Chardin, Teilhard 192
De Fabrègues, Jean 100
De Foucauld, Charles 100, 184
De Gasperi, Alcide 23, 98, 145, 150-154, 157, 160-164, 168, 176, 179, 182, 189, 237, 243, 251, 261-267
De Gaulle, Charles 53, 57, 120, 260
De Lubac, Henri 32, 41
De Man, Hendrik 245
De Mun, Albert 67, 119
De Piaz, Camillo 192

De Provenchères, mgr. 140
De Schryver, August 253
De Soignie, Philippe 29, 31, 39, 42
De Wasseige, Yves 106
Dean, Patrick 255
Delfosse, Antoine 18
Delfosse, Jean 103-104
Deliat, Roger 127-128
Delors, Jacques 58
Depierre, André 96, 125, 133
Desroches, Henri 81, 95, 97
Dewez, Hubert 105-106
Dillard, Victor 122, 125
Dirks, Walter 28, 196-202, 205-206, 212-214, 216-217, 220-227
Domenach, Jean-Marie 183
Dossetti, Giuseppe 22-23, 42, 143, 157-158, 160, 163-164, 174, 177, 179, 182, 237, 244, 250-251, 261, 263-266, 268, 270
Dreyfus, Alfred 100
Dru, Gilbert 52
Duvivier, Julien 190

Einaudi, Luigi 262-263, 266
Elfes, Wilhelm 202
Engels, Friedrich 215
Enriques, Anna Maria 153, 155
Erhard, Ludwig 208, 258

Fabro, Nando 192
Facibeni, Giulio 181
Fafchamps, Joseph 18, 235, 280
Fanfani, Amintore 22-23, 31, 157, 161-163, 168, 250, 264
Favreau, Michel 129
Feltin, Maurice 69, 138, 140-141, 183
Feuerbach, Ludwig 199
Flagothier, Louis 124, 132
Frenay, Henri 20, 51
Frings, Joseph 224

Gaggero, Andrea 187, 193
Galloni, Giovanni 163
Gambino, Antonio 263
Gaudenti, Alberto Canaletti 150, 154
Gedda, Luigi 160, 179, 184
Gentile, Giovanni 144
Gerard, Claude 92, 96
Gérard-Libois, Jules 105-106
Gerlier, mgr. 138, 140-141
Gilibert, Jean 253
Gilson, Arthur 104-105
Gilson, Etienne 32
Giordani, Igino 145, 152-153, 187, 189-190
Girardi, Giulio 169
Godin, Henri 34-35, 121, 124, 274

Gonella, Guido 153
Gouttebarge, Jo 126, 129, 131, 133-135, 137
Gramsci, Antonio 149
Grandi, Achille 166, 237, 243
Gronchi, Giovanni, 150, 163, 265
Guardini, Romano 198
Guareschi, Giovanni 190
Guérin, Georges 67, 69, 71
Guerry, Emile 84
Guetzevitch, Boris Mirkine 152
Guichard, Albert 122
Gurvitch, Georges 152

Habermas, Jürgen 230
Hamon, Léo 58, 99, 242, 253
Harmel, Pierre 104, 111
Haurand, Wilhelm 224
Heller, Vitus 218
Hennebicq, Fernand 242
Henriot, Philippe 120
Hermand, Henri 96
Hitler, Adolf 250
Hohoff, Wilhelm 198-199, 224
Hollande, Father 134-136
Hourdin, Georges 51
Hromadka, Josef 98
Hua, Maxime 42, 72
Hull, Cordell 262
Husch, Jakob 206

Izard, Georges 106

Jadot, Jean 104, 106
John XXIII 194, 227, 269
Josz, Claude 106

Kaiser, Jakob 202, 204, 209-210, 223, 238
Kant, Immanuel 218-219
Kerkhofs, mgr. 34, 124
Ketrzynski, Wojciech 98
Knappstein, Karl Heinz 205-206, 220-221
Kogon, Eugen 28, 198, 205-206, 220-222, 225
Krushchev, Nikita 182

La Pira, Giorgio 22-23, 145, 153, 157, 160, 162-163, 179, 182, 191
Labor, Livio 169
Lacroix, Maurice 53
Ladrière, Jean 106
Lafontaine, Jo 129, 133
Lajolo, Davide 187
Lazzati, Giuseppe 27, 157, 160, 179
Lebret, Louis-Joseph 33-34, 93, 122
Leburton, Paul 106

INDEX

Leclercq, Jacques 103
Legendre, Jean 129, 132, 134
Lemire, Father 113
Lenci, Dante 155
Lenin, Vladimir I. 149
Lenoir, Jean 96
Leo XIII 15, 113-114, 119-120, 200
Leonori, Franco 164
Léopold III 110
Liénart, Achille 120, 137-138, 140-141
Loew, Jacques 33, 34, 122, 124, 127-128, 130, 132-133, 136
Lukács, Georg 199, 219

Magnani, Aldo 167
Malraux, André 20
Maret, Henri 192
Marie, André 260
Maritain, Jacques 16, 25-27, 29-32, 34, 60, 75, 95, 99-100, 145, 152, 155, 161, 183-184, 192, 218, 229, 233, 243
Marlio, Louis 30
Marx, Karl 30-31, 33-34, 198-199, 214-219
Masaryk, Jan 265
Mattei, Enrico 179, 182
Mauriac, François 100
Maurras, Charles 15
Mayer, René 260
Mazzolari, Primo 166, 178-179, 183-184, 187-192, 194
Mei, Aldo 176
Melloni, Mario 168
Menant, Guy 53
Mendès-France, Pierre 100
Merten, Pierre 105
Mertens, Heinrich 197-198, 200, 218
Michel, Ernst 197-200, 212-213, 218
Michiels, Jean 104
Miglioli, Guido 151, 156, 164, 186
Milani, Lorenzo 191, 194
Mitterand, François 20, 59
Moeller, Charles 104
Molitor, André 104
Molotov, Vyacheslav 264
Monari, Elio 176
Montaron, Georges 58
Montesi, Mario 151, 164, 167
Montesi, Pio 164, 186
Montuclard, Maurice 95
Mortati, Constantino 150, 159
Moulin, Jean 120
Mounier, Emmanuel 27-28, 30, 32, 58, 60-62, 93, 95, 99, 106, 152, 156, 184, 233
Münster, Clemens 220
Murri, Romolo 113, 150, 174
Mussolini, Benito 22, 148

Nenni, Pietro 168
Niemöller, Martin 98

Olgiati, Francesco 152
Olivelli, Teresio 177
Olivetti, Adriano 156
Orel, Anton 198
Ossicini, Adriano 21, 147-148, 151, 154, 167
Ottaviani, cardinal 193
Ozanam, Antoine-Frédéric 192

Paoli, Arturo 184
Pappagallo, Pietro 176
Parri, Ferruccio 151, 167
Pastore, Giulio 239, 243
Paul VI 118, 136, 194
Pauwels, Henri 241
Pecoraro, Paolo 147, 154
Pella 182
Perrin, Henri 122, 127, 134, 137
Persoons, François 106
Pesch, Heinrich 204-205
Pétain, Henri-Philippe 53, 119-121
Pezet, Ernest 51
Pfaff, "Bobby" 128, 135
Piasecki, Boleslaw 98
Pinzani 262
Pirker, Theo 28-29, 36, 220, 223-224
Pius IX 114
Pius VI 115
Pius X 65, 113-114
Pius XI 15, 119, 144, 200, 274
Pius XII 115, 136, 138-139, 153, 186, 195, 224, 227, 237, 264, 266, 269, 274-275
Pleven, René 59
Poimboeuf, Marcel 51-52
Poinsignon, Maurice 96
Politi, Sirio 182
Pollarolo, Giuseppe 180
Prigent, Robert 51, 55, 74-76

Ramadier, Paul 58
Ravaioli, Domenico 150, 250
Renard, André 42, 235
Reumont, Damien 105, 124, 130
Ridgeway, Matthew B. 135, 137
Rigaux, Beda 104, 107
Robert, Joseph 96, 126
Rodano, Franco 21, 98, 147-149, 151, 154, 161
Rodhain, Jean 122
Roger, Charles 105
Rollin, Simone 76
Roosevelt, Franklin 162
Rose, Lucien 20
Rosi, Auguste 122

Rossaint, Joseph 224
Rosselli, Carlo 178
Rosselli, Nello 178
Rossellini, Roberto 176
Rossi, Federico 166
Rossi, Mario V. 184
Rousset, David 42, 62
Ryan, James H. 152

Sacchetti, Otello 164, 168
Saliège, mgr 277
Saltini, Zeno 179, 184-186, 193
Sangnier, Marc 45-47, 51, 53, 58, 65, 93, 119, 271
Saragat, Giuseppe 266
Sartre, Jean-Paul 32, 61, 62
Sauvageot, Mme 96
Scelba, Mario 185-186
Scheler, Max 204
Scheyven, Raymond 104
Schmitt, Hermann-Josef 224
Schumacher, Kurt 210, 214, 250
Schuman, Robert 98, 259-260, 265
Schumann, Maurice 53
Schuster, mgr 178
Schwering, Leo 255
Screppel, Jacques 126, 132, 134
Segers, Paul 273
Selvaggiani, Marchetti 187
Serrarens, Joz 233
Serre, Charles 53
Serre, Philippe 53
Siemer, Laurentius 203, 221
Simon, Yves 32
Smith, Adam 31
Spataro, Giuseppe 154
Spiecker, Carl 202, 211
Stegerwald, Adam 202, 209
Steinbüchel, Theodor 197-200, 212, 215-219
Stern, Max 96-97
Strunk, Heinrich 210
Sturzo, Luigi 150, 152, 176
Suhard, Emmanuel 35, 83, 120-122, 136, 141, 165, 183, 274

Taviani, Paolo Emilio 153, 155, 177, 179, 263
Teitgen, Pierre-Henri 265
Tessier, Gaston 243
Tessier, Jacques 232, 236, 243
Thorez, Maurice 233
Tiberghien, Bernard 133
Togliatti, Palmiro 165, 168
Tosatti, Quinto 150
Truman, Harry S. 256-257
Turoldo, David Maria 179, 192-194

Vaissières, Yvette 96
Van der Gucht, Robert 106
Van Lierde, Jean 106
Van Roey, Jozef 41, 241, 279
Van Zeeland, Paul 253
Vanoni, Ezio 163
Vender, Giacomo 180
Verdier, Jean 120
Verlhac, Jean 93, 96
Vico, Francis 133, 135
Vidal, François 133
Vieujean, Jean 104
Vignaux, Paul 94, 235-236, 240
Vittorio Emanuele III 148
von Nell-Breuning, Oswald 214, 219, 224

Weiss, Alice 191
Welty, Eberhard 203-204, 207, 214, 221, 224
Wernier, Jean 128
Wéry, Christiane 96-97
Wirth, Joseph 202, 224
Wurm, Theophil 217

Zaccagnini 178
Zorzi, Silvio 164, 168
Zybura, John S. 152

CONTRIBUTORS

Cole-Arnal, Oscar
Teaches History of Christianity at Waterloo Lutheran Seminary and Wilfrid Laurier University, Waterloo, Ontario, Canada. Research and publications on various aspects of Liberation Theology.

Conway, Martin
Fellow and tutor in Modern History at Balliol College University of Oxford. Research and publications on the history of political Catholicism in Europe and politics in Belgium after Liberation.

Delbreil, Jean-Claude
Docteur d'état in Contemporary History, Professor at the Université de Metz. Research and publications on Christian Democracy and the political and religious history of contemporary France.

Duriez, Bruno
Doctorate in Sociology, Research Director at the Centre National de la Recherche Scientifique (CNRS), France. Member of the Centre lillois d'études et de recherches sociologiques (CLERSE) at the Université des sciences et technologies Lille I. Research and publications on social activism and on the history of confessional organisations.

Gerard, Emmanuel
Doctorate in History and Professor of History at the Faculty of Social Sciences of the Catholic University of Leuven. Research and publications on Christian Democracy, the social sciences and political decision making in Belgium.

Horn, Gerd-Rainer
Senior Lecturer in History at the University of Huddersfield. Publications on socialism in the 1930s, the Catalan Revolution and on social movements in "1968".

Jadoulle, Jean-Louis
Doctorate in History, Bachelor's Degree in Theology. Assistant in the Didactics of History at the Université Catholique de Louvain. Research and publications on the history of the variants of Catholicism in the 19th and 20th centuries, the origins of Christian Democratic ideas in Belgium and the Catholic intellectual progressivist milieus in French-speaking Belgium between the end of World War II and the Second Vatican Council.

Lienkamp, Andreas
Doctorate in Catholic Theology at the Universität Münster, Lecturer at the Katholische Akademie des Bistums Essen, 'Die Wolfsburg', in Mülheim/ Ruhr. Research and publications on various aspects of social ethics, most recently a monograph on the Christian socialist theologian Theodor Steinbüchel.

Parisella, Antonio
Professor of Contemporary History at the University of Parma. Research and publications on rural society, on political parties and on the relationship between popular culture and mass culture in Italy.

Pasture, Patrick
Doctorate in History, Lecturer at the Department of History of the Catholic University of Leuven. Research and publications on trade unions and on the comparative social history of the churches in Western Europe.

Tranvouez, Yvon
Doctorate in History from the Université de Paris IV; Director of Research at the Université de Rennes II; Professor of Contemporary History at the Université de Bretagne Occidentale (Brest). Specialisation in the history of Catholicism in twentieth century France. Research and publications on the milieus of Left Christians and the protest movements within the Catholic Church in the 1960s and 1970s.

Van Kemseke, Peter
Studied History at the Catholic University of Leuven and Hull University; MA in International Affairs from the USC Los Angeles. Doctoral fellowship from the FWO, Belgium. Is preparing a dissertation on "The Cold War and the 'Discovery' of the Third World in International Socialism and Christian Democracy".

Vecchio, Giorgio
Studied Political Science at the Catholic University of Milan. Teaches Contemporary History at the University of Parma and at the Catholic University of Milan. Research and publications on the history of Italian Catholics, the Italian Church and Italian politics and society in the 20th century.

KADOC-JAARBOEKEN AND STUDIES

1. *Cardijn. Een mens, een beweging / Un homme, un mouvement. Handelingen van het colloquium / Actes du colloque Leuven / Louvain-la-Neuve, 18-19/11/1982.* 1983. 318 blz., ill. Uitgeput. Résumé en français. English summary.

2. E. Lamberts, ed. *De kruistocht tegen het liberalisme. Facetten van het ultramontanisme in België in de 19e eeuw.* 1984. 362 blz., ill. Uitgeput. Résumé en français. English summary.

3. M. De Vroede & A. Hermans, ed. *Vijftig jaar Chiroleven 1934-1984. Aspecten uit verleden en heden van een jeugdbeweging.* 1985. 288 blz., ill. Uitgeput. Résumé en français. English summary.

4. E. Gerard & J. Mampuys, ed. *Voor Kerk en werk. Opstellen over de geschiedenis van de christelijke arbeidersbeweging 1886-1986.* 1986. 368 blz., ill. 850 BEF. Résumé en français. English summary.

5. J. De Maeyer, ed. *De Sint-Lucasscholen en de neogotiek 1862-1914.* 1988, 448 blz., ill. 1150 BEF. Résumé en français. English summary.

6. J. Billiet, ed. *Tussen bescherming en verovering. Sociologen en historici over zuilvorming.* 1988. 325 blz., ill. 895 BEF. Résumé en français. English summary.

7. R. Boudens, ed. *Rond Damiaan. Handelingen van het colloquium n.a.v. de honderdste verjaardag van het overlijden van pater Damiaan.* 1989. 317 blz., ill. 650 BEF. Résumé en français. English summary.

8. L. Vints. *P.J. Broekx en de christelijke arbeidersbeweging in Limburg 1881-1968.* 1989. 352 blz., ill. 950 BEF.

9. L. Van Molle. *Ieder voor allen. De Belgische Boerenbond 1890-1990.* 1990. 391 blz., ill. 640 BEF.

9. L. Van Molle. *Chacun pour tous. Le Boerenbond belge 1890-1990.* 1990. 412 blz., ill. 640 BEF.

10. S. Hellemans. *Strijd om de moderniteit. Sociale bewegingen en verzuiling in Europa sinds 1800.* 1990. 287 blz., ill. 1250 BEF. Résumé en français. English summary.

11. E. Gerard, ed. *De christelijke arbeidersbeweging in België 1891-1991.* 1991. 1016 blz., 2 dln., ill. 1950 BEF.

12. K. Dobbelaere, Lambert Leijssen & Michel Cloet, ed. *Levensrituelen. Het vormsel.* 1991. 246 blz., ill. 995 BEF.

13. E. Lamberts, ed. *Een kantelend tijdperk / Une époque en mutation / Ein Zeitalter im Umbruch 1890-1910*. 1992. 282 blz., ill. 1250 BEF. Drietalige publicatie. Publication trilingue. Trilingual publication

14. J. De Maeyer & P. Wynants, ed. *De Vincentianen in België / Les Vincentiens en Belgique 1842-1992*. 1992. 404 blz., ill. 1250 BEF. Tweetalige publicatie. Publication bilingue.

15. R. Burggraeve, J. De Tavernier & L. Vandeweyer, ed. *Van rechtvaardige oorlog naar rechtvaardige vrede. Katholieken tussen militarisme en pacifisme in historisch-theologisch perspectief.* 1993. 312 blz., ill. 995 BEF. Résumé en français. English summary.

16. E. Gerard & P. Wynants, ed. *Histoire du mouvement chrétien en Belgique*. 1994. 1044 blz., 2 dln., ill. 2400 BEF.

17. R. Renson, M. D'hoker & J. Tolleneer, ed. *Voor lichaam en geest. Katholieken, lichamelijke opvoeding en sport in de 19de en 20ste eeuw*. 1994. 296 blz., ill. 800 BEF.

18. J. De Maeyer. *A. Verhaegen 1847-1917. De rode baron*. 1994. 696 blz., ill. 1750 BEF. Résumé en français. English summary.

19. C. Dujardin. *Missionering en moderniteit. De Belgische minderbroeders in China 1872-1940*. 1996. 518 blz., ill. 1650 BEF.

20. L. Leijssen, M. Cloet & K. Dobbelaere, ed. *Levensrituelen. Geboorte en doopsel*. 1996. 336 blz., ill. 1250 BEF.

21. E. Lamberts, ed. *Christian Democracy in the European Union 1945-1995*. 1997. 480 blz., ill. 2200 BEF. Publication plurilingue. Plurilingual publication.

22. P. Heyrman. *Middenstandsbeweging en beleid 1918-1940. Tussen vrijheid en regulering*. 1998. 624 blz., ill. 2950 BEF. Résumé en français. English summary.

23. L. Voyé & J. Billiet, ed. *Sociology and Religions. An Ambiguous Relationship. Sociologie et Religions. Des Relations Ambiguës*. 1999. 263 blz., 1250 BEF. Bilingual publication. Publication bilingue.

24. R. Burggraeve e.a., ed. *Levensrituelen. Het huwelijk*. 2000. 297 blz., 1250 BEF.

KADOC-ARTES

1. J. De Maeyer, L. Van Molle & K. Maes, eds. *Joris Helleputte (1852-1925). Architect en Politicus.* I. *Biografie.* II. *Oeuvrecatalogus.* 1998. 296 + 288 blz.,ill. 4500 BEF

2. A.Bergmans. *Middeleeuwse muurschilderingen in de negentiende eeuw. Studie en inventaris van middeleeuwse muurschilderingen in Belgische kerken.* 1998. 450 blz., ill. 2950 BEF.

3. J. De Maeyer e.A., ed. *Negentiende-eeuwse restauratiepraktijk en actuele monumentenzorg. Handelingen van het Nederlands-Vlaams symposium, Leuven 13-14 september 1996.* 1999. 264 blz., ill. 2200 BEF.

4. P. Anthonissen e.a. *Ast Fonteyne (1906-1991). Een kwestie van stijl.* 1999. 324 blz., ill., foedraal. 2500 BEF.

5. J. De Maeyer & L. Verpoest, eds. *Gothic Revival. Religion, Architecture and Style in Western Europe 1815-1914.* 2000. 304 blz., ill. 2300 BEF.

www.ingramcontent.com/pod-product-compliance
Lightning Source LLC
Chambersburg PA
CBHW050622300426
44112CB00012B/1621